# BLACK PEOPLE IN BRITAIN
## 1555—1833

FOLARIN SHYLLON

# Black People
# in Britain 1555–1833

*Published for*
The Institute of Race Relations, London

*by*
Oxford University Press

LONDON   NEW YORK   IBADAN
1977

*Oxford University Press, Walton Street, Oxford,* OX2 6DP

OXFORD   LONDON   GLASGOW
NEW YORK   TORONTO   MELBOURNE   WELLINGTON
IBADAN   NAIROBI   DAR ES SALAAM   LUSAKA   CAPE TOWN
KUALA LUMPUR   SINGAPORE   JAKARTA   HONG KONG   TOKYO
DELHI   BOMBAY   CALCUTTA   MADRAS   KARACHI

British Library Cataloguing in Publication Data

**Shyllon, Folarin Olawale**

Black people in Britain, 1555–1833.
Bibl. – Index.
ISBN 0–19–218413–x
1. Title 2. Institute of Race Relations
301.45′19′6041        DA125.N4
Blacks in Great Britain—Social conditions

*Printed in Great Britain
by Unwin Brothers Limited
The Gresham Press, Old Woking, Surrey*

TO 'DEỌLA

It is, then, the strife of all honorable men of the twentieth century to see that in the future competition of races the survival of the fittest shall mean the triumph of the good, the beautiful, and the true; that we may be able to preserve for future civilization all that is really fine and noble and strong, and not continue to put a premium on greed and impudence and cruelty. To bring this hope to fruition, we are compelled daily to turn more and more to a conscientious study of the phenomena of race-contact—to a study frank and fair, and not falsified and colored by our wishes or our fears.

W. E. B. DuBois
(*The Souls of Black Folk*, 1903)

# CONTENTS

# ILLUSTRATIONS

# Preface

This book is a complement to my *Black Slaves in Britain*.[1] The legal framework of that book precluded exploration of how black people lived in Britain from the generally accepted date of their arrival in 1555 until Emancipation in 1834. This book, then, describes the experiences, vicissitudes, and achievements of black people, whether slave or free, in Britain during that period. It also examines the legal, economic, social, and cultural aspects of the black situation. The study deals, too, with British attitudes towards the blacks, and has attempted to show that the present-day attitudes of the white British Government and people towards black people are directly comparable with those of the period of this study.

Europe, having annexed ancient Egypt, proceeded to loot and hide in European museums the best of African art and treasures. Evidence of African history and culture safely in the West, leading historians and professors vied with each other for the post of *primus inter pares* in denigrating and degrading Africans and the African past. A venal breed of scholars arose, lying patriots they were and are, to whom honesty and integrity, the much vaunted endowments of the white race, were at a total discount; and who carefully lied and still lie about how Africa had never had any civilization and how her people are 'lesser breeds without the Law'. Taking up, therefore, the 'White Man's Burden', freebooters like Lugard and Leopold came to Africa to brutalize and murder Africans in a very sadistic manner. Meanwhile, Africans of the Diaspora in America and the West Indies met with a similar fate. Dehumanized and degraded, they were told that they had no past. Their inalienable rights to 'life, liberty, and the pursuit of happiness' were brutally trampled upon in the 'lands of the free' because they were black. To enjoy these inalienable rights of man at all, they had to approximate themselves to the whites in words, thoughts, and deeds, while, of course, being denied the ways and the means of approximation. But that did not matter; the horrors of American and Caribbean life were such that people of African ancestry strove nevertheless for the unattainable. They became estranged from and ashamed of Africa, and accepted the Western definitions of their past, present, and future. The myth that there is no African historical past became entrenched. But a lie never stands for ever.

The rise of Nkrumah in what was then the Gold Coast after the Second World War, and the birth of a new country with the symbolic name of Ghana on 6 March 1957, were not irrelevant events in an irrelevant corner of the globe.[2] Today their reverberations are still being felt. The Independence of Ghana was the dawn of a new age for black people all over the world. The name Ghana itself evokes and resurrects the glorious and dignified African past. (The medieval Ghana, several miles north of modern Ghana, was one of the three great empires of the Western Sudan——Sudan meaning the land of the Black People.) Today and only today, Afro-West Indians and Afro-Americans know that they have a past in Africa; and that their ancestors did much to advance world civilization. 'Black' and 'African' are therefore used interchangeably in this book to denote people of African ancestry. The word 'Negro' is a Western creation, invented to cut off Africans of the Diaspora from Africa and Africans, and is now discredited and untenable. George Jackson wrote in *Soledad Brother* in 1967, 'I speak of the African here in the U.S.' And of himself he wrote in 1970, ' I think of myself as a black, and an African.' The great DuBois, born in Great Barrington, Massachusetts, in 1868, took up residence in Ghana in 1961. In 1963 he became a citizen of Ghana and died in the same year. He lies buried in Accra, in the land of his fathers.

This study deals with the black experience in Britain. Four types of source have been used—African, American, Caribbean, and British. The first three have been used to explain, elucidate, or refute the lies, half-truths, and propaganda about the black experience and presence in Britain during the period of this study. This book, too, is propaganda. But it is propaganda of the truth: propaganda of the fact that racism has been the British way of life ever since the first blacks settled in Britain. The black community of the last quarter of the eighteenth century successfully resisted British racism. But they were successful because of their solidarity as black people, and not as Africans, Afro-West Indians, or Afro-Americans. No matter where they had been born, they acted in concert as 'Sons of Africa', conscious of the common experience which their blackness had produced in their lives. This was the key to their success, and it is surely the key today for exorcizing racism and all its barbarities and obscenities from Britain, America, the Caribbean, and Africa.

F. O. Shyllon

1. F. O. Shyllon, *Black Slaves in Britain* (London, 1974).
2. Hugh Trevor-Roper, *The Rise of Christian Europe* (London, 1965), p. 9.

# PART ONE : BLACK EXPERIENCE

# Introduction

In 1555 five Africans were brought into Britain. Over the next century, more and more Africans were imported. By the middle of the seventeenth century at least, a thriving black community had been established, and Britain had ceased to be a white man's country. This part of the book traces the origin of the black community in Britain, and shows how each successive generation suffered legal, economic, and social deprivation because of its blackness. The 'noble savage' has, of course, always had a niche in British hearts, and so there were some exceptions to the rule. But this section of the book is concerned with the roots of British racism and the black response to it. Aided by a small group of Englishmen who genuinely believed in the dignity and worth of the human person, the black response was positive, vibrant, and defiant. I have not concentrated merely on the relatively well-known quintet, Equiano, Sancho, Cugoano, Suleiman, and Barber, but have also sought to show how the anonymous thousands survived in an alien and hostile land.

In 1578 George Best reported, 'I my self have seene an Ethiopian as blacke as cole brought into England, who taking a faire English woman to wife, begat a sonne in all respects as blacke as the father.' Black men marrying white women was and is a root of Anglo-Saxon racism. It had been fine as long as Englishmen went to Africa raping and ravishing black women and girls. But when the black man came to England and started entering the body of the white woman, the white man reacted wrathfully. Such is the twisted contradiction in the thoughts of the white man that he takes the black woman at will, and at the same time believes that his civilization is destroyed when the black man enters the body of the white woman. It is truly astonishing and very sad indeed that such beautiful and basic human behaviour as the sexual act, the union of two beings into one, either for the wonderful act of creation of another human being or as an expression of love, affection, and mutuality, should have been and is the cause of so much pain, sorrow, sadism, and destruction of human beings, particularly in the Anglo-Saxon world.

Next to the emergence of and reaction to the black man as the destroyer of the myth of sacred white womanhood, the supposed threat to the position of the white working people by black people was another cause of morbid racial prejudice against blacks. Most of the blacks were, of course, chattels who were not paid any wages and were exploited as cheap labour. It did not matter to public watchdogs that Africa was being raped and denuded of her most valuable assets—her people. In fact it was the very men who campaigned vigorously against the black presence and competition in Britain, who strenuously advocated the expansion of Britain as the leading slave carrier and slave mistress. In a tract published in London in 1772 Samuel Estwick, Agent for the island of Barbados in London, urged:

There [are] already fifteen thousand Negroes in England; and scarce is there a street in London that does not give many examples of that ... . To this end, let a Bill originate in the House of Lords ... let slavery, so far as property is such in Negroes, be held in America: let the importation of them be prohibited to this country, with such other regulations and provisions as [may be deemed] fit to take place ... by this act you will preserve the race of Britons from stain and contamination; and you will rightly confine a property [in blacks] to those colonies, upon whose prosperity and welfare the independent being of this country rests.

The villainy and rapacity of racists are sometimes too disgusting for words.

In 1949 the then Sir Alfred Denning asserted in *Freedom under the Law*, that it is a cardinal principle of English law that no man shall 'suffer any disability or prejudice by reason of their race and shall have equal freedom under the law'. He made the point even more explicit when he laid it down that 'it is clear beyond peradventure that the common law of England has always regarded a man's race or colour as just as irrelevant in ascertaining his rights and duties as the colour of his hair'. In *Black Slaves in Britain* I demonstrated that, during the period of this study, the Courts fully subscribed to the doctrine that the blacks were 'lesser breeds without the Law'. Blackstone, the great expositor of English common law, was at pains in his *Commentaries* to make it clear that the race and colour of 'the heathen negro', as he chose to call black human beings, was very relevant in determining his rights and duties under the common law of England. Lord Mansfield, one of the great Chief Justices of England, refused to extend the protection of the Habeas Corpus Act to black people until his decision in 1772 in the case of the slave James Somerset. And when, having stayed on the fence for so long as to have outlasted Quintus Fabius Cunctator, he decided that the protection of the Habeas Corpus Act applied to blacks, he persisted in ruling that black servants were not entitled to wages or poor law relief

A subject fraught with emotion is depicted by Hogarth with verve and serious fun

because, as he said, 'The statutes do not relate to them [blacks], nor had they them in contemplation.'

'If you should go into the Hall of Lincoln's Inn or of any other of the Inns of Court,' Lord Denning says, 'you will see men and women of all races and colour, from all parts of the world, often dressed in the costume of their own lands, come here to study our laws under which all are free.'[1] One can only smile at the mention of Lincoln's Inn Hall. It was in Lincoln's Inn Hall one winter evening after dinner in 1729 that two Law Officers of the Crown issued the infamous 'Yorke and Talbot joint opinion', to the effect that a slave did not become free on coming to England, he did not become free by baptism, and, finally, any owner might compel his slave to return with him to the West Indies or America. Although the opinion was overruled in the Somerset case by the Mansfield decree, the 1729 opinion issued at Lincoln's Inn Hall remained the slave owners' Bill of Rights and the slave hunters' charter, and made every black man, woman, or child unsafe and under imminent threat of removal by force into slavery, until Emancipation in 1834.

1. Sir Alfred Denning, *Freedom under the Law* (London, 1949), p. 51.

# 1

# Genesis

Although Beckwith suggests that the first black slaves were brought into England in 1440,[1] other records suggest that the first instance of Africans coming to England was of the five 'blacke slaves' brought by John Lok from West Africa in 1555.[2] And they were not even slaves, but were sent to the country to learn English, so that on their return to Africa, they would 'be a helpe to Englishmen' as interpreters. The first English slave-raiding expedition was, of course, that of Sir John Hawkins, son of William Hawkins. Hawkins left the coast of England in October 1562, 'and passed ... to the coast of Guinea ... where he stayed some time and got into his possession, partly by the sword and partly by other meanes' at least three hundred Africans, who were sold to the Spaniards in the West Indies.

It is not possible to fix with certainty the date when private property in black slaves was established in Britain, although one writer says, without reference, that 'the first slaves sold in the English market were two dozen West Africans who were knocked down to curious English gentlemen in 1553'.[3] Bearing in mind that the first batch of Africans was purchased in Lisbon for the West Indies in 1510, and that the first African slaves, twenty in number, to be landed in what became the United States of America arrived in Jamestown in a Dutch man-of-war during the closing days of August 1619, it would seem safest to say that between these two dates a number of African slaves were imported into England and were probably disposed of by private arrangement. The first instance of blacks as articles of commerce in Britain, if we may trust such authenticated evidence as we have, occurred in 1621, in the 'Petition of William Bragge to the Honorable Sir Thomas Smith, Knight, and all the Company of the East India and Sommer Islands'. Bragge, claiming the sum of £6,875 from the Company, not only petitions but also furnishes his account, and one of the items is as follows:

Item, more, for thirteen Negroes or Indian people, six women, seaven men and boyes, the price of them not be bee vallewed, for why, ... Well, for Estimacion of theis poore Soules, they are not be vallewed at anie price. The cause why, I will shewe unto you, because the Lord Jesus hath suffered Death as well for them as for all you, for in time the

Lord may call them to be true Christians, ... And now for the Thirteen Heathens. ... So farre now my most Worshipful Masters, I most humblie beseeche my heauenlie God, I may not receeve Rewards either of Gold or Silver for such as are Created after the Image, Similitude, and Likenesse of God, our most heauenlie, most sweete Comforter, whom in Troubles is reddy alwaies to bee founde. ... And so much in the name of God as touching that Buisnesse, and touching the Negroes or Indians.[4]

The strong anti-slavery feeling of this British merchant founded on Christian principles is in pleasing contrast to the conduct of British and *Christian* slave dealers and slave holders of half a century later.

The English slave trade remained desultory and perfunctory in character until the establishment of British colonies in the Caribbean and the introduction of the sugar industry. When, by 1660, the political and social upheavals of the Civil War period came to an end, England was ready to embark wholeheartedly on a branch of commerce whose importance to her sugar and tobacco colonies in the New World was beginning to be fully appreciated. In accordance with the economic policies of the Stuart monarchy, the slave trade was entrusted to a monopolistic company, the Company of Royal Adventurers Trading in Africa, incorporated in 1663 for a period of one thousand years. The Earl of Clarendon voiced the hope, current at the time, that the company would 'be found a model equally to advance the trade of England with that of any other company, even that of the East Indies'. This optimistic prediction was not realized, largely as a result of losses and dislocations caused by the war with the Dutch, and, in 1672, a new company, the Royal African Company, was created. The policy of monopoly, however, remained unchanged and provoked determined resistance. The case against monopoly was succinctly stated by the free traders—or interlopers, as they were then called—to the Board of Trade in 1711. The monopoly meant that the purchase of British manufactures for sale in the slave trade, the sale of blacks to the plantations, and the importation of plantation produce—'this great circle of trade and navigation'—on which the livelihood, direct and indirect, of many thousands depended, would be under the control of a single company. The planters in their turn complained of the quality, prices, and irregular deliveries, and refused to pay their debts to the Company. In 1698 the Royal African Company lost its monopoly, and free trade in black slaves was recognized as a fundamental and natural right of Englishmen. With free trade and the increasing demands of the sugar plantations, the volume of the

British slave trade rose enormously. The Royal African Company, between 1680 and 1686, transported an annual average of 5,000 slaves. In the first nine years of free trade, Bristol alone shipped 160,950 black slaves to the sugar plantations. In 1760, 146 ships sailed from British ports for Africa, with a capacity for 36,000 slaves. By 1771 the number of ships had increased to 190 and the total number of slaves to 47,000.[5]

The chief contract for the trade in Africans was the celebrated 'Asiento' or agreement of the King of Spain to the importation of slaves into Spanish domains. The Papal Bull or Demarkation of 1493 debarred Spain from African possessions, and compelled her to contract with other nations for slaves. This contract was in the hands of the Portuguese in 1600; in 1640 the Dutch received it, and in 1701 the French. The War of Spanish Succession brought this monopoly to England. The Asiento of 1713 was an agreement between England and Spain by which the latter granted the former a monopoly of the Spanish colonial slave trade for thirty years, and England engaged to supply the colonies within that time with at least 104,000 slaves at the rate of 4,800 per year. The English counted this prize as the greatest result of the Treaty of Utrecht of 1713.[6]

The result was that England became the leading slave mistress, slave trader, and slave carrier of the world. While British ships were engaged in transporting millions of Africans to their death in the Middle Passage, or to servitude and oppression on the sugar, rice, cotton, and tobacco plantations of the West Indies and America, thousands of blacks were landed on the English shores to be kept in bondage in England. It was the custom to allow captains of slaving vessels to transport a few 'privilege slaves' in each cargo for their personal profit. 'It was doubtless through this custom that so many slaves were brought to England, and lived and died here in servitude.'[7]

1. Martha Warren Beckwith, *Black Roadways* (Chapel Hill, 1929), p. 3.

2. I am aware that between 1548 and 1550, one Sir Peter Negro, also called Captain Negro, Pedro Negro, or Petro Negro, was sent against the Scots with a band of 'souldiours Spanierdes'. It would seem that he had some African blood, and that his band of mercenaries were mixed-blooded men too. But they were Spaniards. At the time it was a common English practice to employ foreign mercenaries—Italians, Albanians, Germans, Spaniards, etc.—to put down uprisings in Scotland, or in the eastern and western counties, while the English army dealt with the hereditary enemy—the French. For references to Peter Negro and his band, see John Roche Dasent, ed., *Acts of the Privy Council of England (New Series) II, 1547-50* (London, 1890), pp. 183, 261, 275, 279, 419, 427-8.

3. Cedric Dover, *Hell in the Sunshine* (London, 1943), p. 159.

4. *Notes and Queries*, 3rd series, II (1 November 1862), pp. 345-6.

5. Facts for this paragraph are taken from Eric Williams, *Capitalism and Slavery* (London, 1964), pp. 30-3.

6. W. E. B. DuBois, *The Negro* (New York and London 1915, reissued 1970), pp. 91 and 110; W. E. B. DuBois, *The Suppression of the African Slave-Trade to the United States of America 1638-1870* (New York, 1896), pp. 3, 207-8.

7. John Latimer, *Annals of Bristol in the Eighteenth Century* (Bristol, 1893), p. 146.

# 2

# Chattels

'We have often heard and read of the bewildered and amazed condition of the swart-hued natives of some far-distant clime,' wrote a contributor in *All the Year Round*, 6 March 1875, 'when in their midst has appeared suddenly—a white man. They were scared at first, then curiosity overcoming fear—they gradually approached to question him, to touch him and his attire, and to make sure, indeed, that for all his strangeness of aspect, he was yet human as themselves. Now, something very much of this kind must have happened, although no one seems to have been at hand to make note of the fact, when there stepped upon our shores, for the first time—a black man. Who can doubt that there was much crowding round him, that he was greatly stared and gaped at, poked and pinched, too, no doubt, that his reality might be ascertained beyond all dispute.'[1]

While doubts exist as to exactly when the first black man stepped off the boat, it seems probable that the black man was not a familiar figure in England until the seventeenth century. A paragraph in *Mercurius Politicus*, 11 August 1659, affords the earliest evidence of the employment of black serving boys in Britain: 'A negro-boy, about nine years of age, in a grey serge suit, his hair cut close to his head,[2] was lost on Tuesday last, August 9th at night, in St. Nicholas Lane, London. If anyone can give notice of him to Mr. Thomas Barker at the Sugar Loaf in that Lane, they shall be rewarded for their pains.'[3]

According to John Latimer, 'the post of captain in a slaving ship was a lucrative one, and those who gained it were prone to make a display of their good fortune ... . They were accustomed to flaunt large silver, and sometimes gold, buttons on their apparel, and their shoes were decorated with buckles of the precious metals. But the most distinguishing mark of a captain in the streets was the black slave who attended him, and who was often sold to a wealthy family when the owners again embarked for Africa.'[4] The taste for black servants spread, until it became quite a custom among the nobility and fashionable ladies, bringing an increase in the population of blacks in the metropolis. Pepys records that when, in 1662,[5] Lord Sandwich brought Catherine of Braganza from Portugal to be the queen of Charles II, he carried in the same ship by way of present to the young ladies of his family 'a little Turke and a negroe'.[6] Some seven years later, Samuel Pepys himself is found employing a black girl in his household as cookmaid: '5th April, 1669. For a cookmaid we have, ever since Bridget went, used a black-a-moor[7] of Mr. Bateliers's Doll, who dresses our meat mighty well, and we mightily pleased with her.'

When, in 1714, George I arrived in England to ascend the English throne, he brought with him black Mohammedan body-servants of whom he was fond. In England they attended to his personal needs, and dressed him, much to the discontent, it is said, of certain Dukes whose prerogative was dressing the king.[8] In bringing his favourite blacks with him, George I followed a practice common among the slave-holding class of his new subjects, for West Indian planters, merchants, and traders returning to England were in the habit of bringing with them one or more of their personal attendants to whom they had grown accustomed.

The blacks thus brought into Britain in their thousands were, except for a few privileged ones discussed in the next chapter, the merest of chattels, obliged to wear collars like dogs, freely and shamelessly bought and sold, and freely and callously bequeathed to relatives.

That a collar was considered to be as essential for a black slave as for a dog is shown by the following 'Hue and Cry' advertisements in *The London Gazette* of 1688 and 1694:

A black boy, an Indian, about thirteen years old, run away the 8th inst. from Putney, with a collar about his neck with this inscription: 'The Lady Bromfield's black, in Lincoln's Inn Fields.' Whoever brings him to Sir Edward Bromfield's at Putney, shall have a guinea reward.

Run away, a Tannymoor [tawny-moor?], with short bushy hair, very well shaped, in a grey livery lined with yellow, about seventeen or eighteen years of age, with a silver collar about his neck, with these directions: 'Captain George Hasting's boy, Brigadier in the King's Horse Guards.' Whoever brings him to the Sugar Loaf in the Pall Mall shall have forty shillings reward.

The newspapers of the last quarter of the seventeenth century and the first seventy years of the eighteenth century contain scores of 'Hue and Cry' advertisements, relating to absconding blacks. For, as on the plantations, the blacks in London, Liverpool, and Bristol made their escape from slavery. For instance, in *The London Gazette* for March 1685, Colonel Kirke advertised the elopement of his black servant, a boy of about fifteen years of age, named John White: 'He has a silver collar about his neck, upon which is the colonel's coat of arms and cipher; he has upon his throat a great scar.' A reward was offered for bringing him back. No explanation is given as to how John White came to have the great scar, which may be the clue to the lad's action, for as we shall see in the case of Jonathan Strong, some masters treated their black chattels in Britain just as brutally as they treated them in the West Indies.

In the issue of *The London Gazette* for 3-6 August 1696 we read: 'Run away from Capt. Robert Wadlow, from on Board the Ship St. Jago, a Black-Moor Fellow named Tony, aged about 24 years. Whoever secures and brings him to Col. Bartholomew Gracedieu, at the Flying Horse in Thames-street, shall have two Guineas Reward.'

A stick-and-carrot advertisement appeared in *The London Gazette* for 7-10 September 1696:

Run away from Captain John Brooke of Barford near Salisbury, about the middle of August last, a middle-sized Negro Man, named Humphrey, aged about 30, in a dark brown Cloath Coat with hair Buttons, a Waste coat of the same with Brass Buttons, and sad-coloured Leather Breeches. If the said Negro will return to his Master he shall be kindly received; or whoever secures him, so he may be had again, and gives notice to the said Capt. John Brooke, or Mr. Waterman, Postmaster in Salisbury, or Mr. Brabazon Aylmer at the Three Pigeons in Cornhill, London, shall have 3 Guineas Reward, and reasonable Charges.

In the plantations, some blacks dared to run away again and again, and to deter this, all kinds of abominations were committed on their persons, such as deliberately crippling them and even sawing off the offending legs. In England, we have at least one instance of a persistent runaway. In the 23-26 March 1691 issue of *The London Gazette*, William Johnson of Bromley, Middlesex, announced the escape of his 'Black Boy named Toby, aged about 19, being pretty tall and slender, and his Hair newly cut off; he wore a blue Livery with Brass Buttons lined with Orange colour, and was seen in Essex the day he went away.' Between the date of the advertisement and the beginning of May 1691, the boy was recaptured, for in *The London Gazette*, 7-11 May 1691, we read again: 'Toby a Black Boy, aged about 19, pretty Tall and Slender, his Hair cut short; Servant to William Johnson Esq; of Bromley in Middlesex, made his escape last Tuesday Morning ... .'

*The Bristol Journal* of 12 March 1757 publishes the elopement of a young black man called Stirling, who 'blows the French horn very well'. His owner, a publican in Prince's Street, offers a guinea reward for his capture. In *The Bristol Journal* of 14 April

1758, Captain Holbrook advertises a 'handsome reward' for the recovery of his black servant named Thomas.[9]

Slave dealing was the natural corollary of slave hunting. In *The Tatler* of 1709 was advertised for sale: 'A Black boy, twelve years of age, fit to wait on a gentleman, to be disposed of at Denis's Coffee House in Finch Lane, near the Exchange.'[10] The following, from *The London Advertiser* in 1756, with its reference to freedom from 'distemper', is painfully like an offer of a young dog for sale: 'To be sold, a Negro Boy, about fourteen years old, warranted free from any distemper, and has had those fatal to that colour; has been used two years to all kinds of household work, and to wait at table; his price is £25, and would not be sold but the person he belongs to is leaving off business. Apply at the bar of George Coffee-house in Chancery Lane, over against the Gate.'[11]

In *The Public Ledger*, 31 December 1761: 'A healthy Negro Girl, aged about fifteen years; speaks good English, works at her needle, washes well does household work, and has had the small-pox.'

*The Liverpool Chronicle*, 15 December 1768, carried the following detailed qualities of the African boy offered for sale: 'A FINE NEGROE BOY, of about 4 Feet 5 Inches high. Of a sober, tractable, humane Disposition, Eleven or Twelve Years of Age, talks English very well, and can Dress Hair in a tollerable way.'

In 1763 one John Rice was hanged for forgery at Tyburn, and among his effects sold by auction after his execution was a black boy. *The Gentleman's Magazine* announced: 'At the sale of Rice the broker's effects, a Negro boy was put up by auction, and sold for [£]32. Perhaps the first instance of the kind in a free country.'[12]

In fact this was not the first instance of a sale by auction or the first occasion of the sale of human property of a deceased person. In *Williamson's Liverpool Advertiser*, 20 August 1756, an auctioneer advertised for sale by candle-light, *inter alia*, 'Three young men slaves to be sold at the same time.'[13] It is, therefore, wrong to assume that the sale of Rice's black boy was the first instance of a black slave in England coming under the auctioneer's hammer.[14] It would seem that sale by private treaty and sale by auction of black slaves in Britain went on hand in hand.

At Lichfield, in 1771, there was offered for sale by public auction: 'A Negro Boy, from Africa, supposed to be ten or eleven years of age. He is remarkably stout, well proportioned, speaks tolerably good English, of a mild disposition, friendly, officious, sound, healthy, fond of labour, and for colour, an excellent fine black.'[15]

In *Williamson's Liverpool Advertiser* for 12 September 1766, it was announced, 'to be sold at the Exchange Coffee-house in Water Street, this day the 12th inst. at one o'clock precisely, eleven negroes, imported per the *Angola*.'[16] In 1788 John Tarleton, an opulent Liverpool slave merchant was in London at the head of the Liverpool delegation lobbying against the passing of a Bill that regulated according to tonnage the number of slaves a slaver was allowed to carry. A letter dated Liverpool 25 June 1788 informed Tarleton that: 'Your Vessel the Mary from Calabar is arrived with 262 Negroes & little mortality—from their being extremely healthy, they have been sold at the high price of £38 a head.'[17]

*The Stamford Mercury* for 1771 states that 'at a sale of a gentleman's effects at Richmond, a Negroe Boy was put up and sold for £32,' adding 'a shocking instance in a free country'. John Latimer cited two similar instances as having occurred in Bristol in the early years of the century. In 1715 in the will of a ship's captain named Nightingale, 'the proceeds of his two boys and girls, then on board his ship' were bequeathed. In October 1718, a merchant, named Becher Fleming, left to Mrs. Mary Becher 'my negro boy, named Tallow'.[18]

The slave hunters and slave dealers conducted their activities openly. In *The London Advertiser* in 1756, Matthew Dyer, working-goldsmith at the Crown in Duke Lane, Orchard Street, Westminster, intimated to the public that he made 'silver padlocks for Blacks or Dog; collars, &c.'.[19] The equipment of the slave merchants, like the muzzle, iron necklace, shackles, chains, collars, and thumb-screws, were boldly exhibited for sale in the shops and advertised in the press.[20] Thus, while the case of James Somerset was pending in the Court of King's Bench in 1772, Granville Sharp (friend of the blacks) sent an Iron Gag-Muzzle to Serjeant Davy, leading counsel for Somerset (Serjeant was a title given to high-ranking barristers). In a note accompanying the muzzle, Sharp told Serjeant Davy that he had sent it to him because it was 'a Brief against Slavery', and proof of the monstrous wickedness of tolerating it. 'It is, indeed an *Iron Argument*, which must at once convince all those whose hearts are not a harder metal, that MEN are not to be entrusted with an absolute authority over their brethren.' Granville Sharp asserted that 'many wholesale Ironmongers in Town keep quantities of them ready in order to supply the Merchants and Planters Orders for the West Indian Islands'.[21] In 1788, when Parliament was debating the Bill to regulate the transportation of black slaves in accordance with the capacity of the ship, *The London Chronicle*, 10 July, reported that:

Mr. Williams, a manufacturer in brass, copper, tin, &c. appeared at the bar [of the House of Lords, on 9 July], and declared that he and his partners had upwards of [£]70,000 invested in works in several parts of Wales, the produce of which was entirely destined for the African market: that upon the present rumours of a check being put upon the trade, there had been a sudden stoppage of his trade, and that at least [£]15,000 in value of goods now lay upon their hands, for which there was no other vent than the African market.

Accordingly, 'the Bishop of Bangor', reported *The Whitehall Evening Post*, 10 July 1788, 'presented a petition against the Bill, from Mr. Williams'.

Small black boys occupied a special position as exotic ornaments. They were the favourite attendants of the great ladies and courtesans of the period. This can be seen from a letter that the Duchess of Devonshire wrote to her mother towards the end of the eighteenth century:

Dear Mama, George Hanger has sent me a Black boy, eleven years old and very honest, but the Duke don't like me having a black, yet I cannot bear the poor wretch being ill-used; if you liked him instead of Michel I will send him, he will be a cheap servant and you will make a Christian of him and a good boy; if you don't like him they say Lady Rockingham wants one. [22]

Sometimes 'Wanted' advertisements for these poor boys appear in the newspapers. Thus in *Williamson's Liverpool Advertiser*, 20 August 1756, was the following: 'Wanted immediately a Black boy. He must be of a deep black complexion, and a lively, humane disposition, with good features, and not above 15, nor under 12 years of age.' [23]

The black, thus obtained, was often made to bear an absurdly pompous classical name, the exalted associations of which contrasted sharply with his lowly estate as a chattel or plaything. Scipio, Zeno, and Socrates were among the more common appellations; Pompey was the favourite, indeed becoming almost a generic sobriquet for black servants both young and old. [24] Describing the mystification he experienced on calling at a friend's house, Horace Walpole illustrates this usage. 'I went, found a bandage upon the knocker, an old woman and child in the hall, and a black boy at the door—Lord! think I, this can't be Mrs. Boscawen's—however, Pompey let me up ... .' [25] The Right Honourable the Earl of Suffolk and Brandon had his black boy named Scipio Africanus. Scipio died on 21 December 1720, aged eighteen years, and was buried in a Bristol cemetery. Why such classical names should have been bestowed upon these poor black lads is hard to say, unless the practice arose from a cruel inclination to mock at them by contrasting their grand appellations with their abject fortunes.[26] The fashion was of attiring them fancifully in oriental dress.[27] It was the duty of the little black boy in the service of the lady of quality to attend his mistress's person and tea-table, to carry her train as she moved to and fro, to take charge of her fan and smelling-salts, to feed her parrots, and to comb her lap-dogs.[28] Hogarth, in the fourth scene of his *Marriage à la Mode*, portrayed a turbaned black boy playing with a collection of china ornaments. In a scene in *The Harlot's Progress* there appears another black boy, wearing a turban, jewelled and plumed, and conveying to his mistress's tea-table her tea-pot. A black boy also appears in *Taste in High Life* dressed exotically.

The returning West Indian and American planters and merchants brought their black chattels with them for a combination of selfish motives: they were reluctant to pay English servants when blacks could be had for nothing; the rigours of the arduous passage to England were invariably lessened by the ministrations of a black body-servant; and having a black servant conferred on the West Indian magnates an air of luxurious well-being. Charles Dunster in his poem *St. James's Street* (1790) observed of the fashionable in London's most exclusive street:

> ... Sometimes at their head,
> Index of Rank or Opulence supreme,
> A sable Youth from Aethiopia's climes,
> In milk-white turban dight, precedes the Train.

In the West Indies and America, the response of the black to his enslavement was not one of passivity and docility, but discontent and rebelliousness. Protest among slaves took individual and collective forms. Among the individual manifestations of protest were 'laziness', 'thievishness',[29] 'irresponsibility', flight, assassination, arson, sabotage of tools and animals, self-injury, infanticide. Among collective protests were group flights, group arson, the existence of maroons—outlying, belligerent fugitive slaves—and conspiracy and uprisings.[30] Protest among black slaves in Britain took almost exclusively the individual form of flight, as the scores of 'Hue and Cry' advertisements testify. When captured, the blacks were usually sent back to the West Indies and America. Pending shipment, it was customary to incarcerate them in the Poultry Compter, a City jail. The slave-hunting and slave-kidnapping activities in the streets of London, Liverpool, and Bristol, and the shipment of runaway blacks to the plantations raised two legal problems. First, was the unqualified slavery and bondage of the blacks permitted by English law? Second, had a master the legal right to kidnap his runaway slave and return him by force to the West Indies or America?

In 1569 it had been decided that English law would not recognize the status of a slave. The case in question is mentioned in Rushworth's *Historical Collections*, and it is there stated, 'That in the 11th of Elizabeth, one Cartwright brought a slave from Russia, and would scourge him; for this he was questioned, and it was resolved, that England was too pure an air for Slaves to breathe in.'[31] But in 1677 in *Butts* v. *Penny*[32] it was held that English law would recognize the status of a slave, on the ground that blacks 'being usually bought and sold among merchants, as merchandise, and also being infidels, there might be a property in them to maintain trover' (an action for trover is an action to recover value of goods wrongfully detained). In 1694 this decision was followed in *Gelly* v. *Cleve*.[33] In a series of decisions, Chief Justice Sir John Holt of the Court of King's Bench gave no countenance to these two cases when he held that slavery is not a status recognized by the law of England. In *Chamberlain* v. *Harvey*,[34] decided in 1698, Holt held that trespass does not lie for a black. Three years later, in *Smith* v. *Browne & Cooper*,[35] Holt declared that 'as soon as a Negro comes into England, he becomes free; one may be a villein in England but not a slave'. But in the same case, Mr. Justice Powell was of the opinion that 'the Laws of England take no notice of a Negroe'. In *Smith* v. *Gould*,[36] decided in 1706, Chief Justice Holt held that, 'By the common law no man can have a property in another.'

Far from clarifying the legal status of black slaves in Britain, these cases confounded the matter. In the first place, the series of cases decided by Holt being in conflict with *Butts* v. *Penny* and *Gelly* v. *Cleve*, it remained uncertain whether English law did or did not recognize slavery. Secondly, if according to *Butts* v. *Penny* and *Gelly* v. *Cleve* the African was a slave because he was a 'heathen', what if he became a Christian? In *Chamberlain* v. *Harvey*, the Court side-stepped the issue of baptism and the African becoming a Christian. The Court avoided the issue, I submit, for the simple reason that it felt that a slave could not become free by baptism. In any event, the Friends of the Africans held the contrary view that by baptism a slave does become free. The Africans, longing to be free, took this simple step to freedom, and all around them they found sympathizers among the clergy and laity willing to perform the baptismal ceremony and stand as godfathers.

The slave owners responded with indignation to this interference with their chattels, and not only forbade their slaves to go through the ritual of baptism, but even prohibited any form of rudimentary Christian instruction being given to them. In 1685 the Revd. Morgan Godwyn, best known as the author of *The Negro's and Indians Advocate* (1680), gave several examples of the infinite pains the English took to prevent their slaves being made Christians:

The first that I shall mention, is of a Gentlewoman, who commending a certain *Negro* Wench that she had, for her towardliness and other good qualities, in the hearing of a Minister; he demanded of her, why she made her not a *Christian*? Whereat, casting her eyes strangely on him, and greatly wondring, she replied, That she had thought he would have given her better Counsel.

The next shall be of a poor Wretch of the like sort, belonging to a certain Lady, at that time residing in a place some seventy miles distant from *London*: With this *Negro*, a religious Gentlewoman condescended to discourse, and to perswade to Christianity, unto which she found him very inclinable; but was interrupted by the Lady, who overhearing the Discourse, thereupon ran in; and, as in a most hideous affrightment, cryed out, *O, for God's* (she might better have said the Devil's) *sake*, say no more to him of that. And so the Discourse ended.

The third instance shall be of a *Negro*, whose Owner lived nearer *London*, viz. within some four or five miles distance of it. This Negro presented himself to the Minister, I think not of his own, but of a neighbouring Parish, desiring Baptism at his hands; For which the Minister finding him not unqualified, did not absolutely refuse it, nor yet at present grant it him; tis possible, as being of another Parish. But however, the Master coming to the knowledge thereof, forthwith sends a peremptory Message to the Minister, charging him upon his peril not to proceed.

The fourth is of a *Negro*, whose Owner resided somewhere near *Bristol*, (the places name I have forgotten); This *Negro* also addressed himself to the Minister, beseeching Baptism; For the which the Minister finding him incompetently fitted, did not deny it him; only deferred it for the present. All which soon after arriving at the Master's jealous ear, he, with the like terrible Menaces, dehorted the Minister; adding withal, this insolent enquiry, *Whether he would baptize his Horse*? But perceiving that the Minister little regarded his Menaces or Arguments, he goes home, and instantly chains the *Negro* under the Table among his Dogs, and there continues him in that double bondage for sometime; till finding him thereby to become unserviceable, which is all they regard; he at length releaseth him of his Chain, but with this strict charge, not to go any more to the Minister. Which the *Negro* not observing, the Minister, like one that understood his Office, and, that believed himself obliged to pay a greater respect to *Christ's* Commands, of *baptizing all Nations*, than to that Infidel *American's* forbidding it, publickly admits him into the Church by the Sacrament of Baptism; ... This again coming to his Masters knowledge, as it could not well be kept from him, the *Negro* upon his return, was welcomed with his former Chain, wherein he was soon after conveyed on Shipboard, and so to *America*: Where 'tis to be presumed, that according to the *general custom* there, he shall never more hear of *Christianity*. Three of these Passages I had from the Ministers themselves, even as the other was told me by the Gentlewoman, an eminent Clergy-man's Wife in those Parts.

I have heard also of a parcel of *Negro's* brought into *England*, concerning whom an especial charge was in the first place given to the Servants, not to mention any thing of Religion to them: Together with an intimation, (which was no other, than to invite some lewd fellow to the Villany) how acceptable a piece of service it would be, to have a certain young *Negro* Wench of the Company got with child. It seems they take this Fornication to be no sin, no not so much as Venial.[37]

In February 1690 Katherine Auker appealed to the Middlesex Sessions under the following circumstances according to the record of the Court:

Upon the petition of Katherine Auker, a black. Shows she was servant to one Robert Rich, a planter in Barbadoes, and that about six years since she came to England with her master and mistress; she was baptized in the parish church of St. Katherine's, near the Tower, after which her said master and mistress tortured and turned her out: her said master refusing to give her a discharge, she could not be entertained in service else where. The said Rich caused her to be arrested and imprisoned in the Pulletry Cempter, London. Prays to be discharged from her said master, he being in Barbadoes.

The Court in its infinite wisdom ordered that Katherine Auker 'shall be at liberty to serve any person until such time as the said Rich shall return from Barbadoes'.[38] Sir William Blackstone, the celebrated legal luminary and commentator of the period, after declaring that baptism did not free a slave, went on to denounce 'the infamous and unchristian practice of withholding baptism from [Black] servants'.[39] There is a curious irony here. The English had sent missionaries to Africa to 'civilize' and baptize the 'savage' and 'heathen' Africans. Englishmen, among other Europeans, had purchased blacks on the African coast and baptized them before embarkation to the plantations. Now that black body-servants of planters and captains of slaving vessels were arriving in England, the 'civilized and Christian' country, they were hunted and hounded, tortured, and turned out into the streets, or bundled into prisons for undergoing baptism and becoming full members of the Christian church. In the case of Dinah Black at Bristol in 1667, she told her mistress, following her baptism, that she wished from henceforth 'to live under the teaching of the Gospel', whereupon the Christian mistress had Dinah Black bound and gagged and put on board a ship going to America. Fortunately for Dinah, some truly pious citizens of Bristol heard of the kidnapping and obtained her release.[40]

The West Indians had brought their black body-servants over, because they presumed that their private rights and property in human flesh would be recognized in England. Now they were not so sure. In 1729, in order to clarify the position, one evening after dinner at Lincoln's Inn Hall, a West Indian deputation approached the Law Officers of the Crown, Attorney-General Yorke and Solicitor-General Talbot, and asked for their opinion as to whether a slave becomes free by being in England or by being baptized. As Charles Stuart pertinently noted, the delegation representing the powerful West Indian interest 'had men to suit their purpose'.[41] These eminent lawyers, each of whom later became Lord Chancellor, categorically declared:

We are of the Opinion, That a Slave by coming from the West-Indies to Great Britain, doth not become free, and that his Master's Property or Right in him is not thereby determined or varied: And that Baptism doth not bestow freedom on him, nor make any Alteration in his Temporal Condition in these Kingdoms. We are also of the Opinion, that his Master may legally compel him to return again to the Plantations.[42]

About the same time the Bishop of London also declared 'that baptism made no sort of change in the political estate of a [Black]'.[43] In the words of Charles Stuart, 'The Church had given it [slavery] their sanction. The most distinguished lawyers crouched beneath the lie, and the Lord Chief Justice of the day [Lord Mansfield] affirmed its validity ... religion and humanity, were trampled upon without remorse. The inalienable rights of man ... were given to the winds. Then exulted the slavemaster. Then sunk the soul of the slave.'[44]

Not quite. The slave owners exulted all right, but, as the 'Hue and Cry' advertisements manifestly make clear, black men, women, and even children opposed the Bill of Rights granted to their owners by Yorke and Talbot in the only way open to them —flight. The Yorke and Talbot Opinion was the slave hunters' charter, and fugitive blacks were now violently hauled back by men who found 'nigger hunting' a very lucrative profession: 'Mischief framed by law, yet against law, thus took deep root in Britain. And the Crown and the nobles—and the monied interests —and the church and the bench and the bar, watered together the deadly plant. The whole nation seemed gone away with one consent, from God, and from law, and from its poor brother.'[45]

Again, not quite. Here and there, the fugitive blacks were sheltered by sympathetic Englishmen. In order to stamp out such acts, it became the practice of slave owners to warn off men of humane feelings from their property. In *The Bristol Journal*, 15 November 1746, Captain Eaton, announcing the escape of his black servant called Mingo, added; 'All persons are hereby forbidden entertaining the said Black at their peril.' In *The Bristol Journal* of 22 September 1757, Captain Ezekiel Nash threatened to prosecute anyone hiding his absconded black servant. On 15 April 1758, the same paper offered £5 for the recapture of a black boy who had absconded from one McNeal, who also menaced legal proceedings against anyone who detained his property.[46]

Reference to England as a 'land of slaves' during the period was indeed genuine: 'the nobility and high-born ladies were actual or potential slave owners. To doubt the justice of the institution would have caused a man to be dubbed a crank.'[47] But an accidental meeting in 1765 between an African boy near to death and an Englishman led the latter to doubt the justice of the institution for the rest of his life.

In 1765 David Lisle, a lawyer and slave master of Barbados, then living in London, nearly killed his slave Jonathan Strong, aged about seventeen, by brutally beating him with a pistol on the head. Jonathan Strong became nearly blind and lame and quite ill. In this condition 'he was turned adrift on the unpitying stones of the great metropolis, lame, blind, and faint, with ague and fever, and without a home. In this plight, while staggering along in quest of medical care, he was met by the Good Samaritan, Granville Sharp.'[48] Granville Sharp got Jonathan Strong admitted to St. Bartholomew's Hospital, through William Sharp, his brother and an eminent surgeon. After three and a half months' treatment, he was partially cured and discharged. He continued to need aid from the Sharp brothers and through them he secured employment in the service of an apothecary named Brown, in Fenchurch Street. He served Brown for about two years, and was gradually recovering, when his former owner, David Lisle, met and recognized him one day in the street. Seeing that his damaged property had recovered, Lisle immediately laid his plan: he had Jonathan Strong seized and lodged in the Poultry Compter, pending his transportation to the West Indies and slavery. As soon as possible, Jonathan Strong made known his case to Granville Sharp who lost no time in enjoining the keeper of the prison, at his peril, not to deliver the African to any person whatever; and then promptly invoked the jurisdiction of the Mayor of London. On 18 September 1767, the cause was tried at Mansion House, and as soon as the case was stated, the Chief

Magistrate of the City gave judgement. 'The lad,' said Sir Robert Kite, 'had not stolen anything, and is not guilty of any offence, and is therefore at liberty to go away.'[49] The agent of the claimant, nevertheless, seized Jonathan Strong by the arm, and still claimed him as property. Whereupon, Granville Sharp retorted: 'Sir, I charge you for an assault.' To avoid immediate commitment, the agent let go his piratical, slave-hunting grasp, 'and all bowed to the Lord Mayor and came away, Jonathan following Granville Sharp, and no one daring to touch him.'

For this procedure, Granville Sharp was charged with *robbery* by David Lisle, and received a challenge to give gentlemanlike satisfaction. 'You are a lawyer,' said Sharp, 'and you shall want no satisfaction which law can give you.' But the lawyers whom Granville Sharp consulted over the suit for trespass brought against him declared that the laws were against him. Sir James Eyre, Recorder of the City, and later Chief Justice of the Court of Common Pleas, whom Sharp retained as his counsel, adduced to him the infamous Yorke and Talbot Opinion, and informed him that Lord Mansfield, the Chief Justice, had concurred with the Opinion, to the odious extent of delivering up fugitive slaves to their claimants. Granville Sharp could not believe that the laws of England were really so injurious to mankind's rights as so many lawyers, for political reasons, had been pleased to assert. Thus, forsaken by his professional defenders, he was compelled, 'through the want of legal assistance, to make a hopeless attempt at self-defence, though I was totally unacquainted, either with the practice of the law or the foundations of it, having never opened a law-book (except the Bible) in my life, until that time.' Granville Sharp's efforts were far from hopeless. For nearly two years, during which time the suit was still pending, he gave himself to intense study of British Constitutional Law in all its bearings on human liberty. During his researches he was confirmed in his original opinion, that slavery is not permitted by English law. 'The word slaves,' he exulted, 'or anything that can justify the enslaving of others, is not to be found there, God be thanked.'[50] The result of his research was embodied in a tract entitled *A Representation of the Injustice and Dangerous Tendency of Tolerating Slavery; or of Admitting the Least Claim of Private Property in the Persons of Men, in England*. By means of copies in manuscript, circulated among the gentlemen of the Bar, the slave owner and his lawyers were intimidated, and the claimant-owner of Jonathan Strong, failing to bring forward his action, was mulcted in treble costs. Granville Sharp had won by default, but his undying hostility towards slavery and the slave trade had been aroused. The battle was but begun.

In 1770 an African named Thomas Lewis had left his master Robert Stapylton, and was residing in Chelsea. Stapylton with the aid of two watermen whom he had hired for the purpose, seized the person of Thomas Lewis on a dark night, and dragged him to a boat lying in the Thames. They gagged him, tied him with a cord, rowed him down to a ship, and put him on board to be sold as a slave in Jamaica. This base action took place near the garden of Mrs. Banks, the mother of Sir Joseph Banks (the botanist). Lewis it appears, on being seized, screamed violently. The servants of Mrs. Banks, who heard his cries, ran to his assistance, but the boat was gone. On informing their mistress of what had happened, she sent for Sharp, who began now to be known as the friend of the helpless Africans, and professed her willingness to incur the expense of bringing the delinquents to justice. Sharp, with some difficulty, procured a habeas corpus, in consequence of which Lewis was brought from Gravesend just as the vessel was on the point of sailing. The vessel on board which Lewis had been dragged and confined had reached the Downs, and had actually got under way for the West Indies. In two or three hours she would have been out of sight; but just at this critical moment the writ of habeas corpus was carried on board. 'The officer, who served it on the captain, saw the miserable African chained to the mainmast, bathed in tears, casting a last mournful look on the land of freedom, which was fast receding from his sight.' The captain, on receiving the writ, was outraged but, knowing the serious consequences of resisting the law of the land, gave up his prisoner, whom the officer carried safely 'but now crying for joy, to the shore'.[51]

On 12 July 1770, a bill was preferred and found by the Grand Jury of Middlesex against Stapylton and the two watermen, Malony and Armstrong, on behalf of Lewis, 'without the least demur or doubt on account of the plaintiff's complexion or idea of *private* property urged against him'. The cause was removed to the Court of King's Bench, and on 20 February 1771, the trial was held before Lord Mansfield, Chief Justice of the King's Bench. But so fraught was Mansfield's mind still with the false views of the day, that, although the jury found Stapylton 'guilty', the Chief Justice refused to proceed to judgement, and the criminals escaped. 'Such is *justice* in human hands! Against this proceeding of the judge, as against an open contempt of the laws of England, Granville Sharp prepared a strong protest.[52] 'Alas! it is the natural influence of slavery to make men hard,' Charles Sumner wrote, 'Gorgon-like it turns to stone.'[53] Lord Mansfield was not alone. His companion in contemporary fame, Blackstone, shared the petrifaction. Relying on Sir John Holt's decision, Blackstone declared in his *Commentaries*, 'that a slave or a Negro, the moment he lands in England, falls under the protection of the laws, and with regard to all natural rights becomes *eo instanti* a freeman.'[54] Paradoxically, however, he also declared the master's rights in the former slave to be undiminished and likened the African's condition to apprenticeship for life.[55] Accordingly, he, too, declined to defend Granville Sharp in the suit instituted by Jonathan Strong's claimant-owner.

Other slaves were rescued by Granville Sharp, but the general right to freedom of black slaves in Britain remained undecided. The case of James Somerset settled the issue.

James Somerset had been brought to England in November 1769 by his master, Charles Stewart, from Boston, Massachusetts, and in process of time, had left him, and claimed his freedom. Stewart had him kidnapped and carried on board the *Ann and Mary*, in order to be taken to Jamaica and there sold for a slave. Through a habeas corpus procured by the friends of the African, Somerset was released from the ship, where he had been detained in irons. The cause was brought by Lord Mansfield who granted the habeas corpus before the Court of King's Bench. On the advice of Granville Sharp, five counsel, Serjeants Davy and Glynn, James Mansfield, Hargrave, and Alleyne, were briefed to represent James Somerset. The question at issue was, 'Is every man in England, entitled to the liberty of his person, unless forfeited by the Laws of England?' Serjeant Davy, leading counsel for James Somerset, boldly declared, 'that no man at this day *is* or *can be*, a slave in England.' The cause of Somerset the Black 'continued from time to time, according to the convenience of counsel and the court, running through months, and occupying different days in January, February, and May, down to the 22d June, 1772, when judgement was finally delivered.'[56] The Chief Justice noted that in the return to the writ of habeas corpus, Stewart had claimed that he was entitled to remove Somerset from England by force, as the latter was his property. He then related the facts of the case, and after much lawyer-like circumlocution, decided as follows:

No master was ever allowed here to take a slave by force to be sold abroad[57] because he deserted from his service, or for any other reason whatever; we cannot say, the cause set forth by this return is allowed or approved by the laws of this kingdom, and therefore the man must be discharged.[58]

Thus through the persistence of Granville Sharp, Mansfield was forced to abandon the sanctity of the Yorke and Talbot Opinion, and declared that black slaves could not forcibly be removed from the country. It is worth emphasizing that the

Somerset case did not decide more than this. For 'much has been made of this case, by people constantly seeking for triumphs of humanitarianism',[59] who maintained that Mansfield by his modest ruling in the Somerset case freed all black slaves in eighteenth-century Britain. Professor Coupland, for example, asserted that from the day judgement was given in the Somerset case, 'all slaves in England, whether or not they chose to remain in their old master's service, were recognized as free men.'[60] This is quite untrue. Within a year of the decision in the Somerset case, the newspapers widely reported the first recorded breach of the Mansfield decree that a slave owner could not forcibly remove his slave from England. 'A black, who a few days before had run away from his master and got himself christened with intent to marry a white woman, his fellow servant, being taken and sent on board a ship in the Thames, took an opportunity of shooting himself through the head.'[61]

In a letter to Horace Walpole, dated July 1790, Hannah More related the kidnapping of an African slave 'in my city of Bristol'. The black girl had run away, 'because she would not return to one of those trafficking islands, whither her master was resolved to send her. To my great grief and indignation, the poor trembling wretch was dragged out from a hole in the top of a house where she had hid herself, and forced on board ship.'[62] *Bonner's Bristol Journal* of 8 December 1792 stated that a citizen had recently sold his black servant girl, who had been many years in his service, for £80 Jamaica currency, and that she had been shipped for that island. 'A bystander who saw her put on board the boat at Lamplighter's Hall says, "her tears flowed down her face like a shower of rain".'[63]

In the case of *The King* v. *The Inhabitants of Thames Ditton*,[64] decided by Mansfield in 1785, the Chief Justice intervened in the course of submission by counsel, and said, 'The determination [in the case of Somerset] go no further than that the master cannot by force compel him [the slave] to go out of the kingdom.' But this ruling of the Chief Magistrate of the land was never enforced. In another intervention in the case, Lord Mansfield revealed that 'where slaves have been brought here, and have commenced actions for their wages, I have always nonsuited the plaintiff' [that is the slave]. So, as he had persisted in delivering up all runaway slaves to their masters until his ruling in the Somerset case, Mansfield persistently ruled that the black slaves in Britain were not entitled to be paid for their labour. Consequently, in the case of *The King* v. *The Inhabitants of Thames Ditton*, Mansfield decided that an African woman who had been bought in America and brought to England by her owner was not a hired servant. Therefore, the African was outside the pauper legislation and not entitled to pauper relief on her owner's death, because, as Lord Mansfield said, 'The statutes do not relate to them [slaves], nor had they them in contemplation.'

The fiat of Lord Mansfield in the Somerset case in 1772 did not run in Scotland, which had and has a separate legal system, but only in England and Wales. As early as 1757, however, the Court of Session had been confronted with the question of whether ownership in slaves continued after they had reached Britain. In about 1750, a Mr. Sheddan had brought to Scotland from Virginia a black slave to be taught a trade. He was baptized, and, learning his trade, began to acquire notions of freedom and citizenship. When the master thought he had been long enough in Scotland to suit his purpose, the black was put on board a vessel bound for Virginia. He got a friend, however, to present for him a petition to the Court of Session. The report of the case in *Morison's Dictionary of Decisions* says: 'The Lords appointed counsel for the Black, and ordered memorials, and afterwards a hearing in presence, upon the respective claims of liberty and servitude by the master and the Black; but during the hearing in presence, the Black died, so the point was not determined.'

Six years after the Somerset decision, another case occurred in Scotland where the question of a master's rights over a black slave in Britain was at issue. The case of *Knight* v. *Wedderburn* acquired notice from the interest taken in it by Dr. Johnson, and the frequent mention of it in James Boswell's *Life of Johnson*. Wedderburn had bought in Jamaica a black boy of about twelve, called Knight. He came to Scotland as Wedderburn's personal servant, married in the country, and for some years seemed contented with his position. Probably at the suggestion of someone who wished to try the question as it had been tried in England, Knight went off, avowing that he was a free man.[65] Wedderburn maintained, however, that their mutual position gave him a right to claim the black's services, as if he had engaged himself as a servant for life. He applied to a Justice of the Peace, who at once issued a warrant for the black's apprehension. The matter came before the Sheriff of Perthshire, who decided that the colonial laws of slavery did not extend to Scotland, and that personal service for life is just another term for slavery. The Sheriff accordingly ruled that Knight was entitled to his freedom. After a tedious litigation the decision of the Sheriff was affirmed by the Court of Session, and Knight was declared free. Thus, in 1778, the highest tribunal in Scotland ruled that slavery was illegal in Scotland. Consequently, the decision of the Court of Session in *Knight* v. *Wedderburn*, went further than the decision of the

Court of King's Bench in the Somerset case.

Although in 1772 it was decreed that a master could not forcibly remove his slave from England and Wales, and in 1778 slavery was declared illegal in Scotland, chattel slavery continued in Britain until the abolition of colonial slavery in 1834. This is illustrated by the case of Grace Jones,[66] tried in the High Court of Admiralty in 1827. Mrs. Allen brought her black body-servant, Grace, from Antigua to England in 1822. Grace lived with her in England until 1823, and was then compelled to return to Antigua with her mistress. In 1825, proceedings were commenced in the Vice-Admiralty Court of Antigua against the owner of Grace alleging illegality with regard to the egress of Grace Jones in 1822 and her ingress in 1823. The myth attached to the Mansfield decree in the Somerset case (that a slave, the moment he lands in England, becomes free) was relied on, on behalf of Grace. The Vice-Admiralty Court of Antigua, of course, rejected the claim. On appeal to Lord Stowell in the High Court of Admiralty in England, Lord Stowell also held that Grace's temporary residence in England without manumission suspended, but did not extinguish, her status as a slave to which she reverted when she was enticed back to Antigua.

Mary Prince was brought from Antigua in 1828 by her owners Mr. and Mrs. John A. Wood of that island, who were visiting England to put their son to school and return with their daughters. Mary Prince, a victim of rheumatism, 'was willing to come to England: I thought that by going there I should probably get cured of my rheumatism.' But she suffered in England from the usual West Indian ill usage. 'They constantly kept cursing and abusing me.' Ultimately, matters came to head when Mary Prince, 'worse than ever' with her rheumatism, was ordered by her mistress to launder 'a great many heavy things'. She refused:

I told her I was too ill to wash such heavy things that day. She said, she supposed I thought myself a free woman, but I was not; and if I did not do it directly I should be instantly turned out of doors. I stood a long time before I could answer, for I did not know well what to do. I knew that I was free in England, but did not know where to go, or how to get my leaving; and therefore, I did not like to leave the house. ... at last I took courage and resolved that I would not be longer thus treated, but would trust to Providence. This was the fourth time they had threatened to turn me out, and, go where I might, I was determined now to take them at their word; though I thought it very hard, after I had lived with them for thirteen years, and worked for them like a horse, to be driven out in this way, like a beggar. My only fault was being sick, and therefore unable to please my mistress, who thought she never could get enough work out of her slaves; and I told them so.[67]

Mary Prince found her way to the meeting house of the Moravian Missionaries at Hatton Garden, and from thence to the Anti-Slavery Office in Aldermanbury. Eventually, the Secretary of the Anti-Slavery Society, Pringle, engaged her as a domestic servant in his household. From a year's observation of her conduct, Pringle found her 'really a well-disposed and respectable woman'.[68]

The cases of Grace Jones and Mary Prince were not exceptional. On the contrary, while the appeal of Grace Jones was pending, the Directors of the African Institution reported, in 1826: 'The Collector of the Customs [in Antigua] has twenty-five [Blacks] of the description under his care, whose future situation, if returned to their masters after this claim of freedom, the vengeance which has been already threatened them, and in one instance even executed, has not left it for mere imagination to conceive.'[69]

Yet Lord Stowell, who said in the course of his judgement in the appeal of Grace Jones that he was a 'stern Abolitionist', threw the black slaves to the wolves. And in 1831, the editor of Mary Prince's *History* declared emphatically, 'The case of Mary Prince is by no means a singular one; many of the same kind are daily occurring in England.'[70]

It is clear that both the import and the effect of Lord Mansfield's decree in the Somerset case have been exaggerated by men who have placed national vanity and pride before evidence of the truth of the Somerset decision and its aftermath. But this should not blind us to the fact that the outcome of the Somerset case was a triumph for the humanitarianism and assiduous zeal of Granville Sharp. Mansfield struggled hard to avoid rendering a judgement. Twice he suggested that Stewart should manumit Somerset so that he might be spared the necessity of deciding the cause. Granville Sharp, masterminding the *cause célèbre* on the side of Somerset, steadfastly refused a compromise. And so Mansfield was forced to make the modest ruling that a slave owner could not forcibly remove his black slave from England. Even so, if the decree had been enforced, it would almost have justified the subsequent lyrical outpourings. And here we must pay tribute to Somerset's counsel, who did not receive a penny for their prodigious effort. Serjeant Davy had opened the cause with the proposition, 'that no man at this day *is* or *can be* a slave in England'. Serjeant Glynn, James Mansfield (afterwards Chief Justice of the Common Pleas), Mr. Hargrave, and Mr. Alleyne were all patiently heard by the Court at length. The argument of Mr. Hargrave, who early volunteered his great learning in the case, is one of the masterpieces of the Bar. This was his first appearance in court; but it is well that Liberty had such support on that day.

Granville Sharp was not the first friend of the blacks, although he was the most renowned among them and best loved by them. The earliest friends were those kind-hearted anonymous English people who gave shelter and protection to runaway blacks and thus precipitated the empty threat, 'Trespassers Will Be Prosecuted', in 'Hue and Cry' advertisements. We must remember, too, the clergy who baptized the blacks and the laity who stood as godfathers to sons and daughters of Africa. The godparents took their duties seriously. Clarkson tells us that, 'When they [black slaves] were seized they usually sent to [their godfathers], if they had an opportunity, for their protection. And in the result, their godfathers maintained that they had been baptized, and that they were free on this account as well as by the general tenour of the laws of England.'[71] Thus, when Jonathan Strong was kidnapped and put in the Poultry Compter, he 'sent, as was usual, to his godfathers, John London and Stephen Nail, for their protection. They went, but were refused admittance to him. At length he sent for Mr. Granville Sharp.'[72] The Yorke and Talbot Opinion was designed to deter godfathers from espousing the cause of the oppressed Africans. But the attempt made by Jonathan Strong's godfathers to rescue him, albeit unsuccessfully, clearly indicates that the Opinion neither deterred nor intimidated them in carrying out their duties. Of the clergymen who baptized them, we read of one, Dr. Mayo (1733-91), Rector of a Stepney church:

He was particularly kind to the Blacks and uninstructed men of colour, who, employed generally on board of ship, occasionally resided in his parish, which is full of seafaring people. I suppose no clergyman in England ever baptized so many black men and Mulattoes; nor did he at any time baptize them without very much previous preparation. ... The attachment of these poor people to him was very great. Several of them never came into the Port of London, without waiting upon him, by way of testifying the respect in which they held him.[73]

An earlier friend of the blacks was Steele, the essayist, who wrote in *The Tatler* in 1710:

As I am a patron of persons who have no other friend to apply to, I cannot suppress the following complaint: Sir—I am a six year-old blackmoor boy, and have, by my lady's order, been christened by the chaplain. The good man has gone further with me, and told me a great deal of news; as that I am as good as my lady herself, as I am a Christian, and many other things; but for all this, the parrot who came over with me from our country is as much esteemed by her as I am. Besides this, the shock dog has a collar that cost as much as mine. I desire also to know whether, now I am Christian, I am obliged to dress like a Turk and wear a turbant. I am, sir, your most obedient servant, Pompey.[74]

It is well known that Dr. Johnson upon one occasion at Oxford, 'in company with some very grave men' as Boswell puts it in the *Life*, gave the toast, 'Here's to the next insurrection of the Negroes in the West Indies.' Towards the conclusion of his *Taxation no Tyranny*, Johnson asked, 'How is it that we hear the loudest *yelps* for liberty among the drivers of Negroes?' It is equally well known that Samuel Johnson was the master of a free black servant, Francis Barber, to whom he was devoted.

On 21 August 1773, Samuel Johnson and James Boswell on their way to the Hebrides, called on Lord Monboddo. When they left on the same day, Gory, the Laird's black servant, was sent as their guide along the high road. Boswell 'observed how curious it was to see an African in the north of Scotland, with little or no difference of manners from those of the natives.'[75] When Gory had guided Johnson and Boswell so far, and was about to depart, Johnson said to him: 'Mr. Gory, give me leave to ask you a question! "are you baptized?"' Gory answered that he was, and volunteered the information that he was confirmed by no less a prelate than the Bishop of Durham. Johnson then gave him a shilling and Gory took his leave of them. Although Johnson despised Monboddo (in point of fact, Johnson had not wanted to call on Monboddo and Boswell had to persuade him to), Boswell observed that the Laird's having a black servant 'was another point of similarity between Johnson and Monboddo'.[76]

Despite what Eric Williams has rightly called Johnson's 'monumental contempt for the savage man',[77] his opposition to slavery and the slave trade was unequivocal. Boswell noted in the *Life* that Johnson was always 'very zealous against slavery in every form', and his zealous opposition is best illustrated by his argument in favour of Joseph Knight, dictated to Boswell while the case of *Knight* v. *Wedderburn* was pending, and reproduced by Boswell in the *Life*:

... It is said according to the constitution of Jamaica he was legally enslaved; these constitutions are merely positive; and apparently injurious to the rights of mankind, because whoever is exposed to sale is condemned to slavery without appeal; by whatever fraud or violence he might have been originally brought into the merchant's power. In our own time Princes have been sold, by wretches to whose care they were entrusted, that they might have an European education; but when once they were brought to a market in the plantations, little would avail either their dignity or their wrongs. The laws of Jamaica afford the Negro no redress. His colour is considered as a sufficient testimony against him. It is to be lamented that moral right should ever give way to political convenience. But if temptations of interest are sometimes too strong for human virtue, let us at least retain a virtue where there is no temptation to quit it. In the present case there is apparent right on one side, and no convenience on the other. Inhabitants of this island can neither gain riches nor power by taking away the liberty of any part of the human species. The sum of the argument is this:- No man is by nature the property of another: The defendant is, therefore, by nature free: The rights of nature must be some way forfeited before they can be justly taken away: That the defendant has by any act forfeited the rights of nature we require to be proved; and if no proof of such forfeiture can be given, we doubt not but the justice of the court will declare him free.

Boswell, who accused Johnson of 'a zeal without knowledge', in his opposition to slavery in every form, naturally rejected Johnson's argument in favour of the African, based on natural rights. After printing Johnson's argument he added:

I beg leave to enter my most solemn protest against his general doctrine with respect to the *Slave Trade*. For I will resolutely say—that his unfavourable notion of it was owing to prejudice, and imperfect or false information. The wild and dangerous attempt which has for some time been persisted in to obtain an act of our Legislature, to abolish so very important and necessary a branch of commercial interest, must have been crushed at once, had not the insignificance of the zealots who vainly took the lead in it, made the vast body of Planters, Merchants, and others, whose immense properties are involved in that trade, reasonably enough suppose that there could be no danger. The encouragement which the attempt has received excites my wonder and indignation; ... To abolish a *status*, which in all ages GOD has sanctioned, would ... be *robbery* to an innumerable class of our fellow-subjects.

As Wylie Sypher pertinently observed, 'Boswell, like many an M.P., has discovered that the slave-trade gains England £300,000 annually at a moment when the nation is impoverished.'[78]

William Roscoe was a consistent and zealous Abolitionist. He was not just a merchant, but a merchant from the slaving port of Liverpool. He was also an author and poet. In *The Wrongs of Africa* (1787), he asked his countrymen:

> Form'd with the same capacity of pain,
> The same desire of pleasure and of ease,
> Why feels not man for man?

Earlier in the Preface to the book, he had warned: 'The spirit of trade may degrade the national character, and endanger our sacrificing the principles of justice and feelings of humanity to the acquirement of wealth. It becomes us therefore to guard against the introduction of those base and sordid maxims which represent every thing as fair that is lucrative, and separate infamy from villainy, provided it is successful.'

31

In the following year, 1788, Roscoe published in prose *A General View of the African Slave Trade demonstrating its Injustice and Impolicy*. In October 1806 Roscoe was elected Member of Parliament for Liverpool in the Whig interest. He spoke in Parliament in favour of the Bill to Abolish the Slave Trade in February 1807, saying, 'for thirty years I have never ceased to condemn this inhuman traffic'.[79] The line Roscoe had taken made him many enemies in Liverpool. In May 1807 he made a sort of public entry into Liverpool attended by his friends. Parties of seamen armed with bludgeons obstructed the procession, and in a scene of great tumult, a magistrate was attacked and his horse stabbed. Roscoe was nominated again as Member for Liverpool at the ensuing election, but the degree of hostility against him ensured his defeat.[80]

In 1809 Roscoe was instrumental in the rescue of nine blacks who were destined for servitude. Some time in the month of September that year, Roscoe was informed that nine black men were confined in the borough gaol of Liverpool for debt. On further inquiry, he learned that they had been arrested by the master of a Portuguese vessel from Brazil—then in the port of Liverpool—for the purpose, as was supposed, of keeping them in safe custody until his ship should be ready for the sea. As it seemed clear that in such a case no debt could exist, Roscoe engaged two friends to put up bail for the defendants. Before an order was obtained for their discharge, the master and his agents, being apprised of these proceedings, surrounded the prison with a great number of armed Portuguese seamen and others, for the purpose of seizing the prisoners, and the attorney for the master of the vessel sent an order to the gaoler to discharge the blacks. The black men, however, had been warned of their danger and, in one of the instances of solidarity between blacks and whites to be met with in this narrative, their fellow-prisoners declared they would not let them be taken away by force. The desperadoes were therefore obliged to depart without their prey. The next day, Roscoe attended on the Magistrates and Recorders of Liverpool when an inquiry into these proceedings took place. Ultimately, the master having undertaken, on his not being prosecuted, that the men should be set at liberty, and that he should pay all the costs, and relinquish further proceedings, the nine black men were immediately released from their confinement. 'In the course of these proceedings, Mr. Roscoe was most ably assisted by Mr. Stanistreet and Mr. Avison, two very respectable solicitors, who strenuously advocated the cause of the prisoners at several hearings on the subject, and generously declined any recompense for their services.' The blacks were evidently of great value, having

James Ramsay:
his *Essay on the Treatment and Conversion of African Slaves in the British Sugar Colonies* (London, 1784) provided the fillip to the rise of the British Anti-Slavery Movement

William Roscoe:
a Liverpool merchant who vigorously opposed the British slave trade in prose and in verse

been bred to the sea, and one of them was actually the boatswain of the ship. 'Eight of these men immediately afterwards entered, most cheerfully, into his Majesty's service; and the ninth, being more infirm, was taken by a friend of Mr. Roscoe's on board of one of his own vessels.'[81]

In 1784 Peter Peckard, Vice-Chancellor of Cambridge University, Master of Magdalene College, and Dean of Peterborough, preached against the slave trade, and in the following year, Peckard set as a subject for the Latin prize essay contest within Cambridge University, the question: *Anne liceat invitos in servitutem dare?* (Is it right to make slaves of others against their will?). The result was one of the great classics of Abolitionist literature, Clarkson's *Essay on the Slavery and the Commerce of the Human Species, particularly the African.*

Peckard was well acquainted with Olaudah Equiano, the black Abolitionist and leader of the African community in England in the last decades of the eighteenth century. Equiano received every assistance from Peckard in his Abolitionist activities, and he may well have met his English wife through Peckard.

In his *Thoughts Upon Slavery*, in 1774, John Wesley made a powerful denunciation of 'that execrable sum of all villanies commonly called the Slave Trade'.[82] 'Liberty is the right of every human creature,' the great divine solemnly affirmed, 'and no human law can deprive him of that right, which he derives from the law of nature.'[83] On Sunday 26 December 1758, Wesley had baptized in Wandsworth two blacks 'belonging to Mr. Gilbert, a gentleman lately come from Antigua'. Again on Sunday 5 March 1786, Wesley baptized a young black 'who appeared to be deeply serious and much affected; as indeed the whole congregation'. At Whitehaven in Scotland in May 1780, Wesley had been very much impressed by the devotion of a black woman he met at a Methodist meeting. 'She seemed to be fuller of love than any of the rest.'[84] When Granville Sharp, Thomas Clarkson, Samuel Hoare, and others joined forces to form the Society for the Abolition of the Slave Trade in 1787, Wesley wrote to Hoare, on 18 August 1787: 'What little I can do to promote this excellent work, I shall do with pleasure.' On Monday 3 March 1788, he gave notice of his intention to preach on the slave trade. In consequence, 'on Thursday, the house from end to end was filled with high and low, rich and poor.' His discourse produced a 'storm':

The people rushed upon each other with the utmost violence, the benches were broken in pieces; and nine-tenths of the congregation appeared to be struck with the same panick. In about six minutes the storm ceased, almost as suddenly as it arose. And all being calm, I went on without the least interruption.

It was the strangest incident of the kind I ever remember; and believe none can account for it, without supposing preternatural influence. Satan fought lest his kingdom should be delivered up. We set Friday apart as a day of fasting and prayer, that God would remember those poor outcasts of men, and (what seems impossible with men, considering the wealth and power of their oppressors) make a way for them to escape, and break their chains in sunder.[85]

The attitude of George Whitefield was in sharp contrast to that of Wesley. For religious conviction and revivalism did not keep Whitefield from being an ardent supporter of slavery or from owning slaves.[86] Whitefield was, in a sense, Wesley's Boswell.

The economist Adam Smith asserted, in *The Wealth of Nations* (1776), that slave labour was dearer than that of freemen, and illustrated conclusively why the service of freemen is to be preferred to that of slaves. Much earlier, in *Theory of Moral Sentiments* (1759), he had claimed in a famous passage, that there was not a black from the coast of Africa who did not possess a degree of magnanimity, which the soul of his sordid owner was too often scarcely capable of conceiving. 'Fortune never exerted more cruelly her empire over mankind, than when she subjected those nations of heroes to the refuse of the gaols of Europe, to wretches who possess the virtues neither of the countries which they come from, nor of those which they go to, whose levity, brutality, and baseness, so justly expose them to the contempt of the vanquished.'

Among the lawyers, apart from Somerset's counsel, Thomas Day was the most vocal friend of blacks. Although called to the Bar, Day never practised his profession. Though nothing was done to punish those who had kidnapped the black man who shot himself on board the ship lying in the Thames in 1773, the incident gave rise to Thomas Day's famous poem *The Dying Negro* (1773). Day wrote eloquently about the black's determination not to drag his body to the West Indies: 'To groan beneath some dastard planter's chain'.

In 1785, in *A Dialogue Between a Justice of the Peace and a Farmer*, Day ridiculed Blackstone's paradoxical judgement on the legal status of black slaves in England. 'I cannot say I perfectly understand that last passage, how the negroe is a free man, and yet his master may possibly have a right to his service.'[87]

Granville Sharp, together with Thomas Clarkson and James Ramsay, were the best known friends of the blacks in the black community in London. Olaudah Equiano paid a memorable tri-

bute to this trinity in his autobiography: 'Granville Sharp, Esq;
the Reverend Thomas Clarkson; the Reverend James Ramsay;
our approved friends, men of virtue, are an honour to their country, ornamental to human nature, happy in themselves, and benefactors to mankind!'[88]

Ottobah Cugoano, another central figure in the African community, referred to Granville Sharp in his book as 'the amiable
and indefatigable friend of mankind'. Clarkson was the 'excellent' author of the *Essay on the Slavery and Commerce of the
Human Species,*[89] and James Ramsay was 'the worthy and judicious author of *An Essay on the Treatment and Conversion of
African Slaves in the British Sugar Colonies'.*[90] Ignatius Sancho,
the golden black boy of the English aristocracy and gentry,
declared that 'Mr. Sharpe's strictures upon slavery [are] of consequence to every one of humane feeling'.[91] Granville Sharp was
undoubtedly the best loved of the trinity. In a letter addressed to
him and signed by twelve Sons of Africa, he was acclaimed as
'Him who has been the great source and support of our hopes.
We need not use many words. We are those who are considered
as slaves, even in England itself, till your aid and exertions set us
free.'[92]

The black community of this period was divided into three
classes: the slaves, the free, and those who occupied the halfway
house between bondage and freedom. This middle class is examined in the next chapter.

1. 'The Black Man', *All the Year Round*, XIII, New Series, a journal edited by
Charles Dickens (1875), pp. 489-93.
2. This suggests that the missing lad's hair was 'polled' or cropped, after the Puri-
tanical fashion of the time.
3. *All the Year Round*, XIII, New Series (1875), p. 490.
4. John Latimer, *Annals of Bristol in the Eighteenth Century*, p. 146.
5. The date of the entry in Pepys' diary is 30 May 1662.
6. *All the Year Round*, p. 490.
7. Which may be a corruption of 'Black as a Moor'.
8. William Makepeace Thackeray, *The Four Georges* (London, 1861), p. 52; J.
A. Rogers, *Sex and Race* (New York, 1940), I, p. 201.
9. John Latimer, op. cit., p. 147.
10. *All the Year Round*, p. 491.
11. 'Black Slaves in England', *Chambers's Journal of Popular Literature,
Science, and Art*, Fifth Series, VIII (1891), pp. 65-7.
12. *The Gentleman's Magazine*, XXXIII, 1763.
13. Gomer Williams, *A History of the Liverpool Privateers with an Account of
the Liverpool Slave Trade* (Liverpool, 1897), p. 474.
14. In *Chambers's Journal*, op. cit., p. 66, the suggestion that the sale of Rice's

black boy was the first instance of a sale by auction was assumed to be correct.

15. Gomer Williams, op. cit., p. 479.
16. Ibid., p. 476.
17. Liverpool Papers, British Library, Add. MSS. 38416, fol. 134.
18. John Latimer, op. cit., p. 15.
19. *Chambers's Journal*, op. cit., p. 66.
20. Gomer Williams, op. cit., p. 473.
21. 'Granville Sharp Letter Book', pp. 34-5, at York Minster Library, York.
22. Victoria Sackville-West, *Knole and the Sackvilles* (London, 1922), p. 191.
23. Gomer Williams, op. cit., p. 474.
24. J. Jean Hecht, *Continental and Colonial Servants in Eighteenth Century England* (Northampton, Mass., 1954), p. 40. According to Victoria Sackville-West, 'the black page at Knole, of which there had always been one since the days of Lady Anne Clifford ... had always been called John Morocco regardless of what his true name might be'. Sackville-West, op. cit., p. 191.
25. Horace Walpole, *The Letters of Horace Walpole* (Oxford, 1903-5), III, p. 122.
26. K. L. Little, in *Negroes in Britain* (London, 1948), suggests that by giving classical names to their chattels the more literary minded among the British were enabled to perpetuate their favourite philosopher (p. 168).
27. The small black boys 'had an exotic charm closely akin to that which the age found so captivating in the art and manufactures of the Orient'. Hecht, op. cit., p. 36.
28. *All the Year Round*, p. 491.
29. On 'thievishness' among slaves, Frederick Douglass said in his own inimitable way: 'We were compelled either to beg, or to steal, and we did both. I frankly confess, that while I hated everything like stealing, *as such*, I nevertheless did not hesitate to take food, when I was hungry, wherever I could find it. Nor was this practice the mere result of an unreasoning instinct; it was, in my case, the result of a clear apprehension of the claims of morality. I weighed and considered the matter, closely, before I ventured to satisfy my hunger by such means. Considering that my labor and person were the property of Master Thomas, and that I was by him deprived of the necessaries of life— necessaries obtained by my own labour—it was easy to deduce the right to supply myself with what was my own ... . To be sure, this was stealing, according to the law and gospel I heard from St. Michael's pulpit; but I had already begun to attach less importance to what dropped from that quarter.' Frederick Douglass, *My Bondage and My Freedom* (New York, 1855), pp. 188-9.
30. Herbert Aptheker, *American Negro Slave Revolts* (New York, 1969), p. 3.
31. John Rushworth, *Historical Collections of Private Passages of State, weighty matters in Law, remarkable proceedings in five Parliaments ... .* (London, 1680-1722), II, p. 468.
32. (1677) 2 Levinz. 201.
33. (1694) 1 L. Raym. 147.
34. (1698) 1 L. Raym. 146.
35. (1701) 2 Salk. 666.
36. (1706) 2 Salk. 666.
37. Morgan Godwyn, *Trade Preferr'd before Religion, and Christ made to give place to Mammon: Represented in Sermon relating to the Plantations. First Preached at Westminster-Abby, and afterwards in divers Churches in London* (London, 1685), pp. 4-5. Although Morgan Godwyn, who was resident in Virginia and Barbados for a time, was very much in favour of the conversion of African slaves into Christianity, he was not an Abolitionist. On the contrary, he vigorously urged the conversion of the slaves because Christianity 'presseth *absolute* and entire *Obedience* to *Rulers* and *Superiours*, as may be collected from almost innumerable places of Scripture; ... It [Christianity] establisheth the *Authority of Masters*, over

their Servants and Slaves, in as high a measure, as even themselves could have prescribed ... . Exacting the strictest *Fidelity* ... Requiring service *with singleness of heart, as unto the Lord, and not unto Men*. ... And so far it is from encouraging Resistance, that it allows them not the *liberty of Gainsaying*, or making undutiful replys to their Masters. And referring them to *future recompense in Heaven*, for their *faithful services done to them upon Earth'*. Morgan Godwyn, *The Negro's and Indians Advocate, Suing for Their Admission into the Church: or a Persuasive to the Instructing and Baptizing of the Negro's and Indians in Our Plantations. Shewing, that as the Compliance herewith Can Prejudice No Mans Interest; so the Wilful Neglecting and Opposing of It, Is No Less than a Manifest Apostacy from the Christian Faith. To which is Added, A Brief Account of Religion in Virginia* (London, 1680), p. 112.

38. William Hardy, *Middlesex County Records* (London, 1905), p. 6.

39. Sir William Blackstone, *Commentaries on the Laws of England* (Oxford, 1765-9), Bk. I, p. 413.

40. John Latimer, *Annals of Bristol in the Seventeenth Century* (Bristol, 1887), p. 344.

41. Charles Stuart, *A Memoir of Granville Sharp* (New York, 1830), p. 6.

42. *The Gentleman's Magazine*, XI (1741), p. 186.

43. During the hearing of the case of James Somerset in 1772, one of the Judges sitting with Lord Mansfield in the Court of King's Bench read the sentiments of the Bishop of London. See, *The Gazetter* and *New Daily Advertiser*, (15 May 1772).

44. Stuart, op. cit., pp. 6-7.

45. Ibid., p. 7.

46. Latimer, op. cit., p. 147.

47. Robert Graham, *Doughty Deeds* (London, 1925), p. 57.

48. Charles Sumner, *Works* (Boston, 1875-83), III, *The Life of Granville Sharp*, pp. 481-519.

49. 'An Account of the Occasion which Compelled Granville Sharp to study Law, and The Defence of Negroe Slaves in England' (MS.); Granville Sharp papers at Hardwicke Court, Gloucestershire, Box No. 54.

50. Prince Hoare, *Memoirs of Granville Sharp* (London, 1828). 2nd ed., I, pp. 54-8.

51. Thomas Clarkson, *A History of the Rise, Progress, and Accomplishment of the Abolition of the African Slave-Trade* (London, 1808), I, 73-5; Hoare, op. cit., II, pp. 78-92; Sumner, op. cit., p. 498.

52. Stuart, op. cit., p. 10.

53. Sumner, op. cit., p. 499.

54. Blackstone, op. cit., Bk. I, p. 123.

55. Ibid. Bk.I, pp. 411-13.

56. Hoare, op. cit., I, p. 113; Sumner, op. cit., p. 501.

57. Granville Sharp, *The Just Limitation of Slavery in the Laws of God* (London, 1776), Appendix No. 8.

58. But Mansfield had, of course, delivered about half a dozen runaway slaves to their owners before Granville Sharp started his defence of the oppressed Africans. See, for example, *The Gazetter* (26 May 1772).

59. Eric Williams, op. cit., p. 45.

60. Sir Reginald Coupland, *The British Anti-Slavery Movement* (London, 1933), p. 50.

61. *The London Chronicle*, XXXIII (1773), p. 597.

62. Latimer, op. cit., p. 492.

63. Ibid.

64. (1785) 4 Doul. 300.

65. Boswell was wrong when he asserted in the *Life* that 'it was officiously suggested to [Knight] that he would be found entitled to his liberty without any limita-

tion. He accordingly brought his action.' It was Wedderburn who started the proceedings.

66. (1827) St. Tr. (N.S.) 273.

67. Mary Prince, *The History of Mary Prince, A West Indian Slave. Related by Herself* (London, 1831), pp. 18-20. T. Pringle, Secretary of the Anti-Slavery Society, and an English lady were her amanuenses.

68. Ibid., p. 26.

69. *The Twentieth Report of the Committee of the African Institution* (London, 1826), p. 31.

70. Mary Prince, op. cit., p. 40.

71. Clarkson, op. cit., I, p. 64.

72. Ibid., p. 65.

73. Obituary Notice of Dr. Mayo in *The Orthodox Churchman's Magazine*, II (1802), p. 30.

74. *All the Year Round*, p. 491.

75. James Boswell, *The Journal of a Tour to the Hebrides* (London, 1785), p. 83.

76. Ibid., pp. 82-3.

77. Eric Williams, *From Columbus to Castro: The History of the Caribbean 1492-1969* (London, 1970), p. 212.

78. Wylie Sypher, *Guinea's Captive Kings: British Anti-Slavery Literature of the XVIIIth Century* (Chapel Hill, 1942), p. 213.

79. *The London Chronicle* (24 February 1807).

80. *Dictionary of National Biography*, s.v. William Roscoe.

81. *Fourth Report of the Committee of the African Institution, 1810* (London, 1814), pp. 23-5. In 1814 two African children were rescued from another Portuguese captain in Plymouth as he was about to take them to Lisbon. 'Through the benevolence of the inhabitants of Plymouth, these two children, as well as another [African] girl rescued in a similar manner from destined captivity, have been comfortably provided for.' *Ninth Report of the Committee of the African Institution, 1815* (London, 1815), p. 68. Twelve years later, in 1826, five more African children were rescued from on board a French vessel, which had been driven by stress of weather into the port of St. Ives, in Cornwall. Two of the children died of measles at Hampstead, two returned to Sierra Leone, and the fifth, Louis Asa-Asa, remained in England, and lived with the Abolitionist George Stephen. See T. Pringle, *Narrative of Louis Asa-Asa* (London, 1831).

82. John Wesley, *Journal*, ed. Nehemiah Curnock (London, 1909-16), V, p. 445.

83. Wesley, *Thoughts Upon Slavery* (London, 1774), p. 51.

84. Wesley, *Journal*, IV, pp. 247-8; VI, pp. 277-8; VII, p. 144.

85. Wesley, *Journal*, VII, pp. 359-60.

86. David Brion Davis, *The Problem of Slavery in Western Culture* (London, 1970), p. 419.

87. Thomas Day, *A Dialogue Between a Justice of the Peace and a Farmer* (London, 1785), p. 4.

88. Olaudah Equiano, *The Interesting Narrative of the Life of Olaudah Equiano, or Gustavus Vassa, the African* (London, 1789), II, p. 248.

89. Ottobah Cugoano, *Thoughts and Sentiments on the Evil of Slavery* (London, 1787), p. 100.

90. Ibid., p. 15.

91. Ignatius Sancho, *Letters of the late Ignatius Sancho, An African* (London, 1803), 5th ed., p. 197.

92. Hoare, op. cit., II, p. 114.

# 3

# Privileged Caste

Not all the black slaves in Britain were as savagely treated as
Jonathan Strong, or as shabbily and callously cast off as the black
girls kidnapped and sold into slavery in Bristol in 1667, 1790,
and 1792, after they had given their masters and mistresses long
years of faithful service. Even on the plantations, as C. L. R.
James has pointed out, not all the slaves suffered from the bestial
practices of slave owners and slave drivers, which were the usual
features of slave life. There was a small privileged caste, the
foremen of the gangs, coachmen, cooks, butlers, maids, nurses,
female companions, and other house servants. 'These repaid their
kind treatment and comparatively easy life with a strong attachment to their masters, and have thus enabled Tory historians,
Regius professors, and sentimentalists to represent plantation
slavery as a patriarchal relation between master and slave.'[1]

The fate of Jonathan Strong, who never really recovered from
the savage cruelty of the man who called himself his master, and
who died on 17 April 1773, may be contrasted with that of Joseph
Harvey. In about 1740, Edward Shanley had brought over to
England (whether from the West Indies or America is not known)
a slave, then only eight or nine years old, and presented him to
his niece, Margaret Hamilton, who had the boy baptized and
changed his name to Joseph Harvey (and not one of the more
usual classical names). Margaret Hamilton did not consider or
treat Joseph Harvey as a chattel or plaything. On the contrary,
she stood *in loco parentis* to the African boy. On 9 July 1752, she
knew she was dying. About an hour before her death, she
directed Joseph Harvey to take out a purse which was in her
dressing table drawer, and, delivering it to him, she made a
*donatio mortis causa*, saying, 'Here, take this, there is £700 or
£800 in bank notes, and some more in money, but I cannot
directly tell what, but it is all for you, to make you happy: make
haste, put it in your pocket, tell nobody, and pay the butcher's
bill.' He then knelt down and thanked her. She said 'God bless
you, make a good use of it.'[2]

Some other black body-servants also had masters who did not
repay years of devoted and faithful service with consignment into
the plantations and slavery. Such was Jack Beef, the servant of
John Baker, diarist and former Solicitor-General of the Leeward

Islands. Jack Beef accompanied Baker on his return to England. He attended his master on horseback, went on messages and did commissions in London, and was in much demand among John Baker's friends and neighbours for cooking turtles and bottling wines. He went out with the hounds, he was on friendly terms with the white servants, and accompanied them to the theatres in London, besides attending 'Balls of Blacks', as dances held by the African community were referred to in contemporary parlance. He left his master's service on 2 January 1771, after his emancipation, and was about to return to the West Indies, a free man with his small savings. Then, four days later, he died in his sleep: 'Jan. 7, 1771. Jack Beef died yesterday after a good dinner, when he said he was better and would take a nap on bed; he did so and seemed to sleep quiet, but went and died in his sleep.' His funeral, for which John Baker gave orders, took place on 10 January at the cemetery near the Foundling Hospital, and was attended by the Baker family, his fellow servants, and at least one of his kinsmen.[3]

When Benjamin Franklin and his brother William were in London in 1760, King, the black servant of William, ran away. In a letter to America dated 27 June 1760, Benjamin Franklin said that the African was soon found in Suffolk, where he had been taken into the service of a lady, who was very fond of the idea of making him a Christian, and contributing to his education and improvement. 'The Lady sent him to School, has taught him to read and write, to play on the Violin and the French Horn,[4] with some other Accomplishments more useful in a Servant. Whether she will be willing to part with him, or persuade Billy to sell him to her, I know not.'[5]

When Lord Mansfield supposedly freed black slaves in their thousands in 1772, he was holding in slavery—at least nominally—his niece by blood, Dido Elizabeth Lindsay, who was the natural daughter of Sir John Lindsay, Lord Mansfield's nephew. Thomas Hutchinson, the Loyalist, visiting the Mansfields at Caenwood on 29 August 1779, wrote in his diary: 'A Black came in after dinner and sat with the ladies, and after coffee, walked with the company in the gardens, one of the young ladies having her arm within the other.'[6] Hutchinson went on to record that 'Sir John Lindsay having taken her mother prisoner in a Spanish vessel, brought her to England, where she was delivered of this girl, of which she was then with child, and which was taken care of by Lord Mansfield, and has been educated by his family.' What Hutchinson did not say was that Dido Elizabeth was the daughter of Sir John. But we know from Sir John Lindsay's obituary notices in *The Morning Herald*, 9 January 1788, and in

*The London Chronicle* for the same day that, 'Sir John Lindsay was the nephew to Lord Mansfield; he has died, we believe, without any legitimate issue, but has left one natural daughter, a Mulatto, who has been brought up in Lord Mansfield's family almost from her infancy.' In fact, Dido Elizabeth had a brother named John. For, in his will, Sir John Lindsay left £1,000 upon trust for John and Elizabeth. Nothing, however, is known about John. According to the obituary notice, Dido Elizabeth was of 'amiable disposition and [her] accomplishments have gained her the highest respect from all his Lordship's relations and visitants.' According to Hutchinson, Lord Mansfield 'has been reproached for showing a fondness for her ... She is a sort of Superintendent over the dairy, poultry yard, &c; which we visited, and she was called upon by my Lord every minute for this and that, and showed the greatest attention to everything he said.' While the Somerset case was pending, Hutchinson recorded that a Jamaica planter, being asked what judgement Mansfield would give, made the impatient remark, 'No doubt, he will be set free, for Lord Mansfield keeps a black in his house which governs him and the whole family.' Precisely because the Somerset judgement was not a declaration of emancipation for the black slaves in England, Lord Mansfield in his will, dated 17 April 1783, confirmed the freedom of Dido. In addition, he gave her an annuity of £100 for life with £500 in money. So she was comfortably provided for.

In common with the great ladies of the period, Elizabeth Chudleigh, the licentious Duchess of Kingston, had a black boy named Sambo as a pet. The Duchess had Sambo when he was five or six years old. She was so fond of him that she dressed him in elegant style, taking him with her to most of the public places she frequented, 'especially to the play, where he sat in the boxes with her'. But all good things come to an end, and as Sambo grew up, 'he was deemed at last too big to be admitted to those favours formerly enjoyed with his mistress'. Instead of riding in the coach, the black boy was obliged to mount outside. The Duchess now sent him to school, but 'he never learned anything'. Which is not surprising, considering the sort of life he had hitherto led. Sambo was now about eighteen or nineteen years old. He started staying out several days and nights at a time, and his haunts 'were chiefly in Hedge-lane amongst a set of whores and ruffians'. Clearly, Sambo had outgrown his usefulness, and in due course, he was dispatched to the West Indies and slavery.[7]

The most celebrated of the privileged caste of black slaves in Britain was undoubtedly Soubise, the protégé of the eccentric Duchess of Queensberry. Soubise was a very interesting youth, in whose welfare the Duchess manifested an uncommon concern.[8] This is well illustrated by a story told a few days after the Duchess died on 17 July 1777. *The London Morning Post*, 22 July 1777, related how 'about two months ago', the African raped one of the Duchess's maids, having enticed her 'to a notorious bawdy-house [in the Strand] for the accomplishment of his designs'. When the injured girl told the Duchess what had happened, 'her Grace offered her money, and told her not to speak of it, and she would take care of her.' Upon the maid's refusal of the bribe, and 'finding the girl determined to appeal to the laws of her country', the Duchess sent for the African, 'and having filled his pockets, sent him off to Harwich, where he might either have the opportunity of escaping, or waiting till such time as the girl's resentment could be softened.' In fact Soubise left England for good on 15 July 1777, that is, two days before the death of the Duchess of Queensberry. But, *The Morning Post* reported in the same article:

The Duchess of Queensberry, finding her dissolution approached very fast, earnestly recommended her favourite black, S[oubise], to the protection of the Duke.—Our correspondent expresses his surprise, how the head of such a noble family, should suffer a miscreant of a Negro to live under his roof, spending large sums of money, and thereby enabling him to indulge the most vicious appetite, that perhaps ever was implanted in the heart of a vile slave.[9]

To put the rape story beyond doubt, *The Morning Post* told its readers that the story 'may be relied on as a known fact', adding, 'And is mentioned to show the unaccountable attachment his noble patroness had for him.' Catherine—'Kitty'—Duchess of Queensberry, 'was one of the most celebrated women of her day, ... The influence of the Duchess over Pitt was supposed to be very powerful.'[10]

In the first volume of his *Reminiscences*, Henry Angelo gives the following account of the life and adventures of Soubise.[11] He was born in St. Kitts, and brought to England by Captain Stair Douglas R.N., who during a conversation with the Duchess mentioned the black boy as being uncommonly smart and intelligent. The Duchess at once felt an interest in the boy and persuaded the captain to give him to her. She named him Soubise, sent him to school, supported him genteelly, and gave him a good education. He was taught to fence and soon became an excellent swordsman. He grew fast and was engaging in his manners. The Duchess's maids, who had little more to do than read novels, romances, and plays, called him young Othello.

An 'Index of Rank' waiting on members of 'The Club' including Johnson, Reynolds, Garrick, Goldsmith, and Boswell

Julius Soubise caricatured fencing with his patroness, Kitty, Duchess of Queensberry

Soubise soon brought himself into the favour of the Duke, as well as the Duchess, and became a pet of both. The Duke sent him to the *manège* of Henry Angelo's father, where he became in a short time a most accomplished rider. 'At the end of the riding-house was a gallery for spectators; hither the old Duchess frequently came, accompanied by other ladies, to see her black protégé perform his equestrian exercises.' Eventually, the Duchess proposed to the elder Angelo that he have Soubise articled to him as his assistant to teach riding and fencing. After some hesitation, the elder Angelo took him on. He hesitated because he feared that Soubise's 'colour and humble birth might have made him repulsive to his high born pupils'. But Soubise's engaging manners and good nature gained him the affection of everyone. After two uneventful years, Soubise suddenly changed. He became one of the most conspicuous fops of the town. He frequented the Opera, and other theatres; sported a fine horse and groom in Hyde Park; became a member of many fashionable clubs. He wore such expensive perfumes that in theatre lobbies the fops would exclaim ' I scent Soubise!' Whenever he was in attendance at Eton, he dined in style at the Castle Inn, took his champagne and claret, and entertained half-a-dozen hangers-on. His bills at the inn were regularly discharged by the Duchess. For nearly two years his excesses proceeded unchecked. The Duchess was now faced with the problem of what to do with her dashing protégé. After the rape scandal and at the suggestion of the elder Angelo, he was sent to India and, being an accomplished master of riding and fencing, he established an academy in Bengal, where he died in a riding accident. Gainsborough made a sketch of the head of the self-dubbed Black Prince, and Zoffany a small whole-length picture of his person, which, though not tall, was well proportioned.

Soubise evokes comparison with another black Don Juan of this period who lived in Paris. *The Morning Post*, 15 December 1786,[12] reported:

There is a Mr. George, a Creole, son to the French Governor of St. Domingo, now at Paris, ... He is so superior at the sword, that there is an edict of the Parliament of Paris, to make his engagement in any duel actual death. He is the first dancer ... in the world. He plays upon seven instruments of music, beyond any other individual. He speaks twenty-six languages, and maintains public theses in each. He walks round the various circles of human sciences like the master of each; and, strange to be mentioned, this Mr. George is a mulatto, the son of an African mother.

In fact, George was only one of that great company of mixed-blooded men: Alexander Pushkin and Alexandre Dumas, George Bridgetower and Samuel Coleridge-Taylor, Frederick Douglass and W. E. B. DuBois, Richard Wright and James Baldwin, Paul Robeson and Louis Armstrong, C. L. R. James and Eric Williams, and many others.

1. C. L. R. James, *The Black Jacobins* (New York, 1963), 2nd ed., p. 19.

2. Of course, Joseph Harvey's former owner tried to claim the money given to him. As the Latin tag suggests, a *donatio mortis causa* is a gift made in contemplation of death upon the condition that the gift is not be be absolute until the donor dies. The moment the good lady died the gift to Joseph Harvey became valid. Ten years after the gift was made, Edward Shanley sought to recover the money from his former slave, or as he evidently thought, from his slave. He appears to have brought the action on two grounds. First, as administrator of the deceased. Second, as the owner of Harvey. The former ground could succeed only if the conditions of a *donatio mortis causa* had not been met, which was not the case. The latter ground could only succeed by his showing that Harvey was still his property. Since the gift was valid, the Court of Chancery decided the issue on the second ground. Lord Northington, the Lord Chancellor, holding that 'As soon as a man sets foot on English ground he is free', dismissed the bill brought by Edward Shanley with costs. Lord Northington also added that a black 'may maintain an action against his master for ill usage, and may have a *Habeas Corpus* if restrained in his liberty'. For the Court proceedings and the Lord Chancellor's observations, see *Shanley* v. *Harvey* (1762) 2 Eden, 126; 28 E.R. 844.

Although Mr. Justice Powell declared in *Smith* v. *Brown & Cooper* that the Laws of England would take no notice of a black, clearly other judges did not share that sentiment. For there are other cases where the Courts accorded a measure of equality before the law to free or virtually free blacks; see the case of Anne Black (1732) 2 Barn. 215; Granville Sharp, 'Remarks on the Case of John Hylas and his Wife Mary' (MS.), 'Granville Sharp Letter Book', York Minster Library, York; *The London Chronicle* (21 February 1788).

3. John Baker, *The Diary of John Baker*, ed. Philip C. Yorke (London, 1931), pp. 15 and 208.

4. *The Bristol Journal* (12 March 1757) published, as we have seen, the elopement of a young black called Starling, who 'blows the French horn very well'; John Latimer, *Annals of Bristol in the Eighteenth Century* (Bristol, 1893), p. 147.

5. Benjamin Franklin, *The Life and Writings of Benjamin Franklin*, ed. Albert Henry Smyth (New York, 1905-7), IV, pp. 23-4.

6. Peter Hutchinson, ed., *The Diary and Letters of His Excellency Thomas Hutchinson Esq* (Boston, 1884-6), II, pp. 274-7.

7. Thomas Whitehead, *Original Anecdotes of the Late Duke of Kingston and Miss. Cudleigh, alias Mrs. Harvey, alias Countess of Bristol, alias Duchess of Kingston* (London, 1792), pp. 86-9.

8. Henry Angelo, *Reminiscences of Henry Angelo* (London, 1904), I, pp. 347-53 (first edition published in 1828).

9. The suggestion of the correspondent of *The Morning Post*, that Soubise was still living with the Duke after the death of the Duchess, is wrong. Soubise had left the country, never to return, two days before her death. I do not dispute the rape story, however.

10. *Dictionary of National Biography*, s.v. Catherine, Duchess of Queensberry.

11. Henry Angelo, op. cit., pp. 347-53.

12. See also *The General Evening Post* (15 December 1786).

# 4

# Princes, Students, and Scholars

When Dr. Johnson, in his argument in favour of Joseph Knight, said, 'In our own time Princes have been sold, by wretches to whose care they were entrusted, that they might have an European education', he was alluding to a common practice among the depraved and corrupted captains of slaving vessels, who without compunction betrayed the trust which Africans reposed in them by committing to their care African princes and other promising young men to be brought to Europe for education. Basil Davidson, in *Black Mother*, cites a long letter of 1539 that Affonso of Congo sent to his 'royal brother', John III of Portugal. Affonso is found explaining to John III that the ship which carried the letter also brings to Portugal five of his nephews and one of his grandsons, two of whom are to be taught to read and write, two to be forwarded to Rome, and two to be prepared in Lisbon for minor holy orders.[1] Then comes a passage which glaringly illustrates the craven conduct Johnson indicted:

We beg of Your Highness to give them shelter and boarding and to treat them in accordance with their rank, as relatives of ours with the same blood ... and if we are reminding you of this and begging of your attention it is because, during the life of the King your father, whom pray God to have in His glory, we sent from this Kingdom to yours, according to his orders with a certain Antonio Veira ... more than twenty youngsters, our grandsons, nephews and relations who were most gifted to learn the service of God. ... The above-mentioned Antonio Veira left some of these youngsters in the land of Panzamlumbo, our enemy, and it gave us great trouble later to recover them; and only ten of these youngsters were taken to your Kingdom. But about them we do not know so far whether they are alive or dead, nor what happened to them, so that we have nothing to say to their fathers and mothers.[2]

Basil Davidson observes that these twenty young Congolese students had gone to Europe in 1516, twenty-three years before the letter was written, and ten of them, as the records show, had been seized by the vassal of São Tomé. Yet so little did the Court in Lisbon care that no official word had reached the Congo of the fate of the young Africans. The case was typical enough.

Then we have the case reported in *The Gentleman's Magazine* of February 1749. An English captain of a slaving vessel went into the West African heartland while on a slaving adventure. He was introduced to the King of Annamaboe, who entertained him and at last reposed such confidence in him as to entrust him with his son and another youth to be brought to England and educated there. The captain, however, basely sold them. The British Government heard of the affair and ransomed them. They were brought to England and put under the care of the Earl of Halifax, first Commissioner of Trade and Plantations. They were educated 'in a very genteel manner', and were received by George II, 'richly dressed, in the European manner' for the occasion. The African youths paid several visits to the theatre. On the first occasion they went to Covent Garden to see the tragedy of Oroonoko. 'They were received with a loud clap of applause, which they acknowledged with a genteel bow, and took their seats in a box.' One of the black youths was so moved by the drama that he left in the middle of the act. The other stayed to the bitter end, 'but wept the whole time'.³

Dr. Johnson may well have had in mind this particular case of the son of the King of Annamaboe and his companion, when he made his scathing remarks regarding wretches who betrayed the trust which African parents reposed in them. For the young Africans were the talk of the town. 'There are two black princes of Annamaboe here,' Horace Walpole wrote in his London diary for 23 March 1749, 'who are in fashion at all assemblies, of whom I scarce know the particulars [of their story] ... though all the women know it and ten times more than belongs to it.'⁴ On 22 November 1749, they 'were baptized by the Revd. Terret, reader of the *Temple*'.⁵ Eventually, the young Africans returned home. Sometime in the summer of 1750, the British Admiralty received a letter of thanks from the King of Annamaboe.

The Swedish Abolitionist, Wadström, rescued another African youth in London in 1788. Peter Panah was the son of the King of Mesurado who had himself been 'educated at Liverpool, by the slave-traders'. The African youth had been basely kidnapped, conveyed to Sierra Leone and finally to the West Indies, where he was purchased by one Johnson, a mulatto dealer in Grenada, who brought him to England. Wadström became aware of the black prince's situation and redeemed him with the intention of restoring him to his father. He placed the freed slave at Dempster's academy in Mitcham, where he gained 'a tolerable proficiency in reading and writing', and was instructed in the first rudiments of Christianity. He was baptized on Christmas Day 1788. 'Though pretty accustomed to European manners, he seemed to retain an unconquerable propensity to return to his ... native country.' But it was not to be. Granville Sharp promised to procure him a free passage to Africa, but for various reasons there was a delay, until he was taken ill at Dempster's school by sleeping one evening on damp grass and died shortly after in Wadström's house in October 1790, 'aged, as near as I could guess, about 18 or 20'.[6]

In the summer after the death of Peter Panah, another African prince, John Naimbanna, arrived in London. Early in 1791, Alexander Falconbridge had been sent to Sierra Leone by the Sierra Leone Company to re-establish the settlement which had been scattered by the indigenous Africans' attack. He was accompanied by his wife Anna. After some initial difficulties, Falconbridge soon struck up a working relationship with the Temne paramount King, Naimbanna. Naimbanna was an enlightened ruler who wanted his children to have the advantages of good education. One son was sent to France, another was placed with an Arabic teacher. The eldest son, John, he decided to send to England. When Falconbridge was returning to England, the King entrusted his son to his care, and at the same time he gave him a letter addressed to Granville Sharp. In his letter, the African father entreated Sharp to supervise the education of his son. According to Prince Hoare, Granville Sharp's first biographer, John was about twenty-nine years of age when he arrived in England.[7] Wadström, who saw the African shortly after his arrival, recorded that he could already read a little English. 'It is that lady', said John, pointing to Mrs. Falconbridge, 'to whom I owe this improvement; for she was kind enough to teach me in the passage from Sierra Leone.' Thereafter, Wadström had several opportunities of conversing with him during his stay in England and was much struck 'with his acuteness and good sense'.[8]

His education was supervised successively by two clergymen who reported that, in the space of a year and a half since arriving in England, he had learned to 'read very fluently, and to write a letter in English without much difficulty'. He, too, was baptized, adopting the name Henry Granville, presumably in honour of Granville Sharp and Henry Thornton (Chairman of the Sierra Leone Company), who together stood as his godfathers. In their report the clergymen who supervised his education observed that a desire for knowledge was the predominant feature of his character. He would continually urge his instructors to prolong the time of their reading together. He would express regret if he had been led into company where the time had been spent without improvement. When he was left entirely by himself, he would employ not less than eight or ten hours of the day in reading. Though affectionate in disposition and uncommonly pleasing in his behaviour, he was quick in all his feelings and his temper was occasionally warm. On one occasion, there having been mentioned in his presence the name of a person who was understood by him to have said something degrading about the African character, 'he broke out into violent and vindictive language'. He was immediately reminded of the Christian duty of forgiving his enemies. The young Naimbanna's reply is a joy to read. 'I cannot forgive the man who takes away the character of the people of my country.'[9]

Wadström recounted that on another occasion, when a Member of Parliament proposed the gradual abolition of the slave trade, he retorted that the Member 'should have his carriage drawn by asses, for they go very gradually'.[10] The spring of the second year of Naimbanna's stay in England had scarcely arrived when he received news from Sierra Leone of the death of his father. In May 1793 he left Plymouth on his return journey to Sierra Leone. Before leaving he sent a letter of thanks to Granville Sharp, who had stood *in loco parentis* to him during his stay. Granville Sharp, who was then living with one of his sisters in Fulham, recorded in his notebook on 18 May 1793, 'Parted with Mr. Naimbanna about three o'clock at Fulham.'[11]

Two or three days before Naimbanna arrived in Sierra Leone, he was taken ill, and he died a few hours after landing.[12] A suspicion arose among his countrymen that he had been poisoned during his voyage, and a long palaver was held, which terminated in an entire removal of their apprehensions. Naimbanna's mother, no less alive to the sentiments of regal generosity than her husband or her son, withdrew the charge which had been brought against the captain of the vessel, and coming herself to Freetown with expressions of the utmost confidence in the Governor and Council, requested them to take another of her sons under their protection.[13] Despite the fate of John Naimbanna other chiefs, too, sent their sons to England. Signor Domingo had already sent his son Anthony; when Governor Dawes went on leave in March 1794 he took Henry Kokelly, a Temne chief's son, and John Wilson. Like the young Naimbanna Henry Kokelly disappointed his sponsors' hopes by dying of smallpox in England. Domingo's son, Anthony, returned rather unwillingly and was employed in the accounts office. Phillis Hazeley, who was also brought to England by Dawes, on her return to Sierra Leone opened a school, teaching reading at three cents a week, with needlework an extra five cents, writing and arithmetic ten cents.[14] As John Matthews observed in *A Voyage to the River Sierra Leone*: 'Africans in most parts where the English trade, were desirous of sending their children to England to learn what they call white man's book; a knowledge which they find necessary for carrying on their trade. There are always several of these children in Liverpool, who are boarded and educated by the merchants and masters of ships trading to Africa.'[15]

Africans took a gamble when they sent their children to Europe for education. On the one hand, they earnestly looked forward to the improvement in life and thought which the education of the sons and daughters of Africa in Europe would mean for their countries and countrymen. On the other hand, there was a real possibility that the young men of Africa might never return to make the expected improvement a reality. From time to time, here and there in Africa, Africans reacted sharply to the craven conduct of Europeans who betrayed their trust.

In 1706 an African 'of some distinction' visited England. The ship on which he embarked to return to Africa put in to Plymouth, and going on shore, he met a Captain Mitford, who filled him with brandy, and then enlisted him in Lord Paston's regiment under the name of Jaco. (As will be seen later, blacks served in the British Army in various capacities during the period.) His failure to return excited the animosity of his countrymen, who naturally thought he had been kidnapped. They seized some English hostages and refused to trade with the English. The Royal African Company thereupon wrote urgently to Lord Paston, pleading that his African private might be discharged forthwith. They paid three guineas to procure a replacement for him, and he was sent back to Africa, where he arrived safely.[16]

Of course, it was in the interest and to the advantage of Britain to have the children of African kings and chiefs in England. For they were hostages for the security of Englishmen trading in Africa. 'The trading, which was the main object of Western enterprise in Africa, depended upon the good will of the coastal chiefs; nor were the Europeans able to rely on force to secure it.' Consequently, the Royal African Company instructed its agents 'if any differences happen, to endeavour an amicable accommodation rather than use force'. They were 'to endeavour to live in all friendship with them', and 'to hold frequent palavers with the Kings and the Great Men of the Country, and keep up a good correspondence with them, ingratiating yourself by such prudent methods' as may be deemed appropriate.[17] For factors, agents, or supercargoes, who were 'too hasty and passionate' had to be removed if the Africans refused to trade with them, or to sell them supplies. Kenneth Dike cites an instance in 1824 when there was a dispute between the British and King Peppel of Bonny. British traders during this crisis treated the African King with great 'deference and respect. They administer to his whims and caprice, as if the advantage derived from their traffic was not mutual; and when his anger is raised, instead of opposing his menaces they try to win him back to good humour by the most servile flattery and gifts.'[18]

Although Europeans could not rely on force to ensure favourable trading conditions, they could rely on sons of Africa held as hostages in Europe or in European forts in Africa to secure the co-operation of Africans. Such a reprehensible use of African people in pursuance of western enterprise ended tragically.

In 1768 the whole trade of the Gambia was interrupted over a free African of Bar, whom the King declared was his son. Three years earlier he had embarked as a linguist on a ship bound for the West Indies. On the way back he was caught aiming a gun at the captain, was put in irons, and was eventually incarcerated in Fort James. The King's application for his release was refused, and he was kept confined until a favourable opportunity should occur of 'making a merit with the King' by setting him at liberty. The next thing that happened was that the King cut off the Fort James water supply. Thereupon the Agent decided to release the captive; but unfortunately the latter jumped into the sea and was killed by a shark. The King, of course, refused to believe he had not been murdered and rejected 'a very considerable present' offered in satisfaction. He seized some of the castle slaves and four Europeans who happened to be on the mainland, and attacked the fort boats. By way of reprisal the Agent was foolish enough to risk defeat by attacking Albreda with an insufficient force, and war broke out 'between the Whites and the Blacks all over the river Gambia'.[19]

Aqua and Sackee, two black boys from what is now Ghana, lived in England from 1753 until 1755. We know from a letter dated 21 November 1753, which the African Committee wrote to the Governor of Cape Coast, that the African boys were 'hostages brought over by Captain Cockburn'. The Committee undertook to have them properly educated. They were instructed in the Christian faith, in reading, writing, and accounts. While in England they were expensively dressed, housed, and fed, and were received by the Earl of Halifax. On the eve of their departure they were given a farewell dinner at the King's Arms, Cornhill.[20]

Eventually, after wining and dining, the 'Two Black Boys' now turned 'Two Black Gentlemen' left London for Plymouth en route for Africa in the last week of July 1755. They drove down to Plymouth in the same coach as the wife of the Captain of the *Humbler*, who 'does them the Honour to accompany them'. On arrival at Plymouth, Captain Scott of the *Humbler* gave them a 'very genteel Reception'. Their berths cost the Company of Mer-

chants Trading in Africa fifty pounds, and several more pounds
were spent while they were detained in Plymouth by contrary
winds. While in London, they had been allowed 10s.6d. each as
pocket money weekly, but in Plymouth it was thought 7s.6d.
each would be sufficient. The Company initially refused to be
responsible for two bureaus which the 'two black Gentlemen had
bespoke', but eventually agreed to pay for one bureau, and other
necessaries which included 'check shirts'. In a letter of 19
December 1755 the Governor of Cape Coast Castle was
informed: 'Aqua and Sackee have cost above £600 for Education, maintenance &c. since their being in England, we must
therefore desire you w[oul]d send us no more black Gent[leme]n
except you find it absolutely necessary for the benefit of the
trade.'

Finally, in a letter dated 20 March 1756, the Governor,
informing the Company of the safe arrival of the 'Black Gentlemen' on the last day of February 1756, delivered the *coup de
grâce*, when he added, 'I shall not fail to give them proper Countenance according to your Directions; but must at the same time
beg leave to inform you, that neither of 'em is a Person of Consequence & will hardly be of any Service.'[21]

The Company's caveat to the Governor of Cape Coast Castle,
to send no more black gentlemen except he find it absolutely
necessary for the benefit of the trade, was, of course, not meant
to be taken seriously. From the beginning to the end of the British
African slave trade, it was beneficial to send black boys to
England. In the words of Hugh Crow, who commanded the last
British slaver (Kitty's *Amelia*) to leave a British port, 'It has
always been the practice of merchants and commanders of ships
to Africa, to encourage the natives to send their children to
England; as it not only conciliates their friendship, and softens
their manners, but adds greatly to the security of the traders.'[22] In
a letter dated from Cape Coast Castle, 8 April 1755, the
Governor informed the Company of Merchants Trading in Africa
that loud complaints had been made to him against Captain Ellis
for taking away a free boy from Annamaboe without leave of his
family. 'I beg that some methods may be fallen upon to prevent
such things for the future, for tho, I'm willing to believe Ellis had
no bad design in humouring this boy by shewing him England,
yet his Ship & Cargo will not pay the Damage the Public will
Sustain sho'd any accident befall him.' When Henry Ellis arrived
in England with the black boy, he asked the Company to reim-
burse him for the expenses he had incurred in bringing the boy to
England, presumably because he thought he was acting according
to the standing instructions and doing the Company a favour. But

the Company, still chafing at having spent above £600 on Aqua and Sackee, would have none of it. The Company's Secretary wrote a couple of stern letters to Ellis, then in Bristol with the black boy. In the Secretary's letter dated 11 September 1755, he told Captain Ellis that the Company could give him no instructions in relation to the boy in question, 'but they are of opinion that as you thought proper to bring him over, it is incumbent on you, to take such Measures for his Return to the Coast, as may best prevent Inconveniences to the Publick, & Troubles to your self.'

The Company was bound to take the danger signal seriously. Writing to the Governor of Cape Coast Castle on 28 May 1756, for example, the Company observed gleefully, 'We are pleased to find that the French Agent met with so bad a Reception at Annamabo: we hope it will deter them from coming there again, or carrying any Black Boys to France.' A case of the pot calling the kettle black.[23]

About the same time that the Company was complaining about the £600 expenses incurred on Aqua and Sackee, a Mr. Roberts carried away from the Gold Coast the son of the King of Popo and a son of a Caboccer of Dixcove, promising to return them in two or three years. After four years the King made enquiries, and the Company of Merchants, becoming alarmed lest it might 'prejudice English interests at Popo', sent the son back to his father, with a present of 'a thick robe, 6 dozen of beer, cheese, 6 anchors of brandy, and a barrel of powder, as a testimony of our goodwill and desire to live in friendship with you, as we have no doubt you will use your influence to serve British trade.' This little affair cost them £100, 'so recommend your avoiding involving us in such charges in the future.'[24] As Basil Davidson comments, 'Indeed, it was familiar British and French practice to win the friendship of local rulers on the Coast by entertaining their sons in Europe. This was part of the slaving network of alliance.'[25] Thus in 1802, a House of Commons committee which considered the Petition of the Court of Directors of the Sierra Leone Company for Government subsidy and assistance, reported that: 'the most important subsidiary assistance will be afforded to the influence of the colony on the neighbouring nations, by giving instruction in England to some African children, who are either most promising themselves, or most important in the Kingdom, who will carry back to their own country minds considerably enlightened, and would be particularly well instructed in the Christian religion.' Several of these were sons of chiefs, and if the colony were to be firmly established, it was necessary for the leading men in Africa to have a warm desire that their children should be educated by the Sierra Leone Company. There is the strongest reason to believe that as a result of this, a large proportion of the kings and headmen of the surrounding countries would have received their education in England or at Freetown, and would value the friendship and in good measure adopt the views of the Sierra Leone Government. 'As the governments in Africa are in a great degree hereditary, these youths would succeed to power; and there would be a fair prospect of their carrying into effect in the countries which they would ... govern, plans more or less similar to those inculcated in them in England.'[26]

In fact, the hope of turning these young Africans into black Englishmen was only partially realized, and that was in spheres in which the British merchants, traders, and Government were the least interested. According to Hugh Crow, the influence which 'European education seems to have upon Africans, after their return to their native country, appears chiefly in their ... endeavour to live and dress in the European stiles, to erect their houses in a comfortable and convenient manner ....'[27] And John Matthews observed that, 'The only apparent influence [European education] has upon [Africans] is in the exterior decoration of their persons, and the interior ornaments of their houses.' Adding, 'those black and Mulatto children (and there are not a few of them) who are sent to Europe for their education, on their return to their native country immediately reassume the manner of living, and embrace the superstitious customs and ceremonies of their countrymen.'[28] Although there are 'educated' Africans who will never admit it (especially within earshot of their white admirers), a million years of infiltration by white Western 'civilization' and Christianity, can never boil down the one thousand and one African Gods into One God.

In 1788 Hugh Crow stated that 'the education of [African children] who have come to this country has, it appears, been confined to reading, writing, and a little arithmetic.' While this might have been true of the majority of those in Liverpool (who were sent to England for the specific purpose of learning enough to be able to conduct business with the English on the African coast), it was not the case with those who were boarded in London and its outlying districts. On the contrary, and in contrast to the later British reluctance in colonial Africa, the 'Saints' made a genuine effort to give the African youths a sound education. Not long after the settlement of Sierra Leone, a school was established for African children. In March 1799, when Zachary Macaulay's term of office as Governor of Sierra Leone ended and he left for England, he brought with him twenty-one boys, and four girls, selected from the schools in Sierra Leone, for further education in England. 'Many of the boys were sons of the Native Chiefs, whom it might be desirable, after their education in this country, to place in such situations as would afford the best means of promoting the great ends of the settlement.'[29]

In 1802 Zachary Macaulay, now Secretary of the Sierra Leone Company, giving evidence before the House of Commons committee investigating the petition of the Company for Government subsidy, testified that there had been, in general, between 150 and 300 African children in the various schools in the colony. The children educated there, he revealed, were instructed in writing and reading, English and arithmetic, and, as might be expected, in the principles of religion. They had shown considerable facility in learning. Those who had been educated in England had been instructed with much more effect than those educated within the colony, owing in some degree to frequent interference by parents in the latter case. Finally, Macaulay confirmed that the twenty-five children he had brought to England in 1799 were still in the country.[30] William Greaves, in his evidence, stated that he lived at Clapham, and had the care of the Africans as their schoolmaster. He had had other boys under his care, but at that time was charged solely with the education of the children in question. He then went on to illustrate the scope of education they were receiving and their progress:

They were placed under his care about two years and a half ago. Their ages are from 10 to 17. He instructs them in reading, writing and arithmetic; and one of them who is the most forward, in mensuration. Almost all of them can speak and read English tolerably well. Pains are taken to give them information on general subjects; as, history, geography, natural philosophy, and mechanics. He had not observed any inferiority of capacity, allowances being made for the deficiencies under which they laboured when they came under his care. They converse together in their own language, but more frequently in English. Three of the children ... have been put out to learn boat-building; and it is proposed to place the others, as they get forward, to learn different trades. They also learn various useful arts within the school.

They retain a strong attachment to their own country; but do not appear to be impatient to return home till their education is completed, being sensible of the advantages to be derived therefrom. The children shew a great disposition to adopt the principles of the Christian religion; and several of them have written letters to their parents in Africa, expressive of their opinions on the subject. Books have been prepared, principally on religious subjects, for the use of the children, with the native language of some of them, called 'The Susoo language' on one side, and the English on the other; which the children now read.[31]

Zachary Macaulay and Mr. Ludlam (also a former Governor of Sierra Leone) confirmed the evidence of William Greaves, and added that this was the first attempt made to reduce to writing the Susoo language, and the orthography had been collected only from the sounds. As now printed, it was perfectly intelligible, not only to the boys and girls now in England, but also to those who read the books in Africa. Some of the books prepared as described above had been sent recently to the colony. It was hoped that by these means, with proper assistance, education might be much facilitated among the Africans. They further stated that it was the intention of the Company to continue to educate the children in England for seven or eight years, in order to prepare them, on their return to Africa, either to fill offices under the Company, or 'to promote civilization in any other way, by means of the advantages which an European education will naturally give to them in their intercourse with their own people. Many of them also will succeed to power, being children of the chiefs of the country.'[32]

The Act which abolished the British slave trade in Africans received the royal assent on 14 April 1807. Three weeks afterwards the African Institution was founded. At its first meeting the Institution's members resolved that they were deeply impressed with a sense of the enormous wrongs which the natives of Africa had suffered in their intercourse with Europe, and wanted to repair those wrongs.[33] Education was of course one of the measures that could be used to atone for the wrongs. Accordingly, in the second annual report of the Institution, it was reported that 'The Committee and the directors of the Institution, having learnt that there were in England two African youths, about the age of nineteen or twenty, who had been educated for the last six or seven years at the expense of the Sierra Leone Company, and that it was intended they should soon return to Africa, thought it proper to take upon themselves the expenses of having them instructed fully in Dr. Bell's System of Education.'

Through the intervention of the Duke of Gloucester, President and Patron of the Institution, the two youths, to whom a third was later added, were allowed to attend for several months the Royal Military Asylum at Chelsea, where about one thousand children were educated in Dr. Bell's System of Education.[34] While at the Chelsea school, they were permitted to act as teachers under the supervision of the superintendents of the seminary. When they had acquired a competent degree of familiarity with the details of the system, they were sent, at the expense of the Institution, to Sierra Leone as school teachers. In a letter to the Governor of Sierra Leone, the Directors of the African Institution informed him that, if there should be promising youths who could benefit from further education in England, they would be disposed to incur the expense which attended their being sent to England, their being instructed, and afterwards sent back to Africa. The Directors urged in the letter that the youths selected for this purpose should be such as had given satisfactory proof of their capacity and disposition to make the most of the advantages proposed to them. Thereafter, African youths were regularly selected and sent to England by the Governor for instruction.[35]

The African Institution and the Sierra Leone Company comprised largely the same people, that is, the 'Saints' such as Granville Sharp, Thomas Clarkson, William Wilberforce, Zachary Macaulay, and Thomas Babington. From its inception, the Institution took over the education work previously carried on by the Company. The expenses incurred for the education of the black youths in England amounted to no small part of the annual expenditure of the African Institution. On the board, education, clothing, and passage-money of the first three African youths, they spent £286.18s.5d. As late as 1821, £220.15s.1d. was spent on the education and board of African youths in England.[36]

Long before the Sierra Leone Company and the African Institution commenced their educational work, the Society for the Propagation of the Gospel in Foreign Parts had started educating African youths in Britain. In 1754 three youngsters sponsored by the S.P.G. arrived in England. They were Philip Quaque, Thomas Coboro, and William Cudjo. Of these three, only Philip Quaque survived his sojourn in England and returned to what is now Ghana.

Philip Quaque was born in 1741.[37] He was the son of Cudjo, the enlightened Cabosheer of Cape Coast, known to the African people as Birempon Cudjo. Quaque's father wanted his children 'educated in some kind of learning'. In 1754 he was sent to England with the two other African youths, Thomas Coboro and William Cudjo, in the charge of the Revd. Thomas Thompson to be maintained and educated at the expense of the S.P.G. The sources do not disclose whether Quaque had been to the school which the missionary Thompson had founded in the Cape Coast, but it is probable that he had.

On their arrival they were placed under the care of Mr. Hickman, a schoolmaster at Islington. They lived with Hickman and were instructed by him; after seven weeks they were brought before the Committee and examined. 'One of them repeated the Lord's prayer and the Apostles' Creed, and the other two answered well to the questions put to them.' The Committee was favourably impressed and agreed to recommend to the Society that £15 per annum each for instruction, boarding, clothing, and other necessaries should be paid to Mr. Hickman. Quaque and his fellows remained in the charge of Mr. Hickman until the beginning of 1759. By that time they had once again appeared before the Committee, on 13 February 1758 when they were examined as to their proficiency in reading and writing and in the church catechism. They answered to the satisfaction of the Committee. Mr. Hickman then informed the Committee that he could not possibly continue to meet the expenses in respect of the boys with £15 per annum; and the Committee agreed to recommend to the Society that £50 for three boys should be allowed for 1758 and £55 per annum for the future.

On 7 January 1759, Philip Quaque and William Cudjo were baptized in the parish church of Islington in which they had regularly attended public worship for four years. In contrast with the other entries in the baptismal register of the church, Bartels notes that 'the names of the parents of the two boys are unrecorded. Two Christian names, Philip and William, against the date "7" are all the information shown. They were the only link with the Church of their adoption.' Shortly after their baptism Quaque and Cudjo were transferred to the care of the Revd. John Moore,[38] a member of the Society, and Curate and Lecturer of St. Sepulchre's Church, for their further instruction in the Christian religion and in order to answer the ends proposed by the Society in maintaining them. In 1762 Birempon Cudjo inquired through the Agents of the Company of Merchants Trading to Africa about the boys 'who had been taken to England by the chaplain [Thompson], to be educated under the auspices of the Society for the Propagation of the Gospel, and who had been there for four years without their relations hearing of them.'[39] At the meeting of the Committee of the Company, held in London on 3 February 1762, a letter from the Revd. Thompson to the Secretary of the Committee was read. Thompson in his letter acquainted the Committee with the news 'That one of the Boys which he brought from the Coast died four years ago; that the other two were well in November last, and were under the care of the Revd. Mr. Moore of Charter House Square, to complete their education', as directed by the S.P.G.

Thomas Coboro was the youth who had died. While suffering from small-pox he had been baptized like the other two. In 1758 he died of consumption. Six years later, in December 1764, Cudjo died in Guy's Hospital, after a period of confinement occasioned by a mental breakdown.

In the meantime, Quaque, the lone survivor of the trio, lived in the home of the Revd. Moore, where he continued to receive instruction. In March 1765 he was ordained deacon by the Bishop of Exeter in the Chapel Royal, St. James's Palace. Two months later, in the same chapel, he was ordained priest by the Bishop of London. On 2 May he was married to Catherine Blunt by his tutor, the Revd. Moore. After his ordination and marriage, his thoughts turned home. On 17 May 1765 he was appointed Missionary, Catechist, and Schoolmaster to the Africans in the Gold Coast at a salary of £50 per annum with effect from 25 March 1765. The Secretary of the S.P.G. and the Revd. Moore were asked to provide him with such things as were necessary for his voyage. Together with his English wife he sailed for the Gold Coast, and arrived in the first week of February 1766. In addition to being the chaplain of the Cape Coast Castle for fifty years, he also set up a school for the education of African children, assisted by his son, who was educated in England under the Revd. Fountayne, and his father's former tutor, the Revd. John Moore. In 1784-5, Quaque visited England for a few months. He died on 17 October 1816 at the age of seventy-five.

There were very few schools in the British West Indies sugar colonies. Although some children of the planter class in the Caribbean received private tuition at home, the majority were sent to England for their education. Among these were the Anglo-Africans, that is, children of the union of members of the white planter class and black women. James Stewart, who arrived in Jamaica on the eve of Abolition and remained on the island until 1821, observed that 'The brown children of the more opulent of the whites are either educated in the island, or sent to Great Britain for that purpose.'[40] These Anglo-African youths formed the second group of black children receiving education in England during the period. They received a different sort of education from that given to their brothers and sisters of the blood who had been sent from Africa. For, being the children of wealthy planters, they were given the education that befitted the children of the English gentility, who were destined to become ladies and gentlemen. They were, however, in an unenviable situation, for on their return to the West Indies, they were subjected to all kinds of discrimination and mortification. The Revd. R. Bickell wrote in his *West Indies as they Are*:

Since I went to Jamaica ... two coloured sons of one of the most respectable men (from his office [Governor] and for talent) in the island, who had been educated in Great Britain, went to a ball at Spanish-Town, when a proud coxcomb ... went to one of the stewards and insisted that these young men should be ordered out of the room; otherwise, he said, his wife should not remain there. After much ado (for others united with him, and some did not like to interfere on account of the father and the respectability of the sons) they were obliged to leave.[41]

James Stewart put the plight of Anglo-Africans who had received a liberal education into perspective:

If a white and brown child should be sent to Europe at the same time, and educated together at the same school, though they be in habits of the greatest intimacy while there, they discontinue that intimacy on their return to the West Indies, ... the white Miss no longer recognises her quondam companion and school-fellow as an equal, because ... the customs and distinctions of the country forbid her cultivating such acquaintance .... It is, therefore, a pity that a parent, after having bestowed on his offspring a genteel and liberal education, in a country where at least they experience a respect and attention equivalent to their merits, should suffer them to be brought back to one where their feelings ... are perpetually liable to be wounded by contumely.[42]

In 1734 Ayuba Suleiman Diallo, otherwise known as Job Ben Solomon, made a splash on the English scene. Suleiman, a member of the Jaloff tribe of the Senegambia, had been kidnapped in 1731 and sold as a slave to a Captain Pyke or Pike, who carried him to Maryland, and sold him there. There is poetical justice in his capture and enslavement. For while he was free in Africa, Suleiman had dealt in slaves himself. In fact, he was himself captured on the coast while endeavouring to sell two of his own flesh and blood. Suleiman's father was of the Islamic faith and the spiritual leader of his African town in Senegambia. Suleiman assisted his father. Thus, by the time he was sold into slavery he had become well versed in the Koran, most of which he could recite from memory. After about a year in Maryland, he wrote a letter in Arabic to his father, acquainting him with his misfortune, and hoping that he might yet be able to redeem him. The letter fell into the hands of James Oglethorpe. Oglethorpe sent the letter to Oxford University to be translated, which, when done, gave him a high opinion of Suleiman. Oglethorpe, then in England, sent directly for Suleiman and ultimately he became a free man.

There are two contemporary accounts of the excitement which Suleiman caused during his stay in England. Thomas Bluett, who was closely associated with Suleiman in America and came over to England with him, reported that he translated several Arabic manuscripts in the collection of Sir Hans Sloane for the antiquarian, and Sloane found Suleiman 'a perfect Master of the Arabic Tongue'. Sloane, whose collections formed the nucleus of the British Museum, introduced him to the Duke of Montagu, who in turn introduced him to the Court. The Queen presented him with 'a rich Gold Watch'. He was also well received by the nobility and gentry, and, when he left England for Africa in June 1734, he was furnished by the Duke of Montagu 'with all Sorts of [farming and garden] Instruments, and several rich Presents', and presents from other sources worth upwards of £500.[43]

Suleiman had a phenomenal memory, a quality highlighted by Bluett and corroborated by Wadström. 'His Memory was extraordinary,' wrote Bluett, 'for when he was fifteen Years old he could say the whole Alcoran [Koran] by heart, and while he was in England he wrote three copies of it without the Assistance of any other Copy, and without so much as looking to one of those three when he wrote the others.'[44] And Wadström confirmed that a Mr. W. Smith, Member of Parliament, had in his possession an MS. copy of the Koran, 'in Arabic, written by the extraordinary [African], when in England, purely from memory, as appears from a Latin certificate, at the end, signed by the Rev. Dr. Chandler, and some other reputable persons, competent to judge the merit and authenticity of this curious performance.'[45]

Several decades after Suleiman's stay in England, another African, apparently equally well learned and versed in the Koran, arrived in England. In 1798 Daniel Hill of Antigua purchased from a slave ship a black slave named Mohammed. It did not take long for Hill to discover that Mohammed had 'a considerable share of Arabic literature', and he was led to treat him with particular indulgence. Mohammed manifested a strong attachment to the Islamic religion, and his owner paid the utmost attention to the religious scruples of his slave. At length Mr. Hill resolved to grant him his liberty, and to procure for him the means of returning to his own country. In June 1811 Mohammed, now a free man, arrived at Liverpool, where he stayed for about three months. Meanwhile, an application having been made on his behalf to the Directors of the African Institution in London, they agreed to bear the expense of conveying Mohammed to Goree, which was the nearest point to the residence of his family in Africa. Towards the end of 1811, Mohammed left England for Africa, furnished with a letter to Colonel Chilsom, the Commandant at Goree, who was a member of the African Institution. Mohammed arrived safely at Goree, from where he was sent by Chilsom to Senegal, with a friendly recommendation to the Commandant of that settlement. Eventually, Mohammed 'reached his native village in safety, to the great joy of himself and his friends'.[46]

The Duke of Montagu was the patron not only of the black

Arabic scholar Suleiman, but also of the black poet and classical scholar, Francis Williams.

Francis Williams[47] was a native of Jamaica, and son of John and Dorothy Williams, free blacks of that island. Francis was the youngest of three sons. Since he was a boy of unusual intelligence, the Duke of Montagu, then Governor of the island, decided as an experiment to have Francis educated in England. He went first to a grammar school, and from there he went to Cambridge University, where he studied mathematics. Upon his return to Jamaica, the Duke tried to obtain an appointment for him to be one of the Governor's council, but this scheme was dropped, on objections offered by Mr. Trelawny, the Governor at the time. Williams therefore set up a school in Spanish Town, which continued for several years, where he taught reading, writing, Latin, and mathematics. He also wrote Latin poems, some of which Edward Long printed in his *History of Jamaica*. Inviting the reader to judge the merit of Williams's celebrated verses, Long suggested that the following rigorous standard be applied: 'To consider the merits of this specimen impartially, we must endeavour to forget, in the first place, that the writer was a *Negroe*; for if we regard it as an extraordinary production, merely because it came from a *Negroe*, we admit at once that inequality of genius which has been before supposed, and admire it only as a rare phenomenon.'

We accept Edward Long's insistence that a black poet must be judged ordinarily as 'a poet' and not as 'a black poet' just as we accept today that the race of an African historian, writer, or scientist is irrelevant in determining his place in his discipline. Long, however, used this eminently sensible yardstick merely as a ploy to enable him to denigrate and degrade Francis Williams and the African race. For, two paragraphs later, Edward Long made clear his real objective:

Should we, or should we not, have looked for something better from one, upon whom (to borrow his own phrase) *omnes* artium scientiarumque *dotes* Atticarum in cumulum accesserunt? or, is it at all superior, in classic purity of style and numbers, in sentiment and propriety, in poetic images and harmony, to any composition we might expect from a middling scholar at the seminaries of Westminster or Eaton? It is true, *poeta nascitur, non fit*: but the principal forte and excellence of this man lay in versification; however, as I mean not to prejudge the cause, I leave it to the fair verdict of a jury of critics.

After having directed the jury to bring in a verdict of guilty, Edward Long had the shameless impudence to say: 'Gentlemen of the Jury the verdict is yours.' *Res ipsa loquitur*.

The crucial point which Long missed (and which any bigoted critic would miss) but which the Abolitionist the Revd. James Ramsay pointed out in a direct reply to Long is that:

Though his verses bear no great marks of genius, yet, there have been bred at the same university a hundred white masters of arts, and many doctors, who could not improve them; and, therefore, his particular success in the fields of science cannot operate against the natural abilities of those of his colour, till it be proved, that every white man bred there outstripped him. But allowance is to be made for his being a solitary essay, and the possibility of a wrong choice having been made of him.[48]

Of Francis Williams's character, Long wrote, 'He was haughty, opinionated, looked down with sovereign contempt on his fellow Blacks, entertained the highest opinion of his own knowledge, treated his parents with much disdain, and behaved towards his children and his slaves with severity bordering upon cruelty.' Being part of the classic literature of race vilification, Long's account must be dismissed as the product of a mind warped by prejudice.[49] And we have the word of James Ramsay, who was in the West Indies for six years longer than Edward Long, that 'other gentlemen of Jamaica speak highly of [Francis Williams's] abilities, and of the favour they procured for him.'[50]

Elsewhere in Europe, two African scholars made their mark. The first was Jacobus Eliza Capitein who was born in what is now Ghana in 1717.[51] He was educated in Holland from 1726 to 1742, and was lionized at Leyden University, which he entered on 22 June 1737, for his skill at Latin and Divinity. He graduated in 1742 with a Latin dissertation proving the lawfulness of slavery from the Holy Writ, which work went through several editions in Latin and Dutch and was widely quoted by apologists for slavery and the slave trade,[52] as was to be expected. He argued that slavery was not incompatible with Christianity and could indeed be its instrument. He practically thanked Europe for the slave trade, but for which he would not be studying at Leyden.[53]

On 17 May 1742 he was ordained a *predikant* by the Classis of Amsterdam, and on 20 May he preached his first sermon at Pieterskerk, now the University Church, Leyden. This and some subsequent sermons were published. He was appointed preacher and schoolmaster to Elmina by the church authorities at the request of the Directors of the West India Company, and arrived at St. George d'Elmina on 8 October 1742, at the age of twenty-five, to begin his work in the Gold Coast. In emoluments as well

Suleiman Diallo: Arabic scholar, and slave dealer who was himself enslaved

Francis Williams: noted Latin poet who studied at Cambridge University

Jacobus Elisa Joannes Capitein: ordained *predikant* by the Classis of Amsterdam. He defended slavery in a Latin dissertation.

Chevalier Georges de St. Georges: son of an African mother and a French Governor of San Domingo. A polymath and polyglot of formidable virtuosity.

as in position Capitein was next to the Governor, who was on a salary of 300 guilders a month. Capitein received 100 guilders a month. He was well received at first, by both the Dutch residents and his countrymen, but soon ran into difficulties. He reported that very few Europeans attended his catechism classes, 'as most of those here are Roman Catholics or Lutherans, and the Reformed are always too occupied with their daily business.'[54] In 1744 he wrote a letter to the Classis in Amsterdam begging to be allowed to marry an African girl who seemed very modest and beautiful, lest the Evil One should triumph over him. The education of the girl was the difficulty. There was no one in Elmina to instruct her, and her parents would not allow her to be sent to Holland. In the end he had to abandon the idea of marrying the African girl, and the Classis sent out Antonia Ginderdoa, native of the Hague, whom he married in 1745.

Apparently discouraged by the small result of his labours in the Lord's vineyard among both blacks and whites, he neglected the service of God for that of Mammon, dying insolvent on 1 February 1747 after some disastrous trading ventures.[55]

Anton Wilhelm Amo was born near Axim about 1700.[56] His parents were converted to the Dutch Reformed Church, and he was sent to Holland through the instrumentality of Johannes van der Star, a preacher in the then Gold Coast, to study and come back as a priest and teacher. In Holland, his patron was the Duke of Brunswick, Anton Ulric. Amo lived in the Duke's house at Wolfenbütell until he entered the University of Halle. In 1729 he publicly defended his dissertation, *De Jure Maurorum in Europa*. He argued that the purchase and enslavement of Africans by European Christians was not right. From Halle, Amo moved on to Wittenberg, and, while Kant was still a boy, became a Master of Philosophy there. Amo was a rationalist philosopher after Leibniz, whom as a boy he had met at the Duke of Brunswick's. His mastery of his discipline was indisputable. The Chairman and Faculty members described him as the most noble and most renowned man from Africa, extraordinarily honest, diligent, and so erudite that he stood well above his colleagues. He was well liked and respected, and in 1733 led a procession at the visit of Frederick of Prussia to Halle.

In 1738 Amo produced his magnum opus, a book on logic, the theory of knowledge, and metaphysics.[57] In 1739 he moved to Jena, where he taught. In all, therefore, Amo taught at the universities of Wittenberg, Halle, and Jena. He knew Hebrew, Greek, Latin, Dutch, French, and German. If he had learnt English more about him would be known in England today. His success in Germany was probably symbolized in his nomination as a Counsellor of the Court of Berlin. He returned to the Gold Coast some time after 1743 and died of boredom. Kwame Nkrumah in his autobiography referred to Amo as 'this scholar, the first from the Gold Coast'.[58]

1. Basil Davidson, *Black Mother* (London, 1970), 2nd ed., p. 139.

2. Ibid., pp. 139-140.

3. *The Gentleman's Magazine*, XIX (1749), pp. 89-90; *The London Magazine*, XVIII (1749), p. 94.

4. Davidson, op. cit., p. 236.

5. *The Gentleman's Magazine*, XIX (1749), p. 522.

6. C[arl] B[ernhard] Wadström, *An Essay on Colonization* (London, 1792), II pp. 269-71.

7. Hoare, *Memoirs of Granville Sharp* (London, 1828), 2nd ed., II, p. 166.

8. Wadström, op. cit., II, pp. 267-8.

9. Hoare, op. cit., II, pp. 166-8.

10. Wadström, op. cit., II, p. 268.

11. Hoare, op. cit., II, pp. 169-70.

12. An Englishman who was on board the ship with him gave the following account of the last days of the young African. 'He had left Plymouth in perfect health; but soon as he reached a warm climate, he began to feel a slight complaint in his throat, and occasional pains in his head. ... The heat also began to affect him very violently, and a fever ensued, which was attended with delirium. In one of his lucid intervals he desired the person who gave this account, to assist him in making his will, by which he entrusted his property to his brother, for the use of a young child, his son; and he introduced into the will an earnest request that his brother would exert every endeavour to put an end to the Slave Trade. When he reached Sierra Leone he was insensible of every thing that passed, and his life was despaired of. His mother together with some younger branches of the family, came down to the Governor's house, where he was laid, and, after a few hours' attendance on his dying bed, they saw him breathe his last.' Ibid., II, pp. 170-1n.

13. Ibid., II, p. 170.

14. Christopher Fyfe, *A History of Sierra Leone* (London, 1962), pp. 54, 74, and 102.

15. John Matthews, *A Voyage to the River Sierra Leone* (London, 1788), pp. 170-1n.

16. PRO: CO/267/14; H.A. Wyndham, *The Atlantic and Slavery* (London, 1935), p. 224. For another hostile African reaction, see, *The Gentleman's Magazine*, XXXIV (1764), p. 177.

17. Wyndham, op. cit., pp. 59-62.

18. Kenneth Onwuka Dike, *Trade and Politics in the Niger Delta: 1830-1885* (Oxford, 1956), p. 17. The words are Captain W. F. W. Owen's. Similarly, another African scholar has reported that, in 1709, the English and French competed vigorously with each other in making servile flattery and gifts to Huffon the King of Whydah. I. A. Akinjogbin, *Dahomey and Its Neighbours 1708-1818* (Cambridge, 1967), pp. 42-3.

19. Wyndham, op. cit., pp. 224-5.

20. *Notes and Queries* (10 March 1928), pp. 173-4; Wyndham, op. cit., p. 24.

21. PRO: T/70/29/fols. 47, 60, 62, 64, 68, 71, and 74; PRO: T/70/30/f. 146; Wyndham, op. cit., pp. 24-5.

22. Hugh Crow, *Memoirs of the late Captain Hugh Crow of Liverpool* (London, 1830), p. 300.

23. PRO: T/70/29/fols. 69, 72, and 86; T/70/30/f. 92.

24. PRO: T/70/29/f. 103; T/70/30/f. 153; Wyndham, op. cit., p. 25.

25. Davidson, op. cit., p. 235.

26. *Reports from Committees of the House of Commons, Miscellaneous subjects: 1785-1802* (London, 1803), X, p. 742b.

27. Crow, op. cit., p. 299.

28. Matthews, op. cit., pp. 170-1.

29. Hoare, op. cit., II, pp. 58-9.

30. *Reports from Committees of the House of Commons, Miscellaneous Subjects: 1785-1802* (London, 1803) vol. X. *Report from the Committee on the Petition of the Court of Directors of Sierra Leone Company. Presented by Lord Viscount Castlereagh, 25th May 1802*, pp. 735-46.

31. Ibid., pp. 744-5.

32. Ibid., p. 745.

33. *[First] Report of the Committee of the African Institution, 1807* (London, 1811), p. 1.

34. Andrew Bell (1753-1832) was the founder of the Madras Education System. In 1789 he became the superintendent of the Madras Male Orphan Asylum, an institution founded in that year by the East India Company for the education of the sons of military men, some of whom were English and some Anglo-Indian. For a time the school made slow progress. It then occurred to Dr. Bell that the work of teaching the alphabet might be done by the pupils themselves, and choosing a clever boy of eight he placed him in charge of the lowest class to teach by writing in the sand. The experiment succeeded, and its success opened out to Dr. Bell the value of the system of mutual instruction. From the alphabet he extended it to other subjects. Soon almost every boy was alternately a master and a scholar; and so far as possible even the arrangements of the school were carried out by the boys. *Dictionary of National Biography*, s.v. Andrew Bell.

35. *Second Report of the Committee of the African Institution, 1808* (London, 1808), p. 5; *Third Report ...* (London, 1809), pp. 1-3.

36. *Third Report ...*, p. 20; *Fifteenth Report ...*, p. 44.

37. F. L. Bartels, 'Philip Quaque, 1741-1818', *Transactions of the Gold Coast and Togoland Historical Society* (1955), vol. 1, pt. 5, pp. 153-77, from which source the biography of Quaque and incidental notes on Coboro and Cudjo are exclusively drawn. The Revd. Thompson's letter of 23 January 1762 is quoted from J. J. Crooks, *Notes and Queries* (10 March 1928), p. 174.

38. Aqua and Sackee were also put into the care of the Revd. Moore for 'Board and Schooling' in 1755.

39. Wyndham, op. cit., p. 25. Wyndham says that four boys were brought over by Thompson. But in the letter quoted above, Thompson clearly indicated that there were three, as Quaque's biographer Bartels says.

40. J[ames] Stewart, *A View of the Past and Present State of the Island of Jamaica ...* (Edinburgh, 1823), p. 328.

41. R. Bickell, *The West Indies as they Are; or a Real Picture of Slavery; but more Particularly as it exists in the Island of Jamaica ...* (London, 1825), p. 226.

42. Stewart, op. cit., pp. 328-9.

43. Thomas Bluett, *Some Memoirs of the Life of Job, the Son of Solomon the Highest Priest of Boonda in Africa; who was a Slave about two Years in Maryland; and afterwards being brought to England, was set free, and sent to his native Land in the Year 1734* (London, 1734), pp. 25, 28, 31-2; Francis Moore, *Travels Into the Inland Parts of Africa* (London, 1738), pp. 202-3. For a full-length biography of Suleiman, see Douglas Grant, *The Fortunate Slave* (London, 1968); see also 'Ayuba Suleiman Diallo of Bondu', Philip D. Curtin, ed., *Africa Remembered*,

*Narratives by West Africans from the Era of the Slave Trade* (Madison, 1967), pp. 17-59.

44. Bluett, op. cit., p. 48.

45. Wadström, op. cit., II, pp. 268-9. Some manuscript writings in Arabic of Suleiman are preserved in the Sloane papers at the British Library. See, for example, Add. MSS. 4053.

46. The history of Mohammed can be traced in: *Sixth Report of the ... African Institution* (London, 1812), p. 14; *Seventh Report of the ... African Institution* (London, 1813), p. 18; and *Eighth Report of the ... African Institution* (London, 1814), p. 68.

47. Notes taken from [Edward Long] *History of Jamaica* (London, 1774), II, pp. 474-85.

48. James Ramsay, *Essay on the Treatment and Conversion of African Slaves in the British Sugar Colonies* (London, 1784), pp. 238-9.

49. David Brion Davis in *The Problem of Slavery in Western Culture* suggests that Long's criticisms 'could be dismissed as prejudiced judgement, although such overcompensations are by no means unusual in individuals who have been subject to rapid acculturation' (p. 498).

50. Ramsay, op. cit., p. 239.

51. Facts taken, unless otherwise stated, from F. L. Bartels, 'Jacobus Eliza Capitein, 1717-47', *Transactions of the Historical Society of Ghana*, IV (1959), I, pp. 3-13.

52. C. R. Boxer, *The Dutch Seaborne Empire 1600-1800* (London, 1973 reprint), pp. 170-1.

53. William Emmanuel Abraham, *The Mind of Africa* (London, 1962), pp. 124-5.

54. C. R. Boxer, op. cit., p. 171.

55. Ibid.

56. Facts about Amo are taken from W. E. Abrahams, op. cit., pp. 128-30.

57. *Tractatus de arte sobrie et accurate philosophandi* ... (Halle, 1738).

58. Kwame Nkrumah, *Ghana* (London, 1959), p. 153n.

# 5

# Visitors

Our earliest example was accorded Very Important Person treatment by the British Government and the Royal African Company, because of the ever-desperate desire of the English to be on the friendliest of terms with African kings and chiefs. The African in question was named Tom, and his story is inextricably linked with that of Captain Bulfinch Lambe.[1]

In 1724 Agaja, the King of Dahomey, ravaged and subdued the Kingdom of Allada. Among those captured was Bulfinch Lambe, an Englishman, who had been seized and made a prisoner by the King of Allada for some alleged offence. Lambe was in Agaja's court for about a year; the King of Dahomey then dispatched him to England with his proposals for trade in commodities instead of a trade in human flesh. The King made him a present of 320 ounces of gold, and eighty slaves, of whom forty were said to be a present to George II. Lambe was accompanied by an African named Tom, a native of Jaqueen, who had been made a prisoner with Lambe at the same time, and who spoke good English. Before Lambe left with Tom, Agaja made him promise with a solemn oath to return within a reasonable time, that is, within twelve moons. Lambe, however, went first to Barbados and other islands, and finally ended up in Maryland where he left Tom. Eventually, Lambe recovered Tom and they arrived in London at the beginning of 1731.

Meanwhile, in Africa, the King of Dahomey had complained to another Englishman, William Snelgrave, that Lambe had broken his oath by failing to return within twelve moons. Soon after his arrival in London, Lambe conferred with Snelgrave, who had also returned there after disposing of his cargo of slaves in the West Indies. Lambe asked Snelgrave for his advice about the wisdom of going back to the King of Dahomey. To this, the latter answered frankly that:

It was my opinion, he had miss'd the opportunity, by not returning in a reasonable time, according to his promise; several years being now pass'd since he came from thence, and the State of Affairs much altered for the worse: Besides, he might justly fear the King's resentment, as Mr. Testesole had experienced lately to his cost, for abusing his Goodness; for tho' he was Governour for the *African* Company at *Whidaw*, yet he had been put to death in a cruel manner.[2]

Lambe thereupon took the following measures. First, he delivered a letter to George II purporting to come from the King of Dahomey, wherein Tom, now called Adomo Tomo by Lambe, was described as the Ambassador sent by the King of Dahomey to see the King and Kingdom of Britain. Secondly, Lambe published his plan for a trade in commodities with Africa in place of a trade in slaves, to which was annexed a brief account of his capture, treatment, and release by the King of Dahomey.[3]

George II referred the letter to the Council of Trades. The Board of Trade and the Commissioners of Trade and Plantations deliberated on the letter, and the Directors of the Royal African Company were also sent for. Ultimately, the Lords of Trade resolved that the letter in their opinion was not genuine. But the Royal African Company admitted that Lambe had indeed brought eighty slaves to their Agent in Whydah. Although the Lords of Trade found the letter not genuine, they argued with British practicality that 'there is so much reality in the message as to look upon it as an opportunity not to be neglected of cultivating a good understanding with that Prince'. Accordingly, they recommended that presents should be sent back to the King of Dahomey, 'together with the black man called Adomo Oroonoco Tomo, and a letter as from the King George II, "desiring that the [King of Dahomey] would give your Majesty's subjects all possible protection and encouragement to carry on their trade in his territories."'[4]

So, first Tom became Adomo Tomo and then Adomo Oroonoco Tomo, Ambassador from His Majesty King of Dahomey to His Majesty King George. Everywhere he went, he was given full ambassadorial honours.

I met with several that believed so, till I satisfied them of the contrary; for the jest was carried so far, that several Plays were acted on his Account, and it was advertised in the News-Papers, that they were for the Entertainment of Prince *Adomo Oroonoko Tomo, &c.* these jingling Names being invented to carry on the Fraud the better.

Their Graces the Dukes of Richmond and Montagu showed the Ambassador 'great Kindness', and procured him a passage on board H.M.S. *Tiger* then bound for the coast of Africa, and 'most generously sent by him several rare Presents to his King'.[5]

John Africa, an opulent African merchant of Bonny, made several business trips to England in the first decades of the nineteenth century. Like most other successful, illiterate African merchants of his time, he was 'endowed with an extraordinary memory'. 'I have known him to have opened running accounts with fourteen or fifteen vessels at the same time,' wrote Captain John Adams, 'wherein the debit sides exhibited long lists of various articles received by him at different periods on credit, yet he would tell ... the exact state of each account when he came to settle it, although he could neither read nor write.'[6]

Paul Cuffee was another extraordinary black man who made several business visits to Britain during the period. He was a successful black American merchant and shipbuilder. In 1806 he built a fine brig called the *Traveller* and, in 1811, having often turned his attention to Sierra Leone, with a view to contributing to the welfare of his fellow blacks in that settlement, he set sail in his new vessel, having first obtained a licence to take a cargo from America to Sierra Leone, and a return cargo thence to England. He arrived in Sierra Leone after two months' passage, and remained there another two months. He arrived at Liverpool in July 1811, his vessel being navigated by eight black men and an apprentice boy.

Soon after his arrival, he visited London; and such of the Directors [of the African Institution] as had an opportunity of conferring with him were much gratified by his general intelligence, the accuracy of his observations and statements, and the apparent elevation of his principles. He was afterwards invited to attend a meeting of the Committee of the Board, specially called for the purpose of conferring with him; which the illustrious Patron of this Society [the Duke of Gloucester] honoured with his presence; and the interview left a very favourable impression of his mental and moral qualities on the mind of his Royal Highness, and all the Directors who attended. He gave a clear and encouraging account of what he had seen in Africa, and suggested to the Directors many considerations which may eventually lead to important results.[7]

On 2 February 1816 the *Traveller* once again arrived in Sierra Leone, having on board seven black families from America, adding up to thirty-four people. On Paul Cuffee's application to the Governor, grants of land were made to the heads of families, and they were allowed as much land as they could cultivate. Paul Cuffee sailed from Sierra Leone on 4 April 1816, having supplied every family with provisions for a year.[8] This 'Back to Africa' enterprise cost 4,000 dollars and Cuffee bore most of the cost.[9]

When the Haitians revolted against King Henry Christophe I on 8 October 1820, he shot himself, according to tradition, with a golden bullet. The revolutionaries murdered Henry's young son so that no pretender to the throne might arise, but they allowed Madame Christophe and her two daughters to leave the country. They sailed for England, and immediately upon their arrival they sought out Thomas Clarkson, who had been a devoted friend, counsellor, and Ambassador (to France) of King Henry. Originally, Clarkson planned to have them as guests for three weeks, but an arrangement was worked out whereby the Clarksons were to be remunerated for extra expenses and the visit was extended for several months. The coming of the former Queen of Haiti and her daughters to England placed Clarkson in a new position. Until this time Clarkson, the friend of slaves and black people in general, had met black people only at arm's length, as it were. He was now called upon to live with the three black ladies in close intimacy.[10]

Catherine, Clarkson's wife, communicated the arrival of the Christophes at Playford Hall (the Clarksons' residence) to her friend Dorothy Wordsworth, sister of the poet. The Wordsworths found the idea of the Clarksons giving shelter to the exiles very entertaining indeed. Dorothy Wordsworth wrote back to Catherine Clarkson:

If you could see the lively picture I shaped to myself of the Sable Queen sitting with her sable daughters beside you on the sofa in my dear little parlour at Playford you would thank the newspapers for being so communicative respecting your visitors! I placed them in the *little* parlour because it is always first in my thoughts whenever I turn them thither; but Sara [William Wordsworth's sister-in-law] says 'No! they will sit in the great room.' I was forced to accede and now my fancy espies them through the window of the court upon the larger sofa—them and you— and your dear Husband talking French to them with his loving kindness. I hope they are good and grateful and know the value of such a Friend. ... Does it not seem strange to you after all your thoughts and cares for this poor Family, during their splendour and after their downfall you should see them seated in humble quiet and happy comfort beside you! —at the end of my letter I must copy a parody (which I hope will make you laugh) that William and Sara threw off last Sunday afternoon. They had been talking of Mr. Clarkson's perseverance in the *African* Cause, *especially*—of his kindness to the distressed Negro Widow and her Family—Withal, tender thoughts of merriment came with the image of the Sable princess by your fire-side—the first stanza of Ben Jonson's poem slipped from W's lips in a parody—and together they finished it with much loving fun—Oh! how they laughed! I heard them unto my Room upstairs, and wondered what they were about—and when it was finished I claimed the privilege of sending it to you.

Ben Jonson's poem beginning 'Queen and Huntress, Chaste and fair.' You *must* know it.

> Queen and Negress chaste and fair!
> Christophe now is laid asleep,
> Seated in a British chair

State in humbler manner keep
Shine for Clarkson's pure delight
Negro Princess, Ebon bright!

Let not 'Wilby's'[11] holy shade
Interpose at Envy's call,
Hayti's shining Queen was made
To illumine Playford Hall
Bless it then with constant light
Negress excellently bright!

Lay thy Diadem apart
Pomp has been a sad Deceiver
Through thy Champion's faithful heart
Joy be poured, and thou the Giver
Thou that mak'st a day of night
Sable Princess, ebon bright!

Were the Clarksons amused? No. Three months passed and
Catherine Clarkson failed to answer the letter. Dorothy
Wordsworth then wrote another letter hoping that the Clarksons
were not displeased with 'our joke'. Correspondence between the
two friends was eventually resumed.

Let not 'Wilby's' holy shade
Interpose at Envy's call.

Far from it. On 11 March 1822 William Wilberforce wrote to
Catherine Clarkson:

... I am persuaded for the benefit of the ladies it is much to be desired
that you should accompany them to town. ... It is obviously of great
importance to females so entirely unacquainted with our manners, characters, etc; to have with them a friend of their own sex, who will give
them the benefit of her experience in forming new acquaintants, and
therefore, I hope you will not suffer any motives of feeling or of delicacy ... to obstruct your rendering our Haytian friends the solid service
they would doubtless receive from your accompanying them. I am sure
I should be cordially glad to render them any benefit, and so would Mrs.
W. also. But I have no time to spare, and she has not at present spirits to
undertake an office which would require a considerable share of them.[12]

This is vintage Wilberforce with 'saintliness' oozing from
every syllable. He had 'no time to spare'. But where there is a
will there is a way. The will was what the Wilberforces lacked. It
was a popular saying in Parliamentary circles at the time that his

vote could safely be predicted, for it was sure to be opposed to his speech. And so was the case in respect of the above letter. Wilberforce's expressed concern for 'our Haytian friends' was opposed to his real sentiments. For, years later, Clarkson confided to the painter Benjamin Robert Haydon that 'when Christophe's wife and daughters, all accomplished women, were brought or introduced by him to Wilberforce, and others in high life, there was a sort of shrink at admitting them into high society'.[13]

At the end of their extended visit the Christophes left Playford Hall grateful for the hospitality and humanity they had received. Shortly afterwards they departed for Italy, but not without a most gracious letter to the Clarksons, thanking them for their help and kindnesses.

In November 1830 a young black man, a native of St. Vincent, arrived in England in his bid to establish his claim to freedom. His name was Ashton Warner and he was about twenty-four years old. At the time of his birth, both his parents were slaves on Cane Grove estate in Bucumar Valley. He was an infant at the breast when the owner of the Cane Grove estate, Mr. Ottley, died. Shortly afterwards the estate was put up for sale, so that the property might be divided among his family. But before Cane Grove was sold, Ashton Warner's aunt bought both his mother and himself. But the new owner of the estate, Mr. Wilson, insisted that only Ashton's mother had been manumitted, and Ashton Warner was his property. Ashton Warner was kidnapped and dumped on the Cane Grove estate as a slave. After several years in servitude, he determined to come to England, where Wilson had in the meanwhile returned, in order to establish his claim that he was a free man. He worked his way to England on board ship. 'I landed at St. Catherine's docks, London, and found myself a stranger in this great city; but the hope of gaining my freedom made every thing pleasant to me.' When, however, Ashton inquired after Wilson he found, to his disappointment, that he was dead, and that his property was left to his children, and in the hands of executors. He went to the executors, told them his case, and showed them his manumission papers. 'They promised to look into the business, and settle it for me as well as they could, according to justice.' But on 25 February 1831, Ashton Warner's enfranchisement was suddenly accomplished by death. He died on that day at the London Hospital of an 'inflammatory complaint', uttering, with his last breath, 'freedom to the slaves'.[14]

Thomas Clarkson's last appearance on a public platform was at the great Anti-Slavery Convention held at the Freemasons' Hall

Clarkson, surrounded by veterans of the Abolition and Emancipation campaign including Sir Fowell Buxton and Dr Stephen Lushington, addressing the Anti-Slavery Convention, 1840. The two blacks in

in June 1840, when he presided and made a short speech. Haydon's picture of this scene is now at the National Portrait Gallery. Among the delegates to the convention were Henry Beckford aged twenty-seven and Edward Barrett aged fifty-seven, both emancipated slaves and delegates from the Western Baptist Union of Jamaica.[15] Both men featured in Haydon's picture and, according to the artist, Beckford's depiction is the salient feature of the picture:

In the centre is Clarkson, in his own natural attitude, concluding his speech. Behind, beneath, about him, are the oldest dearest friends of the cause—whilst a liberated slave [Henry Beckford], now a delegate, is looking up to Clarkson with deep interest, and the hand of a friend is resting with affection on his arm, in fellowship and protection; this is the point of interest in the picture, and illustrative of the object in painting it—the African sitting by the intellectual European, in equality and intelligence, whilst the patriach of the cause points to heaven as to whom he must be grateful.[16]

1. The following account of Tom and Lambe (sometimes referred to as Lamb) is drawn from Akinjogbin, *Dahomey and Its Neighbours 1708-1818* (Cambridge, 1967), pp. 64-5, 73-5; William Snelgrave, *A New Account of Some Parts of Guinea and the Slave Trade* (London, 1734), pp. 7-9, 66-72; *Calendar of Treasury Books and Papers*, [II] (1731-4), pp. 88, 89, 96, 98, 101, 142, and 143. See also, Basil Davidson, *Black Mother* (London, 1970), p. 210; H. A. Wyndham, *The Atlantic and Slavery* (London, 1935), pp. 65-6.

2. William Snelgrave, op. cit., p. 69. For Charles Testesole's case, see PRO: T/70/7/fols. 158, 160, 161, and 166. A case similar to that of Testesole's was the killing of Mr. Meredith, Governor at Winnebah fort in 1812, 'Upon some vague and perfectly unfounded suspicions of his having improperly received a quantity of gold, when the Ashantees visited the neighbourhood of Winnebah, the natives of that place seized his person; and although he offered to give up to them the whole of his property; in lieu of the gold he was unjustly accused of having received, they positively refused to set him at liberty. It appears that, whilst taking his usual morning's walk in his own garden, he was surrounded by a number of the town's people and hurried away as fast as possible. They forced him to walk some miles in the burning heat of the sun; ... The parched grass was set on fire, and he was compelled to walk close to its flame: ... His arms were extended, by tying them to a stake which pressed hard on his throat; ... They ... inflict[ed] more torments, which soon produced a melancholy death.' *Seventh Report of the Committee of the African Institution, 1813* (London, 1813), pp. 25-6.

3. Bulfinch Lambe, *Capt. Bulfinch Lambe's Scheme for Trade with the Emperor of Paupau* (London, 1731).

4. *Calendar of Treasury Books and Papers*, op. cit., p. 88.

5. Snelgrave, op. cit., pp. 70-1.

6. John Adams, *Sketches taken During Ten Years Voyage to Africa Between the Years 1786-1800* (London, 1823), pp. 140-1.

7. *Sixth Report of ... the African Institution*, pp. 26-7; Hugh Crow, *Memoirs of*

*the late Captain Hugh Crow of Liverpool* (London, 1830), pp. 300-6. For a full-length biography, see Henry Noble Sherwood, 'Paul Cuffe', *Journal of Negro History*, VIII (1923), pp. 153-229.

8. *Eleventh Report of the ... African Institution*, pp. 40-1.

9. Benjamin Quarles, *Black Abolitionists* (New York and London, 1969), pp. 4-5.

10. E. L. Griggs and C. H. Potter, eds., *Henry Christophe and Thomas Clarkson: A Correspondence* (Berkeley and Los Angeles, 1952), pp. 143-9, 246-7, 254.

11. 'Mrs Wilberforce calls her Husband by that pretty diminutive—"Wilby"—you must have heard her.' Dorothy Wordsworth's note.

12. Griggs and Potter, op. cit., p. 246.

13. Ibid., p. 246n; Earl Leslie Griggs, *Thomas Clarkson, the Friend of Slaves* (London, 1936), p. 147. In Robin Furneaux, *William Wilberforce* (London, 1974), pp. 398-9, the latest biographer of Wilberforce rather disingenuously sought to justify the conduct of Wilberforce and his wife when he wrote: 'Their [the Wilberforces'] elder daughter had died on 30 December 1821 and Barbara [Mrs. Wilberforce] might well have needed longer than two months to recover enough to face an invasion of royal Haitian ladies.' Anyone who believes Robin Furneaux's alibi will believe anything. It is revealing that Furneaux regarded the Christophes as invaders and not refugees who had like the Wilberforces suffered the loss of a loved one the previous year.

14. Ashton Warner, *Negro Slavery described by a Negro: Being the Narrative of Ashton Warner, a Native of St. Vincent's*, ed. S. Strickland (London, 1831), *passim*.

15. In 1826 Samuel Ajayi Crowther (the first African Anglican bishop), who had been rescued from a slave ship in 1822 and sent to Sierra Leone, paid a short visit to England and for a few months he was at the Liverpool Street School, Islington, London. Also, in 1822 George Liele, the Black baptist minister from Jamaica paid a brief visit to England at the invitation of the Baptist Mission.

16. B. R. Haydon, *Description of Haydon's Picture of the Great Meeting of Delegates, held at the Freemasons' Tavern, June, 1840, for the Abolition of Slavery and Slave Trade throughout the World. Thomas Clarkson, President* (London, 1841), p. 10.

# 6

# Community of Interests

While the transient princes, students, and scholars were being honoured and fêted in the homes of the nobility and gentry, or housed, instructed, and educated by schoolmasters and rectors of parish schools, the permanent black folk in Britain grappled with the practical problems of living and surviving in a foreign country and an alien culture.

London, Liverpool, and Bristol were naturally the centres of the black community, but, as the sale and 'Hue and Cry' advertisements indicate, blacks were to be found in other parts of the country. We have already met Gory and Knight in Scotland. Samuel Bowden wrote an 'Epitaph on a Negro Servant, Who Died at Governor Phipp's, at Haywood near Westbury'. The poet recorded that 'Black guests ... Sit round the funeral room', and continued:

> Releas'd from servitude, and woe,
> Here all my toils are o'er,
> To some green island I shall go,
> And see my native shore.
> . . . . . . . . . . . .
> The good shall live again;
> The wicked man's the truest slave,
> And death a tyrant then.

When Clarkson visited Manchester in 1787, campaigning for the Abolition of the Slave Trade, 'the moral steam engine ... the giant with one idea' recorded with astonishment how, arriving at a church where he was to preach one Sunday, he found 'a great crowd of black people standing round the pulpit. There might be forty or fifty of them. The text that I took, was the following: "Thou shalt not oppress a stranger, for ye know the heart of a stranger, seeing ye were strangers in the land of Egypt".'[1]

The African population in Britain during the period was made up of two groups: the free and the slaves. Until 1772 the great majority were slaves. From then onwards, the number of free blacks increased until 1834 when black slaves in both Britain and the colonies were emancipated.

Of the free blacks, a few were slaves who had been emanci-

pated by their English owners, for example Dido Elizabeth Lindsay and Francis Barber. Some, having been emancipated in the
West Indies or America, worked on board ships in one capacity
or another, such as valets and cooks. Yet another group of free
blacks were musicians and regimental bandsmen in the British
army.[2] The majority of free blacks, however, were black slaves,
who, having eloped, evaded capture and remained free. It was
the activities of this group that helped to swell the number of free
blacks. Having escaped, they banded together and lived in the
East End of London in hovels, where they gave shelter and suc-
cour not only to blacks already on the run, but also to the less
adventurous whom they had encouraged to throw off their shackles. Referring to these belligerent fugitive slaves in 1772, Edward
Long exclaimed with the bitterness and asperity which he always
showed when blacks asserted their rights as men: 'Upon arriving
in *London*, these servants soon grow acquainted with a knot of
blacks, who, having eloped from their respective owners at different times, repose themselves here in ease and indolence, and
endeavour to strengthen their party, by seducing as many of these
strangers into the association as they work to their purpose. Not
unfrequently, they fall into the company ... and thus are quickly
debauched in their morals.'[3]

In 1788 Gilbert Francklyn likewise bitterly complained:

It was permitted to debauch their [the planters'] slaves, to encourage or
entice them to run away, with impunity. The ideas of liberty, the
charms of novelty, and an ignorance of the country they had got to,
where they found themselves upon a perfect equality, at least, with the
inferior white people, could not fail of having pernicious effects upon
their minds, and great numbers ran away from their Masters. They in
general plunged into vice and debauchery, ... The whole of those thus
lost to their owners, and to every useful purpose to the community, cannot have been less in number than 15,000 to 20,000. — As most of
them were prime, young, seasoned, or Creole [i.e. born in the West
Indies] slaves, the loss to their owners, the planters, has not been less
than from [£]1,000,000 to [£]1,200,000 sterling: a large sum to be sacrificed to the mere names of liberty and humanity![4]

Francklyn's estimate of the loss to slave owners might be an
exaggeration, but it undoubtedly involved many thousands of
pounds.

It is interesting to note that, in the seventeenth century, a
period when the closely knit black community of the eighteenth
century had not yet been established, and it was therefore the
more difficult for runaway black slaves to survive at large, the
bold and adventurous usually decamped with their owners'

property. Thus in *The London Gazette* for 23-26 April 1677 we read:

A Negro named Robert Moore about 18 years of age, of middle stature, in Livery of Fawn-Coloured Cloth edg'd and lined with Crimson Bages, having lost his thumb from his left hand, went away from his Master, Paul Nicol Esq; of Hendon in the County of Middlesex, on Sunday morning last, being the 22 instant, and is suspected to have taken with him Goods of his Masters of a considerable value. Whoever apprehends him, and gives notice to his Master at Hendon aforesaid, or to John Nicol Esq; at his house in White-Fryers, or to Mr. William Nicol Woollen-draper at the Golden Fleece and Grace in Grace-Church-street, London, shall have 40s. Reward: and farther satisfaction, if required.

In *The London Gazette* of 11-14 November 1689 is another notice: 'Francis Smith, a middle sized black Man, about 30 years old run away from his Master's Service, having a Scar in his Face, and is suspected to have taken away several Sums of Money. Whoever secures him, and gives notice to his Master Mr. Thomas King of Chalgrave in Oxfordshire, within 7 miles of Oxon, or to Mr. William Saunders at the Peacock in Clare-Market, London, shall have two Guineas Reward, and Charges.'

A year later, the following advertisement appeared in *The London Gazette*, for 16-20 October 1690: 'Anthony Charvill, a Tawny-Moor with long curled Hair, and Winifred his Wife, being a short Woman much pitted with the Small-pox, with a Child about 5 weeks old, went away from their Lodging in Turtle-street Westminster the 14 instant, with a considerable parcel of Laced and Plain Linen. Whoever secures either of them and gives notice to Mr. Lowd Taylor in Cockpit-Alley in Drury-Lane, shall have a Guinea Reward.'

In *The London Gazette* for 9-13 January 1695 the Earl of Anglesey announced that his black servant had decamped with quite a sizeable haul of silverware and offered the high reward of £5 for evidence leading to their recovery. In the issue of 6-9 April 1696, *The London Gazette* published the news that James Webster, a black, and his common law wife, Mary Gould, had absconded with 'divers goods'. Finally, in *The London Gazette* for 21-25 January 1696, an apparently opulent slave owner advertised:

Run away on Tuesday the 19th instant, from Mr. Thomas Weedon, Merchant in Fenchurch-street, London, a Negro Boy, named Caesar, aged about 15, the Wooll off the right side of his Head about the breadth of a Crown piece, he had a Silver Coller about his Neck, wears blue Cloth Coat lined with blue with flat Pewie-Buttons, and buttoned close at hand; a black Cloth Waste Coat, Breeches and Cap and black hose; he hath Robbed his Master of several things. Whoever secures him, or brings him to his said Master's House, shall be Rewarded.

The precise conditions of servitude of the black slaves depended on whether they lived in plantation households or non-plantation households. By the former is meant households of West Indian planters, merchants, and Government officials who had served in the West Indies and had brought back to England some of their household body-servants. Non-plantation households were households of Englishmen who had never been to the West Indies, but had acquired blacks as an 'index of rank'. In the plantation households, the Africans lived under a régime no different from what they were accustomed to in the West Indies— witness the savage punishments of Katherine Auker and Jonathan Strong by their respective Barbadian owners. Those who lived in non-plantation households seem often to have fared better. The reason for the difference is not difficult to discern. Englishmen who had not lived in the West Indies and America had not been so depraved by plantation mentality, and were thus enabled to accord some degree of humanity to their black chattels. But too much cannot be made of this distinction. Jack Beef and Francis Barber (before the latter entered Dr. Johnson's service) lived in plantation households. They were well treated and emancipated by their West Indian owners. However, black boys, like Sambo, who were mainly in non-plantation households, were treated as chattels and playthings and were obliged to wear collars. When they had outgrown their value and usefulness as chattels and curios, they were fit only to be returned to the full rigours of West Indian slavery.

Black people domiciled in Britain during this period, whether free or in bondage, were mostly domestics. A good many were beggars, mendicants, and serenaders.[5] Yet another group was of those apprenticed to tradesmen and artificers.[6] Some blacks, however, were self-employed and able to lead independent lives. For example, in the summer of 1815, an application was made to the Directors of the African Institution on behalf of a native of Old Calabar called John Hanson, who had served his time to the trade of a joiner, and was working at that business in Liverpool till an opportunity should occur of his returning to his own country, 'where he appears to have been of some consideration. The Directors thought themselves justified in ordering a sum of [£]20 to be laid out to procure him a chest of tools, and other articles, for his present subsistence.'[7]

*The London Chronicle*, 6 January 1787, reported that a young

Englishwoman who was convicted of forgery was, before committing the crime, servant to some courtesan in the West End, 'and after leaving her service went to lodge at a Black Hairdresser's who got her some employment as a chamber-milliner'. It seems certain that the black man was not only a hairdresser, but also kept a lodging-house, and would have employed fellow blacks in both undertakings.

There is no doubt that the blacks established a sort of transplant of African communal life in Britain. Thus a visitor to the house of Dr. Johnson when Johnson was not at home wrote: 'When Francis Barber, his black servant, opened the door to tell me so, a group of his African countrymen were sitting round a fire in the gloomy anti-room; and on their all turning their sooty faces at once to stare at me, they presented a curious spectacle.'[8]

One of the Africans with Francis Barber may well have been Sir Joshua Reynolds's black servant who is portrayed by Reynolds in some of his pictures. It is well known that Reynolds and Johnson were close friends. We know that one evening Reynolds's black servant took Mrs. Anna Williams, the old blind lady who lived in Dr. Johnson's house, back home to Bolt Court, Fleet Street, after she had dined with Reynolds's daughter. The black did not get back to Reynolds's house until very late, because, 'on his return he had met with companions who had detained him till so late an hour'.[9] Presumably, he stayed to attend another black caucus at Dr. Johnson's, presided over by Francis Barber, or Frank as Dr. Johnson preferred to call him. A consciousness of racial affinity and a background of common experience were the principal unifying bonds of the black community. This consciousness of racial affinity and identity was exhibited during the Somerset case. The whole black community in London closely followed the proceedings in the case of their brother. At each hearing there had been a black delegation. When Lord Mansfield reserved the judgement of the Court of King's Bench on Thursday 21 May 1772, he was reported in the following day's *London Chronicle* as having said that 'due notice would be given' of the day judgement would be delivered. The news that 22 June was the Judgement Day must have spread widely through the black grapevine. 'A great number of [blacks] were in Westminster-Hall', reported *The Middlesex Journal* the following day, 'to hear the determination of the cause and went away greatly pleased.' In a fuller report, *The London Chronicle* disclosed:

Several [Africans] were in Court to hear the event of the above cause so interesting to their tribe, and after the judgement of the Court was known, bowed with profound respect to the Judges, and shaking each other by the hand, congratulated themselves upon the recovery of the rights of human nature, and their happy lot that permitted them to breathe the free air of England. No sight could be more pleasingly affecting to the mind, than the joy which shone at that instant in these poor men's sable countenances.

According to William Beckford, however, their joy was not unalloyed. For, said he, 'At the time that the trial of Somerset was determined at Westminster-Hall, a [black] very shrewdly remarked, that Lord Mansfield had told them they were free, but did not tell them where to get food.'[10] This can either be dismissed as the sour reflection of a slavocrat (once opulent but languishing in Fleet prison as a bankrupt at the time of writing) or accepted as an accurate report of the comment of a reflective black man. True or not, a few days after the victory of James Somerset, a grand ball ('Ball of Blacks') was held by the black community to celebrate the event. Near two hundred blacks, with their ladies, *The London Packet* reported, gathered: 'At a public house in Westminster, to celebrate the triumph which their brother Somerset had obtained over Mr. Stewart his master. Lord Mansfield's health was echoed round the room, and the evening was concluded with a ball. The tickets to this Black assembly were 5s. each.'[11]

Also indicative of the social life of the blacks of London at the time is the following news item in *The London Chronicle*, 17 February 1764: 'Among the sundry fashionable routs or clubs, that are held in town, that of the Blacks is not the least. On Wednesday night last, no less than fifty-seven of them, men and women, supped, drank, and entertained themselves with dancing and music, consisting of violins, and other instruments, at a public-house in Fleet-street, till four in the morning. No Whites were allowed to be present, for all the performers were Blacks.'

This news item requires some brief observation. The fact that the blacks were able to enforce the 'No Whites' colour bar suggests that the public house was at least managed, if not owned, by a black publican. We have seen that Reynolds's black servant, on his return journey from Dr. Johnson's house in Fleet Street, was detained by his companions. It could be that the black servant of Sir Joshua Reynolds was not detained by Frank and his cronies in Johnson's house as surmised earlier, but that he and his companions went to this public house in Fleet Street. The public house may well have been one of the lively African centres which the querulous Philip Thicknesse had in mind when he said, in 1788, that 'London abounds with an incredible number of ... black men, who have clubs to support those who are out of place'.[12]

An instance of the black solidarity to which Thicknesse referred was the case of the two blacks who were committed to Bridewell in 1773 for begging. The papers reported that not only were they visited by over 300 fellow blacks, but also that the black community contributed largely towards their support while incarcerated.[13] The magnitude of arranging for upwards of 300 blacks to visit their brothers, and the administrative complexity of collecting monies for their maintenance would seem to reveal how well developed was the social and communal life of the blacks. As Hecht has rightly conjectured, the black community undoubtedly had its own leaders who planned and organized the important affairs; and was probably centred in certain taverns and public houses that were exclusively patronized by blacks.[14]

In Africa, christenings, weddings, and funerals were social occasions. Such meagre information as we have suggests that the same was true of the black community in Britain. A black (and possibly others too) was present at the funeral of Jack Beef. Bowden recorded that, after the death of Governor Phipps's black, 'Black guests ... Sit round the funeral room'. And a rather salty report of a black christening ceremony appeared in the *St. James's Evening Post*, in 1726:

1st Came the reputed Father, a Guiney Black, a very clever well-drest Fellow, and another Black who was to be the Godfather. 2ndly, The Midwife or rather her Deputy, a White Woman, carrying the little sooty Pagan, who was to be metamorphos'd into a Christian. 3rdly, The Mother, who was also a Black but not of the Guiney Breed, a well shap'd well dress'd woman. 4thly, The Two intended Godmothers, attended by 6 or 8 more, all Guiney Blacks, as pretty, genteel Girls, as could be girt with a Girdle, and setting aside the Complexion, enough to tempt an old frozen Anchorite to have crack'd a Commandment with any of them.

The black community in Britain, relieved from the rigours of the West Indian slavery, and living as free men or slaves in Britain were not preoccupied solely with the problems of their own survival. They were also spokesmen for their brothers and sisters, children and parents still held in servitude. The leading spokesmen for the black slaves in the West Indies were Olaudah Equiano and Ottobah Cugoano, whose Abolitionist activities in print and deeds are told separately in later chapters.

When blacks gathered together it was not solely for the sake of eating and drinking and dancing. West Indian slavery and the British slave trade loomed large in their thoughts and words. In the second appendix to this book we have a collection of six letters, signed by the leaders of the African community including Equiano and Cugoano, written during these black caucuses between 1786 and 1789.

The leaders of the black community were not content with merely writing to the press and the friends of the blacks, but took part in the public debates on the subject of the slave trade and slavery. One such occasion was the debate held on Thursday 7 May 1789 and continued on the following Thursday at the Society of Coachmakers' Hall, 'which without detracting from the merit of similar institutions, is certainly the most popular assembly for free debate in this country'.[15] The most distinguished characters who have written on slavery and the slave trade took part in the debates, on a motion proposed by the Society of Commercial Men, that: 'Would not the Abolition of the Slave Trade be yielding to the principles of mistaken humanity, and highly injurious to the interest of this country.' In its account of the 7 May debate, *The Diary*, a London newspaper, for 14 May 1789 gave the following report of the proceedings: 'Several Gentlemen with great ability reprobated the Slave Trade as totally repugnant to humanity, and the principles of a free country. One Gentleman only opposed the Abolition, which he did in a speech of great fluency and strength of reasoning. He was replied to by an African, (not Gustavus Vassa) who discovered much strong natural sense, and spoke with wonderful facility.'

*The Diary*'s report makes it clear that while Olaudah Equiano (or Gustavus Vassa) was *the* leader of the black community at the time, there were other able Africans who creditably shared the burden of leadership with Equiano.

Blacks, within their means, also made monetary contributions to the funds of the Abolitionist societies. Indeed, James Martin, who died at Clifton near Bristol in September 1813, left a legacy to the African Institution. He had told his acquaintance the Revd. John Greig of Worcester, a member of the African Institution, that he recollected very well living happily with his family in a small town in Africa. One night a great number of people from a distant town surprised and set fire to the town. He believed many of the inhabitants of his town were taken prisoners, and that he, being young, was carried upon a man's shoulders for several days to the sea coast where he was put on board a ship, taken to the West Indies and bought by a planter. He was eventually purchased by a British officer and was brought by him to England. John Greig, understanding that Martin kept some money in an insecure place, advised him to invest it in public funds, and, as he had no relations in the country to claim his property after his death in case of dying intestate, Greig advised him of the propriety of making a will. After explaining to him the nature of the African Institution, he advised him to leave his property to that Society. James Martin said he would consider it and soon afterwards asked Greig whether there was any society for building churches in Africa. 'Upon being told of the Church Mission Society for Africa and the East, he said he should like to leave his money equally between that Society and the African Institution. His will was drawn and executed accordingly, and his bequest has since been received.'[16]

1. Clarkson, *A History of the Rise, Progress, and Accomplishment of the Abolition of the African Slave-Trade* (London, 1808), I, p. 418.

2. Of whom more later.

3. [Edward Long] *Candid Reflections upon the Judgement lately awarded by the Court of King's Bench, in Westminster-Hall, on what is Commonly called the Negroe-Cause, by a Planter* (London, 1772), p. 47.

4. G[ilbert] Francklyn, *Observations, occasioned by the attempts made in England to effect the Abolition of the Slave Trade ...* (London, 1789) pp. xi-xii.

5. Of whom more later (Chapter 12).

6. See the following chapter.

7. *Tenth Report of the Committee of the African Institution, 1816* (London, 1816), p. 38.

8. Aleyn L. Reade, *Johnsonian Gleanings ...* (London, 1909-46), II, p. 15.

9. James Northcote, *The Life of Sir Joshua Reynolds* (London 1818), I. pp. 204-6.

10. William Beckford, *Remarks upon the Situation of Negroes in Jamaica, impartially made from a local experience of nearly Thirteen Years in the Island* (London, 1788), p. 96.

11. *The London Packet*, (26-29 June 1772).

12. Quoted in Dover, *Hell in the Sunshine* (London, 1943), p. 159.

13. See Chapter 8 for the full story.

14. Hecht, *Continental and Colonial Servants in Eighteenth Century England* (Northampton, Mass., 1954), p. 49.

15. *The Diary; or Woodfall's Register* (6 May 1789).

16. *Eighth Report of the Committee of the African Institution, 1814* (London, 1814), pp. 22-4.

# 7

# The Colour Line

In *The London Morning Post* of 28 November 1786 it was reported that: 'On the 23rd of August, the Academy of Sciences elected for their foreign correspondent one Mr. Listel,[1] a free *black* on the Isle of France, from whom the former had received a series of well calculated meteorological observations. This is the first instance of a man of that Anti-European hue being aggregated to any of our learned companies, and the circumstances is an irrefragable proof, that the Academy can consider merit where-ever it may be found.'

The boast of *The Morning Post* is not quite accurate. About 1730, a black had attended meetings of the Royal Society and had been rejected for membership only because of his colour.[2] And in 1731 the Corporation of London prohibited the teaching of trades to blacks.

### APPRENTICES

*The London Journal*, 16 October 1731, reported that: 'The Lord Mayor and Court of Aldermen have ordered that no Negroes shall be bound Apprentices to any Tradesman or Artificer of this City, and the Copies of the Said Order have been sent to the Clerks of the several Companies.'

From a very early period, there were black artificers and apprentices in London. In Fuller's *Worthies of England* it is stated that 'the first fine Spanish needles in England were made in the reign of Queen Mary, in Cheapside, by a negro; but such his envy, that he would teach his art to none; so that it died with him.'[3]

In 1717 the wife of a black named John Caesar petitioned the Middlesex Sessions. Her husband, she said in her petition, had served Benjamin and John Wood, who were printers and embossers in Whitechapel, as a slave without wages for fourteen years. They had very much abused John Caesar and for the greatest part of the time had imprisoned him in their dwelling-house. Seven years previously he had been baptized, but he was still detained as a slave, though, 'as the petitioner is advised, slavery is inconsistent with the laws of this realm'. She herself was very poor and destitute and likely to become chargeable to the parish unless her husband was released from his slavery and confinement and so enabled to provide for himself and the petitioner. The Court recommended the master to come to some reasonable agreement with regard to wages. It is not made clear by Dorothy George[4] whether John Caesar was originally apprenticed to the printers and embossers. But the facts point that way. First, he had been in the service of the printers and embossers for fourteen years. He was baptized seven years before the presentation of the petition. Since the period of apprenticeship at the time was from five to seven years, it would seem that the black man was baptized after he had completed his apprenticeship. Finally, the fact that the Middlesex Session decided that he must be paid wages meant that he was a printer and embosser himself and not just an office boy. It would seem too, that the brothers must have found his services very valuable, since they refused to let him go. On the other hand, it is reported that, in 1725, an artificer petitioned for the discharge of his black apprentice boy. Anthony Emmannuell had been bound in 1723 to one Samuel Johnson, with the consent of his owner. Two years later his new master petitioned for his discharge as, notwithstanding his kindness, the apprentice had run away, embezzled money, and remained incorrigible.

The Lord Mayor and Aldermen of London passed the discriminatory Ordinance of 1731 for a very obvious reason. There were too many blacks in the trades for the comfort of the native population. Ironically, after the Somerset judgement laid down that black body-servants could legally leave their masters, West Indians bringing their slaves into the country induced them to enter into apprenticeship contracts, thus securing their labour under contracts which they hoped English courts would enforce. But, as Granville Sharp, who highlighted the practice, pointed out, the ruse had one fatal defect:

As it has pleased God that the [Black] slaves have had a solemn decision of the Court in their favour, the West Indian slaveholders have attempted to evade it, by binding their [Black] servants to them as apprentices when they bring them to England. But the law will not endure such an evasion! The servant being in slavery, is incapable of entering into any contract with his master, for the same reason that a contract made in prison is suspected of duress, and is therefore null and void.[5]

Granville Sharp's reasoning is unimpeachable in law. But in the case of *Keane* v. *Boycott*,[6] decided in 1795, the law did endure the evasion. In that case a black slave had bound himself to serve his master, who was coming to Britain, as a servant for five years, and the slaver covenanted to find him food, lodging, clothing, and medical assistance in case of sickness. The Court of Common Pleas, in spite of the elementary rule that a contract with a person in a state of slavery is null and void, upheld the contract of apprenticeship in an action between the master and a third party who had taken the black slave into his service.

Extensive use was made of this loop-hole in the law, and only a fortunate slave with powerful allies could escape from the clutches of his brutal oppressor. Such an exceptional case occurred in 1814. In October of that year, information was received by the African Institution 'through a respectable channel that a Black boy was confined in chains, and otherwise ill-treated by his pretended master, at his lodgings in Long Acre'. An application was made without delay to Mr. Birnie, the Magistrate at Bow Street, for his assistance. In consequence of this application a police officer was dispatched to the slave owner with a request that the black boy be produced before the Magistrate. Soon afterwards the boy came, accompanied by his owner, who claimed that the black boy was his apprentice and stated that he had brought him from the West Indies about two months before, and that since their arrival the black boy had cheated him of some bottles of wine. 'On this account, he had determined to send the boy back to the West Indies by the next fleet, and acknowledged that, to prevent his running away, he had chained him to a table.' The slave owner then stated that he should charge the boy with robbing him. The Magistrate observed that such a charge would now be most unseemly, as he had taken the punishment into his own hands, and especially considering the mode of punishment which he had adopted. 'He must know, that, as soon as the boy landed on British ground, he was no longer a slave; to which the master assented.' (The Magistrate was, of course, wrong. Fortunately, in this case he erred on the side of humanity.)

It was then explained to the boy that he might, if he chose, remain in England, instead of being sent back to the West Indies. Naturally, the black boy replied that he would remain in England. The Magistrate then asked the slave owner whether he had ever paid the boy any wages. He admitted that he had not, since he claimed him as his apprentice. He was required to produce or give some account of his indentures, which he declined. The Magistrate then allowed the boy to depart with the Secretary of the African Institution, upon receiving his assurance that the black boy would always be forthcoming to answer any charge which might be brought against him. The boy was then placed by the Institution in the Borough Road school, in preparation for being sent to Africa as a schoolmaster. The African Institution's report of the black boy's case ended with the sentence: 'It is hardly necessary to add, that the threatened charge has not hitherto been preferred.'[7]

About the same time the Directors of the African Institution came to the aid of another black boy. The boy, William Simmons, about sixteen years old, was again recommended to the Institution by one of their members. He had been kidnapped in Africa about eight years before, sold and transported to the West Indies, where he was resold to a Jamaican planter. The slave owner, intending to come to England and bring the boy with him, had the black youth baptized and bound him as an apprentice. Fearing forcible return to Jamaica, the boy bolted from the house of his owner 'who pursued and overtook him; but some persons interfering, the boy was put under the protection of a constable'. The constable in turn applied to a member of the African Institution for advice and assistance. 'Finding him to possess superior capacity, the gentleman recommended him to the notice of the Board, and the lad had been placed at the same school, in the hope that, with proper instruction, he may hereafter become useful as a schoolmaster in Africa.'[8]

## CHEAP LABOUR

In a scene in Isaac Jackman's farce, *The Divorce* (1781), the black man, Sambo, tells the white lawyer, 'I have brought you my year's wages—ten guineas.' Jackman was merely exercising a dramatist's free hand in describing contemporary events. Black slaves in Britain, as chattels anywhere, were not entitled to and did not receive wages. Only the privileged ones like Soubise and Dido Elizabeth Lindsay could boast of owning anything approaching ten guineas. The Duchess of Devonshire offered a black boy to her mother, because as we have seen, *inter alia*, 'he will be a cheap servant.'

Sir John Fielding remarked that the West Indians brought their blacks to England 'as cheap servants having no right to wages'. Lord Mansfield ruled in *The King* v. *The Inhabitants of Thames Ditton* that black slaves, being property, were not entitled to wages. As 'Henry L.' pointed out in *The Morning Chronicle*, 21 May 1772, the planters brought their black slaves with them 'out of avarice, to save the wages to English servants; and out of tyranny, because they can exercise their rage over them without the law's interposition'. In *Back to Africa* Richard West suggests that, 'The handsome wages earned by black servants may explain the scene [cited above] in the farce *The Divorce*, written by Isaac Jackman in 1781.'[9] This sentence shows the writer's thorough misunderstanding of the position of black slaves in eighteenth-century England. Richard West bases his proposition on a work of fiction—a farce.

Of the blacks not in livery, some earned their living by begging and entertaining, and these are discussed in Chapter 12. 'It is only common fairness to say that negroes', wrote Henry Mayhew, 'seldom, if ever, shirk work. Their only trouble is to obtain it. Those who have seen many negroes employed in Liverpool, will know that they are hard-working, patient, and too often underpaid.'[10]

CRIME

On the one hand, Henry Mayhew affirmed that blacks 'are seldom read of in police reports'.[11] On the other, Dorothy George, examining the Old Bailey Sessions Papers, came to the conclusion that 'from time to time Negroes appeared at the Old Bailey charged with petty thefts.'[12] The only valid point that can be made is that, though there was certainly crime among blacks, there is no evidence to suggest that it exceeded (or was even in *pari passu* with) that of the whites. Thus of the scores of people tried as Gordon Rioters in 1780, Dorothy George was able to report that only one was black. The leaders of the black community, in their letter to Sir William Dolben (see Appendix II), made the declaration that it was the duty of all blacks 'to behave with sobriety, fidelity, and diligence in our different stations' while resident in Britain. (The black slaves who escaped with their owners' property are another matter. A popular saying among the slaves in the West Indies was: 'Massa, me no teevee, me takee.') It is suggested that the close affinity between the blacks at the time ensured that 'dutiful behaviour' among the majority of the blacks which their leaders pledged. But of course there were still delinquent blacks.

In the 17 July 1787 issue of the London newspaper, *The World*, it was reported that a black man and his apparently English common law wife escaped the hangman's noose by the grace of the jury, who committed what was then called 'pious perjury' by deliberately convicting the couple for a non-capital offence instead of a capital offence. The crime report in *The World* reads as follows: 'Thomas, a black man, and Elizabeth Smith, were tried on an indictment laid capital, for stealing a watch, value [£]3 a pair of stone knee buckles, &c. the property of Mr. Jones, in a dwelling house; but the jury found them guilty of stealing to the amount of 39s. which takes off the capital offence.'

HORSES, TIM WISKY, and BLACK BOY.

TO be SOLD, at the Bull and Gate Inn, Holborn, A very good Tim Wisky, little the worse for wear, with good harness, and, if desired, a Horse also, that goes well in it.

A Chesnut Gelding, 14 hands and an half high, is very sightly, and would suit a lady in every respect, extremely well, as he goes safe, pleasant, and steady.

A very good Grey Mare, 15 hands high, mistress of 12 stone, and a very pleasant goer. The above are just come out of the country, are rising five years old, and will be warranted sound.

A well made, good-tempered Black Boy, ; he has lately had the small-pox, and will be sold to any gentleman. Enquire as above.

---

RUN away from Capt. Robert Wadlow, from on Board the Ship St. Jago, a Black-Moor Fellow named Tony, aged about 24 years. Whoever secures and brings him to Col. Bartholomew Gracedieu, at the Flying Horse in Thames-street, shall have two Guineas Reward.

---

AS VALET to a Single Gentleman, or SERVANT in a genteel family, either for a constancy or for a season, a Black Young Man, a native of Africa, who has been mostly brought up in London ; can dress hair incomparably well, and is qualified for the duty of a Servant; is of an active and affable disposition. Direct for J. A. at No. 5, Charles-street, near Baker-street, Portman-square.

Three advertisements from contemporary newspapers show the black man as a chattel, a rebel, and a willing labourer in freedom

A black featured in the crime report of *The London Chronicle*, January 1787:

Sunday night a Black was secured at Highgate by a watchman, who observed him endeavouring to put a sack and other articles behind a return post chaise, in order to come to London; but on his questioning him how he came by the articles, and his answer not being satisfactory, he took him to the Watchhouse. About an hour after, a waggon from Yorkshire coming through Highgate, the waggoner enquired if a Black had been seen to go through there with any bundles, when the Watchman shewed him to the Watchhouse. The articles had all been taken out of the waggon at Bell-bar, when the waggoner went to bed, by the Black, who came a passenger in the waggon.

Monday night a highwayman was shot on Finchley-common by the guard of one of the diligences, as he was robbing passengers.

On Monday night a man was stopped by two fellows at the bottom of Park-lane, Piccadilly, who knocked him down, and robbed him of 17s. and some halfpence, and made off without being pursued.

On Monday night about eleven o'clock a gentleman passing under the wall of the Sessions house Yard, in the Old Bailey, a footpad crossed upon him out of New-court, put a pistol to his head, and robbed him of three guineas and his watch.

It will have been noticed that in the above reports taken from a day's crime report in *The London Chronicle*, only the black was identified racially, although the other culprits could have been Irish or French or Italian or English. ('If some restraint could be laid on the importation of the abandoned Irish,' wrote Sir John Fielding in a letter to the Secretary of State in 1771, 'it would be another means of preventing many robberies in this country. There are certainly a much greater number both of Jews and Irish than can possibly gain subsistence by honest means.')[13] When a black committed a serious crime, the paper reported it in all its gory details. The case of John Hogan, a black (or, as some of the newspaper reports preferred to call him, a mulatto) from Madeira, is an excellent example.

John Hogan was porter to a cabinet maker, from whom Mr. Orrell, Attorney, of Charlotte Street, Portland Place, bought some chairs early in June 1785. Hogan delivered the chairs to Orrell's home and made the acquaintance of Ann Hunt, maid-servant to Mr. Orrell. He often visited her during the absence of the family. On Sunday 26 June 1785, Mr. and Mrs. Orrell returned home and found Ann Hunt propped against the wall of the kitchen, besmeared with blood. A surgeon who called said her condition was hopeless. She was, even so, transferred to the Middlesex Hospital, where she died.[14]

A person answering the description of Hogan having been seen in the neighbourhood, suspicion naturally fell on him. Orrell traced him to his lodgings where he lived with an Englishwoman, Elizabeth Pue. There was 'a spot of blood on one of the sleeves of his coat; which coat had been washed, though the blood on the sleeve remained; and an effort seemed to have been made, but in vain, to rub out the spot of blood from the waistcoat.' He was taken before the Magistrates, and 'there was a long examination'; he was then taken to view the body on the evening of Tuesday 28 June 1785. On seeing it, he said, 'My dear Nanny. I do remember you very well: I never did you harm in my life!' In spite of the strong circumstantial evidence against him, Hogan was released by the Magistrates. Orrell, who was a lawyer, strongly suspected that Hogan was indeed the murderer. Hogan was hauled before the Magistrates again, and after long interrogation he was again 'discharged for want of sufficient evidence to bring the fact home'. Six months later, Hogan was tried for larceny at the London Sessions and found guilty on the evidence of a pawnbroker with whom he pawned the stolen goods. He was sentenced to be transported. Orrell read of the trial and conviction of Hogan in the Session Papers, and, as he still retained his suspicion that Hogan was the murderer of Ann Hunt, it occurred to him to search at the pawnbroker's where Hogan had pawned the property for the theft of which he was convicted, to see if the property which was stolen at the time of the murder had been pledged there also.

Orrell's assiduity was rewarded. He found at the pawnbroker's 'a cloak of his wife's which was left hanging in the parlour on the day of the murder, and which was pawned the morning after by the woman with whom the prisoner cohabited'. Meantime, Elizabeth Pue had absconded, but Mr. Orrell's diligence traced her, and by threatening a prosecution likely to bring her to the gallows, he prevailed upon her to secure her own safety by making a full confession of all that she knew, a part of which was that she had washed the blood from Hogan's clothes as soon as he had committed the murder, and had received and pledged the several articles stolen from Mr. Orrell's house. *The Morning Post* (4 January 1786) reported: 'The perpetration of the horrid murder committed on the servant-maid in Charlotte-Street, some months since, was yesterday most providentially discovered.' On Friday 13 January 1786, John Hogan was tried at the Old Bailey for the wilful murder of Ann Hunt. The trial was fully reported in all the London newspapers, especially in *The London Recorder, and Sunday Gazette*, for 15 January 1786:

## OLD BAILEY INTELLIGENCE

*Friday January 13*

### TRIAL OF THE MULATTO FOR MURDER

THIS MORNING CAME ON, BEFORE A CROWDED COURT, THE TRIAL OF JOHN HOGAN, THE MULATTO, FOR THE WILFUL MURDER OF ANN HUNT, SERVANT TO MR. ORRELL, ATTORNEY, IN CHARLOTTE-STREET, PORTLAND PLACE, WHICH LASTED ABOVE FOUR HOURS.[15]

The principal witness against Hogan was the woman with whom he had cohabited. Elizabeth Pue deposed that he brought home a cloak, which he said he had bought on condition of paying for it at the rate of so much per week. The cloak was produced in Court, and Mrs. Orrell testified that it was her property. After other witnesses had given evidence for the prosecution which established Hogan's guilt beyond doubt, he was asked whether he had anything to say in his defence to which he replied, 'I am innocent, and if any body takes away my life, I will never forgive them.' The Recorder then summed up the trial 'with great impartiality, and the Jury instantly found him guilty', reported *The London Chronicle*. After summing up, *The London Recorder, and Sunday Gazette* told its readers, 'The jury then in one minute brought in the prisoner GUILTY'. Before pronouncing sentence, the Recorder observed that the black had been convicted on the fullest evidence, and noted that when the body of the murdered woman was viewed, it drew tears from those who were accustomed to such sights. *The General Advertiser* reported that, 'The Recorder made one of the best and most affecting speeches we remember to have heard; but the wretch was perfectly unmoved, and perhaps was the only person in Court that was unaffected, but he exhibited more a picture of brutality than ignorance.' The Recorder then pronounced the usual sentence in cases of murder, that the prisoner should, on Monday following, be hanged by the neck till he was dead, and his body to be dissected and anatomized. 'He was directly double ironed' and taken to Newgate.

On the day of the black's execution, 16 January, *The Gazetter* reminded its readers, 'John Hogan, convicted on Friday of the wilful murder of Ann Hunt, servant to Mr. Orrell in Charlotte-Street, near Portland Chapel, will this morning be executed as near to the place where he committed that horrid crime as conveniently may be.' All the London newspapers on the day after the execution carried reports of the public hanging of the black. *The Morning Herald* reported: 'Yesterday morning soon after eight o'clock, John Hogan, a Black, who was condemned last Friday for the barbarous and cruel murder of Ann Hunt, servant to Mr. Orrell, of Charlotte-Street, was brought out of Newgate, and put into a cart, and carried to the place near where he committed the horrid fact, and there executed according to his sentence amidst a vast crowd of spectators.'

*The London Chronicle* described the scene thus:

Yesterday morning John Hogan, a Mulatto, convicted on Friday of the wilful murder of Anne Hunt, servant to Mr. Orrell, of Charlotte-Street, Portland-Place, was taken from Newgate in a cart, and executed on a gibbet erected opposite Mr. Orrell's house. He rode with his face towards the horses, and appeared utterly destitute of sensibility. A great concourse of people attended the execution; but it has been seldom that a malefactor has died so little pitied as Hogan. Just before being turned off, the prisoner bowed four times to the populace, and in an audible voice confessed himself guilty of the murder, for which, he said, he had been justly condemned to die. After hanging the usual time the body was taken to Surgeon's Hall for dissection.

Was the black an unfeeling monster? The woman with whom he had cohabited deposed: 'After Hogan had been twice taken before a Magistrate, and discharged for want of sufficient evidence, he at intervals appeared to be very uneasy; that, particularly, he could not sleep in bed; that she finding him thus restless, said to him one night, "For God's sake what is the matter with you? Surely you are not guilty of what you have been taken up for?'' That his answer was, "Yes, I am!—I am guilty!—I did it!'''[16]

Was the black out of place in a white man's civilization?

*The London Chronicle*, 10 January 1786, reported:

The following instance of savage cruelty happened on Wednesday last, on the St. Alban's road, about five o'clock in the evening: a young woman from St. Alban's, going to see her friends at a farm-house, situated a little distance from the London road, got into a waggon which she overtook, and was carried to the end of a lane that led to the farm. On her getting out, she wished the driver and a soldier (who was also in the waggon) a good evening, and they observed her walk down the lane with two bundles in her hand. The waggon had not proceeded 200 yards from the lane, when both the driver and soldier heard a cry of murder, and stopping the horses, they agreed to get each a stake from the hedge and proceed to the spot from whence the sound issued. — They were just going to enter the lane, when they met a fellow with the girl's two bundles in his hand, who, on being questioned how he came by those bundles, was going to draw a hanger from a side coat pocket, when the waggoner gave him so severe a blow, that he broke the villain's arm, and made him surrender himself immediately. On their going a little way down the lane, they found that this savage barbarian had murdered the poor unfortunate girl, by cutting her throat, and that her breast was most inhumanly mangled.

*The Morning Post*, 22 December 1786, commented in an editorial: 'The ferocious profligacy of the present times calls loudly for the interference of the magistrates: A gentleman was stopped on Monday morning, about one o'clock, in Leicester-fields, and making some resistance, the inhuman desperadoes wounded him so barbarously, that he died the next day.'

Why then was the brutal murder committed by John Hogan, a black, given such extensive coverage in the press, when it was so representative of its time? Then, as now: 'Murder may swagger, theft may rule and prostitution flourish and the nation gives but spasmodic, intermittent and lukewarm attention. But let the murderer be black or the violator of womanhood have a drop of Negro blood, and the righteousness of the indignation sweeps the world. Nor would this fact make the indignation less justifiable did not we all know that it was blackness that was condemned and not crime.'[17]

### BLACK PERIL

The first discriminatory law in Britain was not in fact passed by the Corporation of London during the reign of George II in 1731, but in 1596 during the reign of Elizabeth I. As a result of the Spanish wars, a sizeable number of blacks had arrived in Britain. It was thought that these blacks threatened the purity of the English blood, and accordingly, 'Her Majesty, understanding that there are late divers blackamoores brought into this realme, of which kind there are already too manie, considering how God hath blessed this land with great increase of people of our owne nation ... those kinds of people should be sent forth the lande ...'[18] One Casper Van Senden, a merchant of Lübeck, was engaged to transport the blacks out of the country. But once Cromwell snatched Jamaica from the Spaniards in 1655 and the end of the upheavals of the Civil War signalled England's wholehearted participation in the slave trade, the purity of the national bloodstream could not be maintained.

Another inference to be drawn from the discriminatory law of the Corporation of London, aside from the fact that it indicates there were many blacks in the trades, is that by 1731 the black population of Britain had reached considerable numbers. The Ordinance of the Lord Mayor and Aldermen of London was not aimed at those blacks already in the trades, but only against those seeking apprenticeships. The measure would have been unnecessary if the black population was merely a few score. The disquiet and resentment that the presence of a huge population of blacks occasioned in the eighteenth century were voiced by 'Anglicanus', a newspaper correspondent in *The London Chronicle*, October 1764. 'The folly which is become fashionable, of importing [Blacks] into this country for servants', he observed, 'has long been much talked of as a growing piece of ill policy, that may be productive of much evil.' The policy had produced a situation which, 'Was a full enquiry to be made, it would certainly appear that their numbers now in this kingdom amount to many thousands,' and as they filled the places of so many whites, 'we are by this means depriving so many [Englishmen] of the means of getting their bread, and thereby decreasing our native population in favour of a race, whose mixture with us is disgraceful, and whose uses cannot be so various and essential as those of white people.' He resented the fact the blacks 'do not certainly consider themselves to be slaves in this country, nor will they put up with an inequality of treatment.' He was even more resentful of the fact, that 'It is their general character to be spiteful, sullen, and revengeful.' He was quite certain that:

They never can be considered as a part of the people, and therefore their introduction into the community can only serve to elbow as many out of it who are genuine subjects, and in every point preferable. ... many have been perplexed how to get satisfactorily rid of them. ... It is, therefore, high time that some remedy be applied for the cure of so great an evil, which may be done by totally prohibiting the importation of any more of them, or by laying such a tax on doing it, as may prove an effectual discouragement. [19]

In the same year, a piece of home news in *The Gentleman's Magazine*, which bore the marks of 'Anglicanus', raised the same issues:

The practice of importing Negroe servants into these kingdoms is said to be already a grievance that requires a remedy, and yet it is every day encouraged, insomuch that the number in this metropolis only, is supposed to be near 20,000; the main objections to their importation is, that they cease to consider themselves as Slaves in this free country, nor will they put up with inequality of treatment, nor more willingly perform the labourious offices of servitude than our own people, and if put to do it, are generally sullen, spiteful, treacherous, and revengeful. It is therefore highly impolitic to introduce them as servants here, where that rigour and severity is impracticable which is absolutely necessary to make them useful. [20]

A year later, in *The London Chronicle*, another correspondent, 'F. Freeman', after covering the same familiar ground, that blacks 'of late years are become too abundant in this kingdom', that they 'serve but to obstruct a more eligible population', that 'the mixture of their breed with our own ought by no means to be encouraged, because it cannot be made useful, and besides is disgraceful', and that 'in their employment they stand in the way of our own people', proposed his own solution to the Black Peril, which amounts to killing two birds with one stone. He saw in a capitation-tax levied on all blacks in the kingdom a measure that would simultaneously discourage the importation of blacks and pay off interest on the national debt:

The farther increase of them by all means ought to be discouraged, on the principles of good policy; and this cannot be better done than by subjecting them to a capitation-tax, to be paid by those who own or employ them. I have heard their numbers of both sexes, estimated at the lowest to be thirty thousand in the whole kingdom, on each of whom if an annual tax of forty shillings is laid, this will produce the yearly sum of sixty thousand pounds, which will pay interest of two millions of the new funded debt, with only the additional charge of collecting it, which may certainly be trivial.

He admitted that the proposed tax would be a discriminatory one on account of race. But he did not set his face like flint against racism. On the contrary: 'There can be no just plea for their being put on an equal footing with natives whose birth-right, as members of the community, entitles them to superior dues, and therefore such a tax is necessary to make a right distinction in the qualities and the constitutional rights of persons.'

He was careful, however, to make a distinction between skilled and unskilled blacks, and had no objection to the presence of the former. Rather, 'It may be serviceable to invite over those who practice useful arts, because we are benefited by their skill and labour; but it is far otherwise with menial servants ... they stand in the way of the useful natives, and serve to obstruct a far better population.' Like any modern virulent racist, 'F. Freeman' emphasized that he was only paying 'patriotic attention' to a bad policy that might be productive of much evil. With his hand on his heart, he concluded, 'These are hints which I consider to be deserving of attention; and my design in offering them is good, be they thought of as they may.'[21]

In *The London Chronicle*, 13 March 1773, another correspondent urged the expulsion of blacks already in Britain and no entry for those still outside, in order to 'remove the envy of our native servants, who have some reason to complain that the Blacks enjoy all the happiness of ease in domestic life, while many of those starve for want of places.'[22]

Writers like 'F. Freeman' could point to advertisements in the newspapers by blacks seeking employment to establish their claim that blacks 'stand in the way of the natives'. In *The Daily Advertiser*, 26 April 1765, a young black woman advertised for a place as a laundrymaid in a gentleman's family. In *The Morning Chronicle*, 19 June 1786, a black from Jamaica sought a place as a footman, claiming that he 'understands waiting at table and also the management of horses exceeding well, and will be willing to make himself serviceable to the family he may have the honour to serve.' In *The Morning Herald*, 2 January 1787, the following advertisement appeared: 'A Black Servant, very genteel, would be glad to live with any Lady or Gentleman, where there is more than one servant kept; can have a good Character from his last place, where he lived near two years, and is well known in London. Direct for Mess. Chopin and Butler, Grace-Church Street.'

*The Morning Herald* for 24 January 1787 carried the following: 'As FOOTMAN, to a Gentleman, a Black Man, who has always lived in genteel families, has no objection to going abroad, either to the East or West Indies, or any part of England, and can have a good character from his last place. Enquire at John Clifton's haberdasher, No. 1, Crown street, Soho-Square.'

*The World* for 6 February 1788, carried two notices:

As VALET or UPPER FOOTMAN with a Single Gentleman, or in a Family, a genteel Young Man, a Black, who can shave well, and dress hair in the present taste; has been in that capacity in England many years, and can have an undeniable character from his last place. Please to direct for S.J. No. 7, Gerrard-street, Soho.

A BLACK SERVANT, in a family, or with a Single Gentleman that travels; can wait at table; understands taking care of horses, and dressing hair in a plain manner for travelling; can have a good character from his last place. Enquire for W.I. at No. 6, Delahey-street, Westminster.

Finally, in *The World*, 25 July 1789, the following advertisement by another black in search of employment: 'As VALET to a Single Gentleman, or SERVANT, in a genteel family, either for a constancy or for a season, a Black Young man, a native of Africa, who has been mostly brought up in London; can dress hair incomparably well, and is qualified for the duty of a Servant; is of an active and affable disposition. Direct for J.A. at No. 5, Charles-street, near Baker-street, Portman-square.'

It was Sir John Fielding, half-brother of the writer Henry Fielding, who really got down to the nitty-gritty of the KEEP BRITAIN WHITE approach, in a book called *Penal Laws*, published in 1768. He made no bones about what he thought of the Black Peril in Britain and the plantations; he showed his distaste for black solidarity in friendless England; and frowned on the black man's call for justice and equality. The passage is worth quoting at length:

The immense confusion that has arose in the families of merchants and other gentlemen who have estates in the West Indies from the great numbers of Negro slaves they have brought into this Kingdom ... deserves the most serious attention. Many of these gentlemen have either at a vast expense caused some of their blacks to be instructed in the necessary qualifications of a domestic servant or have purchased them after they have been instructed; they then bring them to England as cheap servants having no right to wages; they no sooner arrive here than they put themselves on a footing with other servants, become intoxicated with liberty, grow refractory, and either by persuasion of others or from their own inclinations, begin to expect wages according to their own opinion of their merits; and as there are already a great number of black men and women who made themselves troublesome and dangerous to the families who have brought them over as to get themselves discharged, these enter into societies and make it their business to corrupt and dissatisfy the mind of every black servant that comes to England; first by getting them christened or married, which, they inform them, makes them free (tho' it has been adjudged by our most able lawyers, that neither of these circumstances alter the master's property in a slave). However it so far answers their purpose that it gets the mob on their side and makes it not only difficult but dangerous ... to recover possession of them, when once they are spirited away; and indeed, it is the less evil of the two to let them go about their business, for there is a great reason to fear that blacks who have been sent back to the plantations, after they have lived some time in a country of liberty, where they have learnt to write and read, been acquainted with use, and entrusted with the care of arms, have been the occasion of those insurrections that have lately caused and threatened such mischiefs and dangers to the inhabitants of, and planters in the Islands in West Indies; it is therefore to be hoped that these gentlemen will be extremely cautious for the future, how they bring blacks to England, for besides that they are defeated in the ends they proposed by it, it is a species of inhumanity to blacks themselves, who while they continue abroad in a degree of ignorance so necessary to render a state of slavery supportable, are in some measure contented with their conditions, and cheerfully submit to those severe laws which the government of such persons makes necessary; but they no sooner come over, but the sweets of liberty and the conversation with free men and christian, enlarge them too soon to form such comparisons of the different situations, as only serve when they are sent back again to imbitter their state of slavery, to make them restless, prompt to conceive, and alert to execute the black conspiracies against their Governors and masters.[23]

John Fielding recognized that for the maintenance of slave labour and cheap labour in the plantations, terror and severe laws had to be imposed. But when the man who is terrorized and oppressed tried to exorcize the terror from his life; when the man who endured severe and cruel laws demanded redress, it was considered the most heinous thing to do. 'Hacked, hawed, lamed, tortured, worked to death, poor Africans do not love their masters! Oh Tyranny, thy name should henceforth be Impudence!'[24]

Edward Long, the father of British racism, was the most bilious and inflammatory writer on the issue of the presence of black human beings in Britain. Expansively and with the flair and panache which were his hallmarks in the prosecution of his racist ideology, Edward Long spelt out the potential ramifications, as his warped and twisted imagination conceived them, of the presence of black people in Britain. After the blacks have deserted their owners:

They do not continue long unemployed; the same zealous friends and low pettifoggers, who drew them from their late master, find means, by the register-offices and other channels, to procure them a place in some family; and herein lies a capital part of the grievance. Many persons of rank and fortune entertain these fugitives on the footing of other servants, and often in preference to them, to the very great injury of the owner; who having paid a sum to the state for his Negroe, his services are as much the owner's property, and a part of his fortune, as the estate of the person harbouring him is that person's. This is a loss to the colonies, as well as to the mother country. In the colony their services might have proved beneficial to both; but in *Britain* we find them a dissolute, idle, profligate crew, retained in families more for ostentation than any *laudable* use. ... If these runaway gentry in *England* are invested with English rights in that absolute sense which most of their advocates assert, it will be no surprising thing, if some among them should, by a fortunate ticket in the lottery, or other means, be able to purchase the legal qualifications, and obtain seats in the *British parliament*. It is certain, their complexion will be no disqualification, and that a £20,000 prize will overcome those scruples which some of our rotten boroughs might otherwise pretend against a Negroe representative. The possibility of this event, or of their becoming landholders in the kingdom, is not to be denied. Let us then consider, how far this unrestrained introduction of them among us is either politic, expedient, or useful—In the first place, they are incapable of adding any thing to the general support and improvement of the kingdom; for few, if any, of them have the requisite knowledge for gaining a livelihood by industrious courses. They are neither husbandmen, manufacturers, nor artificers. They have neither strength of constitution, inclination, or skill, to perform the common drudgeries of husbandry in this climate and country. They apply themselves therefore to domestic service, in which they earn little more than their food and cloathing, except what they may happen to acquire by accident of fortune, by benevolence, or petty larcenies, at which they are remarkably acute and dextrous. They are neither so hardy, intelligent, or useful in menial employments as our white servants: One reason which weighs with some persons who retain them is, that they are glad to serve for less wages; a belly-ful and a life of sloth being their *summum bonum*. ... The offspring of these Negroes, a *linsey-woolsey* race, acquire no credit to the people of Britain, and but little strength; for, by the inability of their father to maintain and bring them up at his own cost, they must needs grow burthensome to the public. There has never existed any complaint of a scarcity of white servants in this country; ... the *renegado blacks* from our plantations, debar our own poor from access into families for their livelihood. Since then there is so much reason to complain of inundations from *France*, as well as from the extreme part of *Great Britain* and *Ireland*,[25] there can be no argument alledged, that will prove the expediency, policy, or utility, of encouraging the importation of Negroe domestics; and, if they are not necessary here in that capacity, for which alone they seem at all qualified, they cannot be deemed, in any view, as a needful or valuable accession to the people of *England*.[26]

Here we have an example of the savage art of blaming the victim, which has always been the hallmark of the enemies of the African race. Here we have West Indian ethics stated in all their indecency by one of their greatest exponents.[27] The passage quoted is replete with the most extraordinary assertions and contradictions. The blacks are 'a dissolute, idle, profligate crew', yet the possibility 'of their becoming landholders in the kingdom is not to be denied.' Blacks are not intelligent, but at the same time 'they are remarkably acute and dextrous.' They are not so 'useful in menial employments as our white servants', but they 'debar our own poor from access into families for their livelihood.' The 'renegado blacks' are indolent and lazy, but they are prepared and 'glad to serve for less wages'. Edward Long wrote with tender feeling, that in England blacks are 'retained in families more for ostentation than any laudable use', but two years later wrote in his *History of Jamaica*:

They [the planters] employ too numerous a tribe of domestic servants, ... From twenty to forty servants is nothing unusual. Perhaps it may not be unpleasant to the reader, to see a list of one of these household establishments. I shall therefore present him with following: 1 Butler, 2 Footmen, or waiting-men, 1 Coachman, 1 Postilion, 1 Helper, 1 Cook, 1 Assistant, 1 Key, or store-keeper, 1 Waiting-maid, 3 House-cleaners, 3 Washer-women, 4 Sempstresses. These amount all together to twenty. If there are children in the family, each child has its nurse; and each nurse, her assistant boy or girl; who make a large addition to the number.[28]

And the 'attendants of the table are very numerous, black and yellow, male and female—perhaps too numerous to serve you well.' But consistency, reason, sympathy, humanity, have never been the formulae for a successful demagogue. Appeal to the crude and base instincts in man, however, and the pedlars of racial superiority and purity are home and dry.

'A Lover of Blacks' ably seconded Edward Long.[29] His letter in *The World*, 9 May 1789, was well timed, appearing as it did three days before William Wilberforce moved his first motion in the House of Commons against the slave trade. It was a despicable and sordid letter. The agitation against the slave trade he argued would in the end lead to the expulsion of the whites from the West Indies. The blacks having taken over the plantations, they would be able to visit Britain as wealthy planters and marry Englishwomen. The dark *brunette*, or rather *noirette*, would soon gain in numbers on the fair, and a wonderful alteration would take place in the complexion of future generations by marriages between the new West Indian planters and the daughters of the English nobility, for the descendants of African Princes could not be expected to accept wives under the rank of Peers' daughters. One of the delightful advantages would be 'the graceful air that the young bucks, our grandchildren, of the *mixed breed*, will have, in walking in St. James's and Bond-streets; —the *cross* will give them the appearance of a swivel in the back side, or circuitous motion of the podex.' It must be obvious to anyone, wrote this anonymous assassin of a whole race, that blacks already in England had in some measure anticipated their future greatness, 'witness the great tremendous *tails* they have affixed to their curly pashes, ... this is a degree of vanity, in assuming what does not belong to them.'[30] While giving the usual socio-economic arguments of slavocrats against Abolition and Emancipation, 'A Lover of Blacks' made it clear that he was primarily concerned with the threat posed by the black phallus. Quite understandably, men who had for generations taken black women at will were bound to over-react to black equality.

In 1816 Joseph Marryat, Member of Parliament and Agent for Grenada, reported that at a dinner held in commemoration of Abolition, in the early part of the entertainment, a black man and a white woman led in their child, 'the fruit of their mutual loves. This interesting group paraded round the room, as a proof of the happy result of that union of colours and races which all true philanthropists are so anxious to promote.'[31] For well over 150 years, and long, long before Granville Sharp, Thomas Clarkson, James Ramsay, William Wilberforce, and others began their Abolition work, thousands of Anglo-Africans had been born in the British West Indies. Yet, note the ease with which Edward Long and his disciples ignored this beam in the West Indians' eyes and saw clearly the mote of the Anglo-Africans in England.

It was in 1801 that John Rickman, a friend of Bentham and the Utilitarians, completed and published a census of the population of England, undertaken at the order of the House of Commons. The census returns revealed that the population of England and Wales was 9,168,000.[32] London, the largest city of the Western world, contained 900,000 people. It had been estimated that the population of London in 1700 was 674,350. In 1750 it was estimated at 676,250.[33] In the absence of official statistics, the number of Africans in Britain was freely conjectured. And when a new and higher figure was suggested, then, as now, it gave great force to the spectre of Black Hordes threatening to swamp the natives.

In *The Gentleman's Magazine* in 1764, it was stated that 'the number in [London] only, is supposed to be near 20,000'. In the same year, in *The London Chronicle*, 'Anglicanus' confined himself to saying that 'their numbers now in this kingdom amount to many thousands'. In the same paper the year after, 'F. Freeman' estimated the black population in the whole kingdom 'at the lowest to be thirty thousand'. In 1768, in the case of John Hylas and his wife Mary, counsel for the slave owner, Sir Fletcher Norton, suggested in the Court of Common Pleas, 'that there are now in town [London] upward of 20,000'. In 1772, however, the estimated number of Africans in England sharply dropped. In the Somerset case the estimate given for the entire kingdom was 14,000 to 15,000 Africans. Lord Mansfield accepted the lower figure, hence his calculation that freeing the blacks would cost the proprietary £700,000 (Lord Mansfield estimated £50 per head for each slave). The higher figure of 15,000 was accepted by Samuel Estwick, a West Indian agent, in a tract published shortly after the decision in the Somerset case, adding, 'scarce is there a street in London that does not give many examples of that'.[34] Edward Long, in his tract on the Somerset case, accepted the figure of 15,000 given by Estwick. Edward Long originally gave the figure of 3,000,[35] but, after reading Estwick's tract, he, too, opted for 15,000. 'My reader, I hope will excuse my having stated their number so low as three thousand,' wrote Long, in the postscript, 'this I did from a want of information on that head.' He concluded the postscript by urging ominously, 'The reader may, therefore, if he pleases, alter three thousand to fifteen thousand in the proper place, and deduce accordingly.'[36] In 1788 Gilbert Francklyn, another virulent slavocrat, asserted without authority that, since the Somerset case (a mere sixteen years previously), not less that 40,000 blacks had been brought into Britain.[37]

In 1768 Granville Sharp, who, more than any other Englishman in Britain at the time, was perhaps qualified to give the most reliable estimate, accepted 20,000 as the population of blacks in Britain.[38] But the figure of 20,000 seems rather too high. The black population during the eighteenth century was in a constant state of flux. While some blacks were arriving from the West Indies and America, others were returning. Ill-treatment, starvation, disease, and poverty took their toll among those who formed the 'permanent' black population. After weighing all these factors carefully, it seems that the black population in Britain throughout the eighteenth century at any given time could not have exceeded 10,000.

Although Sir John Fielding, 'Anglicanus', and others expressed grave disquiet at black servants competing with the native born, relations between black and white servants were cordial. For example, when two blacks fought a duel with pistols behind Montagu House in 1780, their seconds were two white footmen.[39] Colonel John Hill's black servant, Pompey, was popular enough with fellow footmen to consider standing for speaker in their mock Parliament. The footmen in attendance at the Houses of Parliament used at this time to form themselves into a deliberative body and usually debated the same points as in the real assembly.[40] Sir John Fielding wrote that it was 'not only difficult but dangerous' for slave owners to rescue runaway blacks because not only were their brothers and sisters supporting them, but they also had the London 'mob on their side'. This indicates that the same harmony which existed between black and white servants also occurred in the general body of poor blacks and poor whites. And we have already seen how white prisoners in a Liverpool prison prevented the removal of black sailors wrongfully detained by their captain. It must be pointed out, however, that not all was well. A passage in Mrs. Piozzi's anecdotes of Dr. Johnson is illuminating: 'Whenever disputes arose in [Dr. Johnson's] household among the many odd inhabitants of which it consisted, [Dr. Johnson] always sided with Francis [his black servant] against the others, whom he suspected (not unjustly I believe) of greater malignity.'[41]

Just as small black boys were the favourites of countesses and duchesses, so were black men the favourites of other women. According to Dr. Johnson, Francis Barber was 'eminent for his success among the girls. ... When I was in Lincolnshire so many years ago, he attended me thither; and when we returned home together, I found that a female haymaker had followed him to London for love.'[42] Alliances and marriages between Africans and Englishwomen were not unusual; in fact, given the very small number of black women, they were inevitable. Benjamin Silliman, a Yale professor who visited Britain in the early years of the nineteenth century, records with astonishment how he met in Oxford Street: 'A well dressed white girl, who was of ruddy complexion, and even handsome, walking arm in arm, and conversing very sociably, with a [black] man, who was as well dressed as she, and so black that his skin had a kind of ebony lustre.'[43]

Sights such as this, and the issue of the union of black and white, were viewed by writers like 'Anglicanus' with grave disapproval. Their message was clear and simple enough; intermarriage between black and white is evil. 'A race, whose mixture with us is disgraceful' was another cogent reason why 'Anglicanus' felt further importation of blacks must be stopped, and why those already here must be got rid of. Samuel Estwick, in the course of attacking Lord Mansfield's decision in the Somerset case, took the opportunity of urging Mansfield to bring in a Bill to prohibit the entry of blacks into Britain: 'It was in representation, if not in proof, to your Lordship, that there were already fifteen thousand Negroes in England; and scarce is there a street in London that does not give many examples of that, ... let a Bill originate in the House of Lords, under your Lordship's formation; ... let the importation of them be prohibited to this country ... In short, my Lord, by this act you will preserve the race of Britons from stain and contamination.'[44]

A correspondent in *The London Chronicle* in the following year made precisely the same point and hoped that 'Parliament will provide such remedies as may be adequate to the occasion, by expelling Blacks now here, ... and prohibiting the introduction of them in this kingdom for the future; and save the natural beauty of Britons from the Morisco tint.'[45]

In 1788 Philip Thicknesse added his voice: 'London abounds with an incredible number of these Black men, who have clubs to support those who are out of place; and every town, nay in almost every village, are to be seen a little race of mulattoes, mischievous as monkeys, and infinitely more dangerous.'[46]

The early children of the union of black and white in Britain were objects of curiosity to the inquisitive. An article in *The London Chronicle*, 9 September 1766, was informative on this point. Two accounts were given by the author of the article, James Parsons, a doctor and Fellow of the Royal Society. The first was of a black man who married a white woman in York 'several years ago'. She soon proved with child, and in due time 'brought forth one intirely Black, and in every particular of colour and features resembling the father'. The child became a centre of attraction 'as a very singular case', because it had been assumed that the issue of such a marriage would be brown. The second case was of a black man, servant to an Englishman, who lived in the neigh-bourhood of Gray's Inn. The black married a white woman who lived in the same family, and, when she proved with child, took a lodging for her in Gray's Inn Lane. When his wife was delivered of the child, a girl, he was out of town with his master on busi-ness. When he returned ten or twelve days after the birth of his daughter, he was much disturbed at the appearance of the child, who was 'as fair a child to look at as any born of white parents, and her features exactly like the mother's.' He swore the child was not his, but the nurse who attended the mother soon satisfied him, for she undressed the infant, and showed that the baby's 'right buttock and thigh' were as black as the father, and recon-ciled him immediately to both mother and child. 'I was informed of the fact,' wrote James Parsons, 'and went to the place, where I examined the child, and found it true; this was in the spring of the year 1747.'[47]

As might be expected, 'the lower classes' of women were blamed for the presence of what DuBois quaintly described as 'that twilight of the races which we call mulatto'.[48]

James Tobin observed that 'The great number of [blacks] at present in England, the strange partiality shewn for them by the lower order of women, the rapid increase of a dark and contami-nated breed, are evils which have long been complained of, and call every day more loudly for enquiry and redress.'[49]

Edward Long, in his tract criticizing Lord Mansfield's decision in the Somerset case, had this to say on the subject:

We must agree with those who declare, that the public good of this kingdom requires that some restraint should be laid on the unnatural increase of blacks imported into it. ... The lower class of women in England, are remarkably fond of the blacks, for reasons too brutal to mention; they would connect themselves with horses and asses, if the laws permitted them. By these ladies they generally have numerous brood. Thus, in the course of a few generations more, the English blood will become so contaminated with this mixture, and from the chances, the ups and downs of life, this alloy may spread so extensively, as even to reach the middle, and then the higher orders of the people, till the whole nation resembles the Portuguese and *Moriscos* in complexion of skin and baseness of mind. This is a venomous and dangerous ulcer, that threatens to disperse its malignancy far and wide, until every family catches infection from it.[50]

It is frightening to see how prejudice can so far extinguish all feelings of humanity as to make men unreasonable in their very reasonings, and to produce these foul and dark thoughts, these brutal and debased emotions, this produce of minds polluted and perverted by their fixation on the black man as a penis symbol.

As a matter of fact, when Long was writing 'the middle and higher orders' of Englishwomen were no less attracted to black human beings. Kitty, Duchess of Queensberry, Elizabeth Chudleigh, Countess of Bristol and Duchess of Kingston, and the Suffolk lady who would not allow King, William Franklin's black, to go back to his master, were not the 'dregs' of eighteenth-century English society, but its 'cream'. The racist ideology that indicted only the so-called lower orders of women of 'strange partiality shewn for' the black is a shameless lie.

In *Back to Africa*, after quoting the remarks of Edward Long cited above, Richard West asserts: 'The views expressed in the Edward Long pamphlet, although all too common today, were rare, unfashionable even outrageous when written in 1772.'[51] Nothing so vividly shows the author's entire misunderstanding of the position of blacks in eighteenth-century Britain. In this chapter we have come across many similar sentiments expressed by men of Long's persuasion. To 'Anglicanus' Africans were 'a race, whose mixture with us is disgraceful'. 'F. Freeman' used almost identical words. James Tobin was concerned about 'the rapid increase of a dark contaminated breed'. An anonymous correspondent in *The London Chronicle* in 1773, like Samuel Estwick,[52] wanted to 'save the natural beauty of Britons'.

Edward Long was not untypical of his time and no natural desire to gloss over a painful subject can hide this fact. The common experience of reading and hearing[53] the most invidious falsehoods and bilious slanders about their race generated that group loyalty and group solidarity among blacks which Sir John Fielding decried so much. The undeniable truth is that racism has been a way of life ever since the first blacks arrived in Britain. The fact of the matter was that, when the importation of blacks into England had reached substantial proportions, men were proposing the same panacea as today to combat the Black Peril. Then, as now, the Government was urged to stop further immigration, or more precisely, further importation of blacks into the country. Then, as now, the Government was urged to introduce fiscal measures to get rid of the blacks already here, and stem the flow into the country of those still outside. And twice during the period, in 1596 and (as will be seen in subsequent chapters) in 1786, blacks were actually expelled from the country. Then, as now, no objection was raised with regard to the entry into Britain of skilled blacks. Then, as now, it was alleged that blacks were filling positions which by birthright, should be filled by the natives. Then, as now, the number game was played. Then, as now, blacks could not have children without being censured. Suffer little children to come unto me ... provided they are white. Then, as now, the spectre of miscegenation was raised.

In their censure of the 'lower classes' of women, race purists like James Tobin, Samuel Estwick, and Edward Long deliberately ignored the fact that Englishmen were responsible for the presence in Britain at the time of the group now known as Anglo-Indians. As Benjamin Silliman recorded:

We saw several children which have been sent ... from India to England, to receive an education. ... They were the descendants of European fathers and of Bengalese mothers, and are of course the medium between the two, in colour, features, and form. I mention the circumstance because the fact has become extremely common. You will occasionally meet in the streets of London genteel young ladies, born in England, walking with their half-brothers, or more commonly nephews, born in India, who possess in a very strong degree, the black hair, small features, delicate form, and brown complexion of the native Hindus.[54]

It was not that Edward Long and his ilk were ignorant of the existence of these blacks—in eighteenth-century England Indians too were called 'blacks'—but then, as now, it was one thing for a white man to marry a black or brown woman, it was entirely another proposition for a black man to marry a white woman. Thus in Britain today, the question is never: Would you allow your son to marry a black girl? It is always: Would you allow your daughter to marry a black man? Yet more and more Englishmen are marrying black girls. In fact, it may be that marriages between black and white in both permutations are now at an equal rate. But, as Calvin C. Hernton explains in his classic work, *Sex and Racism*, when a black man is intimate with *one* white woman, in the minds and emotions of white men, that black man is intimate with all white women. It is reasonable for a man to be jealous of his wife, or of a particular woman whom he knows personally. But it becomes a different matter when a man is envious and jealous of a whole race of women—women he does not know or may never have laid eyes on. Something is terribly wrong with such a man.[55]

Miscegenation is the constant cry of the racists of that and this time, yet it is basically the white man's 'crime'. Consider the following passage from William Howitt's *Colonization and Christianity*, a book published in London in 1838, but which, as DuBois says, Europe has tried to forget:[56]

Amongst the vast mass of colonial crime, that of the treatment of the half-breed race by their European fathers constitutes no small portion. Everywhere this unfortunate race has been treated alike; in every quarter of the globe, and by every European people. In Spanish America it was the civil disqualification and social degradation of this race that brought on the revolution, and the loss of those vast regions to the mother country. In our East Indies, what thousands upon thousands of coloured children their white fathers have coolly abandoned, and while they have themselves returned to England with enormous fortunes, and to establish new families to enjoy them, and have left their coloured offspring to a situation the most painful and degrading—a position of perpetual contempt[57] and political degradation. In our West Indies how many thousands upon thousands of their own children have been sold by their white fathers, in the slave market,[58] or been made to swelter under the lash on their plantations ... In South Africa, this class of descendants were driven from civilization to the woods ... and a miserable and savage race they became. It was not until 1800 that any attempts were made to reclaim them, and then it was no parental or kindred feeling on the part of the colonists that urged it; it was attempted by the missionaries, ... they have now reduced them to settled and agricultural life; and brought them to live in the most perfect harmony with the Bushmen.[59]

The recent arraignment of the white leaders of a community in South Africa under the Immorality Act attracted world-wide publicity. One of these, a village butcher, committed suicide. As Bloke Modisane writes in *Blame Me on History*:

It has never ceased to interest me nor to become a source of ribald comment from Africans that *a law intended to curb the lusting of Africans for white women should count its greatest offenders among the whites*. Some of the country's most respected citizens have come to court on charges of committing an offence under the Act by having indecent carnal intercourse with black women; highly placed citizens like a Prime Minister's private secretary and a few dominees of the Dutch Reformed Church have confessed a realization of the enormity of the implication of the deed, the dominees bowed with grief and humiliation at their 'enormous contravention'.[60]

In C. J. Edwards's *The Rev. John White of Mashonaland* the following incident is related: 'Last year [1896] an instance was reported to me [John White] where one of the officials [an

Englishman] used the influence of his position to obtain a girl for immoral purposes. By threats of punishment, he compelled the Chief to give him his own daughter. I brought the matter to the notice of the administration, and the accused was found guilty of the charge. Shortly after, he left the country, yet so trivial seemed the offence that within nine months he was back again and held an official position.'[61]

John Griffin, the white reporter who travelled through the South of the United States, posing as a black man, discovered some very shocking things about the Southerners. The following incident is but one:

'You got pretty wife?'
'Yes, Sir.'
He waited a moment and then with lightness, paternal amusement, 'She ever had it from a white man?'
I stared at my black hands, saw the gold wedding band and mumbled something meaningless, hoping he would see my reticence. He overrode my feelings and the conversation grew more salacious. He told me how all of the white men in the region craved coloured girls. He said he hired a lot of them both for housework and in his business. 'And I guarantee you, I've had it in every one of them before they got on the payroll.' A pause. Silence above the humming tyres on the hot-top road.
'What do you think of that?'
'Surely some refuse,' I suggested cautiously.
'Not if they want to eat—or feed their kids,' he snorted.
'If they don't put out, they don't get the job. ... We figure we're doing you people a favour to get some white blood in your kids.'
The grotesque hypocrisy slapped me as it does all Negroes. It is worth remembering when the white man talks of the Negro's lack of sexual morality, or when he speaks with horror about mongrelization and with fervour about racial purity. Mongrelization is already a widespread reality in the South—it has been exclusively the white man's contribution to the Southern Way of Life.[62]

One final quotation from Hernton's *Sex and Racism*. Hernton related that he went to a Southerner with a draft of one of the chapters of the book for advice and scrutiny, because of his background and 'because I respect his writing skill and experience'. He was a poet and novelist. The poet-novelist boasted about how honourably his family's black maid was treated. The Southerner continued:

'Why, she was just like one of the family,' he declared, gesturing. 'In fact, she ruled the house. She told my mother what to do—and, good Lord, I've seen her and my father stand up and argue for hours. And not once did I ever hear my father call her a nigger, or treat her with disrespect in any way. And, as I've told you before, my father was a bigot if ever there was one—he lynched a Negro once.' 'Look,' I said, 'why do you think the maid was able to have a free rein in your house, especially with your father?' 'Because—as they say— in the North the Negro is loved as a race and hated as a person, whereas in the South the Negro may be hated as a race but is loved as a person.'

That was a stereotyped explanation, a cliché. It seemed to have rolled out of his mouth without the control of his brain.

'Listen,' I looked him in the eye, 'the most likely explanation is that your father was intimate with that maid. Was he, as far as you know?'

'Why, yes,' he said, matter of factly. And then, as if he could not stop his tongue, added, 'And when I grew up I had her too.'[63]

It is against this background that DuBois wrote in his essay on 'The Damnation of Women':

I shall forgive the white South much in its final judgment day: I shall forgive its slavery, for slavery is a world-old habit; I shall forgive its fighting for a well-lost cause, and for remembering that struggle with tender tears; I shall forgive the so-called 'pride of race', the passion of its hot blood, and even its dear, old, laughable strutting and posing; but one thing I shall never forgive, neither in this world nor the world to come: its wanton and continued and persistent insulting of the black womanhood which it sought and seeks to prostitute to its lust.[64]

The case of the mythological seventy (sometimes sixty) English prostitutes who supposedly accompanied the black founding fathers of Sierra Leone to Africa in 1787 illustrates how, from the yarn spun by Anna Falconbridge, so much has been made from such a trifling little by white men. With very few exceptions,[65] the myth has been the inevitable spice of any book that has even a paragraph on the founding of Sierra Leone. Yet these white women were the wives and consorts of the blacks; like some twenty black women who also went to Sierra Leone with their white husbands and consorts. The suggestion that Granville Sharp who denounced the *Beggar's Opera* in drag 'as an abomination to God', that Pitt (the British Prime Minister who, as we shall soon see, closely followed the progress of the expulsion of the blacks from England), that the British Government and Whitehall organized or were parties to the kidnapping and transportation to Sierra Leone of the so-called prostitutes is too absurd for further comment. Even Anna Falconbridge who first related the fable was compelled to say, 'I cannot altogether reconcile myself to believe it; for it is scarcely possible that the British Government, at this advanced and enlightened age ...

could be capable of exercising or countenancing such a Gothic infringement of human liberty.'[66] Yet O. A. Sherrard, giving vent to the sick fantasies associated with the Big Black Phallus in the thoughts of whites, wrote, 'Negroes, it is well known, possess a fascination for the more unstable and abandoned types of white women, and some sixty prostitutes from the slums of London were sufficiently attracted to throw in their lot with them.'[67] Nothing so vividly illustrates the lewd and pornographic emotions of whites where black men are concerned as this morbid nonsense.

1. He was not Listel, but Lislet Geoffroy, who was also a member of the French Academy and an officer of artillery in the Isle of France.

2. David Brion Davis, *The Problem of Slavery in Western Culture* (London, 1970), p. 492.

3. Thomas Fuller, *Worthies of England* (London, 1840), II, p. 334.

4. The cases of John Caesar and Anthony Emmannuell are quoted from M. Dorothy George, *London Life in the Eighteenth Century* (London, 1925), pp. 136-7.

5. Hoare, *Memoirs of Granville Sharp* (London, 1828), 2nd ed., I, p. 159.

6. (1795) 2 H. Blackstone, 512.

7. *Ninth Report of the Committee of the African Institution, 1815* (London, 1815), pp. 69-71

8. Ibid., pp. 71-2.

9. West, op. cit., p. 15.

10. Henry Mayhew, *London Labour and the London Poor* (London, 1862), IV, p. 425.

11. Ibid.

12. George, op. cit., p. 134.

13. Ibid., quoted at p. 120.

14. The history of the case and the trial of Hogan may be traced in the following papers: *The Morning Post* (4 January 1786); *The London Chronicle* (5, 14, 16, and 17 January 1786); *The Gazetter* (14 and 16 January 1786); *The Morning Herald* (17 January 1786); *The Public Advertiser* (17 January 1786); *The General Advertiser* (14 January 1786); *The London Recorder and Sunday Gazette* (15 January 1786).

15. Some of the capital letters are supplied.

16. *The London Chronicle* (16 January 1786).

17. W. E. B. DuBois, *Darkwater: Voices from within the Veil* (New York, 1969), pp. 34-5.

18. John Roche Dasent, ed., *Acts of the Privy Council of England (New Series), 1596-7* (London, 1902), XXVL, pp. 16-17.

19. *The London Chronicle*, XVI (29 September-20 October 1764), p. 317.

20. *The Gentleman's Magazine*, XXXIV (1764), p. 495.

21. *The London Chronicle*, XVIII (19-22 October 1765), p. 387.

22. *The London Chronicle*, XXIII (13-16 March 1773), p. 250.

23. Sir John Fielding, *Extracts from such of the Penal Laws, as Particularly Relate to the Peace and Good Order of This Metropolis* (London, 1768), pp. 143-5.

24. Horace Walpole to Horace Mann, 22 December 1772. Horace Walpole, *Letters*, VIII, p. 220.

25. For hostilities towards the French, Germans, Swiss, Irish, etc., see Hecht, *Continental and Colonial Servants in Eighteenth Century England* (Northampton,

Mass., 1954), pp. 1-32; George, op. cit., Chapter III, 'London Immigrants and Emigrants'.

26. [Edward Long], *Candid Reflections ...* (London, 1772), pp. 48-53.

27. There is a crying need for a study of Edward Long's influence on the crystallization of British racism. Edward Long was by no means the pioneer of African denigration. The way had been prepared before his time in travel books written by Englishmen and other Europeans who had visited Africa. It is fair to observe that some of these early accounts were innocent misrepresentations, in the sense that the authors misrepresented Africans and African culture, because as Europeans they were unable to express or convey what they saw in any other than European context. It is quite a different matter, however, when we consider the works of those authors who, in spite of their longer stay in, and familiarity with, Africa and Africans, deliberately distorted the truth. Their reports were fraudulent misrepresentations.

What Edward Long did in his tract on the Somerset case, and two years later in his *History of Jamaica*, was to crystallize and put into a coherent whole in vivid imagery fraudulent misrepresentations and racist ideology. The *History of Jamaica* was quoted by both Abolitionists and Anti-Abolitionists in support of their respective causes. Indeed, William Wilberforce, in his first motion against the slave trade, quoted the *History of Jamaica* in the House of Commons in 1789 (*Parliamentary History*, XXVIII, col. 53). Other leading Abolitionists like Granville Sharp, Thomas Clarkson, and James Ramsay quoted Edward Long (in reprobation), but sometimes in approbation, thereby making his work respectable. Several sections in this three-volume work on Africans and Africa are outrageous lies.

28. Edward Long, *History of Jamaica: or, General Survey of the Ancient and Modern State of that Island* (London, 1774), II, pp. 281-2.

29. Or was it Edward Long seconding Edward Long? From the time of his return to England in 1769 until his death in 1813, Long wrote many anonymous pieces in *The St. James's Chronicle*, *The London Packet*, *The World*, and other London newspapers. His favourite pseudonyms were 'A Planter', 'A West Indian', and 'John Bull'. He preserved several of his anonymous letters to the press which are to be found today at the British Library. See particularly, Add. MSS. 12431. The entire Edward Long Papers presented to the British Museum (as it was then) by his grandson, Charles Edward Long, are under the references Add. MSS. 12402-40, 18269-75, and 18959-63. In my own view 'A Lover of Blacks' was in all probability Edward Long.

30. See also, 'Henry L' in *The Morning Chronicle and London Advertiser* (21 May 1772).

31. Joseph Marryat, *More Thoughts ...* (London, 1816), pp. 105-6. The author, an arch foe of Emancipation, was not present at the dinner, but he assured the reader, 'Two accounts of what passed at this meeting was sent me by Gentlemen who were present. I have ... added nothing to either. So far I can answer for the statement not being overcharged', op. cit., p. 106n. We have no reason to doubt the truth of the above account. An Advertisement in *The Morning Chronicle* (20 March 1816), announcing the dinner at the Freemason's Tavern on 27 March, stated that a number of Africans and Asiatics were expected to dine in an adjoining room, separated from the whites.

32. J. H. Plumb, *England in the Eighteenth Century* (London, 1950), p. 144.

33. George, op. cit., pp. 329-30.

34. Samuel Estwick, *Considerations on the Negroe Cause, Commonly So-Called, Addressed to the Right Honourable Lord Mansfield, Lord Chief Justice of the Court of King's Bench* (London, 1773), p. 94.

35. [Edward Long], *Candid Reflections ...* , pp. 51 and 53.

36. Ibid., pp. 75-6.

37. Francklyn, *Observations ...* (London, 1789), p. x.

38. Granville Sharp, 'Remarks on the Case of John Hylas and his Wife Mary'

(MS.), pp. 14-22.

39. *Lloyd's Evening Post*, XLVI (1780), p. 194.

40. Jonathan Swift, *Journal to Stella* (London, 1901), pp. 76-7.

41. Hester L. Piozzi, *Anecdotes of the Late Samuel Johnson* (London, 1786), p. 212.

42. Ibid., p. 210.

43. Benjamin Silliman, *A Journal of Travels in England, Holland and Scotland ... in the Years 1805 and 1806* (New Haven, 1820), I, p. 272.

44. Samuel Estwick, op, cit., pp. 94-5.

45. *The London Chronicle*, XXXIII (13-16 March 1773), p. 250.

46. Dover, op. cit., p. 159.

47. In 1578 George Best had announced that he had seen 'an Ethiopian as blacke as cole brought into England, who taking a faire English woman to wife, begat a sonne in all respects as blacke as the father was ... ', Richard Hakluyt, *The Principal Navigations, Voyages, Traffiques and Discoveries of the English Nation ... 1598*, (Glasgow, 1903-5), VII, pp. 262-3.

48. W. E. B. DuBois, *Darkwater*, p. 178.

49. James Tobin, *Cursory Remarks upon the Reverend Mr. Ramsay's Essay on the Treatment and Conversion of African Slaves in the Sugar Colonies* (London, 1785), p. 118n. Tobin recognized that of the estimated 12,000 blacks in Britain when he was writing, 'A very small proportion of this number are females.'

50. [Edward Long], *Candid Reflections ...* (London, 1772), pp. 46, 48-9.

51. West, op. cit., p. 14. George, op. cit., p. 137, after citing the famous cases of Francis Barber and Ignatius Sancho, states cautiously: 'There seems to have been little prejudice against [Blacks] on account of their race and colour.'

52. If Richard West had bothered to read Long's book, he would have found Long saying that he and Estwick held the same view that the blacks posed a threat to the purity of the national bloodstream. 'I cannot but rejoice to find my sentiments confirmed by the opinion of one who seems to be a candid and sensible writer,' Long wrote in his postscript (p. 75), referring to Estwick's tract.

53. It must not be assumed that black domestics could not read or write. In the advertisements cited in Chapter 2, we find phrases like: 'speaks good English', 'talks English very well', 'speaks English perfectly well', 'speaks tolerably good English'. As Hecht pointed out, most black domestics 'were taught to read and write as a matter of course, and some, perhaps because their masters wished to test the African genius, were given much more extensive instruction', op. cit., p. 42. Francis Barber, it will be seen, had just such an extensive instruction.

54. Benjamin Silliman, op. cit., p. 271.

55. Calvin C. Hernton, *Sex and Racism* (London, 1969), p. 105.

56. W. E. B. DuBois, *The World and Africa* (New York, 1965), p. ix.

57. In an article on Anglo-Indians in the *Observer Colour Magazine*, 30 April 1972, Sunanda Datta-Ray quotes an Anglo-Indian as saying, 'In India the rich despise the poor, the young despise the old and everyone despises the Anglo-Indians.'

58. 'With a harshness and indecency seldom paralleled in the civilized world white masters on the mainland sold their mulatto children, half-brothers and half-sisters, and their own wives in all but name, into slavery by the hundreds and thousands. They originated a special branch of slave-trading for this trade and the white aristocrats of Virginia and the Carolinas made more money by this business during the eighteenth and nineteenth century than in any other way.' DuBois, *Darkwater*, p. 114.

59. William Howitt, *Colonization and Christianity* (London, 1838), pp. 438-9.

60. Bloke Modisane, *Blame Me on History* (London, 1963), p. 215.

61. C. J. Edwards, *The Rev. John White of Mashonaland* (London, 1935), p. 51.

62. John Howard Griffin, *Black Like Me* (London, 1962), pp. 121-2.

63. Hernton, op. cit., pp. 96-7.

64. DuBois, *Darkwater*, p. 172. The whole essay should be read in conjunction with Alexander Crummell's Address, 'The Black Woman of the South' in Alexander Crummell, *Africa and America* (New York, 1891), pp. 62-82.

65. Christopher Fyfe, *A History of Sierra Leone* (Oxford, 1962), p. 17; Richard West, op. cit., pp. 25-6; Mary Beth Norton, op. cit., pp. 414-15; Fernando Henriques, *Children of Caliban* (London, 1974), pp. 117-18.

66. Anna Falconbridge, *Two Voyages to Sierra Leone during the Years 1791-2-3 in a Series of Letters* (London, 1794), pp. 64-6. The Gothic infringement of the human liberty of black women in slavery in the British West Indies and America was of no concern to the authoress, since she assured us after her stay in the British West Indies, 'I now think it [the slave trade] in no shape objectionable either to morality or religion, but on the contrary consistent with both.' Ibid., p. 235.

67. O. A. Sherrard, *Freedom from Fear* (London, 1959), p. 123.

# PART TWO : BLACK POOR

# Introduction

In 1786 and 1787 a concerted attempt was made by the British Government and Britain's liberal establishment to rid Britain of her black population and make Britain a white man's country. It was the culmination of a campaign which began as early as 1764, when an anonymous correspondent in *The London Chronicle* spoke against the folly, which had become too fashionable, of importing blacks into Britain, and urged 'totally prohibiting the importation of any more of them'. As a result of the American Revolution many blacks who had fought on the British side, and who would have been in danger had they remained in America after the successful revolution, came to Britain. Most were indigent and begged in the streets of London, soon coming to be known as the Black Poor. In January 1786 the Committee for the Relief of the Black Poor was formed, as the name suggests, to relieve the Black Poor by providing them with food, clothing, and shelter. Soon, however, the Committee decided that the best way to relieve the Black Poor permanently was to deport them and rid Britain of this nuisance. The Government agreed.

The Government could afford to ignore anonymous correspondents such as those in *The London Chronicle* of 1764, 1765, and 1773, who demanded the deportation of black people. It was different, however, when men of influence (M.P.s, bankers, etc.) stood forth and called on the Government to deport the Black Poor, especially when, as in this instance, they were ostensibly men of 'liberal sentiments'. There is a parallel here with the demand over recent years for the wholesale deportation of black people in Britain. In *The Times* (2 April 1964) 'A Conservative' wrote: 'To have our laws so far out of relation with realities was the cause of the massive [black] immigration in the last decade which has inflicted social and political damage that will take decades to obliterate. ... a common citizenship of the Commonwealth [is] an outworn fiction.'

It has been suggested[1] that Mr. Enoch Powell was the 'Conservative' author of the article in *The Times*. As long as he hollered anonymously, the Government (Labour or Conservative) could afford to ignore his demands. But after his 'river Tiber foaming with much blood' and Britain building her own 'funeral pyres' speeches, the policies of successive British Governments (Labour and Conservative) on the so-called immigration of Commonwealth citizens have been formed according to what Mr. Powell and his ilk say must be done. No matter that the leader of his own Party dubbed Powell's ugly prognostications examples of man's inhumanity to man.

Out of the approximately 10,000 black people in Britain in 1787, less than 400 ultimately left Britain to form the settlement of Sierra Leone. The majority of the blacks, in spite of the tremendous pressure brought to bear on them to leave Britain, refused to leave. Here is a salutary lesson. It suggests that the aimless shouting today that the Government should KEEP BRITAIN WHITE by the compulsory deportation of blacks is only so much hot air, cant, and rant. I can hear vividly now the raucous, vulgar, obscene shrilling that drowned the voice of Frances Brown, the eighteen-year-old schoolgirl, as she spoke eloquently at the 1973 Conservative Party Conference about the contribution blacks have made to British life. One hopes that Frances Brown is the symbol of the future. If humanity forbids, and if the British were to accept Enoch Powell's interpretations of what the black presence means, and in a fit of madness decide on the final solution of the 'black problem', the price would be very heavy indeed. It is the height of naïvety to assume that the British in Britain would have as good and uninterrupted an innings against the blacks and browns as the Nazis had against the Jews in Germany. In Africa, Asia, and the Caribbean, there are British people. It would be a tooth for a tooth, an eye for an eye. It is not only the Thames, but the Ganges and the Niger that would foam with much blood.

1. By Paul Foot, in *The Rise of Enoch Powell* (London, 1969), pp. 29-30.

# 8

# Origin

In August 1773, two blacks were committed to Bridewell for begging in the streets of London. *The General Evening Post* of 27 August 1773, reporting the arrest of one of the Africans, stated that he had 'for some time past sat under some houses in Smithfield begging'.[1] According to the paper, he was one-eyed, and 'was taken from thence and carried before Alderman Thomas at Guildhall, as a vagrant'. Apparently he was no mean vagrant, for *The General Evening Post* told its readers that 'he kept three white women, whom he supported, as well as himself, by begging'. The two blacks were committed to Woodstreet Compter in order that they might be examined before the Lord Mayor. *The General Evening Post* of 28 August reported the examination before the Lord Mayor. The two blacks, the paper declared, 'were both common impostors, one having two wives and the other three, all of whom they maintained in an extravagant manner by begging.' The details of the extravagant manner in which the Africans and their wives lived are not given. The paper, however, proffered the information that two of their wives 'said their husbands provided them with every thing in season'. While they were in Bridewell they were not only 'visited by upwards of 300 of their countrymen', but the black community 'contributed largely towards their support during their confinement'.[2]

In his lurid *Answer to the Rev. Mr. Clarkson's Essay on the Slavery and Commerce of the Human Species, Particularly the African*, published in 1789, Gilbert Francklyn, a prominent member of that venal breed of writers who in the eighteenth century vehemently justified slavery and the slave trade, and bitterly denounced anyone who dared to champion the cause of the oppressed Africans, deliberately distorted and grossly lied about the origin of the Black Poor when he wrote of 'The injury which Mr. Grenville Sharpe's [sic] indiscreet zeal, to procure the freedom of the Negro servants ... occasioned those unhappy people to suffer by considering themselves freemen, and by that means forfeiting the protection of their masters, without acquiring any other; and from thence undergoing extremities of cold and hunger.'[3]

Francklyn's suggestion that Granville Sharp's victory in the Somerset case in 1772 created a 'black problem' in the last quarter of the eighteenth century was a misrepresentation. It was the slave owners who, out of chagrin, threw most of their slaves out on to the streets after the Somerset decision.

It is true that after the Somerset case, a small number of blacks left their owners, but the case of the apparently affluent beggars clearly indicated that these blacks had contrivance enough to keep body and soul together, and lived just as they would have done in Africa. Undoubtedly, a few of the blacks who left their owners fell on evil days but, as the case of the beggars shows, the closely-knit black community in London of those days ensured that they did not create a 'black problem'. It was not until well over a decade after the Somerset decision that the Black Poor grew really numerous; and when they did, it was due to an influx of blacks from overseas: 'Some of these new arrivals were the attendants of army and naval officers who had served in the American War, some were Loyalists whose lives would have been jeopardized had they remained in the colonies; the majority, however, were seamen who had been disbanded after the peace of 1783.'[4]

Granville Sharp, who was well aware of the lie that he created the 'problem' of the Black Poor by his 'nigger-loving' activities, refuted the calumny in a letter to the Archbishop of Canterbury, dated 1 August 1786. After pointing out that, as a result of Lord Mansfield's modest ruling in the case of Somerset, West Indian slave owners were deterred from bringing their body-servants into Britain, he went on to point out that the present set of unfortunate Africans starving in the streets were brought to Britain on very different occasions: 'Some, indeed, have been brought as servants, but chiefly by officers; others were royalists from America; but most are seamen, who have navigated the King's ships from the East and West Indies, or have served in the war, and are thereby entitled to ample protection, and a generous requital.'[5] And we have the word of Lord Sydney, Pitt's Secretary of State, confirming Sharp's explanation of the origin of the Black Poor. The Black Poor, Sydney wrote on 7 December 1786, consisted mainly of those who 'have been discharged from His Majesty's Naval Service at the Conclusion of the late War, and others after having been employed with the Army in North America, who have since their Arrival in England been reduced to the greatest Distress.'[6]

These blacks were part of a larger contingent of American Loyalists, black and white, who found themselves exiled from their country after the American Revolution. The number involved has been estimated at 60,000 to 80,000. Most of the Loyalists settled either in the British West Indies or Canada.

About 7,000 black and white Loyalists ultimately found their way to the 'mother' country. In her recent study, *The British Americans*, Mary Beth Norton has given us a detailed account of the plight of the Loyalists in England. Here we are concerned mainly with the black Loyalists.

The Government provided financial assistance to Loyalist exiles in two ways. First, the administration continued a somewhat informal pension scheme originally established during the war, with the intention of giving deserving refugees temporary support until they found employment in England or were able to settle elsewhere in the empire. Second, Parliament set up a formal commission to which exiles could submit claims to be reimbursed for property they had lost in America because of their loyalty to the Crown. Blacks and whites both availed themselves of the opportunity to seek financial aid from these two sources. Norton reports that a total of forty-seven blacks formally applied in England for pensions or property compensation. Of these, only one was awarded anything for his property losses; three received minuscule annual allowances; and twenty were given small sums of money, ranging from £5 to £20. The contrast with the response to white claimants is instructive: few whites were denied assistance altogether, although more than half the blacks were; the allowances awarded even to the very poorest whites were usually higher than those given to the most fortunate blacks; and whites compensated only with direct charitable grants rarely received less than £25.

The claims and pensions examiners made no secret of the fact that they were deliberately discriminating against the blacks, nor did they hide their reasons for that discrimination. The same phrase, in various forms, appears again and again in their reports on individual cases: typically, they commented with respect to a Connecticut man that 'he ought to think himself very fortunate in being in a Country where he can never again be reduced to a state of Slavery'. Most of the blacks, the commissioners declared on another occasion, had 'gained their Liberty' in the war 'instead of being sufferers' and consequently, they came 'with a very ill grace to ask for the bounty of Government'. Such men, the commissioners observed with staggering callousness, had 'no right to ask or expect any thing from the Government'. Indeed, their 'Applications hardly deserve[d] a serious Investigation or a serious Answer.' Those few blacks who were awarded pensions or grants were the ones who had been able to enlist the support of well-known white refugees. For example, Peter Anderson, a sawyer from Norfolk, Virginia, was at first denied relief by the pension commissioners. But then he obtained a written statement from Lord Dunmore attesting to the truth of his assertions, and the commission thereupon reversed itself, awarding him £10. But the £10 did not last long; and within a few months he was once again petitioning the commissioners for funds, informing them that 'I endeavour'd to get Work but cannot get Any I am Thirty Nine Years of Age & am ready & Willing to serve His Britinack Majesty While I am Able But I am really starvin about the Streets Having Nobody to give me a Morsal of bread & dare not go home to my Own Country again.' Peter Anderson was not alone; there were hundreds more like him on the streets of London. They were the Black Poor, and not the imaginary Africans freed through Granville Sharp's 'indiscreet zeal'.[7]

Although most of the Black Poor were Africans, a sizeable number were Indians, chiefly Lascars. The circumstances in which East Indians were brought to England as domestics in the eighteenth century were very similar to those in which the majority of blacks were imported.[8] Like the Creoles of the Caribbean Islands, high civil and military officials who had acquired wealth in the service of the East India Company returned home to establish themselves in luxury and splendour, and often they carried Indian servants back with them. Warren Hastings brought over two Indian footmen and four maids. Lesser men, such as the writers and factors of the Company, frequently followed the same course. Indians were brought over for precisely the same reasons as Africans. The most important of these were a conviction that the rigours of the arduous passage from India to England were invariably lessened in some degree by the ministrations of a body-servant, and a desire to enjoy at home the same free labour that had been available abroad. The legal status of most Indian domestics corresponded exactly to that of the majority of Africans. They were completely at the disposal of their masters, and, like Africans, they were bought and sold freely on the open market. Thus in *The Tatler* of 9-11 February 1709 the following advertisement appeared: 'A Black Indian Boy, 12 Years of Age, fit to wait on a Gentleman, to be disposed of at Denis's Coffeehouse in Finch-lane near the Royal Exchange.'

The reference to the Indian boy as 'black' is illustrative of the point made by Wylie Sypher regarding the eighteenth-century 'British habit of calling yellow, brown, or red people "black".'[9] (The same is true today. On the radio and television, in newspapers and books, people as diverse and different as Africans, Indians, West Indians, and Arabs are referred to by that odious word 'coloured'.) Sypher also makes the point that many antislavery writers did not distinguish the noble African from the noble Indian. Thomas Moore lays his scene for *Mangora* (1718) in 'Paraguay in the Indies' and the Indian warrior chants to his Indian maid:

> Black Beauty come on
> I must love thee or none ...
> You see my Face black.[10]

A Court action brought by five Lascars in November 1785 is incontrovertible proof that it was not Granville Sharp who compounded the problem of the Black Poor, but the very merchants from whom came the loudest yelps about Sharp's 'indiscreet zeal'. 'Monday, November 28, 1785, came on to be argued in the Court of Common Pleas', reported *The Morning Chronicle* for 30 November 1785, 'a remarkable motion wherein one Soubaney, a Lascar, was Plaintiff, and William Moffatt, of Queen-square, managing owner of the ship *Kent*, East-Indian ship, defendant.'

The facts were these. 'The poor Lascar, with four others, had been soliciting payment of the balance of the wages alleged to be due to them' since July 1784, not only from the defendant, but from John Mavor his agent. Being refused payment, they commenced proceedings for the recovery of their money. Instead of meeting the plaintiffs on the justice of their demands, Moffatt pleaded five pleas in abatement of the actions, stating that he was not the owner of the ship to be answerable for the payment of the Lascar's demands, but that Timothy Curtis, of Homerton, near Hackney, and James Hunt, of Newman Street, Oxford Street, being joint owners with himself, were liable to pay them.

To support his plea more effectively, Moffatt made an affidavit in Court, that at the time the plaintiff's demands were supposed to commence, viz. on 6 May 1783, Curtis and Hunt were, with himself, joint owners of the ship *Kent*. Counsel for the Lascars, having reason to suspect the truth of the pleas, although supported by Moffatt's affidavit, joined issue, which meant that the jury had to determine the point at issue, namely, whether Hunt and Curtis were joint owners of the ship *Kent*, with Moffatt. 'This circumstance it seems', reported *The Morning Chronicle*, 'rather embarrassed Mr. Moffatt, and he applied to the Court for leave to withdraw his pleas in abatement affecting to wish to try the real merits of the demands.' Counsel for the Lascars, the Recorder of London, censured Moffatt's conduct in pleading such pleas to the demands of strangers, who were in many circumstances of affliction, and readily agreed to the withdrawal. Likewise, the Judges of the Common Pleas, after expressing disapproval of Moffatt's conduct, permitted him to withdraw his pleas in abatement. It requires little imagination to guess that the Lascars won their action at this point. On 30 November the Court sitting at Guildhall found in favour of the indigent Indians, and the verdict given was reported in *The Morning Chronicle*, 1 December 1785, 'so as to intitle each of them to recover the sum of twenty pounds and ten shillings' from Moffatt. And we note with gratitude that the Recorder of London, Serjeant Bolton, who was assisted by Mr. Nares, 'pleaded the cause of the Lascars, without fee or reward.'

The plight of the Black Poor reached crisis point during the very severe winter of 1786. Penniless and friendless, poorly clothed, cold and starving, scores perished in the streets of London. As they wandered through the streets, they gave prominence to the existence of a 'black problem' in Britain. In *The Public Advertiser*, 2 December 1786, 'Truth' complained that when a family returned from India they were generally accompanied by their household blacks, whom they usually discarded on landing in Britain. The number of blacks begging 'proves that the generality of those who bring them over leave them to shift for themselves'. In his reply 'Orientalis', in *The Public Advertiser*, 5 December 1786, exculpated the Nabobs, but blamed the Creoles. The Nabobs always returned their blacks to their native country, in contrast to the West Indians who did not. He suggested that 'Truth' had mistaken West Indian blacks for East Indian blacks. Many of the former, it was true, could be found destitute in the streets of the metropolis, 'to the disgrace of those who brought them here'. In *The Public Advertiser*, 22 December 1786, 'Humanus' predicted that a repetition of these scenes might be expected every winter. Within the past four days he had met, at Aldgate and at Covent Garden, two poor wretches on the point of perishing who were probably dead at the time of his writing. He did not know how to administer relief 'except by the casual benefactions of a few half pence'. They were accompanied by their fellow sufferers, 'whose emaciated figures and emphatical gestures spoke more to the feeling heart than words could ... For pity's sake,' he appealed to the editor of *The Public Advertiser*, 'represent the wretched case to the public of these forlorn wretches—in a strange land, cold, hungry, naked, friendless.' In *The Morning Chronicle*, 26 December 1786, 'Youth' went further. The Black Poor were justly entitled to public charity, having been enticed from their country, where the climate is mild and suitable to their constitutions, and brought to one more cold and inclement:

Considering them as foreigners, independent of any service they have rendered us by navigating our vessels, trading to the East Indies, I think they have a claim to our patronage and hospitality, in the condition in which they are at present permitted to roam about this opulent city, unnoticed, and unrelieved, without a coat to shield them from the extremity of the weather, a shoe to preserve their feet from disaster, or even money to purchase sustenance sufficient to allay the griping pangs of hunger and thirst. With plaintive and emaciated countenances they inspire us to pity, and with silent gesture and tears, signify the poignancy of their afflictions.

1. See also *The London Packet* (27-29 August 1773).

2. In the *Observer* of 13 July 1969, under 'Either Way They Lose', Mr. Robert Stew, the National President of the Institute of Burial and Crematorial Administration, was reported as saying, 'We took a sample over a two-month period. Indigenous funerals attracted eight and ten people. But for immigrant funerals, people turned up sometimes in coachloads. At one we actually had an attendance of 450 recorded. ... In these islands I feel we have the finest funeral system in the world with the impact of death on the community not too apparent. I want it to stay that way.' Apparently, both in life and in death, blacks are a source of trouble for the nice, decent, middle class and middle-minded Englishman.

3. Gilbert Francklyn, *Answer to the Rev. Mr. Clarkson's Essay*, p. 165.

4. Hecht, *Continental and Colonial Servants in Eighteenth Century England* (Northampton, Mass., 1954), p. 45.

5. Hoare, *Memoirs of Granville Sharp* (London, 1828), 2nd ed., II, p. 9.

6. *Parliamentary Papers* (1789), vol. 89. Some modern writers have perpetuated the lie that the Somerset decision and Granville Sharp created the problem of the Black Poor. Thus, in T. N. Goddard's *The Handbook of Sierra Leone* (London, 1925), p. 21, we read that after the Somerset case Africans 'suddenly thrown upon their resources soon fell into a state of destitution'. The same point is made in E. L. Griggs, *Thomas Clarkson, The Friend of Slaves* (Ann Arbor, 1936), p. 65. See also A. P. Kup, *A History of Sierra Leone* (Cambridge, 1961), pp. 118-19. The author also wrongly referred to Lord Mansfield as Lord Chancellor.

7. Mary Beth Norton, *The British Americans: The Loyalist Exiles in England, 1774-1789* (Boston, 1972; London, 1974), pp. 49-61, 185-234; 'The Fate of Some Black Loyalists of the American Revolution', *Journal of Negro History*, LVIII (1973), pp. 402-26. See also PRO: AO 12/99/fols. 23, 82, 354; AO 12/100/fols. 74, 129; AO 12/101/fol. 155; AO 13/27/fols. 226-27. For the plight of black Loyalists in Canada, see Robin Winks, *The Blacks in Canada* (New Haven, 1971), pp. 24-60. Edward Brathwaite, in *The Development of Creole Society in Jamaica 1770-1820* (Oxford, 1971), discusses the impact of the black exiles in Jamaica. For the black contribution to the American Revolution consult Benjamin Quarles, *The Negro in the American Revolution* (Chapel Hill, 1961).

8. This paragraph on Indian servants is based on Hecht, op. cit., pp. 50-1.

9. Wylie Sypher, *Guinea's Captive Kings* (Chapel Hill, 1942), p. 106.

10. Ibid., p. 105.

# 9

# Respite

In the first days of 1786, an *ad hoc* committee of merchants, bankers, and Members of Parliament issued an appeal to the public to subscribe to an emergency fund for the relief of the Black Poor, 'who are perishing in our streets'. This committee of City business people, which soon came to be known as the Committee for the Relief of the Black Poor, held its first formal meeting on 8 or 9 January, at Baston's Coffee-House, opposite the Royal Exchange. The response of the public was immediate and generous, as can be seen from the following press release issued by the Committee, which appeared in *The Public Advertiser* and *The Morning Chronicle* on 10 January 1786:

The Attention of the Public having been called to the BLACK POOR, by an Advertisement last week, they have returned Thanks for the generous support which they have given to this Charity. Originally it was only intended to afford a temporary Relief in the Articles of Subsistence; but as the Public seem to enter into the Sufferings of these distressed Foreigners, it is hoped that will carry this Charity much farther, by not only affording them a present Relief, but preventing them in future. If the Public will generously support this undertaking, no Pains shall be spared to lay out Bounty to their Satisfaction.

'At a numerous meeting', on 10 January the subscribers were informed by the Committee 'that a considerable number of Africans and West Indian Blacks, are reduced to the extremest suffering for want of some relief.' However, the generous response of the public would enable the Committee 'to afford them such assistance as the nature of their case admits.'[1]

By 20 February, the public had subscribed £550.17s.6d.[2] On 25 February the Committee announced that it had received £647.19s.6d.[3] The emergency fund reached the sum of £851.8s. on 2 April. The final account of the Committee published on 18 April showed that in just over four months the public had contributed £890.1s. to the relief fund.[4] All sections of the community contributed to the success of the fund, the least subscriber being 'a servant' who sent in one shilling.[5] The generosity of the public did not surprise *The Public Advertiser* (9 January) because 'the City has never used to be backward in exertions of benevolence and liberality.'

As the emergency fund increased, the nature and quality of the relief provided by the Black Poor Committee improved. On 10 January 1786 the Committee announced in *The Public Advertiser* that 'A Quarter Loaf will be given to every DISTRESSED BLACK, who will call at Mr. Brown's, Baker, Wigmore Street, Cavendish Square, on Saturday next, between the hours of Ten and Four.' In *The General Evening Post*, 21 January 1786, and in *The Morning Post and Daily Advertiser* of the same date, the Committee was in a position to advertise that 'A Two-penny Loaf will be given to every Black in real distress, who will call at Mr. Brown's, ... on Monday next, between the hours of eleven and three.' By 21 February the Committee advertised in *The General Evening Post* that 'Every black in distress may receive daily relief, by applying at the White-Raven, near the London Hospital, Mile End-Green.' In fact, daily relief for the Black Poor had begun earlier. Rendering account of its stewardship in *The Morning Post*, 15 March 1786, the Committee reported that:

From the 24th of January, when they began to give broth, a piece of meat, and a two-penny loaf to each person, they have relieved 140 everyday, till the 5th February; and from that time, at the rate of 210 daily, besides bread sent everyday, to many who were sick at home. They have between 40 and 50 in their Hospital, for whom the expences of bedding and medicines have been a heavy charge. About 250 have had shoes and stockings: to many have been given shirts, trowsers and jackets. Some have been fitted out, and sent to sea, and a place is provided with straw and blankets for such as apply for Lodging.

When the Committee published its final account in *The Public Advertiser*, 18 April 1786, it disclosed that 'they have relieved at different Times, and on divers occasions, to the Amount of 460 Persons.'

As we have seen, the original purpose of the Committee was to provide a temporary relief for the starving blacks. The good public response to the appeal and the expressed desire of some blacks to leave friendless England soon suggested to the Committee the idea of the final solution of the Black Poor Problem— repatriation. In *The General Evening Post*, 21 January 1786, the Committee informed the public that it had already received £550, and had already discovered over 250 blacks who were objects of their charity. Of this number, 180 were African men, 30 African women, and the remainder blacks from the East Indies.[6] The greater part of them were taken into service in America and the West Indies, and discharged in Britain. Some of the blacks expressed a desire to go back to sea, or to return to the places from where they had been brought. 'It is therefore the wish of the Committee to be enabled to provide or procure assistance for all' who wished to quit the country. The expressed desire of some of the blacks soon proved to be the thin end of the wedge. The Committee announced in *The Morning Post*, 13 February 1786,[7] that it was now 'the purpose of the Committee' to furnish the Black Poor with the 'means of comfortable assistance in different settlements abroad as Free men'—as if they were not already free men—'but this salutary plan cannot be effected without the generous assistance of the public.' Henceforth, the repatriation of the Black Poor became an imperative feature of the press statements of the Committee. In *The General Evening Post*, 25 February 1786, the Committee reported that they had found that: 'There are considerable numbers who it might be happy to put in a condition of getting their bread in climates best suited to their conditions. Those who are in extreme distress have been relieved for a season, and there is a prospect of making a beginning in providing for some in proper manner Abroad. What respects future importation of these people must be [left] to the consideration of Government.'

With friends like the humane members of the Committee for the Relief of the Black Poor,[8] it was fast becoming evident to the blacks that they no longer needed the enmity of their eternal foes the West Indian planters and merchants. Again, in *The Morning Post*, 15 March 1786, the Committee, expressing their gratitude to the public on behalf of the Black Poor they had relieved, hoped that: 'The Public will continue their beneficence, that they may be enabled to alleviate the miseries arising from the rigour of the season, and likewise to furnish the means of sending abroad those miserable objects, to such places as may put them in a condition of getting their bread in freedom and comfort.'

It was now only a question of time until the Government and the liberal and reactionary Establishment would coalesce in patriotic enthusiasm to preserve the purity of the English bloodstream by expelling from England the 'lesser breeds without the law'.

1. *The General Evening Post* (14 January 1786); *The Morning Post* (17 January 1786).

2. *The General Evening Post* (21 February 1786); *The Morning Post* (21 February 1786).

3. *The General Evening Post* (25 February 1786).

4. *The Public Advertiser* (18 April 1786).

5. The Earls of Carlisle, Huntingdon, and Hertford, the Duchess of Devonshire, the Countess of Devonshire, Lady Walsingham, Daines Barrington, Thomas Boddington, Henry Thornton, and Samuel Hoare, were among the nobility and gentry who subscribed to the relief fund.

6. Which meant that only forty were from the East Indies. In *The General Evening Post* (21 February 1786) it was reported that the number of the Black Poor being maintained by the Committee had risen to 320, 'of this number 35 only are from the East Indies.'

7. See also *The General Evening Post* (21 February 1786).

8. The original members of the Committee were: Montague Burgoyne (Chairman), Sir Joseph Andrews, Bart., George Peter, Jonas Hanway, John Osborn, John Julius Angerstein, James Pettitt Andrews, Samuel Hoare, George Drake, F. Matthews, William Ward, Richard Shaw, John Cornwall, Samuel Thornton, B. Johnson, Henry Thornton, Thomas Boddington. See *The General Evening Post* (28 January 1786).

# 10

# Repatriation

Henry Smeathman explored the areas around the Sierra Leone river on the West African coast between 1773 and 1774. Back in England and in financial difficulties, and having heard of the intention of the Committee for the Relief of the Black Poor to repatriate the blacks, Smeathman approached the Committee with his plan to found a colony in Sierra Leone. Smeathman's plan was considered by the Committee on 21 March, 5 May, and again on 10 May 1786, when the Committee resolved that it was their opinion that it would be in the interest of the Government and people of Britain to expedite the removal of the Black Poor, 'agreeably to Mr. Smeathman's Proposal, which he apprehends may be accomplished within 6 or 8 Weeks.'[1] On 12 April 1786 Smeathman conferred with George Rose, Secretary to the Treasury Board, and in a letter of the same date, Smeathman informed Granville Sharp that it was settled that the 'Government would pay him £12 for each person for any number that are willing to go and settle with him.'[2] The Government, too, had long regarded the numerous blacks who begged in the streets as a nuisance and, therefore, readily agreed to their repatriation. Smeathman, however, was not destined to accompany the settlers to Sierra Leone, and the expedition did not sail in a matter of weeks, but of months.

Following Smeathman's meeting with Rose, and before the House of Commons had sanctioned it, the Treasury began to subsidize the maintenance of the Black Poor. On 17 April, the Committee received £100; 9 May, £100; 16 May, £50; 23 May, £100; and 30 May, £50. Thus within six weeks the Treasury paid out £400.[3] It was not until 5 July 1786 that the House of Commons sanctioned the payment of public money for the repatriation of the Black Poor, and, pending their deportation, payment of public funds for their maintenance. In all, the Government granted £4,056.2s.10d. 'for the Maintenance, Clothing, and Carrying the Free Blacks from hence to Africa.'[4] The Government's apparent eagerness to get the blacks out of the country cut through Whitehall's red tape at every stage of the proceedings. Although over £4,000 (about £45,000 in today's money) of Government money was expended on the project, no one in the Treasury bothered to read Smeathman's plan for the settlement which the Committee forwarded to the Treasury. The pages of the plan submitted to the Treasury are to this day uncut. The Treasury transmitted the plan to the Navy Board on 24 May and on the same day the Navy Board replied that 'having taken into Our consideration, the said Proposals, ... We are of Opinion they are reasonable. We herewith return the Papers.'[5]

The Committee, having decided on Sierra Leone as the destination of the blacks at its meeting on 10 May, ordered at its meeting the following week that a handbill be printed to inform the blacks of the intention to deport them.[6] The handbill reads:

It having been very maturely and humanely considered, by what means a support might be given to the Blacks, who seek the protection of this government; it is found that no place is so fit and proper, as the Grain Coast of Africa; where the necessaries of life may be supplied by the force of industry and moderate labour, and life rendered comfortable. It has been meditated to send Blacks to Nova Scotia, but this plan is laid aside, as that country is unfit and improper for the said Blacks.

The Committee for the Black Poor, accordingly recommend Henry Smeathman, Esq; who is acquainted with this part of the coast of Africa, to take charge of all said persons, who are desirous of going with him; and to give them all fit and proper encouragement, agreeably to the humanity of the British Government.

> By desire of the Committee,
> JONAS HANWAY, Chairman.

Baston's Coffee-house,
17th May, 1786.

Those who are desirous of profiting by this opportunity, of settling in one of the most pleasant and fertile countries in the known world, may apply for further information to Mr. SMEATHMAN, the Author of the Plan, and Agent for the Settlement, at the Office for Free Africans, No. 14, Canon-Street.

Smeathman's *Plan of a Settlement to be Made Near Sierra Leona, on the Grain Coast of Africa Intended more Particularly for the Service and Happy establishment of Blacks and People of Colour, to be shipped as freemen under the direction of the Committee for Relieving the Black Poor, and under the protection of the British Government* could scarcely have failed to attract the destitute blacks. In 1785 Smeathman had testified before a committee of the House of Commons that the climate of Sierra Leone would kill off a hundred convicts a month should a convict station be established on the Sierra Leone coastline. Now in 1786 he enthused about the fertility of the soil and the mildness of the climate. In his *Plan of a Settlement* he assured the blacks that the climate and the soil would enable them to raise corn, rice, livestock, cotton, tobacco, and other produce to considerable amount annually. In the final remarks, Smeathman exhorted, 'an opportunity so advantageous may perhaps never be offered to them again, for them and their posterity.' Smeathman's *Plan of a Settlement*, as he very well knew, was a dishonest prospectus. It did, however, excite the interest of the indigent blacks, who consulted their well-known patron, Granville Sharp. 'Many of them came to consult me about the proposal: sometimes they came in large bodies together.'[7]

It so happened that Sharp himself, since 1783, had been evolving in his mind a plan for the settlement of Africans in the lands of their fathers.[8] Thus when Smeathman approached Sharp for his support in ensuring the success of his plan, he was soliciting the support of the converted. But while Smeathman's vision of the Sierra Leone venture was primarily economic and commercial, Sharp's was rational and humanitarian.[9] It is worth pointing out, too, that whereas the Committee for the Relief of the Black Poor regarded the indigent blacks as a nuisance to be removed from the country by any means, Sharp did not. On the contrary, in a letter to the Archbishop of Canterbury dated 1 August 1786, Sharp wrote: 'It is my duty to inform your Grace, that I have lately heard several hints of an intention to bring in a Bill for a duty on Blacks in England, and to compel masters, who bring them over, to give a bond for [£]100 that they will carry them away again; which would annul the Habeas Corpus Act, and other equitable laws for the protection of strangers.'[10]

Sharp, then, did not see in the blacks a 'Black Problem', but rightly or wrongly saw in his 'Back to Africa' project a way of returning the blacks to the country from which they had been stolen. While he counselled the blacks to go to Sierra Leone, he never pressurized anyone to go there against his wishes. This point is worth emphasizing in view of the erroneous remarks as to the part played by Sharp in the founding of Sierra Leone made in *Race Today* (October 1971). The writer, in the course of his criticisms of the Immigration Bill 1971 (now Immigration Act 1971), observed that the Bill was characterized by overt racial discrimination and thus the Government was acting on an historical precedent which began two centuries ago when proportionately there were more black people in Britain than there are now.[11] 'The establishment of the state of Sierra Leone and the activities of Grenville Sharpe [sic] (the British politician who campaigned for repatriation) exemplify this.' This is a complete misunderstanding of the role of Granville Sharp in the founding of Sierra Leone. Sharp never campaigned for repatriation, and, incidentally, he was never a politician, but a philanthropist. It was the Committee for the Relief of the Black Poor, which comprised bankers, merchants, and politicians, and of which Sharp was never a member, that campaigned for repatriation. Indeed, if Sharp had used his undoubted influence among the blacks to induce them to go to Sierra Leone, the incident about to be related could not have occurred.

Every Saturday the blacks assembled at Paddington or Mile End to receive the sixpence a day Government allowance for their subsistence pending their repatriation. On Saturday 3 June, Jonas Hanway, then Chairman[12] of the Committee, went to Paddington to perform the task of distributing the hand-outs and more importantly to find out the state of opinion among the Black Poor regarding their repatriation. On Wednesday 7 June, the Committee met as usual at Baston's Coffee-House for the weekly meeting:

Mr. Hanway reported that he had attended at the Yorkshire Stingo at Lisson Green on Saturday last [3 June] on account of the Payment of the Allowance made by Government to the loyal Blacks &c. —That he found them reluctant in regard to their going to the Grain Coast of Africa unless they had some Instrument insuring their Liberty. That he had accordingly formed them into a Ring and harangued them, appealing to God and the Common Sense of Mankind for the pure and benevolent Intentions of Government, as represented by the Right Honble. the Lords Commissioners of the Treasury, and no less for the Charity and Benevolence of the good People of Britain exprest by the Committee for the Black Poor, and that for himself, as an old man[13] on the Confines of Eternity, who had no worldly Interest to serve, he must be the worst of all the wicked on Earth to deceive them. That the fertility of the Coast of Africa appeared to him so superior to that of Nova Scotia, as to be incomparably preferable for them; and that they appeared to be convinced of the Truth of what he had advanced.

That he also attended last Monday at the White Raven at Mile End to confirm what he had said at Lisson Green; and that he had selected Eight of the most intelligent among the Blacks and People of Colour as Head men, having proposed to each of them to produce a List of 12 as far as 24 Persons, as his respective Company, ... the Persons so chosen were [James Johnson, John William Ramsay, Aaron Brookes, John Lemon, John Cambridge, John Williams, William Green, Chas. Stoddard],[14] Who appeared well inclined to take charge. Mr. Hanway also reported that in consequence of his Promise to the Blacks and People of Colour, on Saturday, he had digested a Paper (a Printed Copy whereof is annexed) as an Instrument of Agreement, which he thought competent for the Purpose of the most unequivocal Undertaking.

That a Ninth Man, said to be a Person of weight among the Blacks, left the Room saying he would consider it; but the Eight Persons declared they were satisfied, and that they considered it as the fairest and most just Agreement that ever was made between White and Black People, and hoped that he (as the Present Chairman) would recommend it in the strongest Terms to the Approbation of the Committee.

Resolved,

That the Thanks of the Committee be returned to Mr. Hanway with the highest Approbation of his Zeal and Attention to the Object.[15]

Actually, Hanway's haranguing of the blacks was not as effective as he seemed to think. For, at the same meeting of the Committee on 7 June, 'The Clerk Mr. Taylor reported that at Monday's [5 June] Payment the Number was 156 Men and 52 Women, and that about 30 refused taking the Money alledging they wished for a time to consider.' A good many more of the blacks must have stayed away from the place where the Government hand-outs were distributed, for, a week earlier, the clerk to the Committee had reported that '364 Blacks and People of Colour were paid.'[16] Thus about half of the blacks resented Hanway's bulldozing tactics. His eloquence might have persuaded the handpicked Headmen or Corporals, but certainly not the majority of the blacks.

The meeting that Jonas Hanway had with the Black Poor at Paddington on Saturday 3 June marked the beginning of the naked and undisguised pressure put on the blacks by the Committee, the Government, and the London civil authorities, to persuade them to leave the country. At the meeting of the Committee for the Relief of the Black Poor on 7 June, 'The clerk reported that some of the Blacks had been taken up by the Beadles and chastised as Vagrants.' Garnered from the newspapers of the time and the Proceedings of the Committee for the Relief of the Black Poor, the story of these poor black folk is an unbroken succession of misery and persecution.

At the meeting of the Committee on 14 June, the important decision was made that in order to prevent the countenancing of anybody's emigrating against the rights of his master, 'it be advertised in the Gazette and in two Evening Papers that all Persons, Blacks and People of Colour, intended for an African settlement may be seen at the White Raven behind the London Hospital at the next Payment of their Allowance.'[17] Owners of runaway blacks, of course, flocked there in an endeavour to recover their chattels. How successful they were we do not know, but at this distance of time, one cannot but read the Committee's open invitation with the greatest foreboding. First, was any Creole given the benefit of that old misapprehension that 'they all look alike' whereby many free blacks had been sold into slavery repeatedly in the West Indies and America? Secondly, we recall the following incident related by Olaudah Equiano when, as a free man, he visited Georgia:

I was beset by two white men who meant to play the usual tricks with me in the way of kidnapping. As soon as these men accosted me, one of them said to the other, 'This is the very fellow we are looking for that you lost': and the other swore immediately that I was the identical person. On this they made up to me and were about to handle me, but I told them to be still and keep off, for I had seen those kind of tricks played upon free blacks and they must not think to serve me so. At this they paused a little, and one said to the other—'It will not do'; and the other answered that I talked too good English. I replied, I believed I did, and I had also with me a revengeful stick equal to the occasion, and my mind was likewise good. Happily however it was not used, and after we had talked together a little in this manner the rogues left me.[18]

Equiano was well equipped. For he was one of those blacks who emerged from the cruel pangs of slavery still redoubtable. But how many of the depressed and crushed Black Poor could have stood up to slave hunters in the London of 1786?

The Committee lost no time in printing 500 copies of Smeathman's *Plan of a Settlement*, and 750 copies of the Instrument of Agreement drawn up by Hanway. But towards the end of June Smeathman was taken ill of fever, and he died on 1 July 1786. The Committee immediately told Hanway to inform the Treasury of his death and to ask for a substitute for him. But the Treasury played the ball back into the Committee's court. Rose told Hanway that:

It appears to him that as private Persons first proposed the Relief of the Blacks and sending them out of this Country, that the Lords of the Treasury conceived that those private Persons, consisting of experienced and respectable Committee, would bring the Object to an Issue; & therefore as Mr. Smeathman the Person recommended by several Members of Parliament to their Lordships was dead that the Committee would take the trouble to look out for some other fit Person to conduct this Enterprise.[19]

At the time of Smeathman's death, over 400 blacks had enlisted to go to Sierra Leone. The glowing account of life on the projected settlement had obviously produced the desired result—for the meantime at least. Consequently, when after Smeathman's death the Committee lost interest in Sierra Leone as the site for dumping the Black Poor, and resolved, at its meeting on 7 July, to send them to the Bahamas, the blacks protested. Their Petition, which was signed by fifteen Corporals was read at the Committee's meeting on 15 July. They were disturbed to hear that the Committee now intended to send them to the Bahamas. Their attention had been 'peculiarly directed by the late Mr. Smeathman's Plan' to Sierra Leone and they were not interested in any other spot. Since Smeathman was dead, 'there is no Man in whom they can now repose the same confidence as in Mr. Joseph Irwin, the Gentleman who was recommended to them by the late Mr. Smeathman as a proper Person to embark with and assist him in carrying his Plan to Execution.' Annexed to the Petition to the Committee was another in similar terms addressed to the Lords Commissioners of the Treasury. The Committee having duly considered the Petition, it was determined that they 'do adhere to their Resolution of 7th July' to send the blacks to the Bahamas. The other Petition to the Treasury was nevertheless forwarded to George Rose. The Treasury still thought that Smeathman's plan was viable, and the Committee was soon obliged to discard the idea of sending the blacks to the Bahamas, or to New Brunswick, which was also considered by them as a suitable dumping ground.[20]

By October, the number of enlisted blacks had risen to 500. At the meeting of the Committee on 6 October, 'Mr. Taylor [the Clerk] reported that there were 715 Persons paid on the 20th Ult. and 736 on 2d Inst.' At the same meeting, the Agreement between the blacks and Joseph Irwin, who had been appointed Government Agent as the blacks had asked, was read and approved by the Committee, 'and it was Resolved, That no further Money be given but to such as sign the same.' Apparently, the Committee felt that everyone receiving the sixpence subsistence allowance should enlist, and since only 500 had enlisted to go to Sierra Leone, it was thought necessary to make this decision.[21]

Early in October the Navy Board had commissioned the *Atlantic* and the *Belisarius* to transport the deportees to Sierra Leone, and by the end of October, the 500 blacks had embarked on board both ships. When Irwin informed the Navy Board that the number of the deportees would be at least 750, a third ship, the *Vernon*, was commissioned. Everything seemed to be going on well. In *The General Advertiser*, 25 November 1786, it was reported: 'The *Atlantic*, and *Belisarius*, are two ships appointed to carry the intended settlement of blacks and mulattoes to the coast of Africa.—These ships are now taking them on board at Deptford, and will be ready to sail in about ten days. Several of the black men have white wives and families. This settlement was projected by the late Mr. Smeathman, and he was to have been at the head of the settlement.'[22]

Although some 700 blacks had signed the repatriation agreement, many indigent blacks still wandered through the streets of London. The Committee, absolutely determined to get all the Black Poor out of the country, resolved at its meeting on Friday 1 December, 'that it be immediately communicated to all Blacks on shore, that the two Ships will sail tomorrow morning and that such as have signed the Agreement and received the Money to embark without delay.' On 6 December the Chairman of the Committee, Samuel Hoare, wrote to the Treasury, and urged the issue of a Proclamation enjoining all those who had been 'relieved by the humanity of the British Government to go on board the Ships which are now ready for their reception, and that Ten Days after the Date thereof all Persons of that description who are found begging or lurking about the Streets will be taken up on the Vagrant Act.'[23]

Whereupon the London civil authorities rounded up all the blacks they could lay their hands on who were still roaming the streets. But not all. On 14 December 1787, the Committee issued the following press statement which appeared in *The General Evening Post* of the same day:

The Committee for the Relief of the Black Poor think it necessary to inform the Public, that three ships are now ready, amply supplied with provisions, clothing, and every other necessary, in Order to establish a Free Settlement on the coast of Africa; that seven hundred have signed an engagement to go, and only three hundred are on board. It being apprehended that the remainder are prevented from embarking, by the mistaken, though well intended acts of charity of individuals, in giving relief to such of the Black Poor as are still about the metropolis. The Committee submits to the consideration of the Public, whether it may not be advisable to suspend giving alms to the said persons, in order to induce them to comply with the engagement they entered into.[24]

But many ignored the appeal. As we have seen, 'Humanus' asked *The Morning Chronicle* to 'represent the wretched case to the public of these forlorn wretches ... that they may not perish.' Four days later, in the same paper, 'Youth' asserted that the blacks were 'justly entitled to our beneficence', and appealed 'for the munificence of the public'. In *The Morning Chronicle* (28 December 1786) 'H. L.' wrote, 'I met last Sunday two of them bare-footed and naked almost. I relieved them with something.' Kind and generous English people, these are the people sons and daughters of Africa will remember with gratitude, not the hypocrites who harangued the Black Poor in the name of God to get out of the country, and later had the prime impudence to say that the Committee for the Relief of the Black Poor was 'influenced by the purest Principles of Charity, and the most honourable and pious Regard to the Welfare and Freedom of their Fellow Creatures, of whatever Nation, Language or Colour they may be, under our common Parent the great Lord of the Universe.'[25]

Why did 400 Black Poor suddenly opt out of the expedition? Firstly, they resented the contempt shown for their rights and feelings by the Committee. The Committee ignored the blacks' plea not to be sent to the Bahamas (where slavery was still legal) until the Treasury's intervention. Then the Committee threatened to cut off the subsistence allowance from such blacks as refused to sign the agreement to embark. Secondly, the civil authorities in London continued to harass the Black Poor. At the meeting of the Committee on 6 October it was reported that eleven black men and one black woman had been arrested by the watchmen and were in prison. It happened that one of the men was Paul Clarke, one of the Headmen or Corporals. Affronted by the arrest of one of their leaders, the blacks petitioned the Committee 'in favour of Mr. Clarke not signed requesting the release of the said Clarke, and threatening not to go if he did not accompany them.' But the Black Poor were sadly let down by the other Corporals. At the meeting on 6 October William Green, John Mandeville, William Johnson, Abraham Elliot Griffith, and George Sealey, all Corporals, 'Attended and the abovementioned Petition being read to them they all said they knew nothing of it and totally disavowed the same.' The position of a Corporal was a lucrative one, and where your treasure is, there will your heart be also. The five Corporals were informed that 'the Committee were disposed to render them every service in their Power but that it was entirely out of their power to stop the effects of the Laws.' After the Corporals had left, the Committee resolved 'That a letter be written to Mr. Sherrif Le Mesurier to intercede in behalf of those Persons to get them released.'[26]

However, the harassment by the London authorities and the supercilious behaviour of the Committee were not the fundamental reasons for the opting out of 400 blacks, but rather their questioning of the reasons for their deportation, doubts about the intentions of the British Government, and fears for their own security and safety once they reached Sierra Leone. These considerations were spelt out by Ottobah Cugoano, who was undoubtedly the 'Ninth Man, said to be a Person of weight among the Blacks'. In his *Thoughts and Sentiments on the Evil of Slavery*, he wrote at length:

This prospect of settling a free colony to Great-Britain in a peaceable alliance with the inhabitants of Africa at Sierra Leone, has neither

138

altogether met with the credulous approbation of the Africans here, nor yet been sought after with any prudent and right plan by the promoters of it. Had a treaty of agreement been first made with the inhabitants of Africa, and the terms and nature of such a settlement fixed upon, and its situation and boundary pointed out; then might the Africans, and others here, have embarked with a good prospect of enjoying happiness and prosperity themselves, and have gone with a hope of being able to render their service, in return, of some advantage to their friends and benefactors of Great-Britain. But as this was not done, and as they were to be hurried away at all events, come of them what would; and yet, after all, to be delayed in the ships before they were set out from the coast, until many of them have perished with cold, and other disorders, and several of the most intelligent among them are dead, and others that, in all probability, would have been most useful for them were hindered from going, by means of some disagreeable jealousy of those who were appointed as governors, the great prospect of doing good seems all to be blown away. And so it appeared to some of those who are now gone, and at last, haphazard, were obliged to go; who endeavoured in vain to get away by plunging into the water, that they might, if possible wade ashore, as dreading the prospect of their wretched fate, and as beholding their perilous situation, having every prospect of difficulty and surrounding danger.[27]

What with the death of some of the original promoters and proposers of this charitable undertaking,[28] and the death and deprivation of others that were to share the benefit of it, and by the adverse motives of those employed to be conductors thereof,[29] we think it will be more than what can be well expected, if we ever hear of any good in proportion to so great, well-designed, laudable and expensive charity. Many more of the Black People still in this country would have, with great gladness, embraced the opportunity, longing to reach their native land; but as the old saying is, A burnt child dreads the fire, some of these unfortunate sons and daughters of Africa have been severally unlawfully dragged away from their native abodes, under various pretences, by the insidious treachery of others, and have been brought into the hands of barbarous robbers and pirates, and, like sheep to the market, have been sold into slavery ... Much assiduity was made use to perswade the Black People in general to embrace the opportunity of going with this company of transports; but the wiser sort declined from all thought of it; unless they could hear of some better plan taking place for their security and safety. For as it seemed prudent and obvious to many of them taking heed to that sacred enquiry, *Doth a fountain send forth at the same place sweet water and bitter?* They were afraid that their doom would be to drink of the bitter water. For can it be readily conceived that government would establish a free colony for them nearly on the spot, while it supports its forts and garrisons, to ensnare, merchandize, and to carry others into captivity and slavery.[30]

It is worth emphasizing that Cugoano was not writing with the wisdom and easiness of hindsight. He saw clearly at the time that the expedition was being fitted out in haste and the blacks were being ejected from the country on racial grounds. As will be seen later, Cugoano was a very pious man. And when the devout black Christian saw another professed Christian haranguing the Black Poor to get out of England, small wonder that Cugoano 'left the Room saying he would consider of it' (that is, whether he would allow himself to be used as an instrument of ejecting his brothers and sisters from England).

Cugoano was not alone in his general attack on the repatriation of the Black Poor. *The Morning Herald* (a newspaper, which, as we shall see later, was on friendly terms with Olaudah Equiano and a close friend of Cugoano) was highly critical of the expedition, believing that it was motivated by racial considerations. In the issue of 15 December 1786, *The Morning Herald*[31] reported that some of the leaders of the 700 Black Poor who had signed an engagement to go to the intended settlement on the coast of Africa, had submitted the new system intended for their government there to the consideration of Lord George Gordon, and requested his advice and opinion upon the subject before they sailed from England. Lord George Gordon pointed out to them the various miseries and calamities which had uniformly attended the settlement of foreign colonies, and advised them not to go.

In consequence of this four hundred of them declined the embarkation, and came on shore again. Thus the Sierra Leone expedition is delayed for the present. Three large ships are prepared, it is true, and amply supplied with provisions, clothing, and every other necessary, also engineers, surveyors, ecclesiastics; schoolmasters, midwives and surgeons; but *the Poor Blacks prefer liberty with poverty; and nakedness instead of clothing, rather than submit to the plan intended for their government*,[32] when they arrive on the Grain Coast. ... It seems there is no law to compel them to embark, or to detain them aboard, to be transported to a military government, like the White Felons to New Norfolk.

In the next editorial comment on the subject, *The Morning Herald* linked the proposed expulsion of the Africans with the commercial treaty lately concluded between Britain and France. In 1786 Pitt, after his unsuccessful attempt to enter into a commercial treaty with Ireland, the previous year, concluded a commercial treaty with France, whereby, *inter alia*, British goods were to be exported into France at a reduced rate of duty, and French goods were to be imported into Britain, also at a reduced rate of duty. The treaty which worked to the benefit of both countries continued in operation until the outbreak of the French Revolutionary War in 1793. After tinkering with the matter of the black presence in France for some years, in 1777, the French King issued a decree peremptorily ordering all blacks to leave France and banning any more blacks from entering. In the editorial on the repatriation of the Black Poor in the issue of 29 December 1786, *The Morning Herald* stated that the Black Poor 'have heard of the intention of introducing the arbitrary French laws, with respect to Black people into England, as part of the new French Treaty; and look upon the arts now practised to inveigle them out of a land of liberty, with the utmost jealousy and deliberation.' It will be recalled that Cugoano related that 'Much assiduity was made use to perswade the Black People in general to embrace the opportunity of going ... but the wiser sort declined from all thought of it'. In an editorial on 2 January 1787, *The Morning Herald* commented at length:

The black poor were just in time in discovering the intention of the Ministry and their French party, to make them the first sacrifice of British freedom to the French treaty. It seems there is a tyrannical edict of the French King, now in full force against the admission of Ethiopians [Blacks, that is] into his kingdom, and in England they have the enjoyment of our benevolent, liberal, and impartial legislation, without regard to men's complexions. In such a contradictory system of jurisprudence, between the two countries, it became absolutely necessary, that the barbarous edict of the French King should be revoked; or the laws of English liberty repealed, before the mutual intercourse and mixture of the subjects of both the Kings throughout their respective cities and provinces, could take place agreeable to the new treaty. We see in this instance, that the laws of English liberty were to be yielded and modelled to French bigotry and intolerance; for so severe are the French Court, in regard to the Ethiopians, and so tenacious in abiding by the letter and spirit of the black edict, that the Duke de Chartres himself was lately refused the favour he solicited of the Minister, for a lady of high rank, who had just arrived in one of their sea-ports with a black retinue, 'that her retinue might just be permitted to attend her to Paris'. Is this universal benevolence of the French Ministry, the liberal system of the House of Bourbon, the enlarged policy of the Catholic Powers, which we hear daily from the tools of Mr. Pitt and the French faction? Would it not be dangerous innovation in this land of liberty, to suffer the exclusion of our fellow creatures from the rights of mankind, on account of difference of complexion? It would not only rivet the chains of slavery, and confirm the unequal laws, yet in force in many colonies abroad, against men of colour; but it would involve in continued law suits and enquiries at home, many very respectable East and West Indian families of the brunette physiognomy, who might find it impossible to prove their non-descent from Ethiopian progenitors for two thousand years, as the Spanish grandees at Madrid are compelled to prove their non-descent from the stock of Abraham. The children of our greatest Nabobs, even the Members of both Houses themselves, are not all fair Circassians.

Six of the leaders of these poor deceived people, captains of hundreds and captains of fifties, came up last week from the *Belisarius* and *Atlantic*, at Gravesend, and waited upon Lord George Gordon, to pray the continuance of his protection, and to stop their sailing, till the meeting of Parliament, that the public might know their unhappy situation. *Their poverty is made the pretence of their transportation*[33], and ... [they] are already subjected to a treatment and control, little short of the discipline of Guinea-men [slave traders].

*The Morning Post*, 22 December 1786, on the other hand, condemned the blacks for refusing to leave the country. It resuscitated the miscegenation issue from the days of the Somerset case. With ironic humour, *The Morning Post* commented:

The poor blacks, who refuse to go to Africa, do not consider their own interest; if we could dispatch some of our *dark-coloured patriots* to the same place, it would be for the quiet of society; ... When the late Mr. Dunning was some years ago reasoning against making this country a refuge for all blacks who chose to come here, he observed, 'that the numerous dingy-coloured faces which crowded our streets, must have their origin in our wives being *terrified* when pregnant, by the numerous Africans who were to be seen in all parts of the town, and if the legislature did not take some method to prevent the introduction of any more, he would venture to prophesy, that London would, in another century, have the appearance of an Ethiopian colony.'

The editorial would be laughable were it not so tragic.

*The Public Advertiser* was initially neutral. On 12 December[34] it said in an editorial:

The alarm spread among the Blacks who had engaged to accept from Government the offer of a settlement on the coast of Guinea, has thrown an impediment in the way of the expedition, which will retard it for some time; though we hope it will not defeat it. The *Belisarius*, which dropped down to Gravesend last week, has not in consequence of the breach of engagement on the part of the Blacks, proceeded to sea, as expected: she is now lying at Sea-Reach, waiting the event of such measures as Government may take to dispel the fears of the Blacks, quiet their apprehensions, and prevail upon them to fulfill their engagements, under the most solemn assurances that the Government will in no instance break faith with them. The number of Blacks on board the *Belisarius* is very considerable; but still far short of the complement necessary to form the intended settlement, on the scale proposed by Government. So that if the 400, who have receded from their engagements, persevere in their refusal to perform them, the sailing of the *Belisarius* may be countermanded and the whole project laid aside.

In its next editorial on the matter, *The Public Advertiser* took the gloves off. Phrases like 'We hope it will not defeat it', 'The breach of engagement on the part of the Blacks', and 'prevail upon them to fulfill their engagements', in the editorial just cited foreshadowed what was coming next. On 1 January 1787 the paper stated:

They must be enemies to the public tranquillity, to the police, and also to the Blacks [note the order of priority], who studiously endeavour to fill the minds of these poor people with apprehensions of slavery, in the intended settlement on the banks of Sierra Leone. No Ministry would think of breaking public faith with any body of men, however poor and abject they may be: Faith is kept by a nation, not because the persons to whom it is pledged are considerable and powerful, but because it is dishonourable to a nation to break its faith; and the precedent might be attended with consequences highly injurious to the State. The national honour would rouse its guardians, the House of Commons, to do it justice, and to punish those, who, by a breach of the public faith, should tarnish its lustre. The Blacks, therefore, can have no real cause to apprehend that Government only wants to trepan them to Africa, in order to make them slaves. Ministers have no such view; cannot, dare not have such a view: they have too much virtue themselves to think of it; and they know there is too much virtue in the British nation to suffer them to accomplish what they are too just, too generous, and too politic to think of. The Blacks may therefore embark with confidence: their liberty, so far from being invaded, will be protected by Government; and if they are not deprived of their reason, they will quickly perceive how much more eligible it will be for them to go to a country, where they will have lands assigned to them for their support, and all implements of husbandry supplied to them by the bounty of the nation, than to remain in indigence and want, strolling, wretched spectacles of distress, through our streets; constantly exposed to the temptation of committing felonies, for which they may be either hanged or transported to Africa, and left defenceless on the coast, where they will perish with hunger, be killed by their savage countrymen, or taken by them and sold as slaves:[35] so that they may at length meet real slavery, in consequence of their ill-grounded apprehension of an imaginary one.[36]

The writer had a fine style.

Two days later, on 3 January, *The Public Advertiser* reported with satisfaction that: 'The Mayor has given orders to the City Marshalls, the Marshallmen, and Constables, to take up all the blacks they find begging about the streets, and to bring them before him; or some other magistrate, that they may be sent home, or to the new colony which is going to be established in Africa; near twenty are already taken up, and lodging in the two Compters.'[37]

Characteristically, *The Public Advertiser* commented:

The conduct of the Lord-Mayor in ordering the blacks who are found begging about the streets to be taken up, is highly commendable, and it is to be hoped will be imitated by the Magistrates of Westminster, Middlesex and Surrey, and the other counties. It is however humbly submitted to their judgment, whether instead of mere confinement in a gaol, it would not be preferable to put them to hard labour in Bridewell. The blacks, especially those of the East Indies, are naturally indolent; nothing but the utmost necessity will make them work; and the very thought of being subjected to that would soon reconcile them to the plan proposed by Government.

Reading these passages two hundred years later, there is something familiar about them. These cringing deceptions of two centuries ago are eerily similar to the expressions of race prejudice in today's newspapers. But the Adam Smith dictum that 'a man is of all sorts of luggage the most difficult to be transported' will always operate. Remember, too, that in the eighteenth century many blacks were brought here by force by their owners, just as the twentieth-century blacks did not come to Britain unasked, but were invited here to fill low-paid unpleasant jobs for which workers are scarce. When the blacks outlive their usefulness, they become expendable commodities even to the liberal establishment. The story of the Black Poor told here gives the message loud and clear that the 'pride of race' which urges the wholesale expulsion of black people from Britain today will fail. It would cost too much.

At the meeting of the Committee for the Relief of the Black Poor on 16 January 1787, Irwin reported 'the number on board the *Atlantic* to be 242, and on board the *Belisarius* 184'. The Committee was convinced now that no amount of pressure would compel more blacks to enlist. Accordingly, they advised the Treasury to give directions for the sailing of the transports.[38] The necessary Treasury directions were forthcoming. As early as 19 December 1786, *The Morning Post* and *The London Chronicle* had reported that the Government had determined 'if no more Blacks offered themselves to go to the new settlement on the coast of Africa, that the ships shall sail with those they have on board immediately.' On Wednesday 17 January 1787 both *The Public Advertiser* and *The London Chronicle* reported:

Saturday [13 January] Samuel Hoare, Esq; Chairman of the Committee for relieving and providing a settlement for the Black Poor, had an interview with Mr. Pitt, when he laid before him the proceedings of the Committee from their establishment; at which the [Prime] Minister expressed his satisfaction. The two ships, having on board as many of those people as could be collected, sailed from Gravesend on Thursday [11 January] last, with a fair wind for Sierra Leone, on the coast of Africa, where they are to be landed, in order to form the intended settlement.

As a matter of fact, the *Atlantic*, *Belisarius*, and *Vernon* proceeded to Portsmouth where they were joined by the naval sloop *Nautilus* under the command of Captain Thomas Boulden Thompson, who had been commissioned 'to escort the said Vessels to the River Sierra Leone, directing her Commander, upon his Arrival there, to give every possible assistance to the Superintendent or Overseer[39] who will accompany the said Black Poor, in the Execution of the Plan.'[40] At Portsmouth, fever killed off some sixty pioneers. The exact number of those who died is not known, but as we have seen already, Cugoano complained bitterly that the ships did not leave England, 'until *many* of them have perished with cold, and other disorders, and several of the most intelligent among them are dead'.

Also, two of the ships in the convoy were damaged by storm and the fleet had to put in at Plymouth. 'And so it appeared to some of those who are now gone,' Cugoano wrote, 'and at last, haphazard, were obliged to go; who endeavoured in vain to get away by plunging into the water, that they might, if possible wade ashore, as dreading the prospect of their wretched fate'. Wade ashore where? Plymouth. After a dreadful and harrowing two months in Portsmouth the blacks, on reaching Plymouth, made for the shore. On 29 March 1787, the Captain of His Majesty's ships at Plymouth wrote to the Admiralty Office: 'The Magistrate of Plymouth having this day represented to me that a number of Black men are come on shore from a Transport Vessel now at this Port, and are strolling about that neighbourhood and being apprehensive that on the sailing of the Transport many of these People will be left behind to the great nuisance of the Country. They have requested me to pray their Lordships directions thereupon.'[41]

Efforts were made to round up the blacks, but it is not clear whether some escaped the net. At any rate strict orders were given that those blacks on board the ships must have no communication with the shore. In fact no communication with the shore was the policy of the Navy Board. Thus, while the ships were still in Portsmouth, Captain Thompson sought the permission of the Navy Board to call at Tenerife on the way to Africa; the Navy Board considered his request on 22 January 1787, and 'Resolved that he be permitted to call there for the purpose mentioned [to get a supply of wine], taking care that his stay be as short as possible and that the Black People on board the Transports under his convoy have no communication with the shore.'[42]

On 10 April 1787 the fleet sailed for Africa with 441[43] settlers. To the slavocrats, the whole Black Poor crisis was a boon, another weapon to be used in their desperate struggle to lock and bar the gates of freedom for ever. In 1786, as the crisis was getting under way, without even pausing to ask himself 'who brought them here?' and the other questions that inevitably follow, Gordon Turnbull, author of *Letters to a Young Planter*, wrote gleefully asking the advocates for the emancipation of the slaves in the sugar colonies to cast their eyes, 'for a moment, on those deplorable black objects, at every corner, and in every lurking place, of this great city, who, were it not for the outstretched hand of heaven-born charity, would perish, miserably perish, with hunger, or with cold. These are *freemen*!'[44] In 1788 Gilbert Francklyn began where Gordon Turnbull had stopped in 1786:

What has been the result of thus extending *the blessings of liberty* to so many wretched slaves? Let any body shew scarce a single instance of any one of these people in so happy a situation as they were before. The greater part, it is known, died miserably in a very short time. No parish was willing to receive them, so that the survivors, after begging about the streets of London, ... [the] Government was prevailed upon to undertake the transportation of them to the country from whence they, or their ancestors, had been ravished *by the wicked traders* of London, Liverpool, and Bristol. They were there to be made happy: they were there to possess 'land and beeves', instruments of husbandry, tools, and other necessaries for building. Grain, and the seeds of all sorts of vegetables, proper to the climate, were furnished them; and all that was necessary for their future happiness was, that they should *work*. But so far, it seems, were these ungrateful people from thankfully profiting by the kind disposition of the public towards them, that we are told Mr. Glanville [sic] Sharp, the great promoter of all these *mistaken* acts of *humanity*, found it necessary to distribute hand-bills about the town, to request gentlemen not to relieve their distresses, in order to force them to go to Portsmouth, where the ships were to take them in to carry them to Africa. It is confidently said here [Jamaica], that very few hundreds were prevailed on to proceed to that place, the great part of whom ran away when they got there; of those who ... remained ... there was scarce one who did not express his wish to quit his new abode, *his estate and his liberty*, even although it should be to return to his pristine slavery, in the sugar colonies. ... Equal unhappiness would be the lot of the slaves in the islands, if they were set free.[45]

This is the usual concoction of half truths and opinions blended into a plausible whole. Note his inability to give the name of

Granville Sharp correctly. In an earlier quotation from another of Francklyn's books, he was Grenville Sharpe. Here, he is Glanville Sharp.

Finally, in 1787, James Tobin, a planter and attorney of Nevis, wishing the blacks good riddance, wrote:

A colony of free [blacks], after many delays and difficulties, of a nature it would perhaps be deemed invidious in me to enlarge upon, is at length sailed for the coast of Guinea. For my own part I can readily join in a sincere wish, that this undertaking may answer the most sanguine expectations of its humane projectors, and amply repay the expenses which government has been at to second their benevolent views. I will not even hint a doubt of its success, that may give offence to a set of men, who have I am persuaded, been influenced by the purest motives; but shall leave it to time.[46]

Time, indeed, is the true arbiter. Today Sierra Leone is an independent sovereign Republic and a member of the United Nations.

1. *Proceedings of the Committee for the Relief of the Black Poor, 10th May 1786*; PRO: T/1/631.

2. Hoare, *Memoirs of Granville Sharp* (London, 1828), 2nd ed., II, p. 16.

3. PRO: T/1/631.

4. *Parliamentary Papers* (1789), vol. 82.

5. PRO: T/1/631/132.

6. *Proceedings* (17 May 1786); PRO: T/1/631/1333.

7. Hoare, op. cit., II, p. 9.

8. Granville Sharp, *A Short Sketch of Temporary Regulations (until better shall be proposed) for the Intended Settlement on Gold Coast of Africa, Near Sierra Leona* (London, 1788).

9. John Peterson, *Province of Freedom* (London, 1969), p. 22.

10. Hoare, op. cit., II. p. 9.

11. This is a moot point.

12. It is often stated that Jonas Hanway was the first and only Chairman of the Committee. In fact he was one of many. The first two Chairmen were Montague Burgoyne and Benjamin Johnson. The latter was succeeded by Jonas Hanway. When Hanway ceased to be Chairman, George Peters succeeded him, and when he resigned, Samuel Hoare became Chairman and masterminded the repatriation of the Black Poor.

13. At the time he was speaking, Hanway was seventy-four; he died four months later, on 5 September.

14. Aaron Brookes appears to be the only one who did not sail with the first expedition to Sierra Leone. Others appeared in the final list. The names are in square brackets only because I have omitted such details as their occupation, where born, etc.

15. *Proceedings* (7 June 1786); PRO: T/1/632/105-6.

16. *Proceedings* (31 May 1786); PRO: T/1/632/359-60.

17. *Proceedings* (14 June 1786); PRO: T/1/632/111-12.

18. Olaudah Equiano, *Equiano's Travels* (London, 1969 , pp. 116-17.

19. *Proceedings* (5 July 1786 ; PRO: T/1/633/86.

20. *Proceedings* (15 July 1786₁; PRO: T/1/633/274-5.

21. *Proceedings* (9 October 1786₁; PRO: T/1/636; *Proceedings* (24 October 1786₁; PRO: T/1/638.

22. See also *The Morning Herald* and *The Public Advertiser* (9 December 1786).

23. PRO: T/1/638.

24. A Note adds 'Such Blacks as are desirous to go, must apply to Mr. Irwin, No. 14 Cannon-street'.

25. These words are taken from Jonas Hanway's draft Agreement; see PRO: T/1/632/109.

26. *Proceedings* (6 October 1786); PRO: T/1/636/2430. It is not known whether they were released or not.

27. Points raised in this sentence will be dealt with in the course of the narrative.

28. i.e. Henry Smeathman and Jonas Hanway.

29. As will be seen later in the narrative, Cugoano had in mind Messrs. Irwin, Fraser, and Currie.

30. Cugoano, op. cit., pp. 139-42.

31. *The Public Advertiser* (18 December 1786) published the same report, taken verbatim from *The Morning Herald*.

32. Italics are added. *The Morning Herald* listed, *inter alia*: 'A system of fines and forfeiture for the most trivial offences, is one part of the police intended; a tenth part of the profits of their working days to be appropriated to religious uses. ...'

When Granville Sharp drew up his system of government on the intended settlement in August 1783, he envisaged that 'there will be no necessity to form the plan of government by the constitutional model of England; ... [but] the Israelitish commonwealth under the Theocracy. ... The Israelitish government elected judges and officers; heads of tens and fifties, hundreds and thousands ... Under this form of government, all public works, as entrenchments, fortifications, canals, highways, sewers, &c. &c; may be performed by a rotation of service; in which the value of attendance must be estimated, that defaulters may bear their share, or rather a double share, of the burden. And *watch and ward*, or military service, may be defrayed in the same manner.' Hoare, op. cit., II, pp. 13-15. There does not appear to be anything obnoxious in Granville Sharp's plan and the 'new system' referred to by *The Morning Herald* was probably a corruption of Sharp's plan of 1783. In the end, when the expedition got to Sierra Leone, it was Sharp's plan of heads of tens and fifties that was used for the initial régime. It would seem that lack of communication was responsible for this aspect of the Africans' apprehension.

33. The italics are added.

34. *The London Chronicle* (23 December 1786) published the same report, taken verbatim from *The Public Advertiser*.

35. But compare the following report in *The Public Advertiser* (17 January 1786): 'The new convicts going to Africa are destined to the island of Tasso, at the mouth of the river Sierra Leone, about 10 miles in circumference, where there is plenty of water, wood, and every necessary of life sufficient for the support of more than 1,000 inhabitants. The soil also abounds with cotton, indigo, Camur wood, and other valuable exotics. ... [they will] live in perfect security, by means of few field fortifications, from the natives of Africa.'

36. *The Public Advertiser* (29 January 1786) reported: 'We are informed that the Blacks and Mulattoes destined for Sierra Leone, and the convicts for Cape Coast are to be conducted to their respective parts, by Commodore Philips, on his route to Botany Bay.' Yet the apprehension of the blacks was 'imaginary' and 'ill-grounded'!

37. Namely the Poultry Compter and Woodstreet Compter.

38. PRO: T/1/641/173.

39. The use of the term Overseer was singularly unfortunate in reference to free blacks. The word was synonymous with lashing, thumbscrews, muzzles, shackles, chains, etc., etc.

40. *Parliamentary Papers* (1789), vol. 82.

41. PRO: T/1/644.

42. PRO: Adm/3/102.

43. *Parliamentary Papers* (1789), vol. 82. The figure 411 is usually given. See, for example, Little, *Negroes in Britain* (London, 1948), p. 184; West, *Back to Africa* (London, 1970), p. 24; Dilip Hiro, *Black British, White British* (London, 1971), p. 5. M. Dorothy George, *London Life in the Eighteenth Century* (London, 1925), p. 138, correctly states that of the 700 Blacks who originally offered to go, only 441 embarked.

44. [Gordon Turnbull] *Apology for Negro Slavery: or the West-India Planters Vindicated from the Charges of Inhumanity. By the author of Letters to a Young Planter* (London, 1786), 2nd ed., p. 32. The first edition was also published in 1786.

45. G[ilbert] Francklyn, *Observations, occasioned by the attempts made in England to effect the Abolition of the Slave Trade. ...*, pp. xii-xiii.

46. James Tobin, *A Short Rejoinder. ...* (London, 1787), pp. 98-9.

# 11

# Commissary to the Black Poor

At the meeting of the Committee for the Relief of the Black Poor on 25 August 1786, it was resolved to ask the Government to appoint a Commissary, 'who is acquainted with the Coast [of Sierra Leone], to superintend and see justice done.'[1] The Government acceded to the Committee's request, and on the Committee's recommendation Olaudah Equiano, who was born in what is now Nigeria, was appointed the Commissary to the Black Poor going to Sierra Leone. If any man could 'see justice done' to the Black Poor, Equiano was the man. When he was invited to fill the post, he at first declined. He had many reasons, he said, but 'particularly I expressed some difficulties on account of the slave dealers, as I would certainly oppose their traffic in the human species by every means in my power.' However, his objections were overruled by members of the Committee who particularly wanted him to go. They prevailed and he was recommended to the Navy Board 'as a proper person to act as commissary for the government in the intended expedition; and they accordingly appointed me in November 1786 to that office.'[2]

When Equiano declared that he would oppose the traffic in human flesh with all his might, he was speaking with the special knowledge of one who had borne the cruel pangs of slavery for eleven years. This book closes with an account of Equiano's eventful life in bondage and in freedom, but here we are concerned only with his activities as Commissary to the Black Poor. In pursuance of his determination to oppose slave dealers on the African coast, he applied for permission to take ammunition on board one of the transport vessels. On 1 December 1786, the Committee agreed. 'Mr. Vassa having again applied to the Committee for leave to take one Ton of Powder on board, it is agreed that Captain Stevenson may take it on board his Ship and Stow it in a Place of security.'[3] Equiano certainly meant business.

At the height of the pressure on the Black Poor to leave England in December 1786, the indigent and harassed blacks called a meeting to air their grievances about the arrangements for their deportation. The meeting was, however, banned; but Equiano leaked this fact to the newspaper that had consistently opposed the deportation of the blacks—*The Morning Herald*—which published the news of the ban. On 29 December 1786, *The*

*Morning Herald* commented:

We hear from authority that a Meeting of the Black Poor was to have been held in Whitechapel on Wednesday [27 December], composed of those who are ... to go to Africa ... . The Committee [for the Relief of the Black Poor] and Agent [Irwin], however, interfered, and prevented their intended discussion of that Subject, in such great numbers. ... Some of them applied again yesterday to Lord George Gordon. ... A ministerial paper having denied that our intelligence on this subject is not true, it now behoves us to mention the name of the person who [one word illegible] ... It is Gustavus Vasa, an African from Guinea ... the Commissary of the Expedition.

There is no doubt that *The Morning Herald* genuinely detested the racist reason behind the proposed wholesale deportation of the black people in Britain at the time. And the support given by the paper to the blacks was inestimable. But the conclusion is also inescapable that the paper, strongly opposed to the commercial treaty with France, was using the issue of the Black Poor as a weapon with which to beat Pitt's French policy.

*The Morning Herald*'s opposition to the deportation of the Black Poor was an honourable one. Certainly it has none of the odious hypocrisy of the British Labour Party who, when in government in 1968, peremptorily banned British Asians from entering Britain in the same manner as the French Government in 1777 banned blacks from entering France. In opposition in 1971 the Labour Party opposed the British Conservative Government's Immigration Bill (Immigration Act 1971), which carried the 1968 policy to its logical conclusion. Again there were echoes of *The Morning Herald*'s editorials of 1786 in the British press in 1972, when it was suggested, in the few months just before Britain at last entered the European Economic Community, with the 'permission' of France, that black people living in Britain would not be able to move as freely in the European Community as white British, while black Frenchmen from the Antilles would be free to enter Britain without let or hindrance.

The meeting of the Black Poor having been banned, their leaders wrote to *The Morning Herald*, and their letter was published in the issue of 4 January 1787. Unfortunately, it has not been possible to trace a copy of that issue. But the contents of the letter may be deduced from the reply of Joseph Irwin, the Government Agent, which appeared in *The Morning Herald* of 5 January 1787. It would seem that the two principal points made in the letter by the leaders of the Black Poor were: firstly, that Irwin was using his position for feathering his own nest; and secondly, that the blacks on board the ships, as *The Morning Herald* (2 January 1787) had reported, 'are already subjected to a treatment and control, little short of the discipline of Guinea-men.' We have already seen some evidence as to the latter point; and as to whether Irwin had used his position to enrich himself we have supporting evidence from the writings of Equiano. In his letter to *The Morning Herald*, however, Irwin denied both charges. He had not profiteered in the supply of provisions. 'An exact account of the money issued from the Treasury to the Secretary of the Committee and myself, and the manner in which it was expended, has been from time to time presented to the Committee and transmitted to the ... Treasury.' On the second charge, he was ambivalent. 'The Committee are the best able to judge of the propriety of my conduct with respect to the Blacks.'

As soon as Equiano was appointed Commissary, he proceeded to the execution of his duties on board the transport vessels. Two years later, in his autobiography, he stated that while in the employment of the Government, he was struck by the 'flagrant abuses committed by' Irwin. Stores ordered and paid for by the Government were not available. The Government was not the only object of peculation; the Black Poor 'suffered infinitely more; their accommodations were most wretched; many of them wanted beds, and many more clothing and other necessaries.' Equiano could not silently suffer the Government to be thus cheated 'and my countrymen plundered and oppressed, and even left destitute of the necessaries for almost their existence.' He therefore reported the matter to the Navy Board, at the same time claiming his allegations would be backed by Captain Thompson of the *Nautilus*. 'But my dismission was soon after procured, by means of a gentleman in the city, whom the agent, conscious of his peculation, had deceived by letter.'[4]

Captain Thompson's testimony, to which Equiano appealed, censured both Equiano and Irwin. Thompson's letter, dated Plymouth Sound, 21 March 1787, and addressed to the Navy Board, alleged that since Equiano held the situation of Commissary, he had been 'turbulent and discontented, taking every means to actuate the minds of the Blacks to discord.' He was also chagrined enough to say, 'I do not find Mr. Irwin the least calculated to conduct this business: I have never observed any wish of his to facilitate the sailing of the Ships, or any steps taken by him which might indicate that he had the welfare of the people the least at heart.' Nevertheless, Thompson said that unless some means were taken to quell Equiano's 'spirit of sedition, it will be fatal to the peace of the settlement.'[5]

There is no doubt that Equiano was indeed 'turbulent and discontented'. The crucial point to note, however, is that he was turbulent because he saw clearly from the beginning that Irwin had not 'the least heart' for the welfare of the blacks. As the most articulate of the blacks, Equiano saw it as his duty to speak out and not suffer 'my countrymen [to be] plundered and oppressed'. But, as Paul Edwards notes, 'anyone who put the case of his people persistently and forcefully, as Equiano did, would be likely to win a reputation as a troublemaker.'[6] It should not go unobserved that twentieth-century African leaders like Kwame Nkrumah were sent to jail by the British during their fight for independence because of their 'spirit of sedition'.

The Navy Board forwarded Thompson's letter to the Treasury on 23 March 1787 with its own observations on the matter, which makes it clear that Equiano's only crime was that he was a diligent Commissary. 'In all the Transactions the Commissary has had with this Board,' they declared, 'he has acted with great propriety and has been very regular in his information.'[7] The Treasury had to choose between the competent Equiano and the incompetent and dishonest Irwin. Any black man could have foreseen the outcome, as recorded in the Admiralty Board Minutes dated 27 March 1787: 'Lord Sydney, one of His Majesty's Principal Secretaries of State ... upon laying before the Lords of the Treasury Capt. Thompson's letter ... relative to the misconduct of Mr. Gustavus Vasa Commissary and the probability that the Superintendent Mr. Irwing [sic] would not accompany them to Africa, their Lordships have informed him that Orders have been dispatched for the immediate dismission of Mr. Vasa from his Office, and that Mr. Irwing continues in his design to accompany the Black Poor to the place of their destination.'[8]

Meanwhile, in a letter from Plymouth dated 24 March, Equiano complained bitterly to his close friend Cugoano about the treatment of the blacks and himself. The letter was published in *The Public Advertiser* (4 April 1787).

In the letter, Equiano said that he was coming to London to expose Irwin's roguery. He denied the allegation that he had treated the white people with arrogance and the blacks with civility. He went on: 'Many of the black people have died for want of their due. I am grieved in every respect. Irwin never meant well to the people, but self interest has ever been his end: twice this week they [the Black Poor] have taken him, bodily, to the Captain, to complain of him, and I have done it four times. I do not know how this undertaking will end; I wish I had never been involved in it; but at times I think the Lord will make me very useful at last.'

Equiano was indeed 'very useful at last'. For had he not been dismissed and had he gone to Sierra Leone, he probably would have died in a matter of weeks after landing. And then he would certainly not have been in the vanguard of the Abolitionist movement in England which blossomed shortly after the deportees left.

Eventually, Equiano came to London on or about 29 March, by which time it was already too late to save his position, and he returned to Plymouth on 4 April to pick up his luggage. Two days after his departure from London, his full indictment of Irwin appeared in *The Public Advertiser*.⁹ The serious allegations made by Equiano were soon rejected by 'X' in *The Public Advertiser* for 11 April:

The Public will naturally suspend their disbelief as to the improbable tales propagated concerning the Blacks, especially as the cloven foot of the author of these reports is perfectly manifest. That one of the persons employed in conducting those poor people is discharged, is certainly true, his own misconduct having given too good reason for his dismission. The Blacks have never refused to proceed on the voyage but the ships have been delayed at Plymouth by an accidental damage which one of them received in a gale of wind. To sum up all, should the expedition prove unsuccessful, it can only be owing to the over-care of the committee, who, to avoid the most distant idea of compulsion, did not even subject the Blacks to any government, except such as they might choose for themselves. And among such ill-informed people, this delicacy may have fatal consequences.

There have always been those who will say anything to soothe national conscience on racial matters.

In retrospect, the attack on Equiano by 'X' was mild when compared with the follow-up in *The Public Advertiser*, 14 April 1787:

The expedition of the Blacks to Sierra Leone is not the least retarded by the dismission of V—— the Black who was appointed to superintend the Blacks.

The assertions made by that man that the Blacks were to be treated as badly as West-India blacks, and that he was discharged to make room for the appointment of a man who would exercise tyranny to those unfortunate men, show him to be capable of advancing falsehoods as deeply black as his jetty face. The true reason for his being discharged, was gross misbehaviour, which had rendered him not only disagreeable to the officers and crew, but had likewise drawn on him the dislike of those over whom he had been appointed.

The person since appointed is the purser, a man of good character and unimpeached humanity, under whose care, for control it cannot be called, the Blacks, so far from entertaining any apprehensions, are perfectly happy.¹⁰

The cloven foot, as observed by a judicious correspondent X in Wednesday's paper, is perfectly manifest in the tales propagated on account of the above discharge. No man endowed with common sense can credit for a moment that the committee (all men of acknowledged humanity and honour) would give any countenance to the least ill-treatment of the objects of their compassion, whom they have endeavoured to snatch from misery and place in comfortable situations.

The proceedings of the committee do them the greatest honour and as Christians they have provided for the poor Blacks every necessary of life, and will on their arrival at Sierra Leone place them in such a situation as to enable them to live happily. Another provision they have also made for those men, and one which ought not to be forgotten; they have provided for them schoolmasters[11] to instruct them in reading and writing, and have sent out books to have them instructed in the Christian religion.[12] —Are such the measures which would have been pursued if the intention had been to enslave them? Would inculcating the principles of the Christian religion cause the so instructed tamely to submit to unchristian oppression? Or does it not seem far more probable that such measures were adopted for the purpose of inspiring the intended settlers with such elevated ideas of the blessings of liberty, as to induce them to resist any endeavour which may hereafter be made to encroach on their freedom? Let us hear no more of these *black* reports which have been industriously propagated; for if they are continued, it is rather more probable that most of the dark transactions of a *Black* will be brought to *light*.

Equiano continued exposing the roguery of Irwin, and no 'dark transactions' were ever revealed for the simple reason that there were none to reveal. But, on 2 July 1787, *The Public Advertiser* carried a letter written almost certainly by Patrick Fraser, 'the Parson', and sent while the settlers stopped at Tenerife. 'I have the pleasure to inform you that we are all well,' he wrote, 'and that the poor Blacks are in a much more healthy state than when we left England. Vasa's discharge, and the dismission of Green and Rose,[13] are attended with the happiest effects.'[14] The letter was typical of the deliberate misrepresentations about the Black Poor on board the transports. For when 'Fraser the Parson' exulted that the Black Poor were in a much more healthy state than when they left England, he was lying. Captain Thompson, in his letter to the Navy Board, dated 22 April 1787, at Santa Cruz, on the Island of Tenerife, disclosed that fourteen blacks had died since the convoy left Plymouth. 'As they have been sometime on salt provisions I have thought it necessary to purchase for them a bullock to each ship.'[15]

Without the benefit of Thompson's letter, Equiano made his reply to Fraser's letter in *The Public Advertiser* (14 July 1787) as he thought it necessary to vindicate his character from these misrepresentations 'by informing the public, that the principal crime which caused his dismission, was the information he laid before the Navy Board, accusing the Agent of unfaithfulness in his office, in not providing such necessaries as were contracted for the people, and were absolutely necessary for their existence.' Meanwhile, four days after 'Fraser the Parson's' letter had appeared in *The Public Advertiser*, the Treasury, on 6 July, had authorized the Navy Board to pay Equiano £50 'in full of expences and wages' for the period he had served as Commissary.[16]

The settlers reached Sierra Leone on 9 May 1787. In a letter from Sierra Leone River, 23 July 1787, Captain Thompson reported to the Navy Board that the blacks were obstinate, 'which neither Remonstrance, Persuasion, or Punishment, have yet been able to subdue.' The whole situation was 'mortifying', complicated by the antics of Irwin, who soon after they arrived decided after all not to settle with them. The rains, which set in during the latter half of May, had brought on fevers, fluxes, and bilious complaints. Scores had died and 'others are Daily dying'. Irwin was among the dead.[17]

So at last is revealed the duplicity of the Government, the Committee, and the writer of the editorials in *The Public Advertiser* of 6 and 14 April 1787. Remember how the Government sacrificed an honourable, competent, and honest black employee, Equiano, for the sake of retaining the services of a patently incompetent and dishonest white employee, Irwin. Remember how *The Public Advertiser* said that the Committee for the Relief of the Black Poor were 'all men of acknowledged humanity and honour', who were only endeavouring 'to snatch [the Black Poor] from misery and place [them] in comfortable situations'. Hanway, a man of God and humanity, harangued the blacks in the name of God to get out of the country, and was congratulated by the whole Committee for his conduct. Furthermore, the Committee threatened to withhold the sixpence Government subsistence allowance from those blacks who were not amused by Hanway's antics. What honour, what humanity was there among a set of men who issued notice that the public should stop giving help and assistance to the cold and hungry, the penniless and friendless, the naked and the dying? White 'liberals' have always been prepared to tolerate black people as long as they can use them to advertise their own humanitarianism for all the world to see. When, however, black people cease to be pliable and titillating but assert their rights as human beings, as the Black Poor did, the change in the relationship is always very perceptible. Friends today, enemies tomorrow. What redemption is there for men who could see in the misery, oppression, and repression of fellow human beings only a way for their own glorification on earth and salvation in heaven?

So, although the 'turbulent and discontented' Equiano had been removed that he might not 'actuate the minds of the Blacks to discord', in his absence the blacks were still obstinate, and neither remonstrance, persuasion, nor indeed punishment could subdue them. The fact of the matter was that with the dismissal of Equiano, the Treasury removed the one stabilizing influence among the Black Poor. As Cugoano tartly put it, since 'others that, in all probability, would have been most useful for them were hindered from going, by means of some disagreeable jealousy of those who were appointed as governors, the great prospect of doing good seems all to be blown away.' When Captain Thompson left the Sierra Leone River on 17 September 1787 for England, only 268 of the 441 settlers who embarked remained. 122 had been killed off by fever, etc., and 51 others had made their way to the West Indies or drifted to the coast away from Granville Town, as the original settlement was called after Granville Sharp (it is now Freetown). In October 1787, Granville Sharp, the father of the Province of Freedom, wrote that he 'had but melancholy accounts of my poor ill-thriven swarthy daughter, the unfortunate colony of Sierra Leone.'[18]

The first expedition to Sierra Leone was a disaster which confirmed Equiano's worst forebodings and justified his determination to ensure that the Black Poor did not go out of the frying-pan into the fire. Looking back on it all two years later, Equiano wrote, towards the end of his *Narrative*, with the authority of a sage who had been proved right:

Thus provided, they proceeded on their voyage; and at last, worn out by treatment, perhaps not the most mild, and wasted by sickness, brought on by want of medicine, clothes, bedding &c. they reached Sierra Leone just at the commencement of the rains. At that season of the year it is impossible to cultivate the lands; their provisions therefore were exhausted before they could derive any benefit from agriculture; and it is not surprising that many, especially the lascars, whose constitutions are very tender, and who had been cooped up in ships from October to June, and accommodated in the manner I have mentioned, should be so wasted by their confinement as not long to survive it ... the ... expedition to Sierra Leone ... however unfortunate in the event, was humane and politic in its design, nor was its failure owing to government: everything was done on their part; but there was evidently sufficient mismanagement attending the conduct and execution of it to defeat its success.

I should not have been so ample in my account of this transaction, had not the share I bore in it been made the subject of partial animadversion, and even my dismission from employment thought worthy of being made by some a matter of public triumph. The motives which might have influenced any person to descend to a petty contest with an obscure African, and to seek gratification by his depression, perhaps it is not proper here to inquire into or relate, even if its detection were necessary for my vindication; but I thank Heaven it is not. I wish to stand by my own integrity, and not to shelter myself under the impropriety of another; and I trust the behaviour of the Commissioners of the Navy to me entitled me to make this assertion; for after I had been dismissed, March 24, I drew up a memorial ... [which] was delivered into the hands of their Lordships, who were kind enough, in the space of some few months afterwards, without hearing, to order me [£]50 sterling—that is, ... wages for the time ... I acted a faithful part in their service.[19]

1. *Proceedings* (25 August 1786); PRO: T/1/646.

2. Olaudah Equiano, *The Interesting Narrative of the Life of Olaudah Equiano, or Gustavus Vassa, The African* (London, 1789), II, pp. 230-1.

3. *Proceedings* (1 December 1786); PRO: T/1/638/50-1.

4. Equiano, op. cit., II, pp. 236-7. In his introduction to the reprint of Equiano's *Narrative* (London, 1969), Paul Edwards suggests (at p. xl) that the gentleman in the city was Prince Hoare, Granville Sharp's biographer. This seems to be wrong. Prince Hoare was a dramatic author and artist, and was out of the country at the time of the controversy. It seems certain that the Mr. Hoare in question was Samuel Hoare, the banker, who from January 1787 was the Chairman of the Committee for the Relief of the Black Poor.

5. PRO: T/1/643.

6. Equiano, op. cit. (1969), p. xlv.

7. PRO: T/1/643/681.

8. PRO: Adm/3/102.

9. See Appendix I, Letter III.

10. It was after George Harvey took over from Equiano as Commissary that some of the blacks made their way into the centre of Plymouth after bolting from the ships.

11. One of these was John Mawley whose dismissal Irwin procured, because, as he wrote in *The Morning Herald*, 13 January 1787, Mawley 'laboured at different times to create prejudices against me, to sow dissensions amongst the blacks, and retard or frustrate the execution of the plan.' Apparently everyone was to blame except Irwin himself.

12. In fact this was an undertaking of the Society for the Propagation of the Gospel. See C. F. Pascoe, *Two Hundred Years of the S.P.G.* (London, 1901), I, p. 259.

13. Both were blacks. William Green was a Corporal, but Lewis Rose was not.

14. See also *The London Chronicle* and *The Morning Chronicle* (3 July 1787).

15. PRO: T/1/647.

16. PRO: T/1/646.

17. In Admiralty Letter, 8 October 1787, *Parliamentary Papers* (1789), vol. 82.

18. Hoare, op. cit., II, p. 83.

19. Equiano, op. cit. (1789), II, pp. 236-9.

# 12

# Beggars, Mendicants, and Serenaders

The exit of the founding fathers of Sierra Leone was 'too little and too late'. At the end of the eighteenth century there were still about 10,000 black people in Britain. What became of them? They married and were absorbed into the white population. Their children are now white, with no inkling of their African blood and ancestry.

From the beginning of the nineteenth century, blacks began to be displaced from the position they occupied in eighteenth-century English domestic life. The black coachman, 'a very portly person, with powder over his curly pate', continued to perform a regular service in the social life of the worthies.[1] Others continued as footmen, like Garlo, briefly noticed in a letter in *The Spectator*, 25 July 1925. The correspondent mentioned that ninety years before, that is, in 1835, Garlo served as a footman in his grandfather's house. Another nineteenth-century black footman was Andrew Bogle, a key witness in 1871 in the Tichborne case, one of the most celebrated trials in the annals of imposture.[2] Quite a number of the blacks were army bandsmen. 'There is a splendid [black], wearing an embroidered Oriental dress, who plays the cymbals, gesticulating vivaciously—partly of orchestral necessity, perhaps, but partly, it must be, owing to excessive enjoyment of his situation.' Apparently, these regimental bandsmen had to be jet-black. For, in 1823, one was discharged from the 1st Regiment of Foot Guards 'in consequence of not being of a sufficiently black complexion'. He thereafter supported himself by mending shoes, which trade he had presumably learnt while in the army. Oddly enough he had been in the regiment for four years before it was realized that he was not black enough.[3]

Some of these blacks were wont to desert from their regiments. Thus *The London Gazette*, 1-4 June 1696, reported: 'Deserted out of Cap. Frekes Company of Grenadiers, Tho. Eves, a tall black Man, with black lank hair, a cut on his right Wrist, in a brown Frock much torn, aged about 40.'

And in the 25-29 March 1697 issue of *The London Gazette* was announced: 'Deserted out of Capt. Philip's Company, in Coll. Farrington's Regiment of Foot, from their Quarters at Barnet ... Richard Dalton, a short black Man, his hair cole black, weather beaten in the Face, aged about 24, in a mixt colour Coat, lined with strip'd Silk, and whitish Wastecoat.'

As ever before, black sailors continued to visit British ports, and, from time to time, some found themselves stranded and became objects of Government or private charity, as in the autumn of 1815, when a captain in the Royal Navy made a representation to the Admiralty 'relative to the extremely distressed state of the Black Sailors then lately discharged from his Majesty's ships.' On hearing of the plight of the black sailors, the Directors of the African Institution took the matter up with Lord Sidmouth and Lord Melville, in consequence of which orders were afterwards issued by the Lords of the Admiralty to 'the respective Port-admirals at Greenwich and Portsmouth, to provide for the poor Africans discharged from the Navy upon the production of their discharges, and to take care of them till they can safely be sent to Africa.' In April 1821, the Mendicity Society assisted another black who had been many years with the Navy and had been discharged. When he arrived at the offices of the Society, he was 'fainting with hunger and nearly naked'. It appeared that a considerable sum was due to him for prize money. The Society forwarded his claim and obtained £47.9s.3d. on his account. 'He most cheerfully repaid the Society the sum advanced to him during the time his claim was pending', and expressed the utmost gratitude for the effectual assistance he had received. The report added that there were many other similar cases of blacks in distress who had been 'found entitled to pensions for their services, which it had been frequently the gratifying duty of the Managers to obtain.'⁴

Some blacks swept crossings, some knitted night-caps and socks, and others manufactured garden-nets for their livelihood. The unemployed blacks remained the Black Poor as in the eighteenth century. But they no longer attracted the special notice they had enjoyed in the previous century. In consequence of the change, the writer of the essay 'The Black Man' in *All the Year Round* was moved to ask, 'Can it be that when it was firmly established, not so very long since, that the negro was "a man and a brother", he forthwith ceased to be a friend?' The fact of the matter was that, once the blacks 'fell' from the position of 'grace' they occupied in eighteenth-century English social life, as a result of the Abolition of the British Slave Trade in 1807, and Emancipation in 1834, an epoch ended. The blacks ceased to be a special kind of human being and nothing then could stop their assimilation into the national main stream. The Black Poor were now lumped together with the English poor, the Irish poor, the Greek poor, and the Chinese poor. Thus, in 1817, a magistrate alleged as an excuse for licensing scandals in the Tower Hamlets that 'little good can be done by taking away the licences of houses in Shadwell for this reason, that the population consisting entirely [an obvious exaggeration] of foreign sailors, lascars, Chinese, Greeks, and other filthy dirty people of that description.' A passage in Pierce Egan's *Life in London* symbolizes the change. Writing in 1821, Egan observed that at a party in the East End, 'Lascars, blacks, jack tars, coal heavers, dustmen, women of colour, old and young, and a sprinkling of the remnants of once fine girls ... were all jigging together.' The Ball of Blacks had given way to multi-racial balls. Times had changed and the blacks had changed too.[5]

By the end of the Napoleonic Wars, begging among the indigent blacks and whites in the metropolis had reached such a proportion that two Parliamentary Committees examined the problem. In the report of the Select Committee on the State of Mendicity in the Metropolis, it was cited as an example of how lucrative begging was that 'A Black beggar retired to the West Indies with a fortune, it was supposed of £1,500.' There were indeed some celebrated black beggars, mendicants, and serenaders whose activities in the early decades of the nineteenth century were recorded for posterity. Charles M'Gee was probably the most celebrated. He was born in Jamaica in 1744. It is not known when exactly he arrived in England. 'This singular man usually stands at the Obelisk, at the foot of Ludgate-Hill', John Thomas Smith observed in *Vagabondiana*. He had lost one eye and his hair was almost white. 'His stand is certainly above all others the most popular', Smith asserted, 'many thousands of persons crossing it in the course of the day.' A picture of M'Gee was drawn by Smith in a public house in October 1815. James Grant, another observer of the London scene in the early nineteenth century, noted the death of M'Gee in his *Sketches in London*. Grant said that he left many hundred pounds to Alderman Waithman's daughter. The reason he left his money to Miss Waithman was that she not only gave him a penny or a halfpenny more frequently than anyone else, but she enhanced the value of the gift by accompanying it with a gracious smile. Grant went on to mention two other blacks who swept crossings and amassed large fortunes therefrom. One died in the country, the other returned to the West Indies. The latter, probably the same man mentioned in the Parliamentary report, returned to the West Indies, 'carrying with him, as the savings of a long professional life, from [£]1,500 to [£]1,800'. The other black amassed £8,000 in thirty years, which was found at his death 'in the wretched hovel in which he vegetated'.

The second black man whose picture is featured in *Vagabondiana* was Joseph Johnson. He had served in the Merchant Navy until he retired because of an accident. Having no claim to relief in any parish, he was obliged to gain a living by begging. In order to elude the vigilance of the parochial beadles, he first started on Tower Hill, where he amused the idlers by singing. By degrees he ventured into the public streets, and at length became what was called a 'Regular Chaunter'. Kind-hearted waggoners often enabled him in a few hours to visit the market places of Staines, Romford, or St. Albans, where he never failed to gain the farmer's penny, either by singing 'The British Seaman's Praise' or 'The Wooden Walls of Old England'. Toby was another character well known in the metropolis. He had no toes, his head was bound with a white handkerchief, and he bent himself almost double to walk upon two hand-crutches, with which he nearly occupied the width of the pavement. 'Master Toby generally affected to be tired and exhausted whenever he approached a house where the best gin was to be procured; and was perhaps of all the inhabitants of Church-Lane, St. Giles, the man who expended the most money in that national cordial.'[6]

The black serenaders seemed to have been particularly well patronized, for they were soon overwhelmed by white men disguised as black men. These went by the names 'Lamp-Blacks', 'Ethiopian Serenaders', and 'nigger minstrels'. Ironically, the public reacted unfavourably to these imitation blacks. The whites who dyed themselves black and 'stood pad' as real Africans were regarded as impostors, who were soon detected and punished.[7]

In 1818 an unofficial committee, the Society for the Suppression of Mendicity, was founded, having its headquarters in Red Lion Square. The Society was instituted for the purpose of checking the practice of public begging in the metropolis by enforcing the laws against those who adopt mendicity as a profession, and by affording prompt and effectual assistance to those genuinely in need. In the introduction to the first report of the Society in 1819, 'the wretched condition of many Africans' was noted, 'who, having served this country have lost their own without acquiring another; and the disinclination or inability of parishes to give relief by employment to able-bodied poor; are evils calling aloud for remedy.' In each annual report of the Mendicity Society, a section was devoted to the case histories of persons they had assisted. The following case histories of blacks assisted or arrested by the officers of the Society in the first quarter of the nineteenth century give a good cross-section of the black population and their experience in the early decades of the century. The first case history illustrates that then, as now, blacks were unem-

Joseph Johnson, a prosperous beggar

ployed and forced to seek public assistance not because they so wished but because of institutional racism and racial discrimination. The second example shows, on the one hand, the rough tactics used by the Society's officers when arresting mendicants and, on the other, that black solidarity survived right to the end of the period:

W.J. a native of Jamaica, had been apprehended by the Society's officer, and being committed to the house of correction for seven days, was ordered by the magistrate to be passed to the parish where he was found begging, which was accordingly done. In a few days he was again found in the streets, and inquiry having been made, it was ascertained that the overseer refused to take him into the workhouse when regularly passed to him. The Secretary of the Society having interfered, the overseer was at length compelled to take the man under his care according to law.

J.F. aged 22, a native of St. Domingo, was apprehended in Park-Lane, by four of the Society's officers, after a most desperate resistance, during which, the constables were compelled to use their staves, in consequence of five other blacks attempting a rescue; but failing, they all decamped excepting the prisoner, who was handcuffed to the iron railing until a coach was procured. He however, escaped but was stopped by a Soldier, and eventually lodged at St. George's Watchhouse, ... The Society determined to prosecute so daring an offender, and he was accordingly brought up at Clerkenwell Sessions, sentenced to be imprisoned for three months, and to be twice flogged during that period.

E.B. aged 40, a native of Tortola, in the West Indies, with a wife and child, was referred to [the Society]—their appearance was truly wretched, illness having caused their distress. They had no settlement, therefore the Society set them up with fruit.

J.W. aged 20, a native of Sierra Leone, said that only the last stage of distress could induce him to solicit charity; that he had been in service, and could have a good character. His account was found true, and a situation offering soon afterwards necessary clothing was given, and he thankfully accepted the place. It is pleasing to add that this honest fellow had no sooner received his wages than he returned twenty shillings, part of the sum laid out for the clothing.

J.W. a native of Jamaica, aged 35, was reduced by illness to great distress selling fruits in the street. His means being entirely exhausted, he applied by ticket at the Office. His character having been fully inquired into, the Society replenished his basket; and about six months afterwards he came to the Office very decently clad, expressed his gratitude for the assistance he had received, and was then looking for the situation of servant in a gentleman's family.

G.D. a native of Africa, his tale was as follows:- 'I was stolen from my parents in Africa, and being sold as a slave, was bought by a captain of a vessel in Demarara; on the arrival of the ship at Greenock I ran away, and enlisted as a drummer in the 25th regiment, and was at the taking of Guadaloupe and Martinique; from thence I returned to England, and was discharged after seven years service. Three years after this I went to sea in a merchantman, and was wrecked last winter in my passage home on the banks of Newfoundland; my hands were frostbitten, and my fingers were in consequence amputated in St. John's, when sufficiently recovered, my passage home was paid for by a magistrate there, amounting to three pounds; and on my arrival in Liverpool I gained a livelihood by selling pin cushions, which were made by the woman of the house where I lodged. I remained there about four months and went from thence to Newmarket, where I was apprehended begging and committed to a gaol for a month; on my release a gentleman gave me a guinea which paid my expenses to London, and I have since my arrival met with a little assistance from a gentleman in the East Indian House.' This tale naturally interested the feeling of every one, and inquiry was set on foot, as well to ascertain the truth, as to procure something permanently beneficial for poor D. Among other applications, the African Institution was resorted to, and the Society for Foreigners in Distress. Here we learnt that £5 had been voted to set him up in some little way of business; they had a few days before given him ten shillings, and were duly supporting him with food and paying his lodgings. Of course nothing more could be done for him here, and he was discharged with a reference to that Society.

E.C.; alias J.E.; alias J.J.; an African, came from thence ten years previously; he had been on board a merchantman, and paid off two months before; he said he was unable to procure another berth, was with his wife compelled to beg. He was apprehended by the constables of the Institution, and the magistrate finding he did not give a very good account of himself, committed him for three weeks recommending his wife, however, who was in a state of pregnancy, to the consideration of the Society; a small weekly allowance was accordingly given her; This man however, was no sooner out of gaol, than he was again apprehended begging in Charing Cross; he made a most violent resistance, and behaved exceedingly ill, that the magistrate committed him for three months. His wife again came to the Office for her usual support, but as it was considered that such indulgence would only prove an inducement to the man to follow his usual course, than act as a check, the Managers thought it right to refuse it.[8]

1. *All the Year Round*, p. 493.

2. M. E. Kenealy, *The Tichborne Tragedy* (London, 1913), pp. 221-3.

3. *The Fourteenth Report of the Mendicity Society* (1832), pp. 41-2. There were also black pugilists. The most celebrated of these was Bill Richmond, who ran a boxing academy in St. Martin's Street, Leicester Square, after retiring from the ring. This academy was frequented by Lord Byron. Tom Molineux, a slave from Virginia, arrived in London penniless in 1809, and was 'managed' by Richmond. Jim Johnson and Massa Kendrick also trained under Bill Richmond.

4. *Tenth Report of the Committee of the African Institution, 1816* (London, 1816), p. 37; *Fourth Report of the Mendicity Society* (1822), pp. 9, 51-2.

5. *All the Year Round*, p. 492; George, *London Life in the Eighteenth Century* (London, 1925), p. 362; Pierce Egan, *Life in London* (London, 1821), p. 321.

6. *Parliamentary Papers*, III (1814-15) and V (1816); James Grant, *Sketches in London* (London, 1838), pp. 26-7; John Thomas Smith, *Vagabondiana, or Mendicant Wanderers through the Streets of London; with Portraits of the Most Remarkable, drawn from the Life* (London, 1817), pp. 33-5.

7. Henry Mayhew, *London Labour and the London Poor* (London, 1862), IV, p. 425.

8. *First Report* (1819), p. 33; *Third Report* (1821), pp. 27-8; *Fourth Report* (1822), p. 26; *Seventh Report* (1825), p. 37; *Ninth Report* (1827), p. 40; *Fifth Report* (1823), pp. 39-40; *Eighth Report* (1826), p. 56.

# PART THREE : BIOGRAPHIES

# 13

# Ukawsaw Gronniosaw

*A Narrative of the Most Remarkable Particulars in the Life of James Albert Ukawsaw Gronniosaw, An African Prince, as related by Himself*, published in Bath in or about 1770, is the only extant account of the trials and tribulations of a Poor Black and his family. Gronniosaw was a native of Bornu in what is now Nigeria, and his mother was 'the eldest daughter of the King of Bornous'. He was kidnapped, sold to the captain of a Dutch slaving vessel, and carried to Barbados. There he was sold for fifty dollars to an American, who took him to New York, where he was held in bondage as a domestic slave. When the American died, he confirmed Gronniosaw's freedom in his will. Prior to his emancipation, Gronniosaw had entertained a desire to come to England. 'I imagined that all the Inhabitants of this Island were *Holy*.' When at last he landed in Portsmouth, he was astonished to hear the natives swearing and cursing. Gronniosaw had arrived with thirty pounds, and lodged with a woman who kept a public house. He deposited twenty-four pounds with the publican for safe keeping, but when he wanted the money back, she denied that he ever gave her any money. Eventually, he was able to salvage four guineas from the woman, which she said she was giving him out of charity. Gronniosaw now perceived that he was among bad people, 'who defrauded me of my money and watch; ... all my promis'd happiness was blasted.'

After this initial upset, he moved to London, where he was more circumspect. He lodged at a house in Petticoat Lane, where he met the woman whom he eventually married. Soon after his arrival at the lodging house, he began to entertain a good opinion of her, though he was very reluctant to indulge this inclination, lest she should prove 'like all the rest I had met with at Portsmouth, &c. and which had almost given me a dislike to all white women. But after a short acquaintance I had the happiness to find that she was very different, and quite sincere.' So Gronniosaw married 'my Betty', who was a weaver.

Soon after the marriage, their 'many great troubles and difficulties' began. His wife had been earning a good income as a weaver, but just after their marriage riots broke out among the weavers. Gronniosaw was afraid to let his wife continue weaving, 'lest they should insist on my joining the rioters which I could not think of, and, possibly, if I had refused to do so they would have knocked me on the head.' So they moved to Colchester, where he 'work'd in the road.' They lived in reasonable comfort until winter came, when he was discharged from his work as a navvy. They were now both unemployed. 'The winter prov'd remarkably severe, and we were reduc'd to the greatest distress imaginable.' He earnestly sought work as a farm labourer, but the farm-hand in charge told him it was not in his power to employ Gronniosaw. He gave Gronniosaw, however, four very large carrots. The gift was a boon, for at the time they had virtually no food. They ate the carrots raw, as they had nothing to make fire with. Their youngest child was quite an infant, 'so that my wife was obliged to chew it, and fed her in that manner for several days.' The last carrot eaten, they were back to square one. By almost a miracle, as he put it, they were rescued by Peter Daniel, a Colchester attorney whom he had met while working in the road as a navvy. Daniel had learnt that Gronniosaw had been discharged and feared that he must be in want. He sent for Gronniosaw, found his apprehension had proved correct, and generously gave him a guinea. Furthermore, Peter Daniel employed Gronniosaw to pull down a house and rebuild it. The work occupied him for more than a year, and after that he was employed successively by others, 'and was never so happy as when I had something to do.'

When Gronniosaw was offered work in Norwich with a prospect of earning better wages, they moved there. His wife hired a loom, and wove during all the leisure time she had and they began 'to do very well', till they were overtaken by fresh misfortunes. Their three children became ill of smallpox and one of them, a girl, died. The Baptist Minister at Norwich refused to bury her because they were not members of his church. The vicar of the Established Church in their parish refused to perform the burial too, because the dead child had never been baptized. He applied to the Quakers, but met with no success. 'At length I resolv'd to dig a grave in the garden behind the house, and bury her there; when the Parson of the parish sent for me to tell me he would bury the child, but did not chose to read the burial service over her. I told him I did not mind whether he would or not, as the child could not hear it.' By the time the dead daughter had been buried and the other two children had recovered, Gronniosaw had fallen into arrears 'for several weeks' with his rent. His landlady told him that if he did not pay the arrears immediately, 'she would turn us all into the street'. Henry Gurdney, a Quaker, heard of their distress and paid all the rent outstanding. Gronniosaw was advised by Henry Gurdney:

To follow the employ of chopping chaff, and bought me an instrument for that purpose. There were but few people in the town that made this their business beside myself; so that I did very well indeed and we became easy and happy. But we did not continue long in this comfortable state: Many of the inferior people were envious and ill-natur'd and set up the employ and work'd under price on purpose to get my business from me, and they succeeded so well that I could hardly get any thing to do, and became again unfortunate.

He now moved to Kidderminster, where one Watson 'employed me in twisting silk and worsted together'. Back in Norwich, Betty was taken ill, and, when she eventually recovered and left the city to join her husband in Kidderminster, she was obliged to sell all they had to pay their debts and expenses incurred during her illness. The *Narrative* closes on this sombre note: 'Such is our situation at present. My wife, by hard labour at the loom, does everything that can be expected from her towards the maintenance of our family; and God is pleased to incline the hearts of his People at times to yield us their charitable assistances; being myself through age and infirmity able to contribute but little to their support. As Pilgrims, and very poor Pilgrims, we are travelling through many difficulties.'[1]

1. Ukawsaw Gronniosaw, *A Narrative* ... (Bath, 1770?). pp. 1, 4, 9-10, 23-7, 30-9. Throughout the *Narrative* no dates of the events related therein are given.

# 14

# Ottobah Cugoano

Ottobah Cugoano was born about 1757 in Ajumako, in today's Ghana. When he was about thirteen years old, in 1770, he was kidnapped with twenty others of both sexes, and in the brutish, base, but fashionable way of the slave traffic, consigned to Grenada. His time in Grenada was spent in 'dreadful captivity and horrible slavery'. Fifteen years later he recalled that every day he witnessed 'the most dreadful scenes of misery and cruelty ... my miserable companions often cruelly lashed, and as it were cut to pieces, for the most trifling faults.' The slaves were also lashed for trying to hear the Christian message. 'Even in the little time that I was in Grenada, I saw a slave receive twenty-four lashes of the whip for being seen in church on a Sunday instead of going to work.'[1]

After about ten months in the slave gang in Grenada, and a further year in various parts of the West Indies, his owner, Alexander Campbell, brought him to England towards the end of 1772. Shortly after his arrival in England, he was advised to get himself baptized, that he might not be carried away and sold again. Accordingly he was baptized, and took the name John Stewart. It is interesting to note that, arriving so soon after the Mansfield judgement, Cugoano was still advised to have himself baptized, a clear indication that although the black community celebrated the victory of their brother Somerset, they knew that their security in England was far from safe. Yet when Cugoano was paying tribute to Granville Sharp in the 1791 shortened edition of *Thoughts and Sentiments*, he too subscribed to the myth that the Mansfield judgement freed all black slaves in England: 'It was considered as criminal, by the laws of Englishmen, when the tyrannical paw and the monster of slavery took the man by the neck, in the centre of the British freedom ... The whole of that affair rested solely upon the humane and indefatigable friend of mankind, GRENVILLE SHARP, esq; whose name we should always mention with the greatest reverence and honor.'[2]

After remaining for some time in the service of Alexander Campbell, Cugoano entered the service of Cosway, who was then the first painter to the Prince of Wales. Soon after his arrival in England Cugoano established contact with the close-knit black community of the time, and soon became one of its leaders. He

may well have met Ukawsaw Gronniosaw; at any rate, he certainly read his *Narrative*, for in *Thoughts and Sentiments*
Cugoano mentioned the vicissitudes which marked the life of
Gronniosaw in Britain, noting in particular that 'he was a long
time in a state of great poverty and distress, and must have died at
one time for want, if a good and charitable Attorney had not supported him.' In 1786 Cugoano was instrumental in the rescue of a
black slave, Henry Demane, who had been kidnapped by his
owner and was en route to the West Indies and slavery. Henry
Demane was kidnapped on 28 July 1786, but fortunately for him,
some of the black folk became aware of it. In his capacity as a
leader of the black community, Cugoano and another black, William Green, then a Corporal of the Black Poor, instantly reported
the kidnapping to Granville Sharp. Sharp, who knew there was
not a moment to waste, set in motion the legal process which ultimately secured Demane's freedom. Irwin and Fraser, the
Government Agent and Chaplain respectively to the Black Poor,
also took part in the rescue of Henry Demane. Thus, while he
was strongly opposed to the deportation decision of the Committee for the Black Poor, Cugoano was prepared to work with
people associated with it. Indeed his position as 'a man of weight
among the Blacks' made it imperative that he should and must
work for the release of a kidnapped brother and for the welfare of
the blacks in general. Henry Demane was among the Black Poor
who went to Sierra Leone. Regrettably, when he got to the West
African coast, Demane joined the pack of slave dealers himself
and became a prosperous dealer in human flesh.[3]

It was in his position as a leader of the black community that
Cugoano published his case for Abolition in 1787. While in the
West Indies Cugoano, of course, had no opportunity to learn to
read and write. But after coming to England, he availed himself
of the opportunity to learn reading and writing, and his owner, he
said, sent him to a proper school for that purpose. Five manuscript letters of Cugoano's are printed in the 1969 reprint of
*Thoughts and Sentiments*, and it is clear from the grammatical
errors in these letters that *Thoughts and Sentiments* must have
been edited for him to achieve the flowery English of some passages in the book. Some of the book is identical with Equiano's
letters to the press between 1787 and 1789 which are collected at
the end of this book. We can safely assume, therefore, that
Equiano had a hand in the editing of his friend's book, and indeed
inserted some of his own writings into the text.

Unquestionably, *Thoughts and Sentiments* was propagandist
work 'submitted to the Inhabitants of Great-Britain.'[4] The whole
business of slavery was an evil of the first magnitude, and yet

carried on by men who called themselves Christians. It was a most horrible iniquity to traffic with slaves and souls of men. Slavery, Cugoano asserted, was a vast, extended, hideous, and unmitigated evil. Some slaves it was true met with better treatment and secured their freedom one way or the other. But these were drops in the mighty, gigantic, deformed ocean of bondage. Of course, Africans were themselves in part responsible for the intolerable calamities of blacks in bondage. In a reference to his own enslavement, he wrote with depressing candour, 'I must own, to the shame of my own countrymen, that I was first kidnapped and betrayed by some of my own complexion, who were the first cause of my exile and slavery.' But he added, 'if there were no buyers there would be no sellers.'⁵

One by one, Cugoano demolished the tenets of the gospel according to slavocracy, which proclaimed that blacks were happy in their servitude, were well-treated and better off than the European poor, and that the white man had brought blacks out of Africa into civilization and enlightenment. He revealed that slaves were lashed for being in church and that they were not taught reading and writing. As to the blacks being happy in their shackles and receiving humane treatment from their owners, Cugoano flatly denied these shameless lies. It could not be. For slavery itself was an atrocity. Blacks had been sold to 'profligate wicked men, to torture and lash us as they please, and as their caprice may think fit, to murder us at discretion.' Whatever the circumstances of poor freemen in Europe might be, their situation was much superior to that of the slaves in the West Indies. Such was the abominable situation of the Africans that they were entitled to rebel and fight for their freedom. It was as much their duty to rebel, 'as it is for any honest community of men to get out of the hands of rogues and villains.' And what about European civilization? 'We want many rules of [European] civilization in Africa; but, in many respects, we may boast of some more essential liberties than any of the civilized nations of Europe enjoy; for the poorest amongst us are never in distress for want, unless some general universal calamity happen to us', which is still true today.⁶

Cugoano proposed an immediate Abolition of the slave trade and the Emancipation of the slave. 'Britain having now acquired a greater share in that iniquitous commerce than all the rest together, they are the first that ought to set an example.' He was quite convinced that his plan for Abolition and Emancipation might be effectively carried out by Britain. 'I would propose, that a fleet of some ships of war should be immediately sent to the coast of Africa, and particularly where the slave trade is carried on, with faithful men to direct that none should be brought from the coast of Africa.' He knew that the insidious owners of the human species would certainly object to Emancipation, because they would be deprived of their valuable human commodities thereby. But so let it be. 'It would be but a just commutation for what cannot be fully restored.' When the British slave trade had outlived its economic usefulness, its suppression by Britain followed more or less Cugoano's suggestions. But as long as it was economically viable, his voice, like the voice of Granville Sharp, the voice of Thomas Clarkson, or the voice of James Ramsay would remain a voice crying in the wilderness.[7]

Copies of *Thoughts and Sentiments* were sent by Cugoano to the Prince of Wales and George III. In the letter accompanying the copy sent to the Prince of Wales, he asked the Prince to accept his little tract as being the thoughts and sentiments of an African against all manner of slavery and oppression. Since the helpless Africans had no 'institutions of Ambassadors to demand restitution for the injuries which the Europeans have pursued against us we can no where lay our case more fitly than at the feet of your Highness.' To the King he wrote that concern for the injurious treatment of his countrymen and the cause of justice and humanity were the only motives which induced him to collect his thoughts and sentiments on the evil of slavery, 'with a view to the natural liberties of Men which your Majesty as a Sovereign will be pleased to support.' Another copy of *Thoughts and Sentiments* was sent to Burke. He told Burke that he was a young man and native of Africa, in domestic employment. (His address was given in the letter as 'Pall Mall at Mr. Cosway's'.) He hoped that the arguments in his tract would meet with Burke's approbation.[8]

Cugoano's representations to Burke were as useless as the representations to the Prince of Wales and George III. In the year 1780 the slave trade had attracted Burke's attention, and he had even proceeded to sketch out a code of regulations which provided for its immediate mitigation and ultimate suppression. 'But after mature consideration he had abandoned the attempt, from the conviction that the strength of the West Indian body would defeat the utmost effort of his powerful party, and cover them in ruinous unpopularity.'[9] Thereafter, his conduct on the subject was governed by political expediency. In his intervention in the debates on Sir William Dolben's Bill in 1788, Burke said: '[I am] one of those who wished for the abolition of the Slave Trade. [I think] it ought to be abolished on principles of humanity and justice. If, however, opposition of interests should render its total abolition impossible, it ought to be regulated, and that immediately.'[10] And in 1792 Burke thought that 'the cause of humanity would be far more benefited by the continuance of the trade and servitude, regulated and reformed, than by the total destruction of both or either.' The slave-trading city of Bristol could well afford to share the general admiration of the great liberal![11]

As to the Royal Family, on 11 April 1793 the Duke of Clarence intervened in the debate in the House of Lords on the Abolition of the Slave Trade. In an extraordinary speech, the future William IV attacked Abolitionists dead and alive. Of the noble James Ramsay, who died in 1789, the Duke of Clarence repeated a long discredited libel: 'The business of this sort of freedom was begun by a Mr. Ramsay, who was one of the most tyrannical men that ever governed a plantation in the West Indies, but, who, ... became now as great a tyrant to order and good government as he was before to justice, moderation, and true liberty.'

James Ramsay never governed a plantation. Ramsay originally went to the West Indies as a surgeon, attached to a number of plantations. He was a conscientious doctor. On one occasion when a slaver was infested with plague, and no other doctor dared to go on board, Ramsay volunteered and went on board and into the hellish hold to treat the dying. The sight made a lasting impression on him and gave birth to his undying enmity to slavery and the slave trade. When he began his systematic attack against slavery and the slave trade in 1784, his opponents launched a campaign of libel and slander against Ramsay, the burden of which the Duke succinctly and shamelessly repeated in the above quotation. Ramsay successfully repudiated these libels and wholly unjustified calumnies. Pitt thought his reputation so wholly unblemished that he called him to Downing Street and obtained invaluable information from him about the wickedness of the slave trade. James Stephen, who went to the West Indies and investigated the charges of Ramsay's enemies, reported the result to Wilberforce. 'I have not heard,' he wrote in his testimony, 'a crime or blemish imputed to Mr. Ramsay which has not been refuted afterwards in my presence by some of his most inveterate enemies, better acquainted with the facts.' Of the living Abolitionists, His Royal Highness asserted that they were 'either fanatics or hypocrites, and in one of those classes he ranked Mr. Wilberforce'.[12]

In 1804 Wilberforce wrote that 'it was truly humiliating to see, in the House of Lords, four of the Royal Family come down to vote against the poor, helpless, friendless slaves.' And George III himself once jestingly whispered to Wilberforce, 'How go on your black clients, Mr. Wilberforce?'[13]

In 1791 Cugoano published a much shorter version of his Abolitionist work under the elaborate title: *Thoughts and Senti-*

*ments on the Evil of Slavery; or, the Nature of Servitude as
admitted by the Law of God, compared to the Modern Slavery of
the Africans in the West-Indies; in answer to the Advocates for
Slavery and Oppression addressed to the Sons of Africa, by a
Native.* As we have seen, the 1787 edition was 'submitted to the
Inhabitants of Great-Britain'. In a final note to the 1791 edition,
Cugoano revealed his plan to open a school for Africans in London. After stating that he had printed this abstract in order to convey instructions to his oppressed countrymen, to excite their
attention to the religious observance of the Laws of God, he continued:

[The Author] further proposes to open a School, for all such of his Complexion as are desirous of being acquainted with the Knowledge of the
Christian Religion and the Laws of Civilization. His sole Motives for
these Undertakings, are, that he finds several of his Countrymen, here
in England, who have not only been in an unlawful Manner brought
away from their peaceable Habitations, but also deprived of every
Blessing of the Christian Knowledge, by their various Masters and Mistresses, either through motives of Avarice, or the want of the knowledge
of their own Religion, which must be a great Dishonour to Christianity.
  Nothing engages my desire so much as the Descendants of my Countrymen, so as to have them educated in the Duties and Knowledge of
that Religion which all good Christian People enjoy; these Blessings
cannot be well conveyed without Learning, and as most of my Countrymen are Poor and cannot afford it, and others are so much engaged in
Servitude, that they have little Time to attend to it; my Design, therefore, is to open a Place for the Instruction of such as can attend; but to
accomplish it, I must wholly depend on the humane and charitable Contributions of those Ladies and Gentlemen [14] who are inclinable to Support this undertaking. I am not excluding some other young Persons,
who need to be taught Reading, etc. but my Design is chiefly intended
for my Countrymen. [15]

After 1791 we have no further information about Cugoano,
and, therefore, we cannot say for certain whether his plan to set
up a school came to fruition. [16] But, all told, the picture we have
of Cugoano is of a typical, conscientious African tribal chieftain
who had the welfare of his 'children' much at heart. Like many
other Africans who lived in England during the period, Cugoano
married an Englishwoman, but we do not know whether they had
children or what eventually became of him and his wife. Scipione
Piattoli, who knew Cugoano well in London, spoke highly of
him, extolling 'his piety, his gentle and modest character, his
honest manner and his talents.' [17]

1. Cugoano, *Thoughts and Sentiments* ... (London, 1787), pp. iv, 10-11, 142.

2. Cugoano, op. cit., pp. iv, 6-7.

3. Cugoano, op. cit., p. 22; Hoare, *Memoirs of Granville Sharp* (London, 1828), 2nd ed., I, pp. 369-70.

4. In 1788 the French edition of *Thoughts and Sentiments* appeared in Paris.

5. Cugoano, op. cit., pp. 12, 23-4, 96-7.

6. Ibid., pp. 17-18, 63, 73, 119-20, 138.

7. Ibid., pp. 110, 130-8.

8. Cugoano, op. cit. (1969), pp. xix-xxi.

9. R. I. and S. Wilberforce, *The Life of William Wilberforce* (London, 1838), I, pp. 152-3. Burke's sketch was published in 1792, as 'A letter to the Right Hon. Henry Dundas, One of His Majesty's Principal Secretaries of State; with the Sketch of a Negro Code'.

10. *Parliamentary History*, XXVII, col. 502.

11. Eric Williams, *Capitalism and Slavery* (London, 1964), p. 41; David Brion Davis, *The Problem of Slavery in Western Culture* (London, 1970), p. 430.

12. *Parliamentary History*, XXX, col. 659; R. I. and S. Wilberforce, op. cit., I, p. 235n; *Dictionary of National Biography*, s.v. James Ramsay.

13. R. I. and S. Wilberforce, op. cit., I, p. 343; III, p. 182.

14. In the 1787 edition, Cugoano says, 'I know several ladies in England who refused to drink sugar in their tea, because of the cruel injuries done to the Black People employed in the culture of it at the West Indies', p. 136. Among the list of the subscribers to the 1791 edition were Joseph Nollekens, the sculptor, and Sir Joshua Reynolds.

15. Cugoano, op. cit. (1791), p. 49.

16. There is a remote possibility that he went to Sierra Leone. In the 1787 edition he wrote: 'I wish to go back as soon as I can hear any proper security and safe conveyance can be found; and I wait to hear how it fares with the Black People sent to Sierra Leone', op. cit., p. iv. A letter he wrote to Granville Sharp on or about 1791 shows that he was not only still active in matters relating to Sierra Leone, but that he was actually in correspondence with the Africans in New Brunswick and Nova Scotia, some of whom went to Sierra Leone in 1792. For the letter, see *Thoughts and Sentiments* (1969), Appendix, pp. xxi-xxiii.

17. H. Grégoire, *De la Littérature des Nègres* (Paris, 1808), pp. 215-16.

# 15

# Francis Barber

As everyone who is at all acquainted with Boswell's *Life of Johnson* knows, it was through his friend Dr. Bathurst that Johnson acquired Francis Barber as his servant. Boswell tells us that Francis Barber was born in Jamaica, and was brought to England in 1750 by Colonel Bathurst, father of Dr. Bathurst. In his will, the 'Colonel' (his military title was a local one, showing his rank in the Jamaica Militia) gave Francis his freedom and twelve pounds in money. According to Boswell, Francis entered Johnson's service about a fortnight after the death of Johnson's wife, which occurred on 17 March 1752. Boswell wrote in his great biography that the authentic and artless account of Johnson's situation after his wife's death was given to him by Francis Barber. Boswell printed his exact words, and they show him to have possessed considerable intelligence, as well as an excellent memory. No less than twenty of Johnson's friends of that period are mentioned, with some personal details and even shrewd criticism. The question of Francis Barber's age is a puzzling one. The only definite evidence on this point is provided by a correspondent to *The Gentleman's Magazine* in 1793, who described him as then aged about forty-eight. If that age is correct, then we must place his birth about 1745, and assume that he was only about seven years old when he went into Johnson's service. It is difficult to believe that he was really so young, and it seems unlikely that at that age Francis could have received and retained such clear and intelligent impressions of Johnson's circumstances and state of mind after his wife's death as he conveyed to Boswell.[1]

Twice Francis left Johnson because of differences between master and servant. On the first occasion, in 1756, he went and served an apothecary in Cheapside, but still visited Johnson regularly. On the second occasion, in 1758, Francis ran away to sea. He was not pressed, as was originally supposed, but went away by his own consent. Francis's decision to go to sea is quite intriguing. 'No man,' Johnson said, 'will be a sailor who has contrivance enough to get himself into a jail; for being in a ship is being in a jail, with the chance of being drowned.' And on another occasion, he said, 'A man in a jail has more room, better food, and commonly better company.' It may be that Francis went to sea, as Reade says, because he grew 'weary of the dullness of a lexicographical laboratory'; or there might have been a deeper reason, which may be inferred from Mrs. Piozzi's anecdote, that Johnson, 'when he spoke of [blacks], he always appeared to think of them as of a race naturally inferior, and made few exceptions in favour of his own.' Although Reade says 'Mrs. Piozzi's unsupported anecdotes, ... are hardly the proper material for history', in this instance we have no reason to doubt the accuracy of her story. Johnson's contempt for the so-called 'savage' was monumental. And we have Johnson's word that 'being disgusted in the house [Francis] ran away to sea.' Being disgusted with whom we do not know. But it is perhaps symbolic that he chose to go to sea to underline his disgust. As a sympathetic editorial on Francis in the *Daily Telegraph*, 10 June 1887, pertinently observed: 'Why, of all callings, he should have chosen a maritime one is hopelessly puzzling; his frame was delicate, he had a bronchial affection, and he must have been continually hearing his master rail against ships and sailors.'

The last observation may be the clue to the puzzle. Presumably Francis, tired of Johnson's nannying and condescensions, opted for the very life he had heard his master rail against so often. Johnson lost no time in procuring Francis's release through the intercession of John Wilkes.[2]

In 1767 Johnson sent Frank (his nickname for Francis) to Bishops Stortford Grammar School. Boswell observed that Johnson's attention to the improvement of Frank's education, 'does Johnson's heart much honour', with which sentiment everyone must agree. But Sir John Hawkins, who in everything relating to Frank is a prejudiced witness, said that Johnson, 'for no assignable reason, nay, rather in despight of nature, and to unfit him for being useful according to his capacity determined to make him a scholar', and expended three hundred pounds in an endeavour to have him taught Latin and Greek. The grammar school Frank attended was a respectable institution of old foundation, but at the time Frank was there, it did not occupy as good a position as it had done in the past. Johnson wrote many letters to Frank while he was at Bishops Stortford, but only three were preserved. The first, commencing 'Dear Francis' and signed 'yours affectionately', is dated 28 May 1768. Johnson said he was glad to hear that Frank was well, and he planned 'to come soon to see you'. In the second, dated 25 September 1770, Johnson was 'very well satisfied' with Frank's progress. He asked Frank to let him know what English books he read for entertainment. 'You can never be wise unless you love reading,' he warned Frank. Frank seems to have left the grammar school early in 1772, for on 21 March 1772 Boswell describes himself as 'happy to find myself again in my friend's study, and glad to see my old acquaintance, Mr. Francis Barber, who was now returned home.'[3]

During the last twelve years of Johnson's life, the period which provided most material for biographers, when he was the acknowledged 'great cham of literature', Frank's figure flits across the scene, here giving colour to an incident, and there finding kindly mention in one of Johnson's letters. On 20 June 1771 Johnson, writing to Mrs. Thrale, informed her that 'this night, at nine o'clock, Sam. Johnson and Francis Barber, Esquires, set out in the Lichfield stage; Francis is indeed rather upon it.' Frank's duties are nowhere exactly specified by the biographers, but it is clear that in addition to attending on his master's person and work, he answered the door (we have already come across an instance of this) and waited at table. Boswell recounts how, one day, when he called at Bolt Court, on the way to dinner, Johnson roared, 'Frank a clean shirt', and he was 'very soon drest'. On 4 October 1779, 'Frank,' thundered Johnson from his bedroom when Boswell called to see him, 'go and get coffee, and let us breakfast in splendour.' Frank even waited at the tables of friends of Johnson. 'One day,' the daughter of Reynolds related, 'his man Frank was waiting at Sir Joshua's table, [Johnson] observed with some emotion that [Frank] had the salver under his arm.' If the entry of 'Frank' in Reynolds's diary of sitters is rightly interpreted as a reference to Francis Barber, then we must assign Sir Joshua's portrait of Frank to April 1767. In *A Literary Party at Sir Joshua Reynolds'*, by James E. Doyle, a black is depicted conveying two wine decanters to members of the Club. The artist could have had in mind Frank or Reynolds's black servant. In 1779 Johnson's *Lives of the Poets* appeared. On 22 January 1779, Boswell wrote to Johnson, and mentioned that as Johnson had been so kind as to permit him to have the proof sheets of his *Lives of the Poets*, he had written to Frank to take care of them for him.[4]

Frank was eminent for his success with English girls, and Johnson remarked that 'Frank has carried the empire of Cupid farther than most men.' Eventually, Don Juan settled down and married an English girl. The exact date of Frank's marriage is not known, but on 23 September 1776, Johnson, in a letter to Robert Levett, remarked that 'Francis and his Wife have both given great satisfaction by their behaviour.' In another letter to Levett, from Brighton, dated 21 October 1776, Johnson wrote of his impending return, and concluded, 'Remember me kindly to Francis and Betsy.' Mrs. Barber's Christian name was Elizabeth. According to Mrs. Piozzi, Betsy was 'eminently pretty'. When Boswell first met her, he laconically recorded his first reaction: 'Like black's

wife, tho' she did not make me break the 10 Commandments.'
But Hawkins, never willing to lose an opportunity of deprecating
Frank, cast the foulest aspersions on Elizabeth Barber's honour:

It was hinted to me many years ago, by his master, that he was a loose
fellow; and I learned from others, that, after an absence from his service
of some years, he married. In his search of a wife, he picked up one of
those creatures with whom, in the disposal of themselves, no contrariety
of colour is an obstacle.[5] It is said, that soon after the marriage, he
became jealous,[6] and, it may be supposed, that he continued so, till, by
presenting him first with one, and afterwards with another daughter, of
her own colour, his wife put an end to all his doubts on that score.

As Reade commented:

It may well astonish us nowadays that a lawyer of experience should
accord the widest publicity to such libellous statements; and that he
should be able to do so with impunity. We will not condemn Mrs. Barber upon the testimony of Sir John Hawkins; if for no other reason
because, ... Frank's son, born after Johnson's death, had a strong [Afri-
can] strain in him; and the facts of nature do not render it probable, in
this case, that the elder children were illegitimate. Moreover, the
woman who many years later kept a school for children, and was described by an unprejudiced man of the world as 'sensible and well-
informed' scarcely accords with the picture drawn by Hawkins.

The biographer of Frank's son said he was of African extrac-
tion. And someone who met his grandson said 'his woolly hair
and mulatto features, are fixed in my memory'. We must therefore dismiss the rancorous abuse of Hawkins, and the sly levities
of the worthy English Canon who said Betsy brought Frank both
black and white children alternately. For had Betsy been 'as
chaste as ice, as pure as snow' she could hardly have produced all
her children of a tint so uniform as to provide no mark for the
shafts either of malice or of humour.[7]
With the exception of Hawkins, all the chroniclers make
kindly reference to Frank. 'Faithful' and 'honest' are the adjec-
tives which crop up again and again. On 12 May 1775, Boswell
took possession of the bedroom assigned him by Johnson for
occasional use and recorded that he was 'attended by honest
Francis with a most civil assiduity'. 'Good Mr. Francis', Boswell
called him when recording how, on 18 March 1778, he arrived in
London and was told by Frank that Johnson had gone to Streatham, visiting the Thrales. And we have seen already that Boswell referred to Frank as 'my old acquaintance'. We have seen,
too, Boswell's view on the legitimacy of the slave trade and

slavery. Boswell was a reactionary if ever there was one. In his will, Johnson omitted many of his friends including Boswell. Giuseppe Baretti sought consolation for the fact that Johnson had not mentioned him and other friends in the reflection that, 'if he had taken notice of us all, and left ever so small a token of his friendship to each of us, as, so far, it would have been a diminution of the little, that he bequeathed to my friend Frank, who from his earliest youth served him with the greatest affection and disinterestedness.' Johnson, who left property worth £2,300, gave an annuity of £70 to Francis, and made him residuary legatee. Johnson decided on the annuity of £70 after consulting a friend, to whom he had put the question: What would be a proper annuity to bequeath a favourite servant? The friend answered that the circumstances of the master were the truest measure, and that, in the case of a nobleman, £50 was deemed an adequate reward for many years' faithful service. 'Then,' said Johnson, 'shall I be *nobilissimus*, for I mean to leave Frank £70 a year.' In addition to Hawkins, Sir Joshua Reynolds and Sir William Scott were the executors of Johnson's will. Johnson died on 13 December 1784. His funeral took place in Westminster Abbey on 20 December, and the name of Frank occurs in the list of those present to pay respect to the memory of his master.[8]

Hawkins, in his prejudice against Frank, would admit neither merit to Johnson for his generosity nor qualities in Frank to deserve the bequest. Angrily, he entered 'a caveat against ostentatious bounty, favour to negroes, and testamentary disposition in extremis'.

'Nowhere', says Birkbeck Hill, 'does Hawkins more shew his malignancy of character than in his attacks on Johnson's black servant, and through him on Johnson.'

In his vendetta, Hawkins accused Frank of 'craft and selfishness'. It is amusing to find that the charge of 'craft and selfishness' is strictly applicable to this attorney and self-important dispenser of justice himself. To Edmund Malone we owe a valuable statement affording evidence of this:

After the death of Dr. Johnson, [Hawkins] as one of his executors laid hold of his watch and several trinkets, coins, &c; which he said he should take to himself for his trouble—a pretty *liberal* construction of the rule of law, that an executor may satisfy his own demands in the first instance. Sir Joshua and Sir Wm. Scott, the other executors, remonstrated against this, and with great difficulty *compelled* him to give up the watch, which Dr. Johnson's servant, Francis Barber, now has; but the coins and old pieces of money they could never get. He likewise seized on a gold-headed cane which some one had by accident left in

Dr. Johnson's house previous to his death. They in vain urged that Francis had a right to this till the owner appeared, and should hold it *in usum jus habentes*. He would not restore it; and his house being soon afterwards consumed by fire, he *said* it was there burnt.

Malone, in a letter to James, first Earl of Charlemont, did not hesitate to put his opinion of the transaction into plain words. 'You perhaps have not heard of a very curious fact,' he wrote. 'Sir John wanted to cheat poor Frank, Johnson's servant, of a gold watch and cane, and Frank, not choosing to lose them, from that time became as black again as he was before.' Hawkins's conduct better deserves to be described as dishonest, for 'craft' scarcely covers such a blunt disregard of Frank's legal rights. Small wonder Hawkins did not long remain a member of the Club, for, as it is said, he was an 'unclubbable man'.[9] (The Club was founded by Johnson and Reynolds in 1764. It met once a week for supper at The Turk's Head, Gerrard Street, Soho. The first members were Edmund Burke, Oliver Goldsmith, Topham Beauclerk, Bennet Langton, Sir John Hawkins, Dr. Nugent, Mr. Chamier, Johnson, and Reynolds. Boswell was not elected till 1773.)

After Johnson's death and burial, Frank and his family retired to Lichfield as Johnson had counselled him to. Boswell naturally sought assistance from Frank for his great biography. But in collecting information for his biography, Boswell wanted more than reminiscences. In particular, he needed Johnson's papers which were in possession of Hawkins. In 1787 the 'unclubbable' attorney had published his own 'Life of Johnson', yet he was unwilling to release Johnson's papers to Boswell. Needless to add, he jealously held fast to anything that might assist a rival biographer. 'In this', Boswell wrote with delightful malevolence, 'he has not been very successful.' For on 29 June 1787, Boswell sent a letter to Frank in Lichfield: 'Sir John Hawkins having done gross injustice to the character of the great and good Dr. Johnson, and having written so injuriously of you and Mrs. Barber, as to deserve severe animadversion, and perhaps to be brought before the spiritual court, I cannot doubt of your inclination to afford me all the helps you can to state the truth fairly, in the Work which I am now preparing for the Press.'

Frank's reply was enthusiastic. He had received Boswell's letter with unspeakable satisfaction. 'The aspersions Sir John has thrown out against my master ... are entirely groundless, as also his assertion[s] concerning ... me.' Ultimately, and after much wrangling, Boswell got the Johnson papers from Hawkins, through Frank, the legal owner.[10]

In *The Gentleman's Magazine* for 1793 appeared an interesting description of Frank by a 'journalist' who met him in Lichfield. Frank, he said, was 'low of stature, marked with the small
pox, has lost his teeth; appears aged and infirm; clean and neat,
... Mr. Barber appears modest and humble, but to have associated with company superior to his rank in life.' He spent his
time in 'fishing, cultivating a few potatoes, and a little reading'.
Johnson's idea in recommending Frank to settle at Lichfield no
doubt was that in a small country town he would not be exposed
to the same temptations as in London. But the result was not very
successful. Frank's management of money was not judicious,
and he soon became improvident. Against this, however, must be
mentioned the fact that in retirement his health got steadily
worse, and with an ailing wife and delicate children, his expenses
were naturally greater than would otherwise have been the case.
Boswell occasionally sent money to him, and suggested to Frank
'opening a little shop for few books and stationery wares in Lichfield', but nothing came of it. Frank found himself compelled to
part with some of Johnson's belongings, for which, even at that
date, there would seem to have been a ready market. One of the
articles he sold was the gold watch retrieved from Hawkins with
so much bother. This watch was specially made for Johnson by
Mudge, the celebrated watchmaker, and was the regulator of the
famous Literary Club.

Frank was a celebrity in Lichfield, and no visitor arrived there
without searching for 'Dr. Johnson's faithful servant'. But in or
about 1796, the Barber family moved to Burntwood near Lichfield and Frank taught at a school there. Frank died in the Infir-
mary at Stafford, in January 1801, after undergoing 'a painful
operation'. Mrs. Barber's lot must have been hard when her husband died. His annuity died with him, if he had not already sold
the annuity and spent the capital. She stayed at Burntwood for a
while, but some time later she came back to Stowe Street, in
Lichfield, where she had lived with her husband. In 1810 the
Revd. Thomas Sedgwick Whalley reported in *The European
Magazine* that he had recently met Elizabeth Barber at Lichfield.
She and one of her daughters kept a day school for children. The
poor though 'sensible and well-informed' woman had had in her
possession many articles, formerly the property of Johnson,
which 'her necessities and not her will' had obliged her to part
with.

It is pleasant to have this testimony in favour of Elizabeth Barber from a level-headed man of the world. We cannot imagine
that this 'sensible and well-informed woman', who kept a school
for children, developed out of the shameless creature described

by Hawkins. Frank's widow survived him for fifteen years and died in April 1816, aged sixty.[11]

Francis and Elizabeth Barber had four children. One of their children, Samuel, became a preacher of note in the Primitive Methodist sect in Staffordshire. Samuel Barber and his wife Frances had six children, of whom one died young, and two emigrated to America. There are therefore Frank's descendants on both sides of the Atlantic.[12]

1. This chapter is based on Aleyn L. Reade, *Johnsonian Gleanings Part II: Francis Barber* (London, 1912), and Boswell's *Life of Johnson*, first edition, 1791. As there are several editions of Boswell's *Life*, it is not intended to cite any particular edition.

2. Reade, op. cit., pp. 11-14; Piozzi, *Anecdotes of the Late Samuel Johnson* (London, 1786), p. 212.

3. Reade, op. cit., pp. 17-23; Sir John Hawkins, *The Life of Samuel Johnson* (London, 1787), pp. 328 and 408; Boswell, op. cit.

4. Reade, op. cit., pp. 21, 25-30; Boswell, op. cit.

5. Yet it has been proclaimed that the views of Edward Long were rare!

6. Hawkins was referring to the incident, related by Mrs. Piozzi, when Frank and Betsy together with Johnson were with the Thrales in Streatham and 'Frank took offence at some affections paid his Desdemona'; Piozzi, op. cit., p. 211.

7. Reade, op. cit., pp. 27-9, 91, 99; Piozzi, op. cit., pp. 210-11; Hawkins, op. cit., p. 586n.

8. Reade, op. cit., pp. 33, 35-8, 46-51, 61; Hawkins, op. cit., pp. 586n and 602; Boswell, op. cit.

9. Reade, op. cit., pp. 49-54, 60-1; Hawkins, op. cit., pp. 328, 586n, 596, 601-2; James Prior, *Life of Edmund Malone* (London, 1860), p. 426.

10. Reade, op. cit., pp. 66-9.

11. Reade, op. cit., pp. 76-83; *The Gentleman's Magazine* (1801), I, p. 190; *The Gentleman's Magazine* (1818), I, p. 194.

12. 'Memoir of Samuel Barber', *The Primitive Methodist Magazine*, X (1829), pp. 81-90, 118-28; Reade, op. cit., pp. 95-102.

# 16

# Ignatius Sancho and Phillis Wheatley

Ignatius Sancho was born a slave in 1729, on a slave ship. He was born a few days after the ship carrying his parents away into slavery left the African coast. His mother died soon after his birth, and his father defeated the miseries of slavery by an act of suicide. At Carthagena, he received baptism from the hands of the bishop, and the name Ignatius. When he was little more than two years old, his master brought him to England, and presented him to three maiden sisters who lived at Greenwich. The petulence of their disposition surnamed him Sancho, from a fancied resemblance to the Squire of Don Quixote. In this respect, the maiden ladies reflected contemporary practice. They were thoroughly unpleasant to the African boy, subjected him to rigorous discipline and when angry threatened to return him to slavery in the West Indies. They deemed it imprudent to give him any education. Their prejudices had taught them that maintaining African ignorance was the only way to maintain obedience, and to enlarge the mind of their slave would go near to emancipating him. The views of the maiden ladies coincided perfectly with those of Sir John Fielding and the West Indian plantocracy. They were unhappy days for Ignatius. As he wrote later, 'The first part of my life was rather unlucky, as I was placed in a family who judge ignorance the best and only security for obedience. —A little reading and writing I got by unwearied application.'[1]

While still with the sisters, he attracted the attention of the Duke of Montagu, who lived at Blackheath and visited his mistresses. The Duke became his patron and indulged his turn for reading with presents of books. When about twenty years old, Ignatius Sancho did what many other black slaves did, he ran away from the maiden ladies, and eventually became a butler to the Montagus. His engagement as a butler in 1749 was the beginning of better days. 'The latter part of my life,' he wrote later, 'has been—thro' God's blessing, truly fortunate, having spent it in the service of one of the best families in the kingdom.'[2] Sancho now had abundant opportunities of satisfying his literary predilections. He read widely, studied poetry, and wrote some verses which were published. He also studied music and is said to have written and published a *Theory of Music*. According to the M.P., Joseph Jekyll, Sancho's *Theory of Music* was discussed, published, and dedicated to the Princess Royal. 'Painting was so much within the circle of Ignatius Sancho's judgement and criticism,' wrote Jekyll, 'that Mortimer came often to consult him.' He was visited too by Nollekens, the sculptor, and John Thomas Smith, author of *Vagabondiana* and Keeper of Prints in the British Museum. In November 1768, while at Bath, Gainsborough painted a portrait of Sancho at one rapid sitting. Gainsborough's picture of Sancho engraved by Bartolozzi is now in the National Gallery of Canada in Ottawa. In *Notes and Queries*, 8 June 1889, 'Wigan' expressed wonder that since, from the Gainsborough picture, Sancho 'is certainly a very ordinary looking individual, his lineaments should be handed down to posterity by artists of such eminence as the above-named painter and engraver.' In the 8 July 1889 issue of *Notes and Queries* William Norman replied, pointing out that the fact that several artists paid great deference to his opinion might account for the Gainsborough picture.[3] It is conjectured, too, that Sancho sat to Hogarth in 1742 for the black boy in *Taste in High Life*. At the time the picture was painted, Sancho was certainly older than the 'miniature Othello' depicted in *Taste in High Life*, though possibly Hogarth might have delineated what his stature would have been some years earlier.

Sancho had a passion for gambling and women. A particularly unsuccessful contest at cribbage, however, dampened his enthusiasm for gambling. His opponent won his clothes! He was a passionate theatre-goer too. Sancho loved the theatre to such a point of enthusiasm, Jekyll wrote, 'that his last shilling went to Drury-Lane, on Mr. Garrick's representation of Richard.' He became a friend of Garrick, who offered him the opportunity to play Othello and Oroonoko on the stage, 'but a defective and incorrigible articulation rendered it abortive'. He might have made a successful drama critic. Consider the following passage taken from a letter of his dated 25 August 1777:

I had an order from Mr. Henderson on Thursday night to see him do Falstaff—I put some money to it, and took Mary and Betsy [his daughters] with me—It was Betsy's first affair—and she enjoyed it in truth-—Henderson's Falstaff is entirely original—and I think as great as his Shylock: —He kept the house in a continual roar of laughter: —in some things he falls short of Quin—in many I think him equal. —When I saw Quin play, he was at the height of his art, with thirty years judgement to guide him. Henderson, in seven years more, will be all that better—and confessedly the first man on the English stage, or I am much mistaken.[4]

Sancho was also well acquainted with Garrick's erstwhile

Ignatius Sancho: literary figure
and friend of Johnson, Garrick,
and Sterne

Phillis Wheatley: poet whose
collection of verses *Poems on
Various Subjects* was published in
London in 1773

Olaudah Equiano: black Abolitionist and leader of the black
community

George Augustus Polgreen
Bridgetower: son of an African
adventurer and a Polish Countess:
he was a professional violinist

teacher, Dr. Johnson, to the extent that previous to the publication of Sancho's *Letters* in 1782, Johnson agreed to write a biographical sketch of Sancho to be prefixed to the *Letters*. But Johnson neglected to write the piece, and it was eventually written by Jekyll, in Johnsonian style. We may assume then, that Sancho and Francis Barber must have met, although we have no account of this.[5]

Sancho was on terms of even more intimate friendship with another literary man of the age, Laurence Sterne. He read, on their first publication, Sterne's sermons and *Tristram Shandy*, and was impressed by Sterne's sympathetic reference to the oppressed Africans. 'Consider slavery—what it is—how bitter a draught—and how many millions are made to drink it,' Sancho wrote to Sterne in July 1766, entreating him to give an hour's attention to slavery. For, 'of all my favourite authors, not one has drawn a tear in favour of my miserable black brethren— excepting yourself.' Sancho's hero replied in a sentimental vein, on 27 July 1766. 'I never look *westward* ... but I think of the burthens which our brothers and sisters are there carrying, and could I ease their shoulders from one ounce of them, I declare I would set out this hour upon a pilgrimage to Mecca for their sakes.' Sterne then struck up an acquaintance with his correspondent. In the spring of 1767, Sancho procured promises of subscriptions for the ninth volume of *Tristram Shandy* from the Duke and Duchess of Montagu and their son, Viscount Mandeville. In a letter dated 25 April 1767, Sterne, while thanking Sancho for securing the commitments, pressed 'my good Sancho' to demand the money immediately.[6]

When the Duchess of Montagu died in 1751, he was left £70 in money and an annuity of £30. Sancho now left the Montagu family thanks to the financial independence the bequest left him. But it was not for long. Women and gambling drained Sancho's purse, and after his abortive stage career, he soon resumed service with the Montagu family. Sancho now settled down, cured of his passion for women and gambling, and married a West Indian girl, Anne. Towards the end of 1773, repeated attacks of gout and 'a constitutional corpulence' forced Sancho to withdraw from service with the Montagu family, and he set up in business as a grocer in a shop in Charles Street, Westminster. In his retirement, Sancho had ample time to satisfy his literary tastes, and he spent his last years penning epistles in Sterne's style. Notables like Fox and the Duchess of Queensberry visited him in his shop. In June 1780, Nollekens and John Thomas Smith visited Sancho, and Nollekens made him a present of Sterne's bust. The two visitors 'drank tea with Sancho and his black lady'. And Smith confirmed that when Sancho visited Nollekens's studio 'he spake well of art'.[7]

From his shop, Sancho watched the Gordon Rioters, and his letters in those early days of June 1780 provide something of a brief running commentary on the activities of the mob, perhaps more absorbing than that of Dickens in *Barnaby Rudge*.

### June 6

This—this—is liberty! Genuine British liberty! —This instant about two hundred liberty-boys are swearing and swaggering by with large sticks.

Eight o'clock. —Lord George Gordon has this moment announced to my Lords the mob—that the act shall be repealed this evening: —Upon this, they gave a hundred cheers—took the horses from the hackney-coach—and rolled him full jollily away: —They are huzzaing now ready to crack their throats.

### June 9

The Fleet prison, the Marshalsea, King's Bench, both Compters, Clerkenwell, and Tothill Fields, with Newgate, are all flung open; Newgate partly burned, and 300 felons from thence only let loose upon the world. —Lord Mansfield's house in town suffered martyrdom; and his sweet box at Caen Wood escaped almost miraculously.

Half past nine o'clock.

King's-Bench prison is now in flames, and the prisoners at large; two fires in Holburn now burning.

Hyde Park has a grand encampment, with artillery park, &c. &c. St. James's Park has ditto, upon a smaller scale. The Parks, and our West end of town, exhibit the features of French Government. This minute, thank God! this moment Lord George Gordon is taken, Sir F. Molineux has him safe at the Horse-guards. Bravo! he is now going in state in an old hackney-coach, escorted by a regiment of militia a troop of light horse to his apartments in the Tower.[8]

In the Westminster election of 1780 Sancho campaigned for Fox, as he reveals in his letter of 7 September 1780. 'I attended the hustings from ten to half past two—gave my free vote to the Honourable Charles James Fox and to Sir George Rodney; hobbled home full of pain and hunger.' Two days later, he had the honour of Fox's 'thanks personally'.[9]

On 14 December 1780, in his fifty-first year, Sancho died in his shop and was buried in Westminster Broadway. His death is recorded in *The Gentleman's Magazine* as follows: 'In Charles-str. Westminster, Mr. Ignatius Sancho, grocer and oilman; a character immortalized by the epistolary correspondent of Sterne.'[10]

One of Sancho's correspondents, Miss F. Crewe, collected his letters and published them in 1782, in two volumes, with Joseph Jekyll's memoir of Sancho's life. The *Letters of the late Ignatius Sancho, an African* is, like *Soledad Brother: The Prison Letters of George Jackson*, a distinguished African of our time, an 'unwilled book', to borrow Jean Genet's phrase. In her editorial note, Miss Crewe stated that she thought it proper, in order to obviate an objection which she found had already been made, to say that Sancho's letters were not originally written with a view to publication. She declared categorically that no such idea was ever expressed by Sancho, and that 'not a single letter is here printed from any duplicate preserved by himself, but all have been collected from the various friends to whom they were addressed.' In his fervent preface to *Soledad Brother*, Genet writes, 'From the first letter to the last, nothing has been willed, written or composed for the sake of a book, yet here is a book ... an unwilled book.' 'As to the authenticity of Mr. Sancho's Letters,' the reviewer in the influential *Monthly Review* asserted, 'there is not "a loop to hang a doubt on". They are certainly the genuine productions of his private correspondence.' Miss Crewe expressly admitted that in collecting and publishing Sancho's letters, she had as one of her motives 'the desire of showing that an untutored African may possess abilities equal to an European.' Jekyll in his biographical sketch also drew attention to 'the extent of the intellect' of an African, 'whose species philosophers and anatomists have endeavoured to degrade as a deterioration of the human.' [11]

The subscription list for *Letters of the late Ignatius Sancho* is said to have been of a length unknown since the first issue of *The Spectator*, with well over 600 people subscribing. Numerous members of the British aristocracy were among the subscribers.

*The Monthly Review* could not review the first edition of the *Letters* in 1782 and had to wait for the publication of the second edition in the following year, because the first edition 'was sold with such rapidity that we could not procure a copy'. [12] It was well that the *Letters* was a best-seller. For Miss Crewe stated in her editorial note that, aside from the desire to show that an untutored African had abilities equal to a European, she had 'still [the] motive of wishing to serve his worthy family'. According to a note in Beeton's *Dictionary of Universal Information*, 'From the profits of the first edition, and a sum paid by the booksellers for liberty to print a second edition, Mrs. Sancho, we are well assured, received more than [£]500.' [13]

Sancho left a widow and six children. A year after his death, *The Monthly Review* stated that 'Mrs. [Anne] Sancho still keeps the same shop in Charles-street.' [14] Again and again in his letters

Sancho mentioned his children or 'Sanchonets' as he referred to them. In December 1777 Sancho says he was 'a poor starving Negroe, with six children.'[15] In another letter, he referred to his 'six brats, and a wife'.[16] In a letter dated 1 November 1773 Sancho revealed that 'Mrs. Sancho is in the straw—she has given me a fifth wench'.[17] The sixth child was a boy William (Billy), born 20 October 1775. Reading through the *Letters* we gather that the names of the five girls were Fanny, Mary, Betsy (Elizabeth), Lydia, and Kitty (Katherine). According to Sancho, Billy was 'the type of his father—fat—heavy—sleepy'.[18] For some time Billy worked in the library of Sir Joseph Banks, the botanist, whose mother had co-operated with Granville Sharp in the rescuing of Thomas Lewis in 1770. Eventually, he carried on the business of bookseller in his father's shop, and in 1803 he brought out the fifth edition of his father's *Letters*. Little else is known of Billy and the five girls.

Although Sancho himself never experienced West Indian slavery, he had read and heard about that hell in the sunshine, so that when the maiden ladies threatened to send him there, he made it clear it would be done only over his dead body. After reading Abolitionist tracts a friend had sent to him, Sancho, thanking the friend for giving him the opportunity of perusal, lashed out at the 'most diabolical usage' of his brothers, and denounced 'the horrid wickedness' of the slave trade. He lamented that the grand object of the English navigator, 'indeed all Christian navigators—is money—money—money'. He condemned, too, the treachery of petty chiefs and kings in Africa, who encouraged their Christian customers to supply them with strong liquors to 'enflame their national madness' and with powder and fire-arms, which 'furnish them with the hellish means of killing and kidnapping'.[19] On the whole, however, Sancho managed to contain his anger and anguish at slavery and the slave trade. This has enabled a modern reviewer of his *Letters*, Paul Edwards, to say that 'it must be acknowledged, in spite of occasional hints of tensions and ironies, that Sancho's letters point clearly to his almost complete assimilation into 18th-century English society'.[20] Ignatius Sancho, friend of artists and men of letters, was always a 'nigger' first. To prove the point (if any proof were needed) he began his first letter to Sterne thus, 'I am one of those people whom the vulgar and the illiberal call Negurs.' In another letter to an English friend he wrote, 'I thank you for your kindness to my poor black brethren. ... my soul melts at kindness—but the contrary—I own—with shame makes me almost a savage.'[21] The apology was unnecessary. Again and again, Sancho emphasized his Africanness. At one stage, while reporting the mindless violence of the Gordon Rioters in 1780, he exclaimed, 'I am not sorry I was born in Afric.'[22] In one letter he referred to himself as 'a poor Blacky grocer',[23] and elsewhere, in similar vein, he asked his correspondent, 'Figure to yourself, my dear Sir, a man of a convexity of belly exceeding Falstaff—and a black face into the bargain.'[24] And we have Sancho saying in 1779 that far from being a Black Englishman, he was an African merely domiciled in England. Commenting on British difficulties in that year he observed:

In faith, my friend, the present time is rather *comique*—Ireland almost in as true a state of rebellion as America—Admirals quarrelling in the West-Indies—and at home Admirals that do not chuse to fight—The British Empire mouldering away in the West, annihilated in the North—Gibraltar going—and England fast asleep. What says Mr. B——— to all this? he is ministerialist: —for my part, it's nothing to me, as I am only a lodger, and hardly that.[25]

We have already conjectured that Sancho must have known Frank. There is no doubt, however, that Sancho was well acquainted with Soubise. In his biographical sketch Jekyll tells us, 'The late Duchesses of Queensberry and Northumberland pressed forward to serve the author of [the Letters]. The former intrusted to his reformation a very unworthy favourite of his own complexion.' There is no doubt that the 'unworthy favourite' whom Sancho was asked by Kitty Duchess of Queensberry to reform was Soubise. Letter XIV was clearly written to Soubise, and from the contents we have a good idea of how Sancho went about reforming Soubise, and the latter's reaction to Sancho's admonitions:

To Mr. S———e.

Richmond, Oct. 11, 1772.

Your letter gave me more pleasure than in truth I ever expected from your hands—but thou art a flatterer; —why dost thou demand advice of me? Young man, thou canst not discern wood from trees; —with awe and reverence look up to thy more than parents—look up to thy almost divine benefactors—search into the motive of every glorious action—retrace thine own history—and when you are convinced that they (like the All-gracious Power they serve) go about in mercy doing good—retire abashed at the number of their virtues—and humbly beg the Almighty to inspire and give you strength to imitate them. —Happy, happy lad! what a fortune is thine! Look round upon the miserable fate of almost all of our unfortunate colour—superadded to ignorance, —see slavery, and the contempt of those very wretches who roll in affluence from our labours.[26] Superadded to this woeful catalogue—hear the ill-bred and heart-racking abuse of the foolish vulgar. —You, S[ou-bis]e, tread as cautiously as the strictest rectitude can guide ye—yet must you suffer from this—but armed with truth—honesty—and conscious integrity—you will be sure of the plaudit and countenance of the good. —If, therefore, thy repentance is sincere—I congratulate thee as sincerely upon it—it is thy birth-day to real happiness. —Providence has been very lavish of her bounty to you—and you are deeply in arrear to her—your parts are as quick as most men's; urge but your speed in the race of virtue with the same ardency of zeal as you have exhibited in error—and you will recover, to the satisfaction of your noble patrons—and to the glory of yourself. —Some philosopher—I forget who—wished for a window in his breast—that the world might see his heart; —he could only be a great fool, or a very good man: —I will believe the latter, and recommend him to your imitation. —Vice is a coward; —to be truly brave, a man must be truly good; you hate the name of cowardice—then, S[oubis]e, avoid it—detest a lye and shun lyars—be above revenge; —if any have taken advantage either of your guilt or distress, punish them with forgiveness—and not only so—but, if you can serve them any future time, do it—You have experienced mercy and long-sufferance in your own person—therefore gratefully remember it, and shew mercy likewise.

I am pleased with the subject of your last—and if your conversion is real, I shall ever be happy in your correspondence—But at the same time I cannot afford to pay five pence for the honour of your letters; five pence is the twelfth part of five shillings—the forty-eighth part of a pound—it would keep my girls in potatoes two days. —The time may come, when it may be necessary for you to study calculations;[27] in the mean while, if you cannot get a frank, direct to me under cover to his Grace the Duke of [Montagu] You have the best wishes of your sincere friend (as long as you are your own friend)

IGNATIUS SANCHO.

You must excuse blots and blunders—for I am under the dominion of a cruel head-ache—and a cough, which seems too fond of me.[28]

Two days after Soubise left the country for India the Duchess died. Recording how he heard of her death, Sancho wrote in a letter dated 23 July 1777, 'Never so struck in my life!' A week before her death, 'I had the honor of a long audience in her dressing-room.' On the day after she died, Sancho was just preparing for his 'concluding pipe' when one of the servants of the Montagu family came to his shop to break the bad news. Having seen her so recently, he 'felt fifty different sensations'. Later Sancho wrote to Soubise informing him that his benefactress and patroness 'entered into the bliss, July 17, 1777, just two days after you sailed from Portsmouth'.[29]

In 1761, at the age of eight, an African girl was kidnapped on the African coast and transported to America. There she was sold to John Wheatley of Boston, New England. Phillis Wheatley, the African girl in question, had no formal education, but she received some instruction from her owner's family, and learnt the English language. Within sixteen months from the time of her arrival, she was able to speak and write in perfect English. She soon started writing poems. Phillis also became quite proficient in Latin, and, besides writing verses, she translated Lavallée's *Le Nègre comme il y a peu de Blancs* ('Negroes Equalled by few Europeans').

Phillis Wheatley arrived in England in 1772, and was the guest of the Countess of Huntingdon, to whom she dedicated her book of poems, which was published in London in 1773. She was subsequently entertained by Lord Dartmouth and other members of the English aristocracy.[30] In order to remove any doubt that Phillis really wrote the verses, an attestation of authenticity was inserted in the book. The subscribers were the leading New England men of the time. Heading the list was Thomas Hutchinson, the Loyalist Governor, followed by his Lieutenant-Governor. The name of Phillis's master was last. Three of the subscribers were entitled to the prefix 'Honourable', three were Squires, and five were Doctors of Divinity. The eighteen subscribers attested as follows: 'We, whose names are underwritten, do assure the World, that the Poems specified in the following Pages were, (as we verily believe) written by Phillis, a young African Girl, who was but a few years since, brought an uncultivated barbarian from Africa, and has ever since been, and now is, under the disadvantage of serving as a slave in a Family in this Town [Boston]. She has been examined by some of the best Judges, and is thought qualified to write them.'[31]

It is not known whether Sancho and Phillis ever met, but, since during her stay in England she moved in the circles where Sancho had friends and admirers, they probably did. At any rate, in his letter of 27 January 1778, Sancho had some caustic things to say about the good white folks of Boston who made the attestation:

Phyllis's poems do credit to nature—and put art—merely as art—to the blush. —It reflects nothing either to the glory or generosity of her master—if she is still his slave—except he glories in the *low vanity* of having in his wanton power a mind animated by Heaven—a genius superior to himself. —The list of splendid—titled—learned names, in confirmation of her being the real authoress—alas! shows how very poor the acquisition of wealth and knowledge is—without generosity—feeling—and humanity.[32]

In *Black Abolitionists*, Benjamin Quarles notes that, 'At some time or other an abolitionist weekly would reprint stanzas from Phillis Wheatley, along with the bittersweet story of her life.'[33] The practice was by no means confined to America. For, after all, her book of poems was first published in London. On 14 July 1789, two days after William Wilberforce moved his first motion against the slave trade in the House of Commons, the London daily newspaper, *The Diary*, printed Phillis Wheatley's poem, 'An Hymn to Humanity'. In the issue of 16 May 1789, *The Diary* had reprinted her epistle to William, Earl of Dartmouth, wherein she gives this account of herself:

> Should you MY LORD, while you peruse my song,
> Wonder from whence my love of FREEDOM sprung,
> Whence flow these wishes for the common good
> By feeling hearts alone well understood.
> I, young in life, by seeming cruel fate,
> Was snatch'd from AFRIC's fancy'd happy seat;
> What pangs excruciating must molest,
> What sorrows labour in my parents breast?
> Steel'd was that soul and by no mis'ry mov'd
> That from a father seiz'd his babe belov'd;
> Such—such my case; and can I then but pray
> Others may never feel tyrannic sway?

DuBois, in *Darkwater*, observed that, 'This child, Phillis Wheatley, sang her trite and halting strain to a world that wondered and could not produce her like. Measured today her muse was slight and yet, feeling her striving spirit, we call to her still in her own words: "Through thickest glooms look back, immortal shade."'[34]

In Europe and America, champions of Africans were wont to cite Phillis Wheatley and Ignatius Sancho as examples of African genius and of what the African could achieve and be if freed from his bondage. John Gabriel Stedman in his *Narrative* mentioned the vocal melody, music, and dancing of the Africans which was perfectly to time, and continued, 'that these people are neither divest of a good ear, nor poetical genius, has been frequently proved.' He then alluded to the 'thirty-eight elegant pieces of poetry' by Phillis Wheatley, and, as a specimen, he inserted an extract from 'Thoughts on Imagination'. The sentimental letters of Ignatius Sancho, he avowed, 'would not disgrace the pen of an European'.[35] William Dickson wrote, in his *Letters on Slavery*, 'To the Latin ode of Francis Williams, the beautiful poetical pieces of Phillis Wheatly [sic], and the letters of Ignatius Sancho, we appeal for specimens of *African Literature*. Have their calumniators obliged the literary world with any such specimens?'[36] Likewise, Peter Peckard commented:

Phyllis Whatley [sic], though not a Poetess of the first rank, has written Poems, all circumstances fairly considered, that are of great and uncommon merit. ... As to moral and epistolary writing, Ignatius Sancho in his Letters that are already published, had done honour to himself, and to Human Nature. There are other Manuscripts, yet unpublished, which the author of these pages has seen, that also have great merit. His Epistles in general breathe the purest and most genuine Spirit of Universal Benevolence; and some of those that are still in Manuscript contain most excellent instructions to a young Gentleman of the University [of Cambridge] for his literary, his moral, and his religious conduct in the course of his education. In those that are published we see even an enthusiastic zeal for the undoubted rights of man, and for the interest of true Religion. And this Man, this rational and moral writer, this able assistant, and conductor of youth in liberal education, this enthusiast in the duties of Universal Benevolence and Evangelical Religion, this exalted Being must be thrust down from the ranks of Men, because the tincture of his skin is black. Oh! shame! shame![37]

Clarkson, too, in *Commerce of Human Species*, inserted some of Phillis's verses, after which he wrote, 'I shall only beg leave to accompany it with this observation, that if the authoress *was* designed for slavery, (as the argument must confess) the greater part of the inhabitants of Britain must lose their claim to freedom.' Writing four years after the publication of Sancho's *Letters*, Clarkson remarked that the *Letters* were too well known to make any extract or indeed any further mention of them necessary.[38] He continued: 'But an objection will be made here, that the two persons whom I have particularized by name, are prodigies, and that if we were to live many years, we should scarcely meet with two other Africans of the same description. But I reply, that if these are prodigies, they are only such prodigies as every day would produce, if they had the same opportunities of acquiring knowledge as other people, and the same expectation in life to excite their genius.'[39]

But there were disparaging notes here and there. Thomas Jefferson, in *Notes on the State of Virginia*, brusquely dismissed Phillis Wheatley and Ignatius Sancho. It was his opinion that 'Religion ... produced a Phillis Whatley [sic]; but it could not produce a poet.' Although, in 1776, George Washington had written to Phillis that he would 'be happy to see' at his headquarters at any time a person 'to whom nature has been so liberal and beneficial in her dispensation',[40] Jefferson asserted in *Notes* that her verses were 'below the dignity of criticism'. He said that Sancho affected 'a Shandean fabrication of words', and that, although amongst men of his own colour he might be *primus inter pares*, he was a nonentity when compared with European writers. The conclusion was inevitable since Jefferson was also of the opinion that blacks 'are inferior to whites in endowments both of body and mind'. Gilbert Imlay, in the ninth letter of his *Topographical Description*, pointed out that Jefferson in *Notes* 'has given Europeans a flagrant proof of his prejudices. ... I have been ashamed in reading Mr. Jefferson's book, to see, from one of the most enlightened and benevolent of my countrymen, disgraceful prejudices he entertains against the unfortunate [blacks].'[41] Jefferson's phrase, 'Religion ... produced a Phillis Whatley; but it could not produce a poet', he dismissed as another of Jefferson's prejudiced dogmas. He quoted part of Phillis's poem on Imagination:

> Imagination! who can sing thy force?
> Or who describe the swiftness of thy course?
> Soaring through the air to find the bright abode,
> Th' imperial palace of the thund'ring God,
> We on thy pinions can surpass the wind,
> And leave the rolling universe behind:
> From star to star the mental optics rove,
> Measure the skies and range the realms above;
> There is one view we grasp the mighty whole,
> Or with new worlds amaze th' unbounded soul.

'It will afford you an opportunity', declared Imlay, 'of estimating her genius and Mr. Jefferson's judgement; and I think, without any disparagement to him, that, by comparison, Phillis appears much the superior. Indeed, I should be glad to be informed what white upon this continent has written more beautiful lines.'[42] Imlay also observed that 'Jefferson has been equally severe upon Ignatius Sancho. But, as I have not the honour to be acquainted with Mr. Sancho's writings, I shall conclude that that criticism is equally marked with prejudice.'[43] Jefferson sometimes wrote like an Abolitionist, but at other times he could reel off the gospel according to slavocracy.[44] In *Notes on the State of Virginia* he gave powerful support to the advocates of African inferiority. Nevertheless, after making several moral reflections upon the subject of slavery, he concluded in these famous words: 'Indeed, I tremble for my country, when I reflect that GOD is just: —that his justice cannot sleep for ever: that, considering numbers, nature, and natural means only, a revolution of the wheel of fortune, an exchange of situation, is among possible events: that it may become probable by supernatural interference! The ALMIGHTY has no attribute which can take side with us in such a contest.'

After quoting these words, Imlay observed:

You see, my dear friend, how powerful is the effect of habit and prejudice; that with ideas and principles founded in reason and truth, sufficient to demonstrate that slavery destroys the energy of the human mind, and with a heart which does honour to Mr. Jefferson as a man, his mind is so warped by education and the habit of thinking, that he has attempted to make it appear that the African is a being between the human species and the oranoutang; and ridiculously suffered his imagination to be carried away with idle tales of that animal's embracing the African women, in preference to the females of its own species.[45]

GREAT GOD! how long is the world to be tantalized with such paltry sophistry and non-sense![46]

In 1754, in a famous footnote to his essay 'Of National Character', David Hume dismissed out of hand the suggestion that Francis Williams was a man of parts and learning, and stated disparagingly that ''tis likely he is admired for very slender accomplishments, like a parrot who speaks a few words plainly.' This was to be expected from one who earlier in the same footnote had said that he was apt to suspect that Africans were 'naturally inferior to the whites. ... There never was a civilized nation of any other complexion than white, nor even individuals eminent either in action or speculation. No ingenious manufactures amongst them, no arts, no sciences.' Thus, without knowing it, Hume and Jefferson dismiss the Benin bronzes, the Ife terracottas, the golden stool of the Ashantehenne, the treasures of Tutankhamen, the marvels of Zimbabwe, Black music, and so on.

In an equally famous passage in *Commerce of the Human Species*, Clarkson reminded Hume that in servitude the African race had produced Phillis Wheatley and Ignatius Sancho: 'If the minds of the African were unbroken by slavery, if they had the same expectations in life as other people, and the same opportunities for improvement, either in the colonies or upon the coast, they would be equal, in all the various branches of science, to the Europeans, and that the argument that states them ''to be an inferior link of the chain of nature, and designed for servitude'', as far it depends on the *inferiority* of their capacities, is wholly malevolent and false.'[47]

Clarkson did not feel himself obliged to deal with Hume's assertions with respect to African capability. He had passed them over in silence, as they had been so admirably refuted by the learned Dr. Beattie, in his 'Essay on Truth'. Beattie finished his celebrated essay in 1767. Demolishing the central thesis of Hume's racist ideology, he wrote:

It will be readily allowed that the condition of a slave is not favourable to genius of any kind; and yet the black-slaves dispersed over Europe, have often discovered symptoms of ingenuity, notwithstanding their unhappy circumstances. They become excellent handicraftsmen, and practical musicians ... That a Black slave, who can neither read nor write, nor speak any European language, who is not permitted to do anything but what his master commands, who has not a single friend on earth, but is universally considered and treated as if he were a species inferior to the human; that such a creature should so distinguish himself among Europeans, as to be talked of through the world for a man of genius, is surely no reasonable expectation. To suppose him of an inferior species, because he does not thus distinguish himself, is just as rational, as to suppose any private European of an inferior species, because he has not raised himself to the condition of royalty.[48]

Without doubt Ignatius Sancho inspired the figure of Shirna Cambo in the anonymous *Memoirs and Opinions of Mr. Blenfield* (1790), published ten years after Sancho's death. After Shirna's parents are betrayed into slavery, his father perishes 'by the fury of his own arm', and his mother pines away on board the slave ship. Just as the Duke of Montagu patronized Sancho, the master of Shirna values his 'lively' disposition and 'generous temper', and sends him to England, where he 'asserted his birthright of human nature'. Having, like Sancho, married a black woman and lived with 'domestic virtue', Shirna enters business. Blenfield says of Shirna, 'his philanthropy and integrity were the examples and admiration of his neighbourhood.' (In his memoir, Joseph Jekyll had written that Sancho's life of domestic virtue 'engaged private patronage and merited public imitation'.) Like Sancho, Shirna reveals a 'wild patriotism' with 'indignation flashing from his eye. ... It was in *his* conversation, that I first learned the disgrace, the indelible shame of my country; here I caught that just enthusiasm for freedom, which has accompanied me through life.'[49]

As we have seen, Sancho was just preparing for his 'concluding pipe' when he learnt of the death of Kitty, Duchess of Queensberry. Sancho was well known as a pipe smoker, so much so that one brand of tobacco was named 'Sancho's best Trinidado' after him. In 1888 the journal *Tobacco* published a series of memoirs of 'Some Old Tobacconists'. In the issue of *Tobacco* for 1 June 1888, well over 100 years after his death, Sancho was featured as one of the 'Old Tobacconists'. The Gainsborough portrait of Sancho is reproduced as well as a woodcut depicting a cask of tobacco, over which is inscribed, on a scroll, 'Sancho's best Trinidado'. The article, signed by 'Gillespie', is largely a reproduction of Jekyll's memoir plus a citation of a couple of Sancho's letters. But before reproducing the letters, 'Gillespie' makes the following observation:

It is only in his letters that we are enabled to obtain a glimpse of the true nobility of his mind. Without James Boswell, how little would the world know of the master mind of the great Samuel Johnson! Between Johnson and Ignatius Sancho there was much in common. Physically, they were both corpulent and unwieldy in their persons; intellectually, they were giants, their minds ranging over a large area, and easily assimilating, and quick to appreciate the characters and facts which surrounded them. Socially, they were in their habits domestic, and in their aspirations noble. Johnson, however, had his biographer; it is regrettable that Ignatius Sancho did not meet with his Boswell.

1. Ignatius Sancho, *Letters of the late Ignatius Sancho, An African* (London, 1803), 5th ed., pp. 70-1. Notes on his early life are taken from the memoir of Ignatius Sancho, written by Joseph Jekyll M.P. and prefixed to the *Letters*, pp. i-ix.

2. Ibid., p. 71.

3. *Notes and Queries*, 7th Series, VII (1889), pp. 325, 427, 457; VIII (1889), pp. 32, 296, 336.

4. Sancho, op. cit., Letter XLVIII, pp. 98-9.

5. The account of Frank and 'his African countrymen ... sitting round a fire in the gloomy anti-room', Reade says, is the only record we possess of Frank consorting with his black brethren (Reade, *Johnsonian Gleanings Part II: Francis Barber* (London, 1912), p. 15). Nevertheless, the inference I have drawn is valid and plausible. There is no doubt, too, that Frank must have known Reynolds's black servant very well, although again we have no evidence of this.

6. Laurence Sterne, *Letters*, ed. G. Saintsbury (London, 1894), I, pp. 130-1; II, p. 18.

7. John Thomas Smith, *Nollekens and His Times* (London, 1828), pp. 26-9.

8. Sancho, op. cit., Letters CXXXIV-CXXXVI, pp. 271-7.

9. Ibid., Letters CXLVI-CXLVII, pp. 295-6.

10. *The Gentleman's Magazine* (1780), p. 591.

11. Sancho, op. cit. (1782), I, pp. iii-iv; Sancho, op. cit. (1803), 5th ed., p. vii; George Jackson, *Soledad Brother: The Prison Letters of George Jackson* (London, 1971), pp. 17 and 23; *The Monthly Review*, CXIX (1783), pp. 492-3.

12. *The Monthly Review*, CXIX (1783), p. 492n.

13. Samuel Orchart Beeton, *Dictionary of Universal Information* (London, 1877), p. 97n.

14. *The Monthly Review*, CXIX (1783), p. 494.

15. Letter LVI, (1803), 5th ed., p. 120.

16. Letter VIII, p. 19.

17. Letter XVI, pp. 35-6.

18. Letter XXXIII, p. 66.

19. Letter LVIII, pp. 125-6; Letter LXVIII, pp. 147-51.

20. Sancho, *Letters* (London, 1968), p. xv.

21. Letter XIII (1803), 5th ed., p. 30.

22. Letter CXXXIV, p. 273.

23. Letter CXIV, p. 231.

24. Letter CXVIII, p. 238.

25. Letter CV, pp. 213-14.

26. This is hardly the phrase a black assimilated to eighteenth-century English middle- and upper-class society would use. Note that he used the words 'our labours'.

27. In 1772, the year of the Somerset decree, Sancho was forty-three years old, and Soubise must have been in his twenties.

28. Letter XIV, pp. 31-3.

29. Letter XLIV, pp. 86-8; Letter LXXX, pp. 171-4. The second letter, dated 29 November 1778, was addressed to Soubise in India. If, as Miss Crewe avowed in her editorial note, all the letters printed were from the originals, knowing that Soubise died in India, we are forced to ask the question: How did she obtain the original of the letter Sancho wrote to Soubise? Possibly, after Soubise's death in India, his personal effects were returned to England. Or, less plausibly, Miss Crewe wrote to India, asking for Sancho's letters to Soubise.

30. Phillis Wheatley, *Poems on Various Subjects* (London,1773); *Poems and Letters*, ed. C. F. Heartman (New York, 1913), p. 10.

31. Ibid., ed. Heartman, p. 1.

32. Letter LVIII, pp. 126-7. Yet Wylie Sypher claimed, 'Sancho has little enough, aside from his correspondence with Sterne, to say on the enslaving of his race.' *Guinea's Captive Kings*, p. 149. He could not have read the *Letters* properly, for nothing could be further from the truth.

33. Benjamin Quarles, op. cit., p. 35.

34. W. E. B. Dubois, op. cit., p. 177.

35. J[ohn] G[abriel] Stedman, *Narrative of a Five Years' Expedition, against the Revolted Negroes of Surinam and Guiana* ... (London, 1796), I, pp. 259-60.

36. William Dickson, op. cit., pp. 76-7.

37. [Peter Peckard], *Am I Not A Man? And A Brother? With All Humility Addressed to the British Legislature* (Cambridge, 1788), pp. 18-20. The letters in manuscript adverted to by Peckard were never published. But for an example of Sancho as an able conductor of youth in liberal education, etc., see Letter LXVIII, pp. 147-53.

38. Clarkson was quite right. Thus in March 1789, seven years after the publication of the first edition, one of the subscribers, Mrs. Boscawen, wrote in a letter, 'What do you think I am reading. You will never guess. Sancho's letters, some dated from Richmond, as he was, you know, butler to the Duke of Montagu. They are very curious, for a poor black servant, and amuse me very well. You have seen them long since I dare say.' Quoted from Cecil A. Oglander, *Admiral's Wife* (London, 1940), pp. 138-9.

39. Thomas Clarkson, *An Essay on the Slavery and Commerce of the Human Species, particularly the African* (London, 1788), 2nd. ed., pp. 120-3.

40. W. E. B. DuBois, *Darkwater*, p. 177.

41. Gilbert Imlay, *Topographical Description of Western Territory of North America* (London, 1792), p. 185.

42. Ibid., p. 198. Imlay also stated that 'a black in New England has composed an ephemeris, which I have seen, and which men conversant in the science of astronomy declare exhibits marks of acute reason and genius', op. cit., pp. 196-7.

43. Ibid., p. 199.

44. Jefferson was, of course, himself a slave owner, and is said to have had two daughters, by his housekeeper-mistress, one of his female slaves. William Wells Brown's *Clotel or The President's Daughter*, first published in London in 1853, is

an account of the slave life of one of his daughters.

45. This coming from one who fathered slave children!

46. Gilbert Imlay, op. cit., pp. 200-1.

47. Clarkson, op. cit., p. 126.

48. James Beattie, *An Essay on the Nature and Immutability of Truth, In Opposition to Sophistry and Scepticism* (London, 1770), pp. 481-2; Clarkson, op. cit., p. 126n.

49. Wylie Sypher, op. cit., p. 285.

# 17

# Ira Aldridge

Before Paul Robeson there was Ira Aldridge. Ira Frederick Aldridge was born in New York on 24 July 1807.[1] As a child he attended the African Free School conducted by the New York Manumission Society. Ira Aldridge's father, Daniel, was a clergyman, and he intended his son for the church. But minor roles by Ira Aldridge at the African Theatre, New York, sharpened his appetite for acting, and convinced him that he was meant for the stage rather than the pulpit. However, a black actor had little prospect of furthering his career in America. Accordingly he resolved to try his luck in England. Aldridge shipped as a steward on a vessel bound for Liverpool. It happened that James Wallack, the English actor, was a passenger in the same vessel. Wallack engaged Aldridge as his personal attendant during the voyage. After arrival in Liverpool in 1825, Aldridge made his way to London.

Within a year of his arrival in England, Ira Aldridge made his first appearance in the English theatre, on 10 October 1825 at the Royal Coburg Theatre. He was styled on the posters as 'The African Roscius' after Quintus Roscius Gallus, the great Roman actor. His début was advertised as 'First night of the celebrated American Tragedian in a new and most effective melodramatic romance called *The Revolt of Surinam or a Slave's Revenge*'. The critics flocked to the Coburg to witness the novelty of a black man on the London stage. In a long and contorted review in *The Times* of the following day, the reviewer dismissed Aldridge as an actor, saying 'excepting for his colour, he will not be known from the rest of the *corps.*' But other critics disagreed. *The Globe*, 11 October 1825, observed that Aldridge's 'enunciation is distinct and sonorous, ... he looks his character.' *The Morning Advertiser* reported, 'A very novel performance excited much attention last night. ... [Aldridge was] evidently a man of much observation, and had a very excellent conception of the character, which he performed in a manner so as to receive the approbation of a numerous audience.' Even *The Times* conceded that 'The African Roscius played the part of Oroonoko probably as well as was necessary.' As will be seen later, *The Times* maligned Aldridge's performance because he was black. The fact of the matter was that Ira Aldridge's début was an unqualified success.

He was kept for another week, and appeared in another West Indian melodrama *The Ethiopian, or the Quadroon of the Mango Grove*.

While appearing at the Coburg, he met and married a Yorkshire girl, Margaret Gill. She was twenty-eight years old, ten years older than Aldridge. According to Edward Scobie in *Black Britannia*, this marriage angered the pro-slavery forces in London with the result that the black actor was shunned for one whole year. Many pro-slavery newspapers and journals, which were mouth-pieces for the powerful sugar, coffee, tobacco, and cotton barons, the estate and plantation owners, and slave traders of the West Indies, organized vile smear campaigns against him.[2]

He was forced to try his luck in provincial theatres. His first provincial appearance was at the Theatre Royal, Brighton. Then followed the main towns and cities in Britain: Liverpool, Manchester, Bristol, Newcastle, Edinburgh, Lancaster, Sunderland, Wolverhampton, Northampton, Derby, Aberdeen. He was a great success. But it was at the Theatre Royal, Dublin, on 7 December 1831, that he reached the high point of his tour. When Edmund Kean, the celebrated actor, saw Aldridge play Othello, Kean not only complimented him highly, but gave him a letter of introduction to the manager of the Theatre Royal, Bath. In his letter dated 3 January 1832, Kean wrote: 'Dear Bellamy,—I beg to introduce to your notice Mr. Aldridge, the African Roscius, whose performance I have witnessed with great pleasure. He possesses wondrous versatility, and I am sure, under your judicious generalship, will prove a card in Bath.'

His first performance in Bath was in *Othello*. The *Bath Journal*, 26 January 1832, reported in its review:

We have seen *Othello* by our best actors, whose points dwelling vividly in our remembrance, gave little disparagement in their recurrence, while the African Roscius, in some particulars, gave freshness of novelty and throughout his performance, evinced nothing but the emanations of sterling self-thinking treasures from his own laboratory. In pronunciation, he is exceedingly correct, and in his reading most clear and distinct, in his countenance animated, in expression forcible, in deportment graceful. The whole of the part was exceedingly well executed and our admiration of the actor was felt by all who witnessed him.[3]

After Bath, Aldridge started another provincial tour, proceeding as far as Aberdeen, including a long run, his second, in Hull. His basic repertoire was *Othello*, *Oroonoko*, *The Slave*, *The*

*Castle Spectre*, and *The Revenge*. When these black roles became monotonous, he expanded his repertoire to include roles specifically written for white actors—Macbeth, Shylock, King Lear, Richard III, Titus Andronicus.

On his return to London, Ira Aldridge was billed to play Othello at Covent Garden. His Desdemona was to be Ellen Tree, later the wife of Charles Kean, who was himself cast as Iago. On its being understood that he was about to appear at the premier English theatre in the character of Othello, several newspapers published articles tending to condemn, or rather 'to annihilate him unheard, and to question the propriety of his being allowed a trial upon the boards of the principal London Theatre'.⁴ One newspaper went even further and shouted 'Aldridge shall be jammed to atoms by the relentless power of critical "BATTERING RAM" if his name is not immediately withdrawn from the Bills!!!'⁵ Actor friends of Aldridge from the Garrick Club rallied to his cause. They printed and distributed handbills on behalf of Ira Aldridge pleading, 'To condemn unheard is contrary to the character and known liberality of Englishmen. We beg of a London audience "fair play" on his behalf when he makes his début Wednesday next.' The handbill was signed 'Crito'. Ira Aldridge did appear in *Othello* for two or four nights⁶ at Covent Garden, in April 1833. And in disregard of the plea of 'Crito', some newspapers and critics did subject the black tragedian to their critical 'battering ram'. *The Times* of 11 April 1833 commented:

An experiment and not a remarkably successful one, as the emptiness of the house incontestably proved was last night essayed here. The tragedy of Othello was performed, the part of the Moor [was played] by an individual of Negro origin, ... who calls himself Aldridge, and who has been facetiously nicknamed The African Roscius: Such an exhibition is well enough at Sadler's Wells, or at Bartholomew Fair, but it certainly is not very creditable to a great national establishment.

We could not perceive any fitness which Mr. Aldridge possessed for the assumption of one of the finest parts that was ever imagined by Shakespeare ... Mr. Aldridge's Othello, with all the advantages of *hic niger est*, wanted spirit and feeling. His accent is unpleasantly, and we would say vulgarly foreign; his manner, generally, drawling and unimpressive; and when by chance (for chance it is, and not judgement) he rises to a higher strain, we perceive in the transition the elevation of rant, not the fiery dignity of soul-felt passion.

*The Times*, the supposed symbol of all that is virtuous and noble in British journalism, made no secret of why it hated Ira Aldridge: 'In the name of common propriety and decency, we protest against an interesting actress and lady-like girl, like Miss

Ellen Tree, being subjected to the indignity of being pawed by Mr. Henry Wallack's black servant.'

*The Morning Post* grudgingly admitted that 'His figure is tall and noble, and his manner of walking the stage is dignified, and speaks long familiarity with the board.' Although his enunciation was strikingly un-English, 'he possesses a fine, full, melodious voice.' Then comes the low-down: 'Our opinion of his performance as a whole may be surmised when we say that our impression was, at the conclusion of the play, that any person with sufficient discretion not grossly to overstep the modesty of nature would obtain a certain no. of rounds of applause in *Othello*. ... To sum up its merits, it was doubtless sufficiently good to be considered very curious, but it was not an Othello for Covent Garden Theatre, where we do not, or rather should not go to witness mere curiosities.'

*The Athenaeum* condescendingly reported to its readers that, 'it is extraordinary that under all circumstances, a natural quickness and aptitude for imitation, should enable him to get through such a part as Othello with so little positive offence as he does.' *The Spectator* arrived at the same conclusion after sententiously remarking at the outset that an African was no more qualified to play Othello by the virtue of his colour alone, than a huge fat white man would be competent to play Falstaff. Aldridge, *The Spectator* reported, 'evinced a great deal of feeling and nature in his performance: these, indeed, were its redeeming qualities; but they could not reconcile us to its numerous and glaring defects. Its beauties, however, surprized us more than its faults.'

But there were also unbiased and unprejudiced reviewers. *The Globe* wrote: 'Nature has been bountiful to Mr. Aldridge in more than the identity of complexion which she has given him for the Moor ... he possesses a good figure and a speaking, intelligent countenance ... there are beauties throughout his performance ... and those who go to see the mere novelty of an African Othello will find more than mere curiosity gratified.'

*The Standard* confirmed *The Globe*'s assertion that Aldridge had 'the fire and spirit of a first-rate actor'. Rejecting the bigotry of other newspapers, *The Standard* said 'We at once gladly express our unqualified delight with his delineation of this masterpiece by the divine Shakespeare. ...he succeeded in deeply affecting the feelings of his audience. ...[and] retired amidst enthusiastic cheering.' *The Times* indeed reported, 'It is, however, our duty to state that Mr. Aldridge was extremely well received.' *The Theatrical Observer* of 11 April stated, 'Mr. Aldridge looked the part well, and his acting was more than respectable ....he has certainly the merit of not over-acting his part.'[7]

It is worth recalling that there was the same uproar in 1930 when Paul Robeson played Othello with Peggy Ashcroft as his Desdemona. One Englishman who resented the campaign against Robeson observed, 'Sixty-five years ago, Dame Madge Kendal played Desdemona to the Othello of Ira Aldridge, a Negro Shakespearean tragedian. Dame Madge survived it.'[8] Dame Madge's memoirs confirmed that she survived it. She wrote of the black tragedian:

Mr. Ira Aldridge was a man who, being black, always picked out the fairest woman he could to play Desdemona with him, ... One of the great bits of 'business' that he used to do was where, in one of the scenes he had to say, 'Your hand Desdemona,' he made a very great point of opening his hand and making you place yours in it, and the audience used to see the contrast. He always made a point of it and got a round of applause, how I do not know. It always struck me that he had some species of—well, I will not say genius, because I dislike that word as used nowadays—but gleams of real intelligence. Although a genuine black, he was quite *preux chevalier* in his manners to women.[9]

In spite of his success at Covent Garden, the French manager of the theatre, Pierre François Laporte, was forced by pressure to abandon Aldridge after two (or four) appearances. Aldridge spent the next nineteen years playing in minor London theatres and provincial theatres. At length he became convinced that his colour and his marriage to a white woman were viewed with disfavour among the impresarios of the English theatre. He recorded in his diary: 'Bigotry and fanaticism have excited themselves in all possible shapes to annoy the profession of dramatic art, but I have been very successful, indeed, thank God.'[10]

So on 14 July 1852 Aldridge left England with his family. Still the English papers were cruel to him, one of them writing 'Mr. Aldridge took his farewell of English audiences previous to rejoining his tribe in some distant part of the world.'[11] Actually, he left for Brussels, in which city he made his first continental appearance as Othello at the Theatre Royal St. Hubert. He afterwards played in Frankfurt, Berlin, Potsdam, Dresden, Hamburg, Prague, Vienna, and other principal European cities. Aldridge returned to London in 1857 decorated with honours by the crowned heads of Europe. He had been made a Knight of Saxony, awarded the Medal of Ferdinand by Emperor Franz Joseph of Austria, and made member of the Prussian Academy of Arts and Science. His great success on the continent opened the doors of the London theatres to Aldridge. He was immediately given an engagement at the Lyceum to play Othello. *The Athenaeum* now recanted: 'Mr. Ira Aldridge appeared on these boards in the character of Othello. Not only does the sable artist pronounce our own language distinctly and correctly, but with elocutional emphasis and propriety and his general action is marked with elegance and ease. So far as our own acquaintance with Mr. Aldridge extends we have formed a favourable opinion of his talents.' [12]

The black tragedian must have smiled when he recalled what the same journal had said nearly a quarter of a century earlier. Although Aldridge was at last accepted in the West End, his acceptance was reluctantly made. In any case, his earlier treatment ensured that he could never be completely at home in the English theatre. On his second continental tour he made a stir at St. Petersburg, and became 'the lion of St. Petersburg'. He was made an honorary member of the Imperial Academy of Beaux Arts, St. Petersburg, and holder of the Imperial Jubilee de Tolstoy Medal. He returned to England in the summer of 1859. In 1860 he toured the provinces, appearing at Brighton, Southampton, and Glasgow among other places. In 1862 he was a sensation in Moscow. On his return to England in 1863, he applied for British citizenship, which was granted him on 3 November 1863. The following year, on 25 March, his wife Margaret died. In April of 1865, he married a thirty-one-year-old Swedish opera singer, Amanda Pauline Brandt. In 1865 he also played Othello at Haymarket.

His last years were spent mainly in tours of Russia and the continent with occasional visits back to England. On 7 August 1867 he died in Lodz in Poland while there to play Othello. It was fitting that he died and was buried on the continent where his greatest triumphs were achieved. He was given a military funeral, and buried in the cemetery at Lodz.

Two examples will be enough to illustrate the popularity of Aldridge on the continent. They both confirm that he had indeed 'the fire and spirit of a first-rate actor'. One European critic, after first seeing Aldridge in *Othello*, attended his rendering of *Macbeth*.

His Macbeth shows generally the mighty stamp of his understanding and expression. ... I expected his Macbeth to be not as good as his Othello. ... I did not think he would understand Shakespeare's intentions in *Macbeth* because of its metaphysical development, whereas *Othello* is more familiar and within his scope. I was afraid that this hot-blooded son of the tropics could not cope with the galvanic, the metaphysical, fantastic and ghostlike in the first two acts of *Macbeth*, which was so Nordic; that he would not understand this most peculiar mood, nor would have the strength necessary for this, but with every scene I felt growing in me, to my surprise, the conviction that this original genius is equal to everything. ... the greatness of his acting and the indescribable kingly nobility which is in every feature, in words of majesty, in style so far above the ordinary theatre contours, that we can only express our feeling when we say we have never seen anything more magnificent.[13]

During one of his tours in Russia, one press report told of a procession of Jews headed by the Rabbi coming to the theatre to thank him for his interpretation of Shylock in *The Merchant of Venice*. For the first time in Russian theatrical history they said, Shakespeare's Jew became a human being and not a monster.[14] Eustace Clare Grenville Murray, the natural son of the second Duke of Buckingham and Chandos, was the British Consul-General in Odessa when Aldridge played Shylock in that city in January 1866. In a letter dated 2 February 1866 Grenville Murray wrote:

DEAR Mr. ALDRIDGE; —I called yesterday to congratulate you on your beautiful performance of Shylock. I like Othello better myself as a play; but your rendering of the character of the semi-Oriental Jew of the middle ages was a master piece of art. ... I should have liked to have seen you to talk about it, and am sorry you were out. Pray let me know when you will breakfast with me, though I hardly dare ask you out of town during this unfavourable weather.[15]

The motivating force in Ira Aldridge's work was, as he himself said over and over again, 'the honour of the stage and the dignity of human nature'. And to this cause he devoted his life and talents. In writing about this aspect of Ira Aldridge's life, Owen Mortimer declared: 'This was the man the unhonoured and uncelebrated and unknown people, held in slavery, gave to the world. It was from the epic struggle of his people to overthrow their masters that the great Negro tragedian derived his inspiration, his strength, his genius, all his magnificent art.'[16]

Ira Frederick Aldridge was 'perfectly conscious of his own moral and physical power as compared with those of men who would avail themselves of the mere force of prejudice to "put him down"; and the quiet dignity of manners, gentlemanly address, and deportment of the African seldom failed to check conduct the very reverse.'[17]

1. My main source for this chapter is Herbert Marshall and Mildred Stock, *Ira Aldridge: The Negro Tragedian* (London, 1958). See also Edward Scobie, *Black Britannia: A History of Blacks in Britain* (Chicago, 1972), pp. 128-34.

2. Scobie, p. 131. This picture portrayed by Scobie does not emerge in Marshall and Stock. But Scobie is in a position to know. Scobie was a close friend of Amanda Ira Aldridge, Aldridge's younger daughter. Aldridge's diaries, newspaper clippings, letters, and documents are in Scobie's possession. Unfortunately Scobie gives no reference for his statement. The first part of *Black Britannia* covers the period of this study. No sources are given for any of the statements. Where it has been possible to check these, the author has faithfully reproduced the sources.

3. Marshall and Stock, pp. 107-8.

4. Ibid., pp. 117-18; Scobie, p. 129.

5. Scobie, p. 129.

6. Marshall and Stock give two performances. Scobie, presumably consulting the actor's diary, says four appearances.

7. The reviews are fully reproduced in Marshall and Stock, pp. 120-8.

8. Quoted in J. A. Rogers, *Sex and Race* (New York, 1940), I, p. 204.

9. Marshall and Stock, p. 311.

10. Scobie, p. 131. Scobie fails to indicate the date when Aldridge made the entry.

11. Ibid., p. 132. The name of the newspaper is not indicated. But the quotation rings true.

12. Scobie, p. 132.

13. Marshall and Stock, pp. 181-2.

14. Ibid., p. 288.

15. Ibid., p. 314.

16. Scobie, pp. 133-4

17. Marshall and Stock, p. 131.

# 18

# George
# Augustus Polgreen Bridgetower

George Augustus Polgreen Bridgetower was born in 1779 in Biala, Poland, the son of an African adventurer who called himself John Frederick Bridgetower the African Prince, and a Polish Count's daughter named Maria.[1] The grandfather of George Bridgetower was committed to the care of a Dutch captain, who was well furnished with diamond and gold dust, for his education in Europe. The Dutchman sold the African prince in Jamaica to a planter. The unfortunate boy, however, met a kind owner who alleviated his misfortune. He married an African woman, by whom he had John Frederick Bridgetower. He too found favour with his owner, at whose expense he was instructed in several languages.

Where George Bridgetower passed the earliest years of his childhood is unknown, but, assuming the correctness of the statement that he was a pupil of Haydn, he must have been in the neighbourhood of Vienna before he had completed his tenth year. The child violin prodigy made his first public appearance in Paris at the age of nine at the Concert Spirituel of 13 April 1789. Bridgetower who studied under Barthelemon Giornovichi and Thomas Attwood, in addition to Haydn, made a very successful début. After his great success in Paris the young violinist crossed the Channel with his father, and we next hear of him at Windsor Castle, playing before George III and his Court. Bath, then still a fashionable rendezvous, was where Bridgetower gave his first public performance in England. *The Morning Post*, 25 November 1789, under 'Bath' reported, 'Amongst those added to the Sunday promenade were the African Prince in the Turkish attire. The son of this African Prince has been celebrated as a very accomplished musician.' Then on 8 December 1789 *The Morning Post* reported:

*Bath*
The young African Prince, whose musical talents have been so much celebrated, had a more crowded and splendid concert on Saturday morning than has ever been known in this place. There were upwards of five hundred and fifty persons present, and they were gratified by such skill on the violin as created general astonishment, as well as pleasure. Rauzzini was enraptured, and declared that he had never heard such

execution before, even from his friend La Motte, who was, he thought, much inferior to this wonderful boy. The father was in the gallery, and so affected by the applause bestowed on his son, that tears of pleasure and gratitude flowed in profusion. The profits were estimated at two hundred guineas, many persons have given five guineas for each ticket.

*The Bath Journal* for 7 December 1789 likewise enthused:

The amateurs of music in this city received on Saturday last at the New Rooms the highest treat imaginable from the exquisite performance of Master Bridgtower, whose taste and execution on the violin is equal, perhaps superior, to the best professor of the present or any former day. The Concert Room, Recesses and Gallery were thronged with the very best of company, and scores went away without being able to procure a hearing. Those who had that happiness were enraptured with the astonishing abilities of this wonderful child—for he is but ten years old. He is mulatto, the grandson[sic], it is said, of an African Prince. The greatest attention and respect was paid by the nobility and gentry present to his elegant Father, who is one of the most accomplished men in Europe, conversing with fluency and charming address in its several languages.

In addition to the above concerts, Bridgetower played 'A concerto on the violin between the 2d. and 3d. Acts' of the performance of the *Messiah* given at Bath on Christmas Eve, 1789, for the benefit of Rauzzini. In the meantime the boy had given a concert at Bristol on 18 December 1789 when, according to *Felix Farley's Bristol Journal*, 'he led the band with the coolness and spirit of a Cramer to the astonishment and delight of all present'. He gave a second concert at Bristol on New Year's Day 1790.

Having conquered Bath and Bristol, Master Bridgetower laid siege to London. He made his first appearance in the metropolis at one of the Lenten Oratorio performances in the Drury Lane Theatre, 19 February 1790, when he played a solo between parts I and 2 of the *Messiah*. In referring to the Lenten performances of that year, William Thomas Parke, the gossiping oboist, says: 'Concertos were performed on the oboe by me, and on the violin, for the first time, by Master Bridgtower, son of an African prince, who was attended by his father, habited in the costume of his country. The youth displayed considerable ability, and was much applauded.'[2]

Of the same occasion *The Public Advertiser* for 20 February 1790 reported: 'Sufficient as the Messiah would have been for an high treat, the Managers had provided an additional dish in a Concerto on the Violin by Master Bridgetower son to the African Prince, a youth, as he appeared, not fourteen, but apparently a complete master of the violin; we say, apparently, as it would be arrogantly presumptuous in us to decide on musical abilities. — He gave the utmost satisfaction in his performance, and we imagine the more he is known, he will be more admired.'

And *The London Chronicle*, 20 February 1790, commented: 'Master Bridgetower, son to the African Prince, who has lately figured away so much at Bath on the violin, performed a Concerto with great taste and execution; his father dwelt on every note with rapture, and seemed highly gratified by the reiterated plaudits so warmly bestowed on the young Prince.'

Later in the season he joined Clement, another violinist prodigy, in giving a concert under the patronage of the Prince of Wales (later George IV) at the Hanover Square Rooms on 2 June. The Abbé Vogler, who was present on that occasion, records that the united age of the performers in the string quartet was under forty years, the first violin player, Clement of Vienna being only eight and a half, and the second violinist, 'Bridgetower from Africa', ten years old.[3]

At the Handel Commemoration of 1791, held in Westminster Abbey, Bridgetower and Hummel sat on each side of the organist, clad in scarlet coats, pulling out the stops for him. In the same year we find Bridgetower among the violinists at the Haydn-Salomon concerts. He appeared at several of the Lenten Oratorios given at the King's Theatre in 1792, and on 28 May he played a concerto by Viotti at Barthelemon's concert, the announcements stating that 'Dr. Haydn will preside at the Piano Forte'.[4]

When he was fourteen in 1794, he became one of the first violinists of the Prince of Wales's private orchestra who divided their time between the Prince's residences, in London (Carlton House) and Brighton (the Pavilion).[5] From letters addressed to him there can be no question that at his prime Bridgetower occupied a good position in London musical circles. That he was on intimate terms with some of the leading musicians of the time is proved by his being addressed as 'My dear George' by Viotti (who held him in the highest esteem), François Cramer, Thomas Attwood, and Dr. Charles Hague, Professor of Music at the University of Cambridge, at whose concerts Bridgetower often played. The letters addressed to him by Samuel Wesley and printed in *The Musical Times* for April 1908 show that he was on friendly terms with that distinguished Bach-loving musician. Wesley left the following appreciation of his friend:

George Bridgetower, whom they used to denominate the African Prince, is justly to be ranked with the very first masters of the violin. He practised much with the celebrated Viotti, and imbibed largely of his bold and spirited style of execution. It was a rich treat for a lover of the instrument to hear him perform the matchless and immortal solos of Sebastian Bach, all of which he perfectly retained in memory and executed with the utmost precision, and without a single error. Indeed, whatever the composition, or whoever the author whose music he undertook to perform, he treated in so perfect and masterly a manner as to yield entire and universal delight and satisfaction to every auditor.[6]

In 1802 Bridgetower was granted leave of absence by the Prince of Wales to visit his mother, then residing at Dresden, where he gave concerts in July 1802 and March 1803. His connection with the English Court enabled him to obtain valuable letters of introduction to influential persons abroad, so much so that at Vienna he had a most brilliant reception among the highest musical circles in the Austrian capital. Particularly advantageous to him in Vienna was the fact that he enjoyed the friendship of Beethoven, who introduced Bridgetower to Viennese society. In a letter of introduction to Baron Wezlar dated 18 March 1803 Beethoven wrote:

Though we have never spoken, I take the liberty of recommending to you the bearer of this note, Mr. Brischdower, *a very skilful virtuoso and master of his instrument*. He plays his Concertos and Quartets excellently, and I much wish that you would procure him some acquaintances. With Lobkowitz, Fries, and all other distinguished amateurs, he has become acquainted with advantage.

I think it would not be a bad plan were you to take him one evening to Theresa Schonfeld, where, I know many friends are in the habit of going, or to receive him yourself.

I know that you will thank me for having procured you this acquaintance. Good bye, Herr Baron.

Yours obediently,<br>BEETHOVEN.[7]

By May, Bridgetower was already enjoying the company of Beethoven, as the following two notes written by the master to Bridgetower in May 1803 show.

Be so kind as to wait for me at half past one at Taroni's coffee house, in the Graben. We shall then go to the Countess Guicciardi's [the mother of Beethoven's pupil Giulietta], where you have been invited to dinner.
BEETHOVEN

Go, My dear B[ridgetower], at about noon today to Count Deym's, that is to say, to the same house where we both were the day before yesterday. Those people would probably like to hear you play one of your own compositions. Well, that is for you to decide. I can't turn up there till about half past one. Until then I look forward to seeing you today,

and in the meantime I take pleasure in merely remembering you.
Your friend,
BEETHOVEN[8]

At the concert Bridgetower gave in Vienna those who purchased tickets included the British Ambassador (50), Prince Lobkowitz (20), Count Razumovsky (5), Princess Liechtenstein, and
others; some of these names will be recognized as among those in
Beethoven's aristocratic circle; the total amount realized by the
sale of tickets was 1,140 florins. Bridgetower induced the master
to compose something for his concert. The result was the sonata
for pianoforte and violin in A (Opus 47), known the world over
as the 'Kreutzer Sonata'. When this work was first performed at
the concert given by Bridgetower on either 17 or 24 May 1803 at
the Augarten-Halle, Beethoven himself played the pianoforte
part. The concert took place at eight o'clock in the morning. As
the time for the concert drew near, Bridgetower became anxious
about the new work, the composition of which Beethoven had put
off until the eleventh hour. Ferdinand Ries tells us that Beethoven
called upon him at half-past four on the morning of the concert,
and asked him to copy out with all speed the violin part of the
first *Allegro* (his regular copyist being otherwise engaged) of
which the pianoforte part was only sketched. The lovely varia-
tions were literally finished at the last moment, and Bridgetower
had to play his violin part as best he could from the more or less
illegible manuscript of the composer. The last movement was
ready in good time, as it originally formed the *finale* of the sonata
in the same key (Opus 30), dedicated to Alexander I, Tsar of
Russia. Bridgetower recorded on his copy of the sonata a very
interesting incident in connection with the first performance of
this magnificent work:

When I accompanied [Beethoven] in this Sonata-Concertante at Wien,
at the repetition of the first part of the *Presto*, I imitated the flight, at the
18th bar, of the pianoforte of this movement ... He jumped up,
embraced me, saying: 'Noch einmal, mein lieber Bursch!' ['Once
more, my dear fellow!']. Then he held the open pedal during this flight,
the chord of C as at the ninth bar.
Beethoven's expression in the *Andante* was so chaste, which always
characterized the performance of all his *slow movements*, that it was
unanimously hailed to be repeated twice.[9]

In *The Musical World* for 4 December 1858 is to be found an
interesting light upon the dedication of the sonata. In a letter written to the editor, J. W. Thirlwall, a well known violinist of that
time, wrote: 'In respect to the Kreutzer Sonata, Bridgetower told

me, that when it was written, Beethoven and he were constant companions, and on the first copy was a dedication to his friend Bridgetower; but, ere it was published, they had some silly quarrel about a girl, and in consequence Beethoven scratched out the name of Bridgetower and inserted that of Kreutzer—a man whom he had never seen.'[10]

Bridgetower returned to London via Dresden. His passport dated 27 July 1803 described him as 'a musician, a native of Biala (Poland), aged twenty-four years, medium height, clean shaven, swarthy complexion, dark brown hair, brown eyes, and straight, rather broad nose.'[11]

On 23 May 1805, he gave a concert in London, which was announced thus in *The Morning Chronicle* of that day:

NEW ROOMS, HANOVER SQUARE.

Under the patronage of his Royal Highness the Prince of Wales.

MR. BRIDGETOWER begs leave to inform the Nobility, Gentry and his Friends, that his Concert will take place this evening. Mrs. Billington and Mr. J. Cramer have kindly offered to play the same Duett as at Messers. Cramer's concert on Monday last.

For the next few years he seems to have lived in London. An important event in his life was the taking in June 1811 of the degree of Bachelor of Music at the University of Cambridge, where his name was entered at Trinity Hall.[12] As one of his exercises for his degree, Bridgetower composed an anthem to words written by F. A. Rawdon, which began:

By faith sublime Fair Passiflora steers
Her Pilgrimage along this vale of tears,
The hopes of Heaven alone her thoughts employ,
Christ is her glory, and the Cross her joy.[13]

The exercise was performed on 30 June 1811 at Great St. Mary's Church, Cambridge, as part of the celebrations for the installation of the Duke of Gloucester as Chancellor of the University. *The Times*, reporting the numerous events connected with the installation, referred to the 'anthem composed by Mr. Bridgetower, the celebrated violinist, as an exercise for his Bachelor's degree in Music', adding 'The composition was elaborate and rich; and highly accredited to the talents of the Graduate. The trio struck us, particularly, by its beauty; but Master Hawes was not unequal to his solo parts.'[14]

As a composer, Bridgetower is unknown to fame. The chief of his published compositions is *Diatonica Armonica* (1812). This

217

work, 'dedicated to his pupils', consists of forty-one studies in
scale passages for the pianoforte. There is also a ballad entitled
'Henry', which was 'sung by Miss Feron and humbly dedicated
with permission to Her Royal Highness the Princess of Wales',
the said permission being given in a letter dated 11 December
1810. In the British Library are two printed undated books of
'Minuets, &c; &c; for the Violin, Mandolin, German-Flute, and
Harpsicord, composed by an African', who may in all probability
be Bridgetower. They are inscribed respectively 'to his Grace
Henry, Duke of Buccleuch', and to the 'Right Honble. John Lord
Montagu of Boughton'. Three of these dance tune compositions
are scored for horns, violins, and basses. [15]

In 1812 we find Bridgetower receiving a letter headed 2 Duchess Street, 30 April 1812, from Dr. Crotch, which reads:

MY DEAR SIR, —As I find you are frequently in company with the
Prince Regent, could you do me the favor to mention my Oratorio to his
R.H; or if that is disagreeable to you would you be so kind as to inform
me what is the regular way of proceeding in such cases. It is to be
repeated May 26th, and the Patronage of H.R.H. would add much eclat
to ye business.

> I am Dear Sir, Your most sincerely
> Wm. CROTCH.

The Oratorio above referred to is *Palestine*, first produced at
the Hanover Rooms, 21 April 1812. [16]
Although Bridgetower was not one of the original members or
associates of the Philharmonic Society, his name appears in the
programme of the fourth concert of the first season (3 May 1813),
as leader of Beethoven's quintet. At the sixth concert on 31 May,
he played second violin in a quartet by Mozart. At that time he
was probably an associate, as he was re-admitted to the Society
on 6 November 1819, being then married, for Mr. Watts, the
Secretary, wrote to him saying that, 'by a vote of the General
Meeting [held 14 April 1819] Mrs. Bridgetower is invited to
accompany you as usual to the concerts, &c; until the usual forms
can be gone through for your re-admission.' Little is known
about his wife who was apparently English, except that her
maiden name was Drake. [17]
The remaining years of Bridgetower's life were passed more or
less in obscurity. So far as is known he appears to have lived
abroad from about 1820 to 1843. He was at Rome in 1825 and
1827, evidently moving in aristocratic circles. We find him in
London in August 1843, through a letter addressed to him by
Vincent Novello, who signs himself 'your much obliged old

pupil and professional admirer'. John Ella has recorded that he met him in Vienna in 1845; he was again in London in 1846, and there are letters which prove that Bridgetower was at St. Cloud, Paris, in 1848. In later years he seems to have 'come down in the world' for he died in a back street in Peckham, London, on 29 February 1860 at the advanced age of eighty-one. A few months before his death, on 10 September 1859, Bridgetower made a will in which he bequeathed the whole of his property to a married sister of his late wife. The will was proved on 3 July 1860 by the executor, the testator's friend, 'Samuel Appleby, Esq; Solicitor, of 6, Harpur Street, Red Lion Square', the estate being sworn 'under £1,000'.[18]

Samuel Coleridge-Taylor (1875-1912) once said that Beethoven had black blood in his veins. The supposition, he thought, was supported by the great composer's type of features and many little points in his character, as well as by his friendship for Bridgetower. And he could not avoid a sarcasm: 'I think that if the greatest of all musicians were alive today, he would find it somewhat difficult, if not absolutely impossible, to obtain hotel accommodation in certain American cities.'[19]

Sayers, the biographer of Coleridge-Taylor, gives the following account in support of the African composer's allusion to Beethoven's mixed blood: 'The story is told of a playful prank of Mr. Henry Down's, who decorated the large bust of Beethoven in the Conservatoire with Coleridge-Taylor's sombrero. It was a small hat for so large a head, but it helped to show the remarkable likeness that existed between the sovereign composer and the young coloured one. This likeness in brow and the outlines and general expression of face has been remarked in later photographs of Coleridge-Taylor.'[20]

DuBois, referring to the friendship between Beethoven and Bridgetower, commented on 'the unexplained complexion of Beethoven's own father'.[21] Thayer also alluded to the dark colour and Negroid features of Beethoven. He adds that Beethoven's 'nose, too, was rather broad and decidedly flattened'. But portraits of Beethoven rarely showed his African or 'Negro' aspect, for the simple reason that they always appear 'touched up'. Or as Thayer says: 'A true and exhaustive picture of Beethoven as a man would present an almost ludicrous contrast to that which is generally entertained as correct. As sculptors and painters have each in turn idealized the work of his predecessor until the composer stands before us like a Homeric god—until those who knew him personally, could they return to the earth, would never suspect that the grand form and more noble portraits are intended to represent the short, muscular and pock-pitted face of their old friend.'[22]

Beethoven, then, was not white but Negroid in colour and features. But we do not intend by this assertion to launch a thousand theses by the die-hards of Hitler's Aryan white master race. They can have Ludwig van Beethoven. Other men of indisputable African ancestry have distinguished themselves in nearly every age and land. Rulers and warriors, Queen Nefertiti, Amenhotep III, Sonni Ali, Mansa Musa, Toussaint L'Ouverture, Shaka, the Mahdi, and a host of others were of us. In literature Terence, Pushkin, the elder Dumas, Dunbar were of us. In music and art Bridgetower, Coleridge-Taylor, Ira Aldridge, Paul Robeson were of us. In science, scholarship, and invention Lislet Geoffroy, Amo, Banneker were of us. DuBois, Wright, Padmore, Lumumba, Nkrumah, Nasser, Fanon, Malcolm X, were of us. C. L. R. James, Baldwin, Soyinka, Césaire, Baraka, Achebe, Kani, Ntshona are with us. We shall march prospering whatever the obstacles. We build on a solid foundation cemented with blood, toil, persecution, and fortitude. Even if our petty bourgeois disown us, or criticize or denounce us, just for the sake of a handful of tainted silver they pick from the tables of our oppressors who have gold in abundance, we will march on. They are the pimps and the slaves. We who in our various ways and disciplines have assumed the awesome task and burden of black liberation are the freemen.

1. My main source for this chapter, apart from the contemporary papers, is F. G. Edwards's biography of Bridgetower under the title 'George P. Bridgetower and the Kreutzer Sonata' in *The Musical Times*, XLIX (1908), pp. 302-8. See also Alexander Wheelock Thayer, *The Life of Ludwig van Beethoven*, ed. H. E. Krehbiel (New York, 1921), II, pp. 8-12; Carl Ferdinand Pohl, *Mozart and Haydn in London* (Vienna, 1867), pp. 18, 28, 38, 43, 128, 137, 199; *Dictionary of National Biography*, s.v. George Augustus Polgreen Bridgetower.

2. William Thomas Parke, *Musical Memoirs; comprising an Account of the General State of Music in England, from ... 1784 to the year 1830* (London, 1830), I, p. 129.

3. F. G. Edwards, p. 304; Thayer, II, p. 11.

4. F. G. Edwards, p. 304.

5. The Prince of Wales was a personal friend of Chevalier Georges de St. Georges, son of the Marquis de Langey and an African slave, champion swordsman, and accomplished violinist and equestrian. The Prince of Wales also patronized Prince Saunders, the black American writer from Boston, and one of the itinerant black Abolitionists in Britain in the early decades of the nineteenth century. See further Benjamin Quarles, *Black Abolitionists*, p. 130.

6. British Library, Add. MSS., 27593, f. 109; F. G. Edwards, p. 305. Edwards had access to the collection of letters addressed to Bridgetower and other documents relating to the violinist which were in the possession of Arthur F. Hill, F.S.A., in 1908.

7. Edwards, p. 305. Italics are added. Another version is found in Thayer, II, p. 10.

8. Emily Anderson, *The Letters of Beethoven* ... (London and New York, 1961), I, pp. 91-2.

9. Thayer, pp. 9-10; Edwards, p. 305.

10. Edwards, pp. 305-6; Thayer, II, p. 10.

11. Edwards, p. 306.

12. The Revd. Alexander Crummell, one of the black Abolitionists from America, entered Queens' College, Cambridge, in 1849, sponsored by Sir Benjamin Brodie, and took his B.A. degree in 1853. See further W. E. B. DuBois, *The Souls of Black Folk* (Chicago, 1903), Chapter 10, 'Of Alexander Crummell'. For black Abolitionists in England during and outside the period of this study see Benjamin Quarles, *Black Abolitionists*, Chapter 6, 'Duet with John Bull'.

13. *The Gentleman's Magazine*, LXXXI, Pt. II (1811), p. 158.

14. Ibid., p. 37; *The Times* (2 July 1811).

15. Paul Edwards, in his introduction to the reprint of *Letters of Ignatius Sancho*, says these pieces 'are unlikely to be by anyone other than Sancho.' I think Paul Edwards is wrong. He seems to be oblivious of the existence of Bridgetower.

16. F. G. Edwards, p. 306.

17. Ibid., pp. 306-7. In the *Dictionary of National Biography* it is said he was reputed to have a married daughter who lived in Italy.

18. F. G. Edwards, pp. 307-8.

19. W. C. Berwick Sayers, *Samuel Coleridge-Taylor Musician: His Life and Letters* (London and New York, 1915), p. 203.

20. Ibid., p. 72.

21. W. E. B. Dubois, *The Negro*, p. 84.

22. Thayer, I, pp. 146, 245.

# 19

# Olaudah Equiano

Olaudah Equiano was born in 1745 in an area under the Kingdom of Benin, now Nigeria. At the age of ten he was kidnapped by slave hunters, together with his sister, from whom he was separated while still in Africa, and transported to America. After passing from one owner to another, enslaved in America, in the Caribbean, and in England, he purchased his freedom with his own savings in 1766, at the age of twenty-one. In 1789 his autobiography, *The Interesting Narrative of the Life of Olaudah Equiano, or Gustavus Vassa, The African*, was published in London. This was an account of his eventful life from the time he was kidnapped in 1755 until 1787. It was a successful book which ran into several editions. Between 1789 and 1827 seventeen editions were published in Britain and in the United States. It was translated into Dutch and German. In 1968 Heinemann Educational Books published an abridged version of the *Narrative*, and, in the following year, Dawsons of Pall Mall issued a reprint of the first edition.[1]

The *Narrative* begins with an account of Equiano's family and his native village. He then describes his arrival on the West African Coast, the horrors of the slave ship and the Middle Passage, and his first experience of hell on earth in Barbados. All the abominations he witnessed led him to ask, 'O, ye nominal Christians! might not an African ask you, Learned you this from your God who says unto you, Do unto all men as you would men should do unto you?'

Equiano stayed in Barbados for about a fortnight, before he was transported with the remnant of slaves who remained unsold to Virginia. There he was bought by one Campbell, on whose plantation he worked for a few weeks, 'weeding grass and gathering stones'. Captain M. H. Pascal R.N. bought Equiano from Campbell and brought him to England, arriving about the beginning of 1757. On his becoming another man's property, Equiano was called first Michael and then Jacob, and finally Pascal bestowed the name Gustavus Vassa on him. After staying for a short while in Falmouth, Pascal took Equiano to Guernsey. He remained in Guernsey till the summer of 1757, when his owner took him to sea again on board H.M.S. *Roebuck*. After two years at sea, Equiano returned to England, and was sent to wait on two sisters, for whom it appears his master had originally 'meant me for a present'. The arrangement was temporary, and the two sisters, the Misses Guerin (one married later), were kind to the African boy. They sent him to school, and 'often used to teach me to read'. The elder Miss Guerin, with whom Equiano was a favourite, persuaded Pascal to allow him to be baptized, 'so I was baptized in St. Margaret's Church, Westminster, in February 1759, ... On this occasion Miss Guerin did me the honour to stand as godmother and afterward gave me a treat.' The time that Equiano spent with the Misses Guerin was a happy one, but Pascal again went to sea and Equiano with him.[2]

It was during the Seven Years War (1756-63) and Pascal served under Admiral Boscawen in the Mediterranean. While on board various ships during the war, Equiano had the opportunity of furthering his education. On the *Namur* there was a school, and Equiano improved on his reading and learned how to write. When Pascal was appointed captain of the fireship, *Aetna*, Equiano became the captain's steward. The captain's clerk not only taught him how to write properly, but 'gave me a smattering of arithmetic'. Another sailor on the *Aetna* taught Equiano to shave and dress his hair. Equiano returned with his owner to England in 1760, and was stationed at Cowes on the Isle of Wight till the beginning of 1761. In March 1761 they fitted out again for another expedition destined for Belle Isle, off the Breton Coast. Thus Equiano witnessed the destruction of the French fleet and the capture of Belle Isle. 'During the siege,' Equiano wrote, 'I have counted above sixty shells and carcasses in the air at once.' The end of the war came, and Equiano was hopeful that Pascal would free him in consideration of years of devoted and unpaid service. Pascal, however, suspected that he planned to run away:

He swore I should not move out of his sight, and if I did he would cut my throat, at the same time taking his hanger. I began, however, to collect myself, and plucking up courage, I told him I was free and he could not by law serve me so. But this only enraged him the more, and he continued to swear, and said he would soon let me know whether he would or not ... just as we got a little below Gravesend, we came alongside of a ship which was going away the next tide for the West Indies; her name was the *Charming Sally*, Captain James Doran, and my master went on board and agreed with him for me, and in a little time I was sent for into the cabin. When I came there Captain Doran asked me if I knew him; I answered that I did not; 'Then,' said he, 'you are now my slave.' I told him my master could not sell me to him, nor to anyone else. 'Why,' said he, 'did not your master buy you?' I confessed he did. 'But I have served him', said I, 'many years, and he has taken all my wages and prize-money, for I only got one sixpence during the war; besides this I have been baptized, and by the laws of the land no man has a right to sell me.' And I added that I had heard a lawyer and others at different times tell my master so. They both then said that those people who told me so were not my friends, but I replied, 'It was very extraordinary that other people did not know the law as well as they.' Upon this Captain Doran said I talked too much English, and if I did not behave myself well and be quiet he had a method on board to make me. I was too well convinced of his power over me to doubt what he said, and my former sufferings in the slave-ship presenting themselves to my mind, the recollection of them made me shudder. However, before I retired I told them that as I could not get any right among men here I hoped I should hereafter in Heaven, and I immediately left the cabin, filled with resentment and sorrow.[3]

When the incident just described occurred Equiano was a boy of sixteen. It is in crises that the character of a man can be measured, and already at sixteen this African boy was an opponent worthy of any adversary's steel. Defenceless and unarmed, while his opponent had a sword in hand, few men, let alone a boy of sixteen, would have dared to pluck up courage and tell the villain that 'I was free and he could not by law serve me so.' One moment he was the property of one man, and the next, without as much as a consultation of the chattel, the power of life and death over the property was transferred to another. But the shattering change did not break him. Instantly he retorted: 'I have been baptized, and by the laws of the land no man has a right to sell me.' Evidently, Equiano had heard all about the controversy as to whether baptism did or did not emancipate. The owner and prospective owner of property in human flesh, of course, subscribed to the Yorke and Talbot Opinion.

And so it came to pass on 13 February 1763 that the ship taking Equiano back to the land of slaves came in sight of her destined island of Montserrat: 'At the sight of this land of bondage, a fresh horror ran through all my frame and chilled me to the heart. My former slavery now rose in dreadful review to my mind, and displayed nothing but misery, stripes, and chains; and, in the first paroxysm of my grief, I called upon God's thunder and his avenging power to direct the stroke of death to me rather than permit me to become a slave, and sold from lord to lord.'[4]

Equiano was, however, spared the traumatic experience of being sold from lord to lord and was saved from the worst horrors of West Indian slavery. When Captain Doran was ready to sail for England in May 1763, he sold Equiano to Robert King, a Quaker from Philadelphia, who owned many vessels. Equiano worked on board his owner's vessels, criss-crossing from America to the Caribbean, and became familiar with such places as St. Eustatius, St. Kitts, Guadeloupe, Grenada, Montserrat, Santa Cruz, Charleston, the Bahamas, New Providence, and Georgia.

In 1766 Equiano bought his way to freedom and was manumitted by his Quaker owner. After a seven-week voyage Equiano was once again in 'Old England' in the middle of March 1767. On landing in London, he searched for the Misses Guerin, and found them at Greenwich. He told them how their cousin Pascal had sold him and sent him back to West Indian slavery. They freely acknowledged that their cousin's conduct did him no honour. Very soon after his arrival, Equiano met Pascal in Greenwich Park. Pascal was a good deal surprised to see him, and asked Equiano how he came back. He answered drily, 'In a ship.' To which Pascal replied, 'I suppose you did not walk back to London on the water.' Equiano, seeing that Pascal was not at all sorry for his craven conduct, told Pascal that he had used him 'very ill after I had been such a faithful servant to him for so many years, on which, without saying any more, he turned about and went away.'

A few days after this confrontation, they met again at the Guerins, and Equiano asked Pascal for his prize-money. He told Equiano that he was entitled to none, that even if his prize-money had been £10,000, he Pascal had the right to it all. Equiano told him that he had been informed otherwise. Upon which in a bantering tone, Pascal told Equiano he could commence a law-suit. 'There are lawyers enough,' said Pascal, 'that will take the case in hand.' Equiano replied that he would do so, which enraged Pascal very much. However, in deference to the Guerins, he forbore.

During the next twenty years, Equiano was a hairdresser in Coventry Court, Haymarket, assistant to Dr. Charles Irving, in Pall Mall, who was celebrated for his successful experiments in making sea-water fresh, and was a roving sailor. As a sailor, Equiano went to Turkey, Italy, Portugal, Madeira, Barbados, Jamaica, Grenada, Nevis, and the Archipelago islands. In 1773 he took part in Phipps's expedition to the Arctic. For four months in imminent danger of their lives, 'we explored nearly as far towards the Pole as 81 degrees north, and 20 degrees east longitude, being much farther by all accounts than any navigator had ever ventured before, in which we fully proved the impracticability of finding a passage that way to India.' In 1775 Equiano accompanied Dr. Irving to the Mosquito Shore and returned to England in 1777. Although till 1786 Equiano worked from time to time on merchant ships sailing between England and the Caribbean, and England and America, he seems to have settled more or less permanently in England after his return from the Mosquito Shore in 1777.

When Robert King had asked Equiano to stay in Montserrat after his manumission, and held out to him the prospect of his owning his own land and slaves, nothing could have been further from Equiano's mind. He was already a committed Abolitionist. He was anxious to return to England partly to settle his account with Pascal and partly, and more importantly, in order to start his campaign against slavery and the slave trade. The evening schools and special tuition he had had in England in 1767 were part of the education of a black Abolitionist.[5] When he had first returned to England in 1767, he had become a member of the close-knit African community. It was not until 1774, however, that Equiano began his Abolitionist work. *The London Chronicle* of 27 April 1774 reported one of the kidnappings in violation of the Mansfield decree of 1772:

A few days ago a Merchant, who had kept a Black Servant some years, having some words with him they parted by consent, and the Black had his Master's leave to go; he accordingly went, and entered himself as a Cook on board a West India ship; the Master hearing where he was, went with two Gentlemen and two Watermen and took the poor Fellow by violence, tying his hands and legs, and carried him on board a ship bound to St. Kitt's, on which he was put in chains to be carried into slavery; but several Gentlemen seeing the transaction, employed an Attorney to serve the Merchant with a habeas corpus to produce the body: the habeas corpus was returned that the body was not to be found, though it is said the ship did not sail through the Downs for St. Kitt's till some days after the habeas corpus was served; therefore the Gentlemen have ordered the Attorney to proceed against the Master; and also on the Captain's return to proceed against him for violently and by force taking a man out of the kingdom.

In several respects the report of the kidnapping in *The London Chronicle* was inaccurate. The black man kidnapped in this instance was a friend of Equiano, who was the person responsible for bringing the matter to public notice. In his *Narrative*, Equiano gave a fuller account of the kidnapping and of his efforts to regain his friend's freedom. In December 1771, just before the drama of the Somerset case began, the ship on which Equiano was serving, sailed from England for Nevis in Jamaica. He arrived back in England in August 1772, a couple of months after Lord Mansfield handed down his decision in the Somerset case. Undoubtedly, on his arrival, he must have heard of the Mansfield ruling from his fellow Africans. In 1773, as we have seen, Equiano took part in the Phipps expedition to the Arctic and he was back in England by the end of that year. It was not long before he 'thought of visiting old ocean again'. The *Narrative* continues:

It was now spring 1774. I sought for a master, and found a captain John Hughes, commander of a ship called Anglicania, and bound to Smyrna, in Turkey; I supplied myself with him as a steward; and at the same time I recommended to him a very clever black man, John Annis, as a cook. This man was on board the ship for near two months doing his duty: he had formerly lived many years with William Kirkpatrick, a gentleman of the island of St.Kitts, from whom he departed by consent, though, he afterwards tried many schemes to inveigle the poor man. He had applied to many captains who traded to St. Kitts to trepan him; and when all their attempts and schemes of kidnapping proved abortive, Mr. Kirkpatrick came to our ship at Union Stairs on Easter Monday, April the fourth, with two wherry boats and six men, having learned that the man was on board; and tied, and forcibly took him away from the ship, in the presence of the crew and the chief mate, who had detained him after he had notice to come away. I believe that this was a combined piece of business: but at any rate, it certainly reflected great disgrace on the mate and captain also, who, although they desired the oppressed man to stay on board, yet did not in the least assist to recover him, or pay me a farthing of his wages, which was about five pounds. I proved the only friend he had, who attempted to regain his liberty if possible, having known the want of liberty myself. I sent as soon as I could to Gravesend, and got knowledge of the ship in which he was; but unluckily she had sailed the first tide after he was put on board. My intention was then immediately to apprehend Kirkpatrick, who was about setting off for Scotland; and, having obtained a *habeas corpus* for him, and got a tipstaff to go with me to St. Paul's church yard, where he lived, he, suspecting something of this kind, set a watch to look out. My being known to them occasioned me to use the following deception: I whitened my face, that they might not know me, and this had its desired effect. He did not go out of his house that night, and next morning I contrived a well plotted stratagem not withstanding he had a gentleman in his house to personate him. My direction to the tipstaff, who got admission into the house, was to conduct him to a judge according to the writ. When he came there, his plea was, that he had not the body in custody, on which he was admitted to bail. I proceeded immediately to that philanthropist, Granville Sharp Esq. who received me with the utmost kindness, and gave me every instruction that was needful on the occasion. I left him in full hope that I should gain his liberty, with the warmest sense of gratitude towards Mr. Sharp for his kindness; but, alas! my attorney proved unfaithful! he took my money, lost me many months employ, and did not do the least good in the cause; and when the poor man arrived at St. Kitts, he was, according to custom staked to the ground with four pins through cord, two on his wrists, and two on his ancles, was cut and flogged most unmercifully, and afterwards loaded cruelly with irons about his neck. I had two very moving letters from him, while he was in this situation; and also was told of it by some very respectable families now in London, who saw him in St. Kitts, in the same state in which he remained till kind death released him out of the hands of his tyrants.[6]

*The Morning Chronicle and London Advertiser*, 18 March 1783, published an anonymous letter reporting the lurid case of the slave ship *Zong*, from on board which 132 African slaves were thrown alive into the sea on the pretext of shortage of water, in order to claim the insurance money on them. The writer of the letter was present in Court during the hearing of the action between the insurers and the owners of the slave ship, for the determination of the insurers' liability. The description of how *parcel* after parcel of living Africans were cast into the sea, he said, 'seemed to make every one present shudder'. But the 'Jury, without going out of Court, gave judgement against the Underwriters'. The Court of King's Bench subsequently ordered a new trial, and the outcome of the new trial is not reported.[7] On 19 March 1783 Equiano called on Granville Sharp, with an account of 132 Africans thrown alive into the sea. It is fair to assume that Equiano heard of the tragic affair through the letter in *The Morning Chronicle*. Equiano earnestly solicited the assistance of the victor of the Somerset case, 'to avenge the blood of his murdered countrymen'.[8] Sharp could hardly believe that 'this most inhuman and diabolical deed actually happened.' With characteristic speed, on the day following Equiano's visit, 20 March, he called on Dr. Bever, the Oxford law teacher and legal practitioner, 'to consult about prosecuting the murderers' of the Africans.[9] The influential *Gentleman's Magazine*, hearing of Sharp's efforts, told its readers 'that a true patriot, a true christian, has nobly stepped forth, and, at his own expence, instituted a criminal process against those workers of wickedness; the event of which, we hope, will put away this evil among us.'[10] But the action did not get off the ground. Blacks were property. And that was that.

Although nothing was done by the authorities to punish the murderers of so many innocent individuals, the efforts of Equiano and Sharp brought the matter to public notice, and the cruel and disgraceful incident reverberated through the writings of several Abolitionists. Clarkson referred to it as 'this atrocious and unparalleled act of wickedness'.[11] Equiano did not refer to the *Zong* case in his *Narrative*, but Cugoano did in his *Thoughts and Sentiments*. He contended in his usual forceful manner that such perpetrators of murder and fraud should have been sought after from one end of the world to the other, until brought to justice. 'But our lives are accounted of no value.'[12]

It was in 1783, the year of the *Zong*, that the Quakers established a committee on Abolition and presented a petition to Parliament for the Abolition of the slave trade. Lord North, the Prime Minister, commended the Quakers for their humanity, but regretted that it was impossible to abolish the slave trade. The trade in human flesh was necessary.[13]

The African community was well aware of the endeavours of the Friends on behalf of their brothers and sisters. Equiano, who had always held the Friends in special regard and had bought his freedom from one of their number, composed an address of thanks to the Quakers in October 1785, and, accompanied by some of his brothers, he presented it to the Friends at their meeting house in Lombard Street. 'These gentlemen received us very kindly, with a promise to exert themselves on behalf of the oppressed Africans.'[14] The first Appendix to this book is a collection of eighteen letters that Equiano wrote in his campaign for Abolition, and the address presented to the Quakers in 1785 is given as Letter II.

As a black Abolitionist, Equiano came to know several white Abolitionists. The most prominent, of course, was Granville Sharp. Equiano had met the Revd. James Ramsay in the West Indies, and the acquaintance was continued in England. He was also on friendly terms with Clarkson, who must have obtained first-hand information concerning the lot and treatment of black slaves in the West Indies from Equiano. We have already mentioned, in an earlier chapter, the close liaison with Peter Peckard.

On 9 May 1788 William Pitt moved a resolution in the House of Commons pledging the House to consider the circumstances of the slave trade early in the following session.[15] The British Prime Minister carefully refrained from giving his opinion on the merits of the trade, saying that the appropriate time would be in the next session, and he urged Members to emulate his example. But various speakers expressed their views on the merits and demerits of the slave trade. When Fox spoke, he observed that some of the several petitions presented to the House held that the trade should be abolished outright, others that it only needed regulation. For his own part, '[I have] no scruple to declare, in the onset, that [my] opinion of this momentous business is that the Slave Trade ought not to be regulated, but destroyed.'[16] When it became apparent that the Abolition of the slave trade would not after all be discussed in that session, old Sir William Dolben, the Member for the University of Oxford, brought in a Bill to regulate the carrying of African slaves to the plantations. In a long speech on 28 May 1788, Sir William Dolben said that the purpose of his introducing the Bill was, 'to save the lives of hundreds and thousands that must necessarily perish, if some such regulations as he had adverted to, were not adopted without delay. ... These miserable wretches had not a yard square allowed them to live in, while, in that narrow space they were loaded with shackles, and fastened hand to hand and foot to foot to one another.'[17] The Bill had the powerful support of Fox. Initially, Pitt was lukewarm, but the disgraceful opposition of Members for Liverpool, Bristol, and London, eventually forced Pitt to back this modest measure, the purport of which, as one Member said, was merely to ensure 'that those whom you allow to be robbed of all things but life, may not unnecessarily and wantonly be deprived of life too.'[18] When Pitt came out in favour of the Bill, he said: 'The regulation proposed would not tend to the abolition of the Trade; but if it did even go to the abolition of the Trade, [I have] no hesitation to declare, that if the Trade could not be carried on in a manner different to that stated by the hon. Members opposite me, [I will] retract what [I] said on a former day against going into the general question, and, waving every other discussion ... give [my] vote for the utter abolition of a Trade which [is] shocking to humanity.'[19]

Opposition to the Bill diminished after this outburst. In the House of Lords, every possible road block was placed in the way of the Bill. Again, Pitt had to cajole and issue threats before the Lords passed the measure.

The black community followed the debates in both Houses closely and Equiano, who was in constant consultation with Sir William Dolben, led several black delegations that attended the Houses of Parliament to listen to the debates and the examination of witnesses. (See Appendix II, Letters III, IV, and V.) He was received by the Speaker of the House of Commons and by the Prime Minister. In addition to the several consultations he had with Members of Parliament, Equiano found time to write to and for the press. On 19 June his letter (Letter XI) to the 'Worldly Members of the BRITISH SENATE', appeared in *The Public Advertiser*. On 25 June he was in the House of Lords, where he heard Lord Sydney's speech in favour of the slave trade. During his speech, Lord Sydney, Pitt's Secretary of State, made some inane remarks about the fiasco of the first expedition to Sierra Leone.[20] In *The Public Advertiser* (28 June), as politely as he could, Equiano told Lord Sydney that he had talked nonsense in the Lords (Letter XIII).

In May 1787, the Society for the Abolition of the Slave Trade was instituted by twelve individuals, most of whom were London merchants, and all but two of whom were Quakers. The two non-

Quakers were Granville Sharp and Thomas Clarkson.[21] Granville Sharp, as England's earliest Abolitionist, was invited to be Chairman. By June 1788, through the propaganda mounted by the Society, at least 100 petitions had been presented to Parliament, some calling for the outright abolition of the trade, others calling for its regulation. Thus, by 9 May 1788, when Pitt moved his resolution that the Commons should debate the subject of the slave trade in the next session, 'There was an apparent enthusiasm in behalf of the injured Africans.' Clarkson commented, 'It was supposed by some that there was a moment, in which if the Chancellor of the Exchequer [the official title of the Prime Minister at the time] had moved for an immediate abolition of the Trade, he would have carried it that night.'[22] But Abolition was a dream deferred. As Pitt's Lord Chancellor, Lord Thurlow, put it in his own rough, disparaging way, it was merely a 'five days fit of philanthropy'.[23]

Equiano took an active part in the Abolitionist campaign in the summer of 1788, and an acquaintance was to write a few years later that he was an important influence in bringing about the motion. That was not all. *The Public Advertiser*, 28 January 1788, published his review (Letter VI) of the pro-slavery tracts by James Tobin, *Cursory Remarks upon the Reverend Mr. Ramsay's Essay on the Treatment and Conversion of African Slaves in the British Sugar Colonies* (1785) and *A Short Rejoinder to the Reverend Mr. Ramsay's reply to J. Tobin's 'Cursory Remarks'* (1787). These two books, as the titles indicate, were scurrilous attacks on James Ramsay whose *Essay on the Treatment and Conversion of African Slaves in the British Sugar Colonies* had been published in 1784, and was based on nineteen years of experience in the West Indies. In his book, Ramsay exposed the heavy mortality among slaves on the plantations; he refuted the myth that the slave trade was the nursery of the British Navy, and affirmed, 'As far as I can judge, there is no difference between the intellects of whites and blacks.'[24] Tobin violently denied Ramsay's assertions, launched bitter personal attacks on Ramsay, and roundly denigrated the Africans.

Although the subject of dispute between Ramsay and Tobin was the treatment of African slaves in the British sugar colonies, somehow Tobin brought into the contention Africans resident in Britain at the time. And it is axiomatic that a writer of his ilk would draw attention to 'the great number of [blacks] at present in England, the strange partiality shewn for them by the lower order of women, and the rapid increase of a dark and contaminated breed'. Moreover, Tobin had written earlier in the same book about 'the promiscuous commerce too common between the

231

English managers and overseers, and the female slaves under their charge.'[25]

When Equiano was working on Robert King's slave ships sailing around the Caribbean, he recounted:

I was often a witness to cruelties of every kind, which were exercised on my unhappy fellow slaves ... It was almost a constant practice with our clerks, and other whites, to commit violent depredations on the chastity of the female slaves; and these I was, though with reluctance, obliged to submit to at all times, being unable to help them. When we had some of these slaves on board my master's vessels to carry them to other islands or to America, I have known our mates to commit these acts most shamefully, to the disgrace not of Christians only, but of men. I have even known them gratify their brutal passion with females not ten years old; and these abominations some of them practised to such scandalous excess, that one of our captains discharged the mate and others on that account. And yet in Monserrat I have seen a black man staked to the ground, and cut most shockingly, and then his ears cut off bit by bit, because he had been connected with a common prostitute: as if it were no crime in the whites to rob an innocent African girl of her virtue; but most heinous in a Black man only to gratify a passion of nature, where the temptation was offered by one of a different colour, though the most abandoned woman of her species.[26]

Equiano rejected Tobin's shameless lie that only British overseers and managers were responsible for mulattoes in the West Indies. On the contrary, Equiano declared, 'some of our most wealthy Planters [are] their fountain'. It is remarkable that, in spite of the flogging of black women into prostitution that Equiano had witnessed, his reply to the spectre of 'miscegenation' luridly painted by Tobin was that of a humanist (see Appendix I, Letter VI). 'As the ground work, why not establish inter-marriages at home, and in our Colonies? and encourage open, free, and generous loves upon Nature's own wide and extensive plain, subservient only to moral rectitude, without distinction of colour of a skin?'

Five years after Equiano wrote these words, he married an English girl.

Equiano also reviewed Gordon Turnbull's *Apology for Negro Slavery* (1786). Clarkson in the preface to *Commerce of the Human Species*, noted that Turnbull's book 'is almost too despicable a composition to merit a reply'. Equiano, too, thought that 'In this enlightened age, it is scarcely credible that a man should be born and educated, in the British dominions especially, possessed of minds so warped as the author of the Cursory Remarks and yourself.' Equiano felt obliged to attack Turnbull and Tobin in the same breath, because Turnbull in the *Apology* had praised Tobin as the 'impartial and well informed' author of *Cursory Remarks*, who had fully answered James Ramsay's ill-founded assertions.[27]

Samuel Jackson Pratt published his poem *Humanity* in 1788, and *The Morning Chronicle* during June 1788 carried some of the verses. It was after Equiano had read some of these that he wrote Letter XII. In the preface to the poem, Pratt wrote: 'I felt myself called upon by all the awakened emotions of HUMANITY, to consider SLAVERY ... Humanity requires that the Rights of Nature should be enjoyed by every Human Being.' He was contending against the shocking barbarity, the unquestionable cruelty, and the too well-attested horror of slavery. 'Abolition of *these enormities* is absolutely necessary. For the rest, whether the commerce flourishes or falls, is a matter of no moment to the Philanthropist ... the *wealth of worlds* cannot justify the least wanton infraction of the *laws of Humanity*.'

> The rights of man by nature still are due,
> To men of ev'ry clime and every hue.

After reading some of the verses, Equiano sat down and wrote, 'In the name of the poor injured Africans, I return you my innate thanks.' In an editorial note beneath the letter, the paper stated, 'We cannot but think the letter a strong argument in favour of the *natural abilities*, as well as *good feelings*, of the [African] Race, and a solid answer in their favour, though manifestly written in haste, and we print it exactly from the original.' As a matter of fact, Equiano had copied a passage from his earlier letter to *The Public Advertiser*, 13 February 1788 (Letter VIII), which he incorporated into his letter to *The Morning Chronicle*.

In Letter IX, Equiano put forward his case for trade in commodities instead of trade in human flesh between Africa and Britain. Similar ideas had been put forward by the King of Dahomey (1727, through Captain Bulfinch Lambe), Malachy Postlethwayt (1757), Ramsay (1785), and Clarkson (1786). Equiano wrote at least three letters on the subject. The first was to Lord Hawkesbury (Letter IX). This letter was included in the Privy Council report relating to Trade and Foreign Plantations.[28] The letter was reprinted in *The Public Advertiser*, 30 March 1788. And in the *Narrative*,[29] a year later, Equiano repeated almost word for word his letter to Lord Hawkesbury. The chief interest of the letter lies not in the contents, but in the person to whom it was addressed, for it shows Equiano's grasp of the politics of the time and his knowledge of individuals who could be influenced on particular issues. Lord Hawkesbury, born Jenkinson, was a West Indian proprietor, and, as President of the Privy Council for Trade, he lent consistent support to the cause of the slave owners and slave traders. For this devotion tracts in favour of the slave trade were dedicated to him, and Liverpool conferred on him the freedom of the city in gratitude for the essential services rendered to the city by his exertions in Parliament in support of the slave trade. 'Hawkesbury symbolized the connection by assuming the title Earl of Liverpool when raised to the peerage and accepting the Corporation's offer to quarter its arms with his own.'[30] Five months after Equiano sent his letter to Hawkesbury, *The Public Advertiser*, 18 August 1788, referred to him as 'that prompt actor of every part in the political drama'. Equiano could not have chosen a more appropriate politician to send his letter to than Hawkesbury.

After his dismissal as Commissary to the Black Poor in March 1787, Equiano must have commenced the writing of his *Narrative*. The *Narrative*, which is in two volumes and 526 pages long, was published in 1789. In *The Monthly Review* for June 1789, a reviewer commented: 'The Narrative wears an honest face; and we have conceived a good opinion of the man, from the artless manner in which he has detailed the variety of adventures and vicissitudes which have fallen to his lot. His publication appears very seasonably, at a time when negroe-slavery is the subject of public investigation; and it seems calculated to increase the odium that has been excited against the West-India planters, on account of the cruelties that some are said to have exercised on their slaves, many instances of which are here detailed.'

*The General Magazine and Impartial Review*, July 1789, observed that 'The Narrative appears to be written with much truth and simplicity. ... and the reader, unless perchance he is either a West-India planter or Liverpool merchant, will find his humanity often severely wounded by the shameless barbarity practised towards the author's hapless countrymen in all our colonies.'

And a modern reviewer has said that 'Equiano has many of the characteristics of the 18th-century literary hero or narrator, emerging from his narrative as a wholly convincing, living personality prepared to reveal the truth about himself whether or not it is entirely pleasant.'[31] Although the reviewer in *The Gentleman's Magazine* commented on the 'very unequal style' of the *Narrative*, the reviewer in *The Monthly Review* thought that 'it is not improbable that some English writer assisted him in the compliment, or at least the correction of his book, for it is sufficiently well written'. The modern critic, Paul Edwards, disagrees:

> We must remember that Equiano had received schooling even when a slave, had mixed constantly with Englishmen, and from the age of twenty-one had been a free man working as a valet, regularly in the company of educated people. There is no reason why he should not, at the age of forty-four, be perfectly fluent in English. Apart from one or two purple patches, in fact, Equiano's English is very plain, and occasionally even clumsy. ... Had the book been revised in any detail, we might have expected generally a much more elaborate style and certainly the removal of all awkward or ungrammatical expressions. In fact, these are not removed, and it is this simplicity and naturalness which gives the book much of its character. If the book was revised, the revisions probably consisted of little more than working up of occasional rhetorical climaxes. Striking evidence of Equiano's own hand is to be found in a poem which he prints immediately after his account of his conversion to Calvinism. It is a fairly competent though dull piece of religious verse, and bears the unmistakable imprint of a West African author in its rhymes—rhymes which are false unless spoken with a West African English accent, and which can still be found in modern West African verse. ... But the most distinctive evidence of all is a manuscript letter of Equiano's [Letter XVII] ... The letter was written at great speed, as Equiano says himself several times in the letter, and there are a few minor errors in it. But not only are these errors fairly insignificant in this context (they resemble errors made by British students writing at speed in examination); whenever an error of grammar occurs, at some point in the letter the same grammatical form occurs correctly, which indicates that haste, not ignorance of the correct form, caused the mistake. Here, then, is decisive evidence that Equiano was fluent and articulate in written English.[32]

There are other decisive pieces of evidence. Equiano's Memorial to the Lords Commissioners of His Majesty's Treasury (Letter IV), written in his own hand, can be seen at the Public Record Office, London (T/1/646/123-5). Furthermore, as we have seen, the letter to *The Morning Chronicle* of 28 June 1788 was 'manifestly written in haste'.

With the publication of his book, Equiano travelled widely through the British Isles selling copies and addressing Abolitionist meetings. From the letters of introduction and recommendation printed in the sixth and subsequent editions of the *Narrative*, we know that he visited Birmingham in 1789. In the following year he was in Manchester, Nottingham, and Cambridge. In a note in the 1792 edition, Equiano wrote:

Since the first publication of my Narrative, I have been in a great variety of scenes in many parts of Great Britain, Ireland and Scotland, an account of which might well be added here, but this would swell the volume. I shall only observe in general, that in May 1791, I sailed from Liverpool to Dublin where I was very kindly received and from thence to Cork; and then travelled over many counties in Ireland. I was every where exceedingly well treated, by persons of all ranks. I found the people extremely hospitable, particularly in Belfast, where I took my passage on board a vessel for Clyde, on the 29th January [1792], and arrived at Greenock on the 30th. Soon after I returned to London, where I found persons of note from Holland and Germany who requested me to go there; and I was glad to hear that an edition of my Narrative had been printed in both places, and also in New York. I remained in London till I heard the debate in the House of Commons on the Slave Trade on April 2 and 3.[33] I then went to Soham in Cambridgeshire, and was married on the 7th April to Miss Cullen daughter of James and Ann Cullen, late of Ely.

In his letter of 27 February 1792 (Letter XVII), Equiano intimated that after giving his bride 'about 8 or 10 days Comfort, I mean Directly to go to Scotland—and sell my 5th Editions—I Trust that my going has been of much use to the Cause of Abolition.' He also visited Durham, Hull, and Stockton in 1792, and Bath and Devizes the following year. Several thousand copies of the *Narrative* were sold during Equiano's lifetime, and many more after his death. He said that, during his stay of eight and a half months in Ireland in 1791-2, he sold 1,900 copies. And in a note in the later editions of the *Narrative*, he expressed his gratitude for 'the kind reception which this Work has met with from many hundred persons'.

Everywhere he went, Equiano kindled or increased hostility to slavery and the slave trade. Thus in *A Century of Birmingham Life*, we are told, 'Gustavus Vasa, the African, visited Birmingham this year [1789], and increased the indignation of the friends of the slaves by the circulation of his narrative.'[34] The *Narrative* was the last secular book John Wesley read, as he recorded in his *Journal*: 'Wed. 23 Feb 1791, read Gustavus Vasa.' He was particularly struck by Equiano's statement that in the West Indies the evidence of a black man was inadmissible against a white man. 'What villany is this!' he exclaimed.[35] Wesley's name appears in the long list of subscribers to the *Narrative*. He not only read the book on his way to his last service at Leatherhead, but in all probability it led him to write his last letter to Wilberforce on 24 February 1791. The slave trade, he solemnly avowed in this letter written in expectation of death, 'is the scandal of religion, of England, and of human nature. ... Go on in the name of God and in the power of His might, till even American slavery, the vilest that ever saw the sun, shall vanish before it.' On his death bed, his own strength failing, Wesley desired both James Rogers and Elizabeth Ritchie to read aloud to him from the *Narrative*.[36]

Clearly, Equiano's character and ability did much to advance and win support for Abolition. Thomas Digges, in his letter of introduction, dated Belfast, 25 December 1791, wrote that Equiano was 'an enlightened African, of good sense, agreeable manner, and of excellent character'. During his residence in England, Digges wrote that he had seen him 'with Sir William Dolben, Mr. Granville Sharp, Mr. Wilkes, and many other distinguished characters. He supported an irreproachable character, and was a principal instrument in bringing about the motion for a repeal of the Slave-act.' William Eddis in his letter of 25 October 1792 introduced Equiano as 'An African of distinguished merit. ... To the principal supporters of the Bill for the Abolition of the Slave-trade he is well known; and has, himself, been very instrumental in promoting a plan so truly conducive to the interests of Religion and Humanity.'

Because Equiano did much to advance the cause of Abolition, he incurred the bitter displeasure of the dealers in human flesh, who tried to discredit him and neutralize his influence. But they failed. The story of their craven conduct and ignoble failure is well told by the editor of the 1814 (Leeds) edition of the *Narrative*:

Being a true relation of occurences which had taken place, and of sufferings which he had endured, [the Narrative] produced a degree of humane feeling in men's minds, to excite which the most animated addresses and the most convincing abstract reasoning would have laboured in vain.

Some judgement may be formed of the popularity of this narrative, and of the ability with which it is written, for the circumstance of its having raised the indignation, and engendered the hatred of many persons interested in the prosperity of the slave-trade. In various ways the author was persecuted: They tried to asperse his character, by representing him as an impostor; and to invalidate his testimony, by accusing him of wilful falsehoods. They carried the violence of their passions to such a height as to assert that he was not a native of Africa, but that he was born in the Danish Island of Santa Cruz, in the West Indies. His dismissal, by government, from his situation of *Commissary to the black poor going to Africa*, furnished these inveterate adversaries with another opportunity of pouring contumely on an innocent man, and of insinuating crimes against him of which he was never guilty. But they failed in this, as in their former attacks. For it appeared in explanation, that the only circumstance which bore the colour of a charge against him in the affair, was his determination not *silently* to sit and connive at the frauds which were committed by others.

Whenever he defended himself, FACTS were the foundation of his as-

237

sertions; and no statement was made by him, for which he had not some voucher or authority. He appealed to these, and to persons that had known him in early life; and the envious shafts of his opposers fell pointless. If his enemies possessed arrogance and industry, his favourers in a righteous cause were courageous and indefatigable. They traced several injurious reports to their polluted sources; and compelled the editor of one paper, in which his character had been traduced, to make a suitable apology for his conduct,[37] though he was not himself the author of the offensive paragraph.

The Editor of another paper, in which the same calumny was copied, in making his apology, says, 'After examining the paragraph which immediately follows the one in question, I am inclined to believe that the one respecting Gustavus Vassa may have been fabricated by some of the advocates for continuing the slave-trade, for the purpose of weakening the force of the evidence brought against the trade; for I believe, if they could, they would stifle the evidence altogether.'

But Equiano refuted the 'invidious falsehood' that he was not born in Africa, which appeared in *The Oracle*, 25 April 1792, and in *The Star*, 27 April 1792.[38] He went on to offer the sixth edition 'of my Narrative to the candid reader, and to the friends of humanity, hoping it may still be the means, in its measure, of showing the enormous cruelties practised on my sable brethren, and strengthening the generous emulation now prevailing in this country.'

Little is known about his activities between the publication of the sixth edition of his book in 1792, and his death in April 1797. There is no doubt, however, that he remained a zealous labourer in the cause of Abolition, for he was visited by Granville Sharp during his last illness: 'He was a sober, honest man—and I went to see him when he lay upon his death bed, and had lost his voice so that he could only whisper.'[39]

Half a century after Equiano travelled round Britain, advancing the cause of the Abolition of the slave trade and Emancipation of black slaves in British colonies, Frederick Douglass, William Wells Brown, Alexander Crummell, and other black Abolitionists and leaders from America travelled the length and breadth of Britain, soliciting and winning support for the emancipation of black slaves in America. Certainly these mission-bent blacks who crisscrossed the British Isles were most cordially received. 'Small in number and transients for the most part, they posed no threat to the labouring man or to the purity of the national blood stream. Hence they received that heartiest of welcomes that comes from a love of virtue combined with an absence of apprehension.'[40] Olaudah Equiano, the first itinerant black Abolitionist in Britain, did his pioneering work in less auspicious circumstances. He was resident in Britain, he believed in inter-marriage between black and white and married an English girl by whom he had at least one daughter. He earned his living as a valet, hairdresser, sailor, and writer. Above all, Olaudah Equiano was the first national leader of black people in Britain who stood uncompromisingly for black Manhood, Dignity, and Freedom.

Today it is well worth reading *Letters of a Black Abolitionist* (Appendix I) and *The Interesting Narrative*. Olaudah Equiano's Calvinism and religious fervour will not go down well with many today. But 'the zeal of this worthy African, in favour of his brethren, would do honour to any colour, or to any cause.'[41]

1. Olaudah Equiano, *Equiano Travels*, ed. Paul Edwards (London, 1969), 2nd ed.; Olaudah Equiano, *The Interesting Narrative* ... (London, 1969), 2 vols., with introduction by Paul Edwards. Unless otherwise stated, citations are from the abridged edition. Passages omitted in this edition are quoted from the first (1789) edition.

2. Equiano, *Equiano Travels*, pp. 32, 35-6, 40-1, 44-5.

3. Ibid., pp. 49-50, 55-60.

4. Ibid., p. 62.

5. Ibid., pp. 63-8. 91-7, 118-34.

6. Equiano, *The Interesting Narrative* ... (1789), II, pp. 119-23.

7. The case is reported under the title *Gregson* v. *Gilbert* (1783). 3 Dougl. 233; 99 E.R. 629.

8. Hoare, *Memoirs of Granville Sharp* (London, 1828), 2nd ed., I, p. 363.

9. Ibid., I, p. 352.

10. *The Gentleman's Magazine*, LIII, Pt. II (1783), p. 859.

11. Clarkson, *History of the ... Abolition of the African Slave Trade*, I, p. 96.

12. Cugoano, op. cit., pp. 111-12.

13. *Parliamentary History*, XXIII, cols. 1026-7.

14. Equiano, *The Interesting Narrative* ... (1789), II, p. 228.

15. Five years earlier Lord North, then Prime Minister had said that the trade was necessary. The dramatic change in British policy was due to the miraculous growth of San Domingo, as C. L. R. James has so lucidly demonstrated in *The Black Jacobins*, pp. 51-7.

16. *Parliamentary History*, XXVII, col. 499. It was a Fox coalition Government that eventually abolished the British slave trade in 1807.

17. Ibid., col. 580.

18. Ibid., col. 597.

19. Ibid., col. 598.

20. Ibid., cols. 646-7.

21. The ten Quakers were William Dillwyn, Samuel Hoare, George Harrison, John Lloyd, Joseph Wood, Richard Phillips, John Barton, Joseph Hooper, James Phillips, and Philip Samson. See Clarkson, *History of the ... Abolition of the African Slave Trade*, I, p. 256.

22. Ibid., I, p. 524.

23. *Parliamentary History*, XXVII, col. 643.

24. James Ramsay, op. cit., p. 203.

25. James Tobin, op. cit., p. 37.

26. Equiano (1789), I, pp. 205-7.

27. [Gordon Turnbull] *An Apology for Negro Slavery* (1786), p. 20.

28. *Parliamentary Papers* (1789), part 2.

29. Equiano (1789), II, pp. 249-54.

30. Eric Williams, *Capitalism and Slavery* (London, 1964), pp. 94-5.

31. Equiano, p. xvi.

32. Ibid., pp. xiv-xv.

33. Equiano was referring to the debates on one of Wilberforce's Bills for the abolition of the slave trade. When the Bill was rejected, the bells of Bristol churches pealed merrily. *The Public Advertiser*, 27 April 1797, reported, 'On Sunday [24 April], at Bristol, upon the arrival of the Morning Papers, which gave an account of the fate of the Slave Trade Bill in the House of Commons, the bells were set a ringing, ... a number of cannons were discharged from Brandon Hill, and a bonfire and fireworks were given in the evening.'

34. J. A. Langford, *A Century of Birmingham Life* (Birmingham, 1868), I, p. 440.

35. Equiano (1789), I, p. 250.

36. John Wesley, *Journal*, VIII, p. 128.

37. See letter printed in the sixth edition of the *Narrative*.

38. The letters appeared in these London newspapers while Equiano was in Glasgow selling his *Narrative*.

39. Equiano, p. xiii.

40. Benjamin Quarles, *Black Abolitionists*, p. 136.

41. *The County Chronicle, and Weekly Advertiser for Essex, Herts, Kent, Surrey, Middlesex, &c.* (19 February 1788).

# Epilogue

Black people are human beings just as white people are. Yet almost from the beginning of contact between the African people and the Europeans, the whites have relied on greed and impudence and cruelty to further their sordid and pecuniary interests. In the last quarter of this century, the African awakening has reduced and is reducing the greed, cruelty and bestiality of the whites towards black people. But there is still a long way to go before the good and the beautiful can triumph when black and white meet. The cancer of racism has eaten too deeply into the psyche of Western man.

The cankerworm of racism still gnaws relentlessly at the vitals of the British nation. Black children are being railroaded daily into schools for the 'Educationally Sub-Normal', and their fathers and mothers, brothers, and sisters are driven to prisons. Black men are denied jobs because they are black. Policemen brutalize black people because they are black. In April 1969 David Oluwole, a Nigerian, was dragged out of a Leeds canal, dead. Two and a half years later, two English policemen, Ellerker and Kitching, were tried for the manslaughter of Oluwole. During the trial witnesses testified that they saw two police officers chase a man resembling Oluwole into the river Aire, but the Judge directed the jury as a matter of law to return verdicts of not guilty to charges of manslaughter. Geoffrey Ellerker was, however, found guilty on four charges of assaulting David Oluwole and causing him actual bodily harm. Kenneth Kitching was found guilty of three charges of assaulting Oluwole, including urinating on the black man. In the course of his evidence Kitching said he regarded Oluwole as an animal. It would be a gross injustice to the animal creation to call this pathetic little Frankenstein an animal, for the animal creation have an innate sense of decency that prevents them urinating on their kind. Illustration after illustration could be given in further proof that racism in all its bloated nakedness reigns supreme in Britain.

Black people in their contact with the whites have struggled for all that is fine and noble and human. As black people we must know that racism is an insanity, a disgrace to humanity, and a negation of man. The expulsion of British Asian citizens from Uganda is therefore a tragedy for Africa. It was not a tragedy for the Asians expelled, most of whom are of the ilk of the Asian who wrote in *The Times*, 22 November 1968: 'As an Asian, I take strong objection to the fact that we are bracketed together— as "coloured" immigrants—with people of African origin. What do we have in common? We are as different in our looks and in our habits (indeed in colour too), from the Africans as we are from the Europeans, perhaps less so in the latter case as we are both of Caucasian origin. We have five thousand years of civi- lized history behind us, the Africans have a lot fewer.'

Yet we remember with pain, sorrow, and anger that during the period of that cowardly phenomenon called 'Paki-bashing' in Britain in 1970, it was the Asians who are of Caucasian origin who were maimed and murdered by the yobs and louts.[1] For such people as the writer of this letter, who, as browns, have been bru- talized and degraded, too, by the West, there is no need to waste one syllable in sympathy when they are kicked out of Africa. There is no need either to waste one drop of ink in regard to the bilious and hypocritical reaction in the British press over the expulsion of British Asians from Uganda. Let it not pass unob- served, however, that when Idi Amin Dada seized power he was hailed as a friend of Britain, who would reverse the anti-British policies of Milton Obote. He had the best press perhaps ever given to an African leader in Britain. His government was recog- nized with indecent haste by Britain. When Amin came to Britain not long afterwards, he had hardly got off the aircraft which brought him to England when he had tea with the Great White Mother. He was honoured and fêted by the British Government. When Amin the good sergeant, Amin the officer material, Amin the friend of Britain, Amin 'our boy' turned against Britain, he became Amin the madman. Such are the ways of imperialism and imperialists. Meanwhile, authenticated evidence of the massacres of Africans in Uganda was ignored by the British press (except the *Observer*) and Government. The British Government even sent a military training mission to Uganda. But, then, the life of the African has never been held to be of any account by the Brit- ish in the pursuit of their squalid and mercenary interests in Africa.

Kenyatta, yesterday's 'leader of darkness' in the view of the British, is now today's man of light and enlightenment. We demand black power in Africa, America, and Britain not as a means to rival the West in greed, inhumanity, cruelty, brutality, and murder. The West holds the world records for these insani- ties; and in a million years black people cannot beat the records of the West. We demand black power because we are resolutely and irrevocably determined to ensure that we shall no longer be beasts of burden, born to be exploited by the whites for inordinate profits; that the fruits of our labours shall no longer be taken from our mouths; that the lands of our fathers are ours to hold and to cherish and improve and preserve; that black women are not born to be brutally violated by whites; that we shall no longer tolerate orgies and bestialities of racism. In the long march towards the extermination of these obscenities of racism black people must shun like the plague that 'pride of race' in whites which for centuries has been the cause of the destruction of millions of black human persons. It would be the easiest and cheapest thing indeed to become black racists. For before us lie centuries of white expertise in the field. As we march forward day after day, week after week, month after month, year after year, decade after decade, the blackest thing in the history of the contact between the blacks and the whites must never be the black people.

1. Those Asians who are of the same opinion as the writer in *The Times* should read Joan Leopold's article 'British Applications of the Aryan Theory of Race to India, 1850-1870', *English Historical Review* (LXXXIX, July 1974), pp. 578-603.

# Appendix I

# Letters of a Black Abolitionist

## LETTER I[1]

To the Right Reverend Father in God, ROBERT, Lord Bishop of London:

The MEMORIAL of GUSTAVUS VASSA

SHEWETH,

THAT your memorialist is a native of Africa, and has a knowledge of the manners and customs of inhabitants of that country.

That your memorialist has resided in different parts of Europe for twenty-two years last past, and embraced the Christian faith in the year 1759.

That your memorialist is desirous of returning to Africa as a missionary, if encouraged by your Lordship, in hopes of being able to prevail upon his countrymen to become Christians; and your memorialist is the more induced to undertake the same, from the success that has attended the like undertakings when encouraged by Portuguese through their different settlements on the coast of Africa, and also by the Dutch: both governments encouraging the blacks, who, by their education are qualified to undertake the same, and are found more proper than European clergymen, unacquainted with the language and customs of the country.

Your memorialist's only motive for soliciting the office of a missionary is, that he may be a means, under God, of reforming his countrymen and persuading them to embrace the Christian religion. Therefore your memorialist humbly prays your Lordship's encouragement and support in the undertaking.[2]

GUSTAVUS VASSA.

At Mr. Guthrie's taylor,
No. 17 Hedge-lane. (1779)

## LETTER II[3]

In October 1785 I was accompanied by some of the Africans, and presented this address of thanks to the gentlemen called Quakers, in Gracechurch-Court Lombard-Street:

GENTLEMEN,

By reading your book, entitled a Caution to Great Britain and her Colonies, concerning the Calamitous State of the enslaved Negroes: We the poor, oppressed, needy, and much-degraded [blacks], desire to approach you with this address of thanks, with our inmost love and warmest acknowledgment; and with the deepest sense of your benevolence, unwearied labour, and kind interposition, towards breaking the yoke of slavery, and to administer a little comfort and ease to thousands and tens of thousands of very grievously afflicted, and too heavy burthened [blacks].

Gentlemen, could you, by perseverance, at last be enabled, under God, to lighten in any degree the heavy burthen of the afflicted, no doubt it would in some measure, be the possible means, under God, of saving the souls of many of the oppressors; and, if so, sure we are that the God, whose eyes are ever upon all his creatures, and always rewards every true act of virtue, and regards the prayers of the oppressed, will give to you and yours those blessings which it is not in our power to express or conceive, but which we, as a part of those captived, oppressed, and afflicted people, most earnestly wish and pray for.

These gentlemen received us very kindly, with a promise to exert themselves on behalf of the oppressed Africans, and we parted.

## LETTER III

### *The Public Advertiser*
### 4 April 1787

We are sorry to find that his Majesty's Commissary for the African Settlement has sent the following letter to Mr. John Stewart, Pall Mall:

At Plymouth, March 24, 1787.

Sir,
These with my respects to you. I am sorry you and some more are not here with us. I am sure Irwin, and Fraser the Parson, are great villains, and Dr. Currie. I am exceeding much aggrieved at the conduct of those who call themselves gentlemen. They now mean to serve (or use) the blacks the same as they do in the West Indies. For the good of the settlement I have borne every affront that could be given, believe me, without giving the least occasion, or ever yet resenting any.

By Sir Charles Middleton's letter to me, I now find Irwin and Fraser have wrote to the Committee and the Treasury, that I use the white people with arrogance, and the blacks with civility, and stir them up to mutiny: which is not true, for I am the greatest peace-maker that goes out. The reason for this lie is, that in the presence of these two I acquainted Captain Thompson of the Nautilus sloop, our convoy, that I would go to London and tell of their roguery; and further insisted on Captain Thompson to come on board of the ships, and see the wrongs done to me and the people; so Captain Thompson came and saw it, and ordered the things to be given according to contract—which is not yet done in many things—and many of the black people have died for want of their due. I am grieved in every respect. Irwin never meant well to the people, but self-interest has ever been his end: twice this week [the Black Poor] have taken him, bodily, to the Captain, to complain of him, and I have done it four times.

I do not know how this undertaking will end; I wish I had never been involved in it; but at times I think the Lord will make me very useful at last.

> I am, dear Friend,
> With respect, your's,
> 'G. VASA.'
> The Commissary for the Black Poor.

## LETTER IV

To the Right Honourable the Lords Commissioners of His Majesty's Treasury.

The Memorial and Petition of Gustavus Vassa, Black Man, late Commissary to the Black Poor, going to Africa.

HUMBLY SHEWETH,

That your Lordships' Memorialist was by the Honourable the Commissioners of His Majesty's Navy on the 4th December last appointed to the above Employment by Warrant from that Board, That He, accordingly proceeded to the execution of his Duty on board of the *Vernon* being one of the Ships appointed to proceed to Africa with the above Poor. That your Memorialist to his great grief and Astonishment received a Letter of Dismission from the Honble. Commissioners of the Navy by your Lordships' Orders. That conscious of his having acted with the most perfect Fidelity and the greatest Assiduity in discharging the Trust reposed in him he is altogether at a loss to conceive the Reasons of your Lordships' having altered the favourable opinion you were pleased to entertain of him. Sensible that your Lordships would not proceed to so severe a measure without some apparent good Cause, he therefore has every reason to believe that his Conduct has been grossly misrepresented to your Lordships and he is the more confirmed in this Opinion because by opposing measures of others concerned in the same Expedition which tended to defeat your Lordships' humane intentions and to put the Government to a very considerable additional expence he created a number of Enemies whose misrepresentations he has too much reason to believe laid the foundation of his Dismission.

Unsupported by Friends and unaided by the advantages of a liberal Education he can only hope for Redress from the Justice of his Cause. In addition to the mortification of being removed from his Employment and the advantage which he might reasonably have expected to have derived therefrom he has the misfortune to have sunk a considerable part of his little property in fitting himself out and in other expences arising out of his Situation an account of which he herewith annexes.* Your Memorialist will not trouble your Lordships with a Vindication of any part of his Conduct because he knows not what crimes he is accused, he however earnestly wishes that you will be pleased to direct an Enquiry into his behaviour during the time he acted in the Public Service and if it shall be found that his Dismission arose from false Representations he is confident that in your Lordships' Justice he will find redress.

Your Petitioner therefore humbly prays that your Lordships will take his Case into Consideration and that you will be pleased to order Payment of the above referred to Account Amounting to £32.4.0 and also the Wages intended me.

> Which is most humbly
> Submitted
> GUSTAVUS VASSA.

P.S. This Account the Navy Board do not think themselves authorized to allow without the order of the Lords of the Treasury.——

London 12th May 1787.[4]

*a List of sundry Expences of Gustavus Vasa the late Commissary for the Black Poor going to Africa, not allowed by the Navy Board.

|  |  | £ | s. | d. |
|---|---|---|---|---|
| 13 Febry. 1787 | To paid for a Flag for the Settlement in Africa | 5. | 5. | 0. |
| 4 Aprl. | To his Expences from London to Plymouth | 2. | 16. | 0. |
| 28 | To Dr. from Plymouth with his Baggage | 4. | 6. | 0. |
|  | To withdrawing the Insurance on £400 | 2. | 0. | 0. |
|  | To a Letter of Attorney and Policy | 1. | 4. | 6. |
|  | To Discount on Goods | 13. | 7. | 6. |
|  | To Dr. on Provisions | 3. | 5. | 0. |
|  |  | £32. | 4. | 0. |

## LETTER V

### *The Public Advertiser*
### 14 July 1787

An extract of a letter from on board one of the ships with the Blacks, bound to Africa, having appeared on the 2nd and 3rd inst.[5] in the public papers, wherein injurious reflexions, prejudicial to the character of Vasa, the Black Commissary, were contained, he thinks it necessary to vindicate his character from these misrepresentations, informing the public, that the principal crime which caused his dismission, was an information he laid before the Navy Board, accusing the Agent [Irwin] of unfaithfulness in his office, in not providing such necessaries as were contracted for the people, and were absolutely necessary for their existence, which necessaries could not be obtained from the Agents. The same representation was made by Mr. Vasa to Mr. Hoare, which induced the latter, who had before appeared to be Vasa's friend, to go to the Secretary of the Treasury, and procure his dismission. The above Gentleman impowered the Agent to take many passengers in, contrary to the orders given to the Commissary.

(Mr. Vasa).

## LETTER VI

For *The Public Advertiser.*
28 January 1788

To J.T. Esq; Author of the BOOKS called CURSORY REMARKS &
REJOINDERS.

Sir,

That to love mercy and judge rightly of things is an honour to man,
no body I think will deny, but 'if he understandeth not, nor sheweth
compassion to the sufferings of his fellow-creatures, he is like the beasts
that perish.' Psalm LIX verse 20.

Excuse me, Sir, if I think you in no better predicament than that exhibited in the latter part of the above clause; for can any man less ferocious than a tiger or a wolf attempt to justify the cruelties inflicted on
the [blacks] in the West Indies? You certainly cannot be susceptible of
human pity to be so callous to their complicated woes! Who could but
the Author of the Cursory Remarks so debase his nature, as not to feel
his keenest pangs of heart on reading their deplorable story? I confess
my cheek changes colour with resentment against your unrelenting barbarity, and wish you from my soul to run the gauntlet of Lex Talionis at
this time; for as you are so fond of flogging others, it is no bad proof of
your deserving a flagellation on yourself. Is it not written in the 15th
chapter of Numbers, the 15th and 16th verses, that there is the same law
for the stranger as for you?

Then, Sir, why do you rob him of the common privilege given to all
by the Universal and Almighty Legislator? Why exclude him from the
enjoyment of benefits which he has equal right to with yourself? Why
treat him as if he was not of like feeling? Does civilization warrant these
incursions upon natural justice? No. —Does religion? No. —
Benevolence to all is its essence, and do unto others as we would others
should do unto us, its grand precept—to Blacks as well as Whites, all
being children of the same parent. Those, therefore, who transgress
those sacred obligations, and here, Mr. Remarker, I think you are
caught, are not superior to brutes which understandeth not, nor to beasts
which perish.

From having been in the West Indies, you must know that the facts
stated by the Rev. Mr. Ramsay are true; and yet regardless of the truth,
you controvert them. This surely is supporting a bad cause at all events,
and brandishing falsehood to strengthen the hand of the oppressor.
Recollect, Sir, that you are told in the 17th verse of the 19th chapter of
Leviticus, 'You shall not suffer sin upon your neighbours', and you will
not I am sure, escape the upbraidings of your conscience, unless you are
fortunate enough to have none; and remember also, that the oppressor
and oppressed are in the hands of the just and awful God, who says,
Vengeance is mine and I will repay—repay the oppressor and the justi-
fier of the oppression. How dreadful then will your fate be? The studied
and torturing punishments, inhuman, as they are, of a barbarous
planter, or a more barbarous overseer, will be tenderness compared to
the provoked wrath of an angry but righteous God, who will raise, I

have the fullest confidence, many of the sable race to the joys of Heaven, and cast the oppressive white to that doleful place, where he will cry, but will cry in vain, for a drop of water!

Your delight seems to be in misrepresentation, else how could you in page 11 of your Remarks, and in your Rejoinder, page 35, communicate to the public such a glaring untruth as that the oath of a free African is equally admissible in several courts with that of a white person? The contrary of this I know is the fact at every one of the islands I have been, and I have been at no less than fifteen: But who will dispute with such an invective fibber? Why nobody to be sure; for you'll tell, I wish I could say truths, but you oblige me to use ill manners, you lie faster than Old Nick can hear them. A few shall stare you in the face:

What is your speaking of the laws in favour of the Blacks?

Your description of the iron muzzle?

That you never saw an infliction of a severe punishment, implying thereby that there is none?

That a [black] has every inducement to wish for a numerous family?

That in England there are no black labourers?

That those who are not servants, are in rags or thieves?

In a word, the public can bear testimony with me that you are a malicious slanderer of an honest, industrious, injured people!

From the same source of malevolence the freedom of their inclinations is to be shackled—it is not sufficient for their bodies to be oppressed, but their minds must also? —Iniquity in the extreme! If the mind of a black man conceives the passion of love for a fair female, he is to pine, languish, and even die, sooner than an intermarriage be allowed, merely because the complexion of the offspring should be tawney—A more foolish prejudice than this never warped a cultivated mind—for as no contamination of the virtues of the heart would result from the union, the mixture of colour could be of no consequence. God looks with equal good will on all his creatures, whether black or white—let neither, therefore, arrogantly condemn the other.

The mutual commerce of the sexes of both Blacks and Whites, under the restrictions of moderation and law, would yield more benefit than a prohibition—the mind free—would not have such a strong propensity toward the black females as when under restraint: Nature abhors restraint, and for ease either evades or breaks it. Hence arise secret amours, adultery, fornication and all other evils of lasciviousness! hence that most abandoned boasting of the French Planter, who, under the dominion of lust, had the shameless impudence to exult at the violations he had committed against Virtue, Religion, and the Almighty— hence also spring actual murders on infants, the procuring of abortions, enfeebled constitution, disgrace, shame, and a thousand other horrid enormities.

Now, Sir, would it not be more honour to us to have a few darker visages than perhaps yours among us, than inundation of such evils? And to provide effectual remedies, by a liberal policy against evils which may be traced to some of our most wealthy Planters as their fountain, and which may have smeared the purity of even your own chastity?

As the ground work, why not establish intermarriages at home, and in our Colonies? and encourage open, free, and generous loves upon Nature's own wide and extensive plain, subservient only to moral rectitude, without distinction of the colour of a skin?

That ancient most wise, and inspired political Moses, encouraged strangers to unite with the Israelites, upon this maxim, that every addition to their number was an addition to their strength, and as an inducement, admitted them to most of the immunities of his own people. He established marriage with strangers by his own example—The Lord confirmed them—and punished Aaron and Miriam for vexing their brother for marrying the Ethiopian—Away then with your narrow impolitic notion of preventing by law what will be a national honour, national strength, and productive of national virtue—Intermarriages!

Wherefore, to conclude in the words of one of your selected texts, 'If I come, I will remember the deeds which he doeth, prating against us with malicious words.'

> I am Sir,
> Your fervent Servant,
> GUSTAVUS VASSA, the Ethiopian,
> and the King's late Commissary for the
> African Settlement.

Baldwin's Garden, January, 1788.


## LETTER VII

### For *The Public Advertiser*
### 5 February 1788

To Mr. GORDON TURNBULL, Author of an 'Apology for NEGRO SLAVERY'.

Sir,

I am sorry to find in your Apology for oppression, you deviate far from the Christian precepts, which enjoin us to do unto others as we would others should do unto us. In this enlightened age, it is scarcely credible that a man should be born and educated, in the British dominions especially, possessed of minds so warped as the author of the Cursory Remarks and yourself: Strange that in a land which boasts of the purest light of the Gospel, and the most perfect freedom, there should be found advocates of oppression—for the most abject and iniquitous kind of slavery. To kidnap our fellow creatures, however they may differ in complexion, to degrade them into beasts of burthen, to deny them every right but those, and scarcely those we allow to a horse, to keep them in perpetual servitude, is a crime as unjustifiable as cruel; but to avow and defend this infamous traffic required the ability and the modesty of you and Mr. Tobin. Certainly, Sir, you were perfectly consistent with yourself attacking as you did that friend to the rights of mankind, the Rev. James Ramsay. Malignity and benevolence do not well associate, and humanity is a root that seldom flourishes in the soil of a planter. I am therefore surprised that you have endeavoured to depreciate his noble Essay on the Treatment and Conversion of African Slaves &c. That learned and elegant performance written in favour of a much injured race of men, we are happy to think has had a good effect in opening the eyes of many of his countrymen to the sufferings of their African brethren; for the Apostle calls us all brethren; but if I may form a conjecture from your writings; the Apostles have very small credit either with you or your worthy partner in cruelty, Mr. Tobin; for can any man be a Christian who asserts that one part of the human race were ordained to be in perpetual bondage to another? Is such an assertion, consistent with that spirit of meekness, of justice, of charity, and above all, that brotherly love which it enjoins? But we trust that inspite of your *hissing* zeal and impotent malevolence against Mr. Ramsay, his noble purpose of philanthropy will be productive of much good to many, and in the end through the blessing of God, be a means of bringing about the abolition of slavery. To the Reverend Gentleman we return thanks and heartfelt gratitude, and we also feel ourselves much indebted to all those gentlemen who have stepped forward in our defence, and vindicated us from the aspersions of our tyrannical calumniators.

You and your friend, J. Tobin, the Cursory Remarker, resemble Demetrius, the Silversmith, seeing your craft in danger, a craft, however, not so innocent or justifiable as the making of shrines for Diana, for that though wicked enough, left the persons of men at liberty, but yours enslaves both body and soul—and sacrifices your fellow-creatures on the altar of avarice.[6] You, I say, apprehensive that the promulgation of truth will be subversive of your infamous craft, and destructive of your iniquitous gain, rush out with desperation of assassins, and attempt to wound the reputation of the Reverend Essayist by false calumnies, gross contradictions of several well-known facts, and insidious suppression of others. The character of that Reverend Gentleman to my knowledge (and I have known him well both here and in the West Indies for many years) is irreproachable. Many of the facts he relates I know to be true, and many others still more shocking, if possible, have fallen within my own observation, within my own feeling; for were I to enumerate even my own sufferings in the West Indies, which perhaps I may one day offer to the public, the disgusting catalogue would be almost too great for belief. It would be endless to refute all your false assertions respecting the treatment of African slaves in the West Indies; some of them, however, are gross; in particular, you say in your apology page 30, 'That a Negro has every inducement to wish a numerous family, and enjoys every pleasure he can desire.' A glaring falsehood! But to my great grief, and much anguish in different islands in the West Indies, I have been a witness to children torn from their agonized parents, and sent off wherever their merciless owners please, never more to see their friends again. In page 34 of the same elaborate and pious work, you offer an hypothesis, that the [African] race is an inferior species of mankind: Oh fool! See the 17th chapter of the Acts, verse 26, 'God hath made of one blood all nations of men, for to dwell on all the face of the earth, &c.' Therefore, beware of that Scripture, which says, Fools perish for lack of knowledge.

GUSTAVUS VASSA, the Ethiopian,
and late Commissary for the African
Settlement

Baldwin's Gardens.

## LETTER VIII

For *The Public Advertiser*
13 February 1788

To the Senate of GREAT BRITAIN.

Gentlemen,

MAY Heaven make you what you should be, the dispensers of light, liberty and science to the uttermost parts of the earth; then will glory to God in the highest—on earth peace and goodwill to man: Glory, honour, peace, &c. to every soul of man that worketh good; to the Britons first (because to them the Gospel is preached) and also to the nations: To that truly immortal and illustrious advocate of our liberty, Granville Sharp, Esq. the philanthropist and justly Reverend James Ramsay, and the much honoured body of gentlemen called *Friends*, who have exerted every endeavour to break the accursed yoke of Slavery, and ease the heavy burthens of the oppressed [blacks]: 'Those that honour their Maker have mercy on the Poor', —and many blessings are upon the heads of the just. May the fear of the Lord prolong their days, and cause their memory to be blessed, and may their numbers be increased, and their expectations filled with gladness, for commiserating the poor Africans, who are counted as beasts of burthen by base-minded men. May God ever open the mouths of these worthies to judge righteously, and plead the cause of the poor and needy—for the liberal devise liberal things, and by liberal things shall stand; and they can say with the pious Job, 'Did I not weep for him that was in trouble? Was not my soul grieved for the Poor?'

It is righteousness that exalteth a nation, but sin is a reproach to any people. —Destruction shall be to the workers of iniquity—and the wicked shall perish by their own wickedness. —May the worthy Lord Bishop of London[7] be blessed for his pathetic and humane sermon on behalf of the Africans, and all the benevolent gentlemen who are engaged in the laudable attempt to abolish Slavery, and thereby prevent many savage barbarities from being daily committed by the enslavers of men, to whom the Lord has pronounced wrath, anguish, and tribulation, &c. to the sons of Britain first (as having the Gospel preached amongst them) and also to the nations———

AETHIOPIANUS.

## LETTER IX

Letter from Gustavus Vassa, late Commissary for the African Settlement, to the Right Honourable Lord Hawkesbury.

My Lord,                                                    London, 13th March 1788.

As the illicit Traffic of Slavery is to be taken into consideration of the British Legislature, I have taken the Liberty of sending you the following Sentiments, which have met the Approbation of many intelligent and commercial Gentlemen.

Sir,

A SYSTEM of commerce once established in Africa, the Demand for Manufactories will most rapidly augment, as the native Inhabitants will sensibly adopt our Fashions, Manner, Customs, &c. &c.

In proportion to the Civilization, so will be the Consumption of British Manufactures.

The Wear and Tear of a Continent, nearly twice as large as Europe, and rich in Vegetable and Mineral Productions, is much easier conceived than calculated. A Case in point. It cost the Aborigines of Britain little or nothing in Cloathing, &c. The Difference between our Forefathers and us in point of Consumption, is literally infinite. The Reason is most obvious. It will be equally immense in Africa. The same Cause, viz. Civilization, will ever produce the same Effect. There are no Book or outstanding Debts, if I may be allowed the Expression. The Word Credit is not to be found in the African Dictionary; it is standing upon safe Ground.

A commercial Intercourse with Africa opens an inexhaustible Source of Wealth to the manufacturing Interest of Great Britain; and to all which the Slave Trade is a physical Obstruction.

If I am not misinformed, the manufacturing Interest is equal, if not superior to the landed Interest as to Value, for Reasons which will soon appear. The Abolition of the diabolical Slavery will give a most rapid and permanent Extension to Manufactures, which is totally and diametrically opposite to what some interested People assert.

The Manufactories of this Country must and will in the nature and Reason of Things have a full and constant Employ by supplying the African Markets. The Population, Bowels, and Surface of Africa abound in valuable and useful Returns; the hidden treasuries of Countries will be brought to Light and into Circulation.

Industry, Enterprise, and Mining will have their full Scope, proportionably as they civilize. In a Word, it lays open an endless Field of Commerce to the British Manufactures and Merchant Adventurer.

The manufacturing Interest and the general Interest of the Enterprise are synonimous; the Abolition of Slavery would be in reality an universal Good, and for which a partial Ill must be supported.

Tortures, Murder, and every other imaginable Barbarity are practised by the West India Planters upon the Slaves with Impunity. I hope the Slave Trade will be abolished: I pray it may be an Event at hand. The great Body of Manufactories, uniting in the Cause, will considerably facilitate and expedite it; and, as I have already stated, it is most substantially their Interest and Advantage, and as such the Nation at large. In a short Space of Time One Sentiment alone will prevail, from Motives of Interest as well as Justice and Humanity.

Europe contains One hundred and Twenty Millions of Inhabitants; Query, How many Millions doth Africa contain? Supposing the Africans, collectively and individually, to expend Five Pounds a Head in Raiment and Furniture yearly, when civilized, &c.—an Immensity beyond the Reach of Imagination: This I conceive to be a Theory founded upon Facts; and therefore an infallible one. If the Blacks were permitted to remain in their own Country they would double themselves every Fifteen Years: In Proportion to such Increase would be the Demand for Manufactures. Cotton and Indigo grow spontaneously in some Parts of Africa: A Consideration this of no small Consequence to the manufacturing Towns of Great Britain.

The Chamber of Manufactories of Great Britain, held in London will be strenuous in the Cause. It opens a most immense, glorious, and happy Prospect.

The Cloathing, &c. of a Continent Ten thousand Miles in Circumference, and immensely rich in Productions of every Denomination, would make an interesting Return indeed for our Manufactories, a free Trade being established.

> I have, my Lord, the Honour to subscribe myself,
> Your Lordships very humble and devoted Servant,
> GUSTAVUS VASSA,
> the late Commissary for the African Settlement.

No. 53, Baldwin's Gardens, Holborn.

## LETTER X

March the 21st, 1788, I had the honour of presenting the Queen with a petition on behalf of my African brethren, which was received most graciously by her Majesty:

To the QUEEN's most Excellent Majesty.

MADAM,

YOUR Majesty's well known benevolence and humanity emboldens me to approach your royal presence, trusting that the obscurity of my situation will not prevent your Majesty from attending to the sufferings for which I plead.

Yet I do not solicit your royal pity for my own distress; my sufferings, although numerous, are in a measure forgotten. I supplicate your Majesty's compassion for millions of my African countrymen, who groan under the lash of tyranny in the West Indies.

The oppression and cruelty exercised to the unhappy [blacks] there, have at length reached the British legislature, and they are now deliberating on its redress; even several persons of property in slaves in the West Indies, have petitioned Parliament against its continuance, sensible that it is as impolitic as it is unjust—and what is inhuman must ever be unwise.

Your Majesty's reign has been hitherto distinguished by private acts of benevolence and bounty; surely the more extended the misery is, the greater claim it has to your Majesty's compassion, and the greater must be your Majesty's pleasure in administering to its relief.

I presume, therefore, gracious Queen, to implore your interposition with your royal consort, in favour of the wretched African; that, by your Majesty's benevolent influence, a period may now be put to their misery; and that they may be raised from the condition of brutes, to which they are at present degraded, to the rights and situation of freemen, and admitted to partake of the blessings of your Majesty's happy government, so shall your Majesty enjoy the heart-felt pleasure of procuring happiness to millions, and be rewarded in the grateful prayers of themselves, and of their posterity.

And may the all-bountiful Creator shower on your Majesty, and the Royal Family, every blessing that this world can afford, and every fulness of joy which divine revelation has promised us in the next.

I am your Majesty's most dutiful and devoted servant to command,

GUSTAVUS VASSA,
The Oppressed Ethiopean.[8]

No. 53, Baldwin's Gardens.


## LETTER XI

*The Public Advertiser*
19 June 1788[9]

To the Honourable and Worldly Members of the BRITISH SENATE.

Gentlemen,

Permit me, one of the oppressed natives of Africa, thus to offer you the warmest thanks of a heart glowing with gratitude for your late humane interference on the behalf of my injured countrymen. May this and the next year bear record of deeds worthy of yourselves! May you then complete the glorious work you have so humanely begun in this, and join with the public voice in putting an end to an oppression that now so loudly calls for redress! The wise man saith, Prov. xiv. 34, 'Righteousness exalteth a nation, but sin is a reproach to any people.' May all the noble youths I heard speak in our favour in the Senate, be renowned for illustrious deeds, and their aspiring years crowned with glory! May the all bountiful Creator, the God whose eyes are ever upon all his creatures, who ever rewards all virtuous acts, and regards the prayers of the oppressed, make you that return, which I and my unfortunate countrymen are not able to express, and shower on you every happiness this world can afford, and every fullness of which Divine Revelation has promised us in the next! Believe me, Gentlemen, while I attended the debate on the Bill for the relief of my countrymen, now depending before you, my heart burned within me, and glowed with gratitude to those who supported the cause of humanity. I would have wished for an opportunity of recounting to you not only my own sufferings, which, though numerous, have been nearly forgotten, but those of which I have been a witness for many years, that they might have influenced your decision; but I thank God, your humanity anticipated my wishes, and rendered such recital unnecessary. Our cries have at length reached your ears, and I trust you are already in some measure convinced that the Slave Trade is as impolitic as inhuman, and as such must ever be unwise. The more extended our misery is, the greater claim it has to your compassion, and the greater the pleasure, you must feel in administering to its relief. The satisfaction, which, for the honour of human nature, this distinguished act of compassion gave you, was as visible as felt, and affected me much. For the particular favours shewed me by many of your worthy Members, especially your Honourable Chairman Mr. Whitebread, Sir P. Burrell, Sir William Dolben, the Hon. Pitt, &c. &c. &c. I beg thus to express my most grateful acknowledgments, and I pray the good and gracious God ever to distinguish them by his choicest blessings! And if it should please Providence to enable me to return to my estate in Elese, in Africa, and to be happy enough to see any of these worthy Senators there, as the Lord liveth, we will have such a libation of pure virgin palm wine, as shall make their hearts glad!!! —And we will erect two altars—one to Pity*—the other to Freedom—to perpetuate their benevolence to my countrymen.

> I am, with the most devoted respect,
> Honourable and Most Worthy Senators,
> Your grateful and lowly Servant,
> GUSTAVUS VASSA, the African

Baldwin's Gardens, June 18, 1788.

*J.R. and T.C.

[The only sense I can make out of the two initials is that Equiano was referring to James Ramsay and Thomas Clarkson. F.O.S.]

## LETTER XII

*The Morning Chronicle and London Advertiser*
27 June 1788

To the Author of the POEM ON HUMANITY.

Worthy Sir,

In the name of the poor injured Africans, I return you my innate thanks; with prayers to my God ever to fill you with the spirit of philanthropy here, and hereafter receive you into glory. During time may you exert every endeavour in aiding to break the accursed yoke of slavery, and ease the heavy burthens of the oppressed Africans. Sir, permit me to say, 'Those that honour their Maker have mercy on the poor'; and many blessings are upon the heads of the Just. May the fear of the Lord prolong your days, and cause your memory to be blessed, and your expectations filled with gladness, for commiserating the poor Africans, who are counted as beasts of burthen by base-minded men. May God ever enable you to support the cause of the poor and the needy. The liberal devise liberal things, and by liberal things shall stand; and may you ever say with the pious Job, 'Did not I weep for him that was in trouble? Was not my soul grieved for the poor?' May the all-seeing God hear my prayers for you and crown your works with abounding success! pray you excuse what you here see amiss. I remain with thanks and humble respect.

> Yours to Command,
> GUSTAVUS VASSA,
> The Oppressed African,

Now at No. 13, Tottenham-Street,
Wednesday June 25, 1788.

Editorial Note:
'We cannot but think the letter a strong argument in favour of the *natural abilities*, as well as *good feelings*, of the [African] Race, and a solid answer in their favour, though manifestly written in haste, and we print it exactly from the original. As to the question of their *stupidity*, we are sincere friends to *commerce*, but we would have it flourish without *cruelty*.'[10]

## LETTER XIII

### For *The Public Advertiser*
### 28 June 1788

To the Right Hon. LORD SYDNEY.

My Lord,

Having been present last Wednesday [25 June] at the debate of the Slave Bill, now depending in the House of Lords, I with much surprize heard your Lordship combat the very principle of the Bill, and assert that it was founded in mistaken humanity. At first such assertion would appear rather paradoxical. If imposing a restraint on the cruelties practised towards wretches who never injured us, be mistaken humanity, what are the proper channels through which it ought to be directed? However, as your Lordship gave reasons for your opinion, I do not wish either to tax your humanity or candour, but on the contrary believe you were misled by your information. Your Lordship mentioned you had been told by Captain Thompson, under whose convoy the natives of Africa were lately sent out to Sierra Leona, that shortly after their arrival there, some of them embraced the first opportunity of embarking for the West Indies, some of the Lascars, rather than work, lay down among the bushes and died, and that the humane intentions of the

Government were frustrated, and the expectations of all concerned in the enterprize disappointed. Now, my Lord, without impeaching the veracity of that gentleman, or controverting the facts he related, permit me to explain the cause of the ill success of that expedition, which I hope will sufficiently obviate the inferences your Lordship drew from them.

When the intention of sending those people to Sierra Leona was first conceived, it was thought necessary by Government to send a Commissary on their part to Superintend the conduct of the Agent who had contracted for carrying them over, and I being judged a proper person for that purpose was appointed Commissary by the Commissioners of the Navy, the latter end of 1786. In consequence I proceeded immediately to the execution of my duty on board one of the vessels destined for the voyage, where I continued till the March following.

During my continuance in the employment of Government, I was struck with the flagrant abuses committed by the Agent, and endeavoured to remedy them, but without effect. One instance, among many which I could produce, may serve as a specimen: Government had ordered to be provided all necessaries (slops as they are called included) for 750 persons; however not being able to muster more than 426, I was ordered to send the superfluous slops, &c. to the King's stores at Portsmouth, but when I demanded them for that purpose from the Agent, it appeared they had never been bought, tho' paid for by Government. —But that was not all, Government were not the only objects of peculation; these poor people suffered infinitely more—their accommodations were most wretched, many of them wanted beds, and many more cloathing and other necessaries. —For the truth of this, and much more, I do not seek credit on my assertion. I appeal to the testimony of Captain Thompson himself, to whom I applied in February 1787, for remedy, when I had remonstrated to the Agent in vain, and even brought him to a witness of the injustice and oppression I complained of. —I appeal also to a letter written by these wretched people, so early as the beginning of the preceeding January, and published in *The Morning Herald* of the 4th of that month, signed by twenty of their Chiefs.

My Lord, I could not silently suffer Government to be so cheated, and my countrymen plundered and oppressed, and even left destitute of the necessaries for almost their existence—I therefore informed the Commissioners of the Navy of the Agent's proceedings—but my dismission was soon after procured by means of his friend, a Banker in the City, possibly his partner also in the contract. By this I suffered a considerable loss in my property, and he, it is said, made a fortune; however, the Commissioners were satisfied with my conduct, and wrote to Captain Thompson, expressing their approbation of it.

Thus provided they proceeded on their voyage, and at last worn out by treatment, perhaps not the most mild, and wasted by sickness, brought on by want of medicine, cloathes, bedding, &c. &c. they reached Sierra Leona, just at the commencement of the rains—At that season of the year, it is impossible to cultivate the land; their provisions therefore were exhausted before they could derive benefit from agriculture. —And it is not surprising that many, especially the Lascars, whose constitutions are very tender, and who had been cooped up in a ship from October to June, and accommodated in the manner I have mentioned, should be so wasted by their confinement as not long to survive it. —As for the native Africans who remained, there was no object for their industry; and surely, my Lord, they shewed a much less indulgent spirit in going to the West Indies than staying at Sierra Leona to starve.

The above facts and many more instances of oppression and injustices, not only relative to the expedition to Sierra Leona, but to the Slave Trade in general, I could incontrovertibly establish, if at any time it should be judged necessary to call upon me for that purpose.

> I am, my Lord,
> Your Lordship's most respectful and obedient Servant,
> GUSTAVUS VASSA, the African.

Tottenham Street No. 13, June 26.

## LETTER XIV

*The Public Advertiser*
14 February 1789

To the Committee for the Abolition of the Slave Trade at Plymouth.

Gentlemen,

Having seen a plate representing the form in which [Africans] are stowed on board the Guinea ships, which you are pleased to send to the Rev. Mr. Clarkson,[11] a worthy friend of mine, I was filled with love and gratitude towards you for your humane interference on behalf of my oppressed countrymen. Surely this case calls aloud for redress! May this year bear record of acts worthy of a British Senate, and you have the satisfaction of seeing the completion of the work you have so humanely assisted us. With you I think it the indispensable duty of every friend of humanity, not to suffer themselves to be led away with the specious but false pretext drawn from the supposed political benefits this kingdom derives from the continuance of this iniquitous branch of commerce. It is the duty of every man, every friend to religion and humanity, to assist the different Committees engaged in this pious work; reflecting that it does not often fall to the lot of individuals to contribute to so important a moral and religious duty as that of putting an end to a practice which may, without exaggeration, be stiled one of the greatest evils now existing on earth—The wise man saith, 'Righteousness exalteth a nation, but sin is reproach to any people.' Prov. xiv. 34.

Permit me, Gentlemen, on behalf of myself and my brethren, to offer you the warmest effusions of hearts over flowing with gratitude for your pious efforts, which it is my constant prayer may prove successful.

With the best wishes for health and happiness,

> I am, Gentlemen,
> Your obedient, humble Servant,
> GUSTAVUS VASA, the African.

Feb. 7, 1789, No. 10, Union Street,
Middlesex Hospital.


## LETTER XV[12]

To the Lords Spiritual and Temporal, and the Commons of the Parliament of Great Britain.

My Lords and Gentlemen,

PERMIT me with the greatest deference and respect, to lay at your feet the following genuine Narrative; the chief design of which is to excite in your august assemblies a sense of compassion for the miseries which the Slave-trade has entailed on my unfortunate countrymen. By the horror of that trade I was first torn away from all the tender connexions that were naturally dear to my heart; but these, through the mysterious ways of Providence, I ought to regard as infinitely more than compensated by the introduction I have thence obtained to the knowledge of the Christian religion, and of a nation which, by its liberal sentiments, its humanity, the glorious freedom of its government, and its proficiency in arts and sciences, has exalted the dignity of human nature.

I am sensible I ought to entreat your pardon for addressing to you a work so wholly devoid of literary merit; but, as the production of an unlettered African, who is actuated by the hope of becoming an instrument towards relief of his suffering countrymen, I trust that *such a man*, pleading in such a cause, will be acquitted of boldness and presumption.

May the God of Heaven inspire your hearts with peculiar benevolence on that important day when the question of Abolition is to be discussed, when thousands, in consequence of your determination, are to look for Happiness or Misery!

> I am,
> MY LORDS and GENTLEMEN,
> Your most obedient,
> And devoted humble servant,
> OLAUDAH EQUIANO, or
> GUSTAVUS VASSA.

Union Street, Mary-le-bone, March 24, 1789.

## LETTER XVI[13]

Extract from a letter to a Birmingham newspaper in 1789.

I beg you to suffer me thus publicly to express my grateful acknowledgments for their Favours and for the Fellow-feeling they have
discovered for my very poor and much oppressed countrymen; these
Acts of Kindness and Hospitality have filled me with a longing desire to
see these worthy Friends on my own Estate in Africa, when the richest
Produce of it should be devoted to their Entertainment; they should
there partake of the luxuriant Pine-apples and the well-flavoured virgin
Palm Wine, and to heighten the Bliss, I would burn a certain kind of
Tree, that would afford us a Light as clear and brilliant as the Virtues of
my Guests.

I am Sir, your humble Servant,
GUSTAVUS VASA, the African.

## LETTER XVII

London Feby the 27.th 1792

Dr. Revd. & Worthy friends &c.

This with my Best of Respects to you and wife with many Prayers
that you both may ever be Well in Souls and Bodys—& also your Little
Lovely Daughter—I thank you for all kindnesses which you was
pleased to show me, may God ever Reward you for it—Sir, I went to
Ireland & was there 8 months—& sold 1900 copies of my narrative. I
came here on the 10th inst.—& I now mean as it seem Pleasing to my
Good God!—to leave London in about 8—to 10 Days more, & take me
a Wife—(one Miss Cullen—) of Soham in Cambridge shire—& when I
have given her about 8 or 10 Days Comfort, I mean Directly to go to
Scotland—and sell my 5th. Editions—I Trust that my going about has
been of much use to the Cause of the abolition of the accu[r]sed Slave
Trade—a Gentleman of the committee the Revd. Dr. Baker has said
that I am more use to the Cause than half the People in the country—I
wish to God, I could be so. A noble Earl of Stanhope has Lately Consulted me twice about a Bill which his Ld. ship now means to bring in to
the House to allow the sable People of the wt Indias the Rights of taking
an oath against any White Person—I hope it may Pass, tis high time—
and will be much use. —May the Lord Bless all the friends of Humanity. Pray Pardon what ever you here see amiss—I will be Glad to see
you at my Wedg. —Pray give my best Love to the Worthy & Rev. Mr.
Robinson, & his—also to my friends Coltman—and Mr. & Mrs. Buxton—I Pray that the Good Lord may make all of that family Rich in
faith as in the things of this World—I have Great Deal to say if I ever
have the Pleasure to see you again—I have been in the uttermost hurry
ever since I have being in this wickd. Town—& I only came now to
save if I can, £232, I Lent to a man, who now Dying. Pray Excuse ha[s-
te]—will be Glad to hear from you—& do very much beg your Prayers
as you ever have mine—& if I see you no more here Below may I

see you all at Last at Gods Right Hand—where parting will be no more—Glory to God that J. Christ is yet all, & in all, to my Poor Soul——

> I am with all Due Respects
> yours to Command——
> GUSTAVUS VASSA
> The African

——at Mr. Hardys No. 4 Taylors Building
Chandos street, Covent Garden

[Reverse side]
P.S. you see how I am confused—Pray excuse this mistake of the frank—
for Mr. Houseman
Pray mind the Africans from the Pulpits[14]

## LETTER XVIII

### TO THE READER

An invidious falsehood having appeared in the *Oracle* of the 25th, and the *Star* of the 27th of April 1792, with a view to hurt my character, and to discredit and prevent the sale of my Narrative, asserting, that I was born in the Danish island of Santa Cruz, in the West Indies,[15] it is necessary that, in this edition, I should take notice thereof, and it is only needful for me to appeal to those numerous and respectable persons of character who knew me when I first arrived in England, and could speak no language but that of Africa.*

Under this appeal, I now offer the sixth edition of my Narrative to the candid reader, and to the friends of humanity, hoping it may still be the means, in its measure, of showing the enormous cruelties practised on my sable brethren, and strengthening the generous emulation now prevailing in this country, to put a speedy end to a traffic both cruel and unjust.

London, Dec. 30, 1792.

* My friend Mrs. Baynes, formerly Miss. Guerin, at Southampton, and many others of her friends.
John Hill, Esq. Custom-house, Dublin.
Admiral Affleck.
Admiral George Belfour, Portsmouth.
Captain Gallia, Greenock.
Mrs. Shaw, James-street, Covent-Garden, London.

1. Quoted from the *Narrative* (London, 1789), II, pp. 218-20.
2. The Memorial was accompanied by two letters of recommendation from Governor Matthew MacNamara and Dr. Wallace (see the *Narrative*, II, pp. 220-2),

men who had lived in Africa for several years and who thought highly of Equiano as 'a good moral man' and who shared his sentiments on the subject of an African mission. Equiano's application for ordination was unsuccessful. 'He received me with much condescension and politeness, but, from certain scruples of delicacy, and saying the Bishops were not of opinion of sending a new missionary to Africa, he declined to ordain me.' (*Narrative*, II, p.222.)

In a profile of Equiano which appeared in *The Morning Herald*, 29 December 1786, his unsuccessful application for ordination to the Bishop of London was mentioned: 'Gustavus Vasa [is] an African from Guinea; whom Governor MacNamara of Senegambia, recommended in 1780 [it was in 1779] to the Bishop of London to be admitted to the Lutheran Order of the Church of England, ordained a Priest with habiliments, and sent out as a Missionary or Bishop to the Africans. The Bishop of London refused the request and since that time Gustavus Vasa generally resorted among the different dissenting [one word blurred, probably—Christians] till the Ministry gave him the Commissary of the Expedition to transport the poor black of England ... to Sierra Leone.'

3. Quoted from the *Narrative*, II, pp. 226-8.

4. The Memorial reached the Treasury on 25 May 1787. A minute on the backsheet to the Memorial dated 6 July 1787 reads: 'Write to Comm. Navy to pay him £50 in full of expenses and wages.'

In the *Narrative*, Equiano printed the Memorial but without the Postscript and Account (II, pp. 239-43.). After the Memorial he wrote in the *Narrative*, 'The above petition was delivered into the hands of their Lordships, who were kind enough, in the space of some few months afterwards, without hearing, to order me [£]50 sterling—that is [£]18 wages for the time upwards of four months I acted a faithful part in their service. Certainly the sum is more than a free [black] would have had in the western colonies!!!'

5. See *The Public Advertiser* (2 July 1787); *The London Chronicle* (3 July 1787); *The Morning Chronicle and London Advertiser* (3 July 1787).

6. See Cugoano, *Thoughts and Sentiments* ... , p.14, where the same phrases occur.

7. Dr. Beilby Porteus, successively Bishop of Chester and London. Equiano was referring to Porteus's famous sermon preached on 21 February 1783 (while still Bishop of Chester) at the anniversary meeting of the Society for the Propagation of the Gospel. The sermon was delivered in the Vestry-Room of St. Mary-le-Bow, on 'the Civilization, Improvement, and Conversion of the Negroe-Slaves in the British Islands'. He referred to the slave trade as 'that opprobrious traffic, in which this country has for too long taken the lead'. He ended with an injunction to slavers: 'Let then our countrymen make haste to relieve, as far as they are able, the calamities they have brought on so large a part of the human race; let them endeavour to wipe away the reproach of having delivered over so many fellow-creatures to a most heavy temporal bondage. ...' Equiano probably attended the Bow church on the day Porteus preached the sermon.

Porteus also took a special interest in Sir William Dolben's Slave Carrying Bill, and it is said that while it was being debated in the Lords 'attended the House daily for a month. ... the measure indeed fell far short of the whole extent of his wishes, but, as under the existing circumstances, more could hardly be expected, he considered.' See Beilby Porteus, *Works*, ed. Robert Hodgson (London, 1823), I, pp. 102-3.

8. Quoted from the *Narrative*, II, pp. 243-6. In a footnote Equiano says he includes the petition 'at the request of some of my most particular friends'.

9. The same letter appeared in *The Morning Chronicle and London Advertiser* (20 June 1788).

10. A short profile of Equiano was published in *The Morning Chronicle* (1 July 1788): 'Gustavus Vasa, who addressed a letter in the name of his oppressed coun-

trymen, to the author of the popular poem on Humanity, which devotes several pages to that now universal subject of discussion, the Slave Trade, is, notwithstanding its romantick sound the real name of an Ethiopian now resident in this metropolis, a native of Eboe [Ibo], who was himself twice kidnapped by the English, and twice sold to slavery. He has since been appointed the King's Commissary for the African settlement, and besides having an irreproachable moral character, has frequently distinguished himself by occasional essays in the different papers, which manifest a strong and sound understanding.'

In the *Narrative* (I, p. 96), Equiano explained how he acquired his European names, 'My captain and master named me *Gustavus Vasa*. I at that time began to understand him a little, and refused to be called so, and told him as well as I could that I would be called Jacob; but he said I should not, and still called me Gustavus; and when I refused to answer to my new name, which at first I did, it gained me many a cuff; so at length I submitted and was obliged to bear the present name, by which I have been known ever since.'

11. For the plate, see Clarkson, *History of Abolition*, II, facing p. 111.

12. Dedication to the *Narrative*.

13. Quoted from J. A. Langford, *A Century of Birmingham Life* (Birmingham, 1868), I, p. 440.

14. Reproduced by courtesy of Liverpool City Libraries.

15. The libel in the first paper reads as follows:

'It was well observed by Chubb, that there is no absurdity, however gross, but popular credulity has a throat wide enough to swallow it. It is a fact that the Public may depend on, that Gustavus Vasa, who has publicly asserted that he was kidnapped in Africa, never was upon that Continent, but was born and bred up in the Danish Island of Santa Cruz, in the West Indies. *Ex hoc uno disce omnes*, What, we will ask any man of plain understanding, must that cause be, which can lean for support on falsehoods as audaciously propagated as they are easily detected?

'Modern Patriotism, which wantons so much sentiment, is *really* founded rather in private interested views, than in a regard for the Public Weal. The conduct of the friends to the Abolition is a proof of the justice of this remark. It is a fact, of which, perhaps, the People are not apprised, but which it well becomes them to know, that WILBERFORCE and the THORNTONS are concerned in settling the Island of Bulham in Sugar Plantations; of course their interests clash with those of the present Planters, and, hence their clamour against the Slave Trade.

'"Old Cato is as great a Rogue as You."'

The libel in the second paper reads:

'The Negroe, called GUSTAVUS VASA, who has published an history of his life, and gives so admirable an account of the laws, religion, and natural productions of the interior parts of Africa; and in which he relates his having been kidnapped in his infancy; is neither more nor less, than a native of the Danish island of Santa Cruz.'

The scandalous attacks were made when Equiano was in Glasgow. But his friends took the matter up on his behalf. The following letters were printed in the sixth edition of the *Narrative*.

ALEXANDER TILLOCH TO JOHN MONTEITH, ESQ. GLASGOW

DEAR SIR,

Your note of the 30th ult. I would have answered in course; but wished first to be able to inform you what paper we had taken the article from which respected GUSTAVUS VASSA. By this day's post, have sent you a copy of the *Oracle* of Wednesday the 25th—in the last column of the 3d page, you will find the article from which we inserted the one in the *Star* of the 27th ult.—If it be erroneous, you will see it had not its origin with us. As to G.V. I know nothing about him.

After examining the paragraph in the *Oracle*, which immediately follows the one in question, I am inclined to believe that the one respecting G.V. may have been fabricated by some of the advocates for continuing the slave-trade, for the purpose of weakening the force of the evidence brought against that trade; for, I believe, if they could, they would stifle the evidence altogether.

Having sent you the *Oracle*, we have sent all that we can say about the business, I am,

> DEAR SIR,
> Your most humble servant,
> ALEX. TILLOCH.

Star Office, 5th May 1792.

FROM THE REV. DR. J. BAKER, OF MAY FAIR CHAPEL, LONDON, TO MR. GUSTAVUS VASSA, AT DAVID DALE'S, ESQ. GLASGOW.

DEAR SIR,

I went after Mr. Millan (the printer of the Oracle), but he was not at home. I understood that an apology would be made to you, and I desired it might be a proper one, such as would give fair satisfaction, and take off any disadvantageous impressions which the paragraph alluded to may have made. Whether the matter will bear an action or not, I do not know, and have not inquired whether you can punish by law; because I think it is not worth while to go to the expence of a lawsuit, especially if a proper apology is made; for, can any man that reads your Narrative believe that you are not a native of Africa? —I see therefore no good reason for not printing a fifth edition, on account of a scandalous paragraph in a newspaper.

> I remain,
> DEAR SIR,
> Your sincere friend,
> J. BAKER.

Grosvenor-street, May 14, 1792.

[I have read through the issues of the *Oracle* from 15 May to 15 June; no apology appears to have been published. F. O. S.]

# Appendix II

# Letters of Sons of Africa

## LETTER I[1]

### To Granville Sharp, Esq.

Sir,

Being assembled (few and insignificant as we are) for the purpose of offering grateful thanks to our benefactors, it was impossible to forget HIM who has been the great source and support of our hopes. We need not use many words. We are those who were considered as slaves, even in England itself, till your aid and exertions set us free. We are those whose minds and bodies are bartered from hand to hand on the coast of Africa, and in the West Indies, as the ordinary commodities of trade. But it is said that we are the factors of our own slavery, and sell one another at our own market for a price. No doubt but in our uncivilized state we commit much evil; but surely the trader cannot believe that the strong on the coast of Africa are entitled to deprive the weak of every right of humanity, and to devote to the most cruel slavery them and their prosperity for ever; or that it belongs to him, more enlightened than we, to execute so horrid a doom. But our cause is in better hands than our own; and humbleness and sobriety, we are sensible, will best become our condition: and this, also, we know to be the return desired by you, looking for your own peculiar reward in the consciousness of doing good.

But yet, Sir, you may allow us to believe that the name of GRANVILLE SHARP, our constant and generous friend, will be drawn forth by our more enlightened posterity, and distinguishingly marked in future times for gratitude and praise.

(Signed)

THOMAS COOPER.
GEO. ROBT. MANDEVILLE.
JOHN STUART.
DANIEL CHRISTOPHER.
BERNARD ELLIOTT.
JAMES FORSTER.

JOHN SCOT.
JORGE DENT.
THOS. OXFORD.
JAMES BAILEY.
JAMES FRAZER.
THOMAS CARLISLE.

## LETTER II

The Address of Thanks of the Sons of Africa to
the Honourable Granville Sharp, Esq.

Honourable and Worthy Sir,                    December 15, 1787.

Give us leave to say, that every virtuous man is a truly honourable man; and he that doth good hath honour to himself: and many blessings are upon the head of the just, and their memory shall be blessed, and their works praise them in the gate.

And we must say, that we, who are a part, or descendants, of the much-wronged people of Africa, are peculiarly and greatly indebted to you, for the many good and friendly services that you have done towards us, and which are now even out of our power to enumerate.

Nevertheless, we are truly sensible of your great kindness and humanity; and we cannot do otherwise but endeavour, with the utmost sincerity and thankfulness, to acknowledge our great obligations to you, and, with the most feeling sense of our hearts, on all occasions to express and manifest our gratitude and love for your long, valuable, indefatigable labours and benevolence towards us, in using every means to rescue our suffering brethren in slavery.

Your writings, Sir, are not of trivial matter, but of great and essential things of moral and religious importance, worthy the regard of all men; and abound with many great and precious things, of sacred writ, particularly respecting the laws of God, and the duties of men.

Therefore, we wish, for ourselves and others, that these valuable treatises may be collected and preserved, for the benefit and good of all men, and for an enduring memorial of the great learning, piety, and vigilance of our good friend the worthy Author. And we wish that the laws of God, and his ways of righteousness and truth set forth therein, may be as a path for the virtuous and prudent to walk in, and as a clear shining light to the wise in all ages; and that these and other writings of that nature, may be preserved and established as a monument or beacon to guide and to warn men, lest they should depart from the paths of justice and humanity; and that they may more and more become means of curbing the vicious violators of God's holy law, and to restrain the avaricious invaders of the rights and liberties of men, whilever the human race inhabits this earth below.

And, ever honourable and worthy Sir, may the blessing and peace of Almighty God be with you, and long preserve your valuable life, and make you abundantly useful in every good word and work! And when God's appointed time shall come, may your exit be blessed, and may you arise and for ever shine in the glorious world above, when that Sovereign Voice, speaking with joy, as the sound of many waters, shall be heard, saying, 'Well done, thou good and faithful servant: enter thou into the joy of thy Lord!' It will then be the sweetest of all delights for ever, and more melodious than all music! And such honour and felicity will the blessed God and Saviour of his people bestow upon all the saints and faithful servants who are redeemed from among men, and saved from sin, slavery, misery, pain, and death, and from eternal dishonour and wrath impending upon the heads of all the wicked and rebellious.

And now, honourable Sir, with the greatest submission, we must beg you to accept this memorial of our thanks for your good and faithful services towards us, and for your humane commiseration of our brethren and countrymen unlawfully held in slavery.

And we have hereunto subscribed a few of our names, as a mark of our gratitude and love. And we are, with the greatest esteem and veneration, honourable and worthy, Sir, your most obliged and most devoted humble servants.

| | |
|---|---|
| OTTOBAH CUGOANO. | JASPER GOREE. |
| JOHN STUART. | GUSTAVUS VASA. |
| GEO. ROB. MANDEVILLE. | JAMES BAILEY. |
| WILLIAM STEVENS. | THOMAS OXFORD. |
| JOSEPH ALMAZE. | JOHN ADAMS. |
| BOUGHWA GEGANSMEL. | GEORGE WALLACE. |

# LETTER III

*The Morning Chronicle and London Advertiser.*
15 July 1788

TO THE Honourable Sir WILLIAM DOLBEN, Bart.

SIR,

We beg your permission to lay in manner our humble thankfulness before you, for a benevolent law obtained at your motion, by which the miseries of our unhappy brethren, on the coast of Africa, may be alleviated, and by which the lives of many, though destined for the present to a cruel slavery, may be preserved, as we hope, for future and for great mercies.

Our simple testimony is not much, yet you will not be displeased to learn, that a few persons of colour, existing here, providentially released from the common calamity, and feeling for their kind, are daily pouring forth their prayers for you, Sir, and other noble and generous persons who will not (as we understand) longer suffer the rights of humanity to be confounded with ordinary commodities, and passed from hand to hand, as an article of trade.

We are not ignorant, however, Sir, that the best return we can make, is, to behave with sobriety, fidelity, and diligence in our different stations whether remaining here under the protection of the laws, or colonizing our native soil, as most of us wish to do, under the dominion of this country; or as free labourers and artizans in the West India islands, which, under equal laws, might become to men of colour places of voluntary and very general resort.

But in whatever station, Sir, having lived here, as we hope, without reproach, so we trust that we and our whole race shall endeavour to

merit, by dutiful behaviour, those mercies, which, humane and benevolent minds seem to be preparing for us.

> THOMAS COOPER.
> GUSTAVUS VASSA.
> OTTOBAH CUGOANA STEWARD.
> GEORGE ROBERT MANDEVIL.
> JOHN CHRISTOPHER.
> THOMAS JONES.

For ourselves and Brethren

Sir W. DOLBEN is highly gratified with the kind acceptance his
endeavours to promote the liberal designs of the Legislature have met
from the worthy natives of Africa; whose warm sense of benefits, and
honourable resolution of showing their gratitude by their future conduct
in steadiness and sobriety, fidelity, and diligence, will undoubtedly
recommend them to the British Government, and he trusts, to other
Christian powers, as most worthy of their further care and attention; yet
as he is but one among many who are equally zealous for the accomplishment of this good work, he must earnestly desire to decline any
particular address upon the occasion.

Duke-Street, Westminster, 1788.

## LETTER IV

*The Morning Chronicle and London Advertiser*
15 July 1788

To the Right Honourable WILLIAM PITT.
SIR,

We will not presume to trouble you with many words. We are persons of colour, happily released from the common calamity, and desirous of leaving at your door, in behalf of our Brethren, on the Coast of
Africa, this simple, but grateful acknowledgment of your goodness and
benevolence towards our unhappy race.

> THOMAS COOPER.
> GUSTAVUS VASSA.
> OTTOBAH CUGOANA STEWARD.
> GEORGE ROBERT MANDEVIL.
> JOHN CHRISTOPHER.
> THOMAS JONES.

For ourselves and Brethren

## LETTER V

*The Morning Chronicle and London Advertiser*
15 July 1788

To the Right Honourable CHARLES JAMES FOX.

SIR,    We are men of colour, happily, ourselves, emancipated from a general calamity by the laws of this place, but yet feeling very sensibly for our kind, and hearing, Sir, that, in their favour, you have co-operated with the Minister [Pitt], and have nobly considered the rights of humanity as a common cause, we have thereupon assumed the liberty (we hope, without offence) of leaving this simple, but honest token of our joy and thankfulness at your door.

> THOMAS COOPER.
> GUSTAVUS VASSA.
> OTTOBAH CUGOANA STEWARD.
> GEORGE ROBERT MANDEVIL.
> JOHN CHRISTOPHER.
> THOMAS JONES.

For ourselves and Brethren

## LETTER VI

*The Diary; or Woodfall's Register*
25 April 1789

To Mr. WILLIAM DICKSON, formerly Private Secretary to the Hon. Edward Hay, Governor of the Island of Barbadoes.

SIR,

We who have perused your well authenticated Book, entitled LETTERS ON SLAVERY, think it a duty incumbent on us to confess, that in our opinion such a work cannot be too much esteemed; you have given but too just a picture of the Slave Trade, and the horrid cruelties practised on the poor sable people in the West Indies, to the disgrace of Christianity. Their injury calls aloud for redress, and the day we hope is not far distant, which may record one of the most glorious acts that ever passed the British Senate—we mean an Act for the total Abolition of the Slave Trade.

It is the duty of every man who is a friend to religion and humanity (and such you have shewn yourself to be) to shew his detestation of such inhuman traffick. Thank to God the nation at last is awakened to a sense of our sufferings except the Oran Otang philosophers, who we think will find it a hard task to dissect your letters. Those who can feel for the distresses of their own countrymen, will also commiserate the case of the poor Africans.

Permit us, Sir, on behalf of ourselves and the rest of our brethren, to offer you our sincere thanks for the testimony of regard you have shewn for the poor and much oppressed sable people.

With our best wishes that your praise-worthy publication may meet with the wished-for success, and may the all-bountiful Creator bless you with health and happiness, and bestow on you every blessing of time and eternity.

> We are,
> SIR,
> Your most obedient humble servants,
> OLAUDAH EQUIANO, OR GUSTAVUS VASA.
> OTTOBAH CUGOANO, OR JOHN SUARR.
> YAHNE AELANE, OR JOSEPH SANDERS.
> BROUGHWAR JOGENSMEL, OR JASPER GOREE.
> COJOH AMMERE, OR GEORGE WILLIAMS.
> THOMAS COOPER.
> WILLIAM GREEK.
> GEORGE MANDEVILLE.
> BERNARD ELLIOT GRIFFITHS.

1. Letters I and II quoted from Hoare, *Memoirs of Granville Sharp* (London, 1828), 2nd ed., II, pp. 114-15, 175-7.

# Appendix III

# Essay on Sources

## PRIMARY SOURCES (MANUSCRIPT)

### 1. Public Record Office, London

Treasury Papers. These have been very valuable indeed for the second part of the section on the Black Poor. The call numbers are T/1/630-T/1/646.

Admiralty in Letters and Admiralty Board Minutes. The Admiralty Papers have been used to supplement the Treasury Papers on the Black Poor. The call numbers are Adm/1 and Adm/3. Other PRO sources are cited in the notes.

### 2. British Library, London

Liverpool Papers. Though these are of very great importance to the student of the British slave trade, the Liverpool Papers have been of slight importance in this study.

Sloane Papers. These papers contain Ayuba Suleiman Diallo's writings in Arabic.

### 3. York Minster Library, York

Granville Sharp Letter Book. This manuscript volume contains short reports and notes on cases of black slaves in England whose freedom Granville Sharp obtained in the English Courts. 'We want words to express our gratitude to you for all your labours of love to our afflicted nation. You were our advocate when we had but few friends on the other side of the water. We request you to accept of our thanks for all your kind and benevolent exertions in behalf of the people of our colour, and in particular for your late humane donation to our church.' Thus wrote the Officers of the African Church of Philadelphia to Granville Sharp in a letter dated 25 November 1793 copied into the Letter Book. Of what the gift mentioned in this letter consisted is not known. It is clear, however, that Granville Sharp extended his benevolent work to the black people in the United States of America.

### 4. Hardwicke Court, Gloucester

Granville Sharp Papers. These give a blow by blow account of the prodigious effort of the indefatigable early English Abolitionist and Emancipationist to free black slaves in Britain, the British West Indies, and America. 'An Account of the Occasion which Compelled Granville Sharp to Study Law, and the Defence of Negroe Slaves in England' gives in a nutshell his legal battles to outlaw slavery in England which culminated in the famous Somerset case in 1772.

## 5. Rhodes House Library, Oxford

In the Rhodes House Library is 'A MS volume, Entirely in Ramsay's Hand, Mainly concerned with his Activities Towards the Abolition of the Slave Trade'. James Ramsay ranks in importance in the Abolition movement with Granville Sharp and Thomas Clarkson. The work of Wilberforce pales into insignificance when compared with the efforts of this trio either singly or in combination. While Granville Sharp and Thomas Clarkson have had their biographers, quite astonishingly, James Ramsay has not hitherto been complimented with a biography. I hope my *James Ramsay: the Unknown Abolitionist* (Edinburgh, forthcoming) will fill a glaring gap and put Ramsay in his rightful place in the British Anti-Slavery Movement. I have used Ramsay's manuscript volume here for general background information and to dismiss the deplorable and wholly unjustified libel of the dead by the Duke of Clarence.

# PRIMARY SOURCES (PRINTED)

## 1. Newspapers

These are the most important single source for this study. The newspapers of the time are in rather small print and reading through them strains the eyes, being an exercise in looking for a needle in a haystack. But, as I hope the text testifies, it is a rewarding exercise. All the newspapers quoted here are in the Burney Collection in the British Library.

## 2. Olaudah Equiano

Paul Edwards has done a very useful job with his introductions to both the abridged and unabridged reprints of Equiano's *Narrative*. The abridged edition is number 10 in Heinemann Educational Books African Writers Series. I have only one complaint about this edition—it would have been more helpful if there had been indications to signify where deletions from the original text have been made. My first Appendix, *Letters of a Black Abolitionist*, is far from comprising all the letters Equiano wrote to the press. *The County Chronicle* of 19 February 1788, for example, regretted that 'the want of room prevents us from giving place to the favours of GUSTAVUS VASSA on the Slave-trade'. I also have no doubt that I have missed some of Equiano's letters in the volumes I have examined. I hope, however, that the few letters spotted fully justify and corroborate the fine compliment paid to Equiano by James Ramsay in his manuscript volume:

Gustavus Vasa, is a well known instance of what improvement [an African] is capable. ... He has learned to read and write; and in vindication of the rights of his colour has not been afraid to contend in Argument with men of high rank [Lord Sydney for example], and acuteness of parts. But the extent of his abilities appeared very clearly, when Government resolved to return the [Black Poor] lately to Africa. Those to whom the management of the expedition was committed, dreaded as much his influence over his countrymen, that they contrived to procure an order for his being sent ashore. In particular, his knowledge of the Scriptures is truly surprising, and shows that he could study and really understand them.

### 3. Ottobah Cugoano

Benjamin Quarles has well observed in *Black Abolitionists* that slave narratives moved well in the book markets in America. No blacks 'before or since have ever experienced less difficulty in getting published'. The same is true of Britain. The pity is therefore that there were not many more blacks in Britain during the period of this study who could read and write. Cugoano's *Thoughts and Sentiments* was a forceful and angry denunciatory attack on the slave trade and slavery, which did much to advance the cause of Abolition, and was published not only in Britain but also in France. Lowell Joseph Ragatz, however, in *The Fall of the Planter Class in the British Caribbean, 1763-1833* (New York, 1928), dismissed *Thoughts and Sentiments* as 'a mediocre enough attack on the slave trade'. *The Fall of the Planter Class* is a dangerous combination of scholarship and racism by an American professor. As the dedication to the book tells us, Ragatz had the best education and it is therefore to be expected that he could not perceive what it takes for someone disadvantaged at every turn to pull himself up by his bootstraps and make good. In the chapter headed 'Caribbean Society' we read, 'The West Indian negro had all the characteristics of his race. He stole, he lied, he was simple, suspicious, inefficient, irresponsible, lazy, superstitious, and loose in his sex relations' (p. 28). Ragatz was, of course, writing at a time when lynching was endemic in America and blacks were seldom referred to in the daily newspapers except in the crime columns. Accordingly, Ragatz could not rise above the level of gutter historiography when writing about black people. In spite of all the advantages that education had conferred on him, Ragatz considered his work well done by applying the lynch law, cutting and mangling the character of the African race without compunction in print, just as African human beings had been cut and mangled in the flesh.

### 4. Ignatius Sancho

Sancho's *Letters*, though of slight interest today, show that he was a man of many parts and well familiar with the mores of the ruling class in eighteenth-century Britain. The memoir of Sancho by Joseph Jekyll is quite useful, but here too we meet with sweeping nonsense from an apparent friend of the African, as in the assertion by Jekyll that Sancho's passion for gambling was a 'propensity, which appears to be innate among his countrymen'. He had read, he wrote, that in Benin and Dahomey an African 'will stake at play his fortune, his children, and his liberty'. At that time, Jekyll, as an M.P., ought to have known that Englishmen wagered at the drop of a hat. In *The Age of Scandal* (London, 1950), T. H. White states that, in three years, Charles James Fox lost £140,000 (at least three million pounds today) in games of chance. 'The gaming', wrote Walpole in 1770, 'is worthy the decline of an Empire. The young men lose five, ten, fifteen thousand pounds in an evening. Lord Stavordale, not one-and-twenty, lost eleven thousand last

Tuesday, but recovered it by one great hand at hazard. He swore a great oath—"Now, if I had been playing deep, I might have won millions!"'

## 5. Francis Barber

With a thoroughness and completeness which are really astonishing, Aleyn Lyell Reade gives us a fascinating portrait of Francis Barber and defends him against the libels of Sir John Hawkins and his daughter. But, in the course of doing so, Reade, too, perpetrated his own libels on the African race. Very early in the narrative he refers to Frank as 'a nigger boy'. Later, he dismissed any suggestion that Frank had been extravagant with his £70 annuity, but he preceded his defence of Frank with the assertion that Africans 'as a rule, certainly shew a fondness for display'. Several examples can be cited in response to this light rubbish. In *The Age of Scandal* it is reported that Lord Durham once remarked that one could 'jog along on £40,000 a year', and thereafter became 'King Jog'. In 1768, at a time when the finances of Denmark were in a tottering state, the King of Denmark made a tour through Holland, Great Britain, France, and Germany, and spent £200,000 in doing so. Today the latter sum would be the equivalent of at least five million pounds.

## 6. Thomas Clarkson

Clarkson's *An Essay on the Slavery and Commerce of the Human Species, particularly the African* (London, 1st ed. 1786, 2nd ed. 1788) and *An Essay on the Impolicy of the African Slave Trade* (London, 1st and 2nd eds. 1788) are the best testimonies of Clarkson's great work to crush the infamous British slave trade and the infamy of slavery. His two-volume *History of the Rise, Progress and Accomplishment of the Abolition of the African Slave Trade* (London, 1808) is still the best account of the humanitarian contribution to Abolition.

The account given in the *History ... of Abolition* remained unchallenged for twenty-five years. In 1833 William Wilberforce died. In 1838 Wilberforce's sons produced their rambling and affected five-volume biography of their father. Out of a perverted sense of filial piety they denounced the aged Clarkson as having arrogated to himself in *History ... of Abolition* the honour and glory due to their father. Thomas Clarkson, in poor health and with bad sight (he was seventy-eight years old), made an effective and calm reply to the cheap nonsense written by the sons of the deeply hypocritical Wilberforce. Earl Leslie Griggs, in *Thomas Clarkson, the Friend of Slaves* (Los Angeles, 1936), has a chapter headed 'The Attack by the Sons of Wilberforce', which gives a rather poor account of the controversy. The best way to follow the dispute is to read the perverse attack by the Wilberforce sons in the first volume of their biography, and then Clarkson's reply in *Strictures on the Life of William Wilberforce, by the Rev. W. Wilberforce and the Rev. S. Wilberforce ...* (London, 1838).

The surest way to appreciate fully Clarkson's Abolitionist achievements is by reading his three works cited above, as biographies of him are rather inadequate. For example, Griggs says that until the Clarksons welcomed the Christophes to Playford Hall in 1821, Thomas Clarkson had never met any black people although he had championed their cause for years. But, as we have seen, in 1788 Clarkson met and preached to about forty blacks in a Manchester church. He knew Equiano very well, and when Equiano left London on his journey through Britain to sell his *Narrative*, Clarkson gave him a letter of introduction to people he, Clarkson, had met the year before.

### 7. Granville Sharp

Of his numerous tracts and pamphlets, *A Representation of the Injustice and Dangerous Tendency of Tolerating Slavery; or of Admitting the Least Claim of Private Property in the Persons of Men, in England* (London, 1769) is all that is needed for this study and the title explains the book.

## SECONDARY SOURCES

The students of Black History will always be in debt to the works of W. E. B. DuBois, C. L. R. James, and Eric Williams. Before writing anything on any aspect of Black History it is obligatory that the novice black historian reads *The Autobiography of Malcolm X* and George Jackson's *Soledad Brother: The Prison Letters of George Jackson*, and goes back to them from time to time for a renewal of faith.

Until quite recently—cursory references in the local histories of London, Liverpool, and Bristol apart—British historians have ignored the historical fact of the black presence in Britain since the sixteenth century. The few traces of blacks in John Latimer's *Bristol in the Seventeenth Century* (Bristol, 1887) and *Bristol in the Eighteenth Century* (Bristol, 1893) are illuminating, as is Gomer Williams's *History of the Liverpool Privateers with an Account of the Liverpool Slave Trade* (Liverpool, 1897). In *London Life in the Eighteenth Century* (London, 1925), Dorothy George gives a short summary of the position of blacks in eighteenth-century London. Sir Reginald Coupland, in *The British Anti-Slavery Movement* (London, 1933), discussed the Somerset case at some length in his sentimental vein, but left out any discussion of the existence of the black community which made the case inevitable. In his introductions to the reprints of Sancho's *Letters*, Cugoano's *Thoughts and Sentiments*, and Equiano's *Narrative*, Paul Edwards has done valuable service by indicating in broad outline the existence of an active black community in eighteenth-century London.

James Walvin's *The Black Presence: A Documentary History of the Negro in England, 1555-1860* (London, 1971) and *Black and White: The Negro and English Society 1555-1945* (London, 1973) are two hastily written books which for the first time deal with the history of blacks in Britain. Written by an English academic liberal, they have the defect of English histories of black people—lack of ordinary human sensibilities towards blacks. Although the following observations are made in relation to the latter work, they are equally applicable to Walvin's first book.

*Black and White* is marred by errors of fact and snap judgements. The errors of fact first: on p. 50, a remark of Lord Stowell in 1827 in the case of the slave Grace Jones is attributed to Lord Mansfield in the Somerset case. As we have seen, Miss Crewe, one of Sancho's correspondents, collected and edited his *Letters* and Joseph Jekyll wrote the memoir prefixed to the *Letters*. But according to Walvin, it was Dr. Joseph Jeckyll [sic] who edited the *Letters*. On p. 93 Walvin states that it was because of shortage of water that over one hundred slaves were thrown overboard from the slave ship *Zong* in 1781. The alleged want of water was a pretext. The mass murder of the Africans on board the *Zong* was in fact committed in order to claim the insurance money on the slaves who had become worth next to nothing as a result of an epidemic. Grace Jones, who was kidnapped and shipped back to Antigua and slavery, went back, according to Walvin, of her own free volition, not showing 'the slightest sign ... that she wished to stay in England or to become free' (p. 137). As we have seen, Jonas Hanway was the fourth Chairman of the Committee for the Relief of the Black Poor. Walvin, however, on p. 146 states that the 'committee sprouted ... under the chairmanship of Hanway'. On p. 179 of *Black and White*, Walvin mentions the fact that Thomas Day's poem *The Dying Negro* (1773) was dedicated to Rousseau, but fails to point out that it was the second edition of *The Dying Negro* (1774) that was dedicated to Rousseau. Chapter Seven of *Black and White* is called 'The Somerset Case, 1772'. Although Walvin says the chapter was written after 'careful scrutiny' of the relevant documents, it is riddled with inaccuracies, some admittedly carried over from the mistakes of Granville Sharp, one of the principal actors in the Somerset case. If Walvin had been less gullible, perhaps he might have spotted some of Sharp's mistakes. Because Lord Stowell in one of his letters to Joseph Story said 'I am rather a stern Abolitionist', Walvin, without examining Stowell's conduct and judgement in the case of Grace Jones, says on p. 138 'Stowell was an abolitionist'. Yet Stowell's conduct in the case of Grace Jones is nothing short of scandalous, as has been demonstrated in *Black Slaves in Britain*. When Stowell's judgement reached the West Indies, one of the newspapers exulted that the judgement 'stamps a value and consistency upon West India property. ... His Lordship has laid the saddle on the right horse.' Serious students of history would be well advised to be careful when reading or citing *Black and White*.

Walvin's citation of his sources leaves much to be desired. He purports to have used a book by Thomas Cooper, *Facts Illustrative of the Condition of Negro Slaves in England* (London, 1824). But Thomas Cooper wrote only *Facts Illustrative of the Condition of Negro Slaves in Jamaica* (London, 1824). The bibliography also states that Walvin used a book by R. Harris, *Scriptural Researches on the Treatment and Conversion of Slaves* (Liverpool, 1788). Dr. Walvin's students will look for ever in vain for such a book. But they would be able to find the following by James Ramsay, *An Essay on the Treatment and Conversion of African Slaves in the British Sugar Colonies* (London, 1784), and by R[aymond] Harris, *Scriptural Researches on the Licitness of the Slave-*

*Trade, Shewing its conformity with the Principles of Natural and Revealed Religion, Delineated in the Sacred Writings of the Word of God* (Liverpool and London, 1788). So what Walvin has done is to take a bit from the title of a book published in 1784 and another bit from the title of a book published in 1788 and has merged them into one to form the title of a non-existent book. Actually, in one of the notes on p. 78, Walvin cites R. Harris, *Scriptural Researches on the Licitness of the Slave Trade* (London, 1824). I am not aware, however, that Harris's *Scriptural Researches* was re-issued in 1824. The first and second editions of *Scriptural Researches* were published in the same year, 1788.

Finally, on pp. 139-40 and 180-1, Walvin asserts that humanitarianism freed the slave. This is an utterly deplorable attempt to excuse the shame of British participation in slavery and the slave trade of Africans. Any economic system comes to end when it has outlived its usefulness, and/or the exploited and the oppressed are powerful enough to overthrow it. Both these factors combined to bring about the Emancipation of black slaves in the United States of America. And, as Benjamin Quarles, one of the fathers of Black History, has demonstrated in *Black Abolitionists*, whatever was done to free the slaves, blacks were in the vanguard. In Haiti (San Domingo), in the most ferocious race war in history, the slaves regained their freedom. By 1763, British West Indian slavery had outlived its economic usefulness. The American Revolution and Haitian Independence, and the consequent scarcity of plantation produce, propped up an economic régime rotten to the core. Blacks in the British West Indies closely followed the Haitian War of Emancipation and subsequent Independence from France. Thus, in 1804, Mrs. Nugent, the wife of the then Governor of Jamaica, recorded in her diary: 'People here are so very imprudent in their conversation. The splendour of the black chiefs of St. Domingo, their superior strength, their firmness of character ... are common topics at dinner; and the blackies in attendance seem so much interested, that they hardly change a plate, or do anything but listen. How very imprudent, and what *must* it all lead to!' It indeed led to rebellions and the cutting off of the slavocrats all over the British West Indies. When Emancipation was conceded in 1834, the black slaves were poised to throw off their shackles. The slaves were not freed, therefore, because of any moral movement on the part of the British Government to end the heinous crime that had festered and endured for three centuries. The Government was forced to free the slaves. Otherwise, the infernal régime would have continued until the present day, and so for that matter would its successor, colonialism.

# Index

slavery—*contd.*
 ability of, 31; legal confusion
 concerning, 17, 20
slaves: advertisements, 10–16;
 baptism of, 17–20, 39; as chattels and playthings, 11, 16, 41;
 as cheap labour, 4, 15, 25, 84,
 86–8, 96, 98–9; collars for, 11,
 14; cruelty to, 18–21, 84, 86; de-
 camp with property of owners,
 76–8; dispersal of, 75; favoured
 and privileged ones, 39–43;
 hunted down, 16, 20, 87; in
 Bristol, 12–14, 18; in Liverpool,
 13–14; in London, 10–12; in
 non-plantation households, 78;
 in plantation households, 78;
 in Scotland, 26, 30; insurance
 of, 228; kidnapping of, 21, 23,
 25, 226; legal status of, 4–5, 17,
 44n.; manumission of, 40–1,
 59–60, 72, 78, 169, 179; opposition to being made Christians,
 17–20, 177; property, 17, 20,
 228; rescued from transportation to the West Indies, 86–7;
 runaways, 11–13, 76–8, 87;
 sale, 6, 13–14
slave trade: abolition of, 55, 160;
 attacked, 31–3, 82, 230–1, 236,
 257; defended, 230, 234, 258;
 movement to ban, 230–1; parliamentary debates on, 229–31;
 Quaker petition against, 229;
 regulated by Act of Parliament,
 14, 230; Sir John Hawkins'
 expedition, 6
Sloane, Sir Hans, 59
Smeathman, Henry, 130–2, 135–6
Smith, Adam, 34, 144
Smith, John Thomas, 161, 188–9
Smith, Sir Thomas, 6
Smith, William, 60
*Smith* v. *Browne and Cooper*, 17
*Smith* v. *Gould*, 17
Snelgrave, William, 67–8
Society for the Propagation of
 the Gospel in Foreign Parts
 (S.P.G.), 56–8

Society for the Suppression of
 Mendicity, 162
Society of Friends, 229, 245–6
*Soledad Brother: The Prison Let-
 ters of George Jackson*, x, 191
Solomon, Job Ben, *see* Diallo,
 Ayuba Suleiman
Somerset, James, 4, 24–5, 80
Soubaney, 123
Soubise, Julius, 41–3, 87, 193–4
Soyinka, Wole, 220
Stanistreet, Mr., 32
Stapylton, Robert, 23
Steadman, John Gabriel, 196
Steele, Richard, 29
Stephen, James, 176
Sterne, Laurence, 189–90, 192
Stewart, Charles, 24, 80
Stewart, James, 58
Stoddard, Chas., 133
Stowell, Lord (William Scott),
 27–8, 183, 278
Strong, Jonathan, 21–2, 29, 39, 78
Stuart, Charles, 20
Sydney, Lord, 120, 153, 230, 258,
 274
Sypher, Wylie, 31, 122

Talbot, Lord (Charles Talbot), 5,
 20
Tarleton, John, 14
*Taste in High Life*, 16, 188
Taylor, Mr., 134, 136
Terence, 220
Terret, Mr., 46
Testesole, Mr., 67, 73n.
Thayer, A. W., 219
*The Times*, 206–7
*Theory of Moral Sentiments*, 34
Thicknesse, Philip, 80, 103
Thirlwall, J. W., 216
Thompson, Thomas, 56–7
Thompson, Thomas Boulden, 145,
 152–3, 155–7, 246, 258–9
Thornton, Henry, 47
*Thoughts and Sentiments on the
 Evil of Slavery*, 138, 176–7
*Thoughts upon Slavery*, 33